William Dunbar
Selected Poems

Longman Annotated Texts

General Editors:

Charlotte Brewer, Hertford College, Oxford
H.R. Woudhuysen, University College London
Daniel Karlin, University College London

Published Titles:

Michael Mason, *Lyrical Ballads*
Alexandra Barratt, *Women's Writing in Middle English*
Tim Armstrong, *Thomas Hardy: Selected Poems*
René Weis, *King Lear: A Parallel Text Edition*
James Sambrook, *William Cowper: The Task and Selected
    Other Poems*
Joseph Phelan, *Clough: Selected Poems*
Douglas Brooks-Davies, *Edmund Spenser: Selected Shorter Poems*
Priscilla Bawcutt, *William Dunbar: Selected Poems*

William Dunbar
Selected Poems

Edited by
Priscilla Bawcutt

LONGMAN

London and New York

Addison Wesley Longman Limited
Edinburgh Gate, Harlow, Essex CM20 2JE, England
and associated Companies throughout the world.

*Published in the United States of America
by Longman Publishing, New York*

First published 1996

ISBN 0 582 06188.1 CSD
ISBN 0 582 06187.3 PPR

British Library Cataloguing-in-Publication Data

A catalogue record for this book is
available from the British Library

Library of Congress Cataloging-in-Publication Data

Also available

Set by 33 in 10/11 Ehrhardt Roman
Produced by Longman Singapore Publishers (Pte) Ltd.
Printed in Singapore

Contents

Acknowledgements

My thanks are due to the staff of the following libraries: the British Library; Cambridge University Library; Edinburgh University Library; the National Library of Scotland; the Pepys Library, Magdalene College, Cambridge; and the Sydney Jones Library, University of Liverpool.

This edition of Dunbar differs greatly from previous ones, not only in the transcription of texts and choice of variants but in the interpretation of the sense; nonetheless I owe much to my predecessors, particularly Professor James Kinsley. I am also greatly indebted to the editorial staff of the *Dictionary of the Older Scottish Tongue*, and to its former editor, Professor A.J. Aitken. I am grateful for the information and advice on specific points that I have received from the following scholars: Professor Francis Cairns, the late Professor Ian Cowan, Miss Judith Cripps, Dr John Durkan, Mr Jonathan Foster, Professor William Gillies, Mrs Bridget Henisch, Dr Emily Lyle, Professor A.A. Mac-Donald, Professor Hector MacQueen, Dr David Sellar, and Professor D.E.R. Watt. To Dr Sally Mapstone I am particularly grateful: she read the whole work in its final stages, and made numerous valuable comments and suggestions. I have profited also from Dr R.G. Fallon's meticulous copy-editing. Above all, I am indebted to my husband, for constant encouragement, scholarly stimulus, and much practical assistance.

Chronology

1460	Death of James II.
c. 1460	Probable birth-date of Dunbar.
1460–69	Minority of James III.
1473	17 March: Birth of James IV.
1477–79	Dunbar studies at St Andrews University.
1479	Dunbar *licentiate* at St Andrews.
1485	Battle of Bosworth; accession of Henry VII.
1488	Battle of Sauchieburn; death of James III; accession of James IV.
1493	Suppression of the Lordship of the Isles.
1494	Gavin Douglas *licentiate* at St Andrews.
1500	Dunbar granted annual pension of £10.
1501	Dunbar returns from England.
1502	Peace treaty between England and Scotland.
1502	15 February: Dunbar a *procurator* for Sir John Wemyss.
1503	8 August: Marriage of James IV and Margaret Tudor (see **41**).
1504	17 March: Dunbar celebrates first mass.
1506	Rebellion in Highlands crushed (see **22**).
1506	27 January: Dunbar receives £5 'for caus he wantit his goun at Yule' (see **55**).
1507	June: First tournament of the Black Lady (see **23**).
1507	Dunbar's pension raised to £20.
1508	May: Second tournament of the Black Lady.
	May: Arrival of Bernard Stewart (see **45**).
1508	11 June: Death of Bernard Stewart (see **18**).
1508	Chepman and Myllar prints published (see **45** and **47**).
1509	Death of Henry VII; accession of Henry VIII.
1509	Dunbar styled 'chaplain'.
1510	Dunbar's pension raised to £80.

1511   May: Queen Margaret's visit to Aberdeen (see **6**).
1513   14 May: Last mention of Dunbar in *Treasurer's Accounts*.
1513   9 September: Battle of Flodden; death of James IV.
1513–28   Minority of James V.

A Note on
Editorial Procedure

This edition contains seventy of Dunbar's finest poems. Each is complete; *The Flyting* (**54**), however, excludes the long, second section written by Kennedy. Only a handful of Dunbar's poems can be dated, so that it is impossible to arrange them chronologically. They have been placed in an alphabetical sequence, therefore, according to first line rather than title. (Two exceptions to this are **37** and **61**, which immediately follow the poems with which they are closely connected.) Few of the titles for Dunbar's poems are early or authoritative; most were invented by editors, from the eighteenth century onwards. Since many readers will be still familiar with them, I provide an index of these largely editorial titles and of the refrains from which many derive.

The poems are provided with headnotes, which discuss theme, genre, metrical form, text, and whatever evidence exists as to their date. All are supplied with annotation (in the form of endnotes) and glosses (in the form of footnotes), the first three poems being glossed particularly fully, and Latin is translated into English. The Introduction is a brief, preliminary guide to important aspects of Dunbar and his poetry; it provides references to fuller studies. Each poem has been freshly edited from the manuscript or print specified in the headnote, and collated with other witnesses. It should be noted that my choice of copy-text differs from that of Kinsley in several cases (e.g. **2**, **9**, **20**, **24** and **70**), and that I value the Asloan and Maitland manuscripts more highly than he does. Only important textual variants and emendations are recorded; fuller discussion will appear in my edition of Dunbar's complete poems for the Association for Scottish Literary Studies. The spelling follows the original text, but is slightly modernized. *ȝ* is replaced by *y*; and *i*/*j* and *u*/*v* are distinguished in accord with modern practice. The Scots usage with *u* and *w* is similarly normalized: MS *wnto* thus appears as *unto*, and MS *tua* as *twa*. Final unetymological *-t* has been removed in words such as *witht* and *baitht*, and *off* is normalized to *of*. Punctuation and capitalization are editorial, as is the numbering of lines and stanzas.

Introduction

'Not Burns – Dunbar!' This was the slogan of Hugh MacDiarmid, when he sought a new model for Scottish poetry in the 1920s – tough, witty, sophisticated and unsentimental. Affinities with Dunbar may indeed be detected in modern Scottish poets, such as Robert Garioch, Edwin Morgan and Douglas Dunn. But his appeal is by no means confined to Scotland. T. S. Eliot coupled him somewhat sardonically with Byron, as 'a *poète contumace* in a solemn country', and W. H. Auden celebrated his versatility: 'Whatever your taste, pious, gay, melancholy, bawdy; he will write a poem for you, apt and elegant. The first gift of such a poet is verse technique, and Dunbar is unfailingly brilliant' (MacDiarmid 1927: 35; Eliot 1957: 206; Auden 1933: 677). Despite the lapse of five centuries, Dunbar has a remarkable power to excite, amuse, and indeed infuriate readers – his attitudes to women and Highlanders, for instance, are far from politically correct. Although firmly grounded, 'heir at hame' in late-medieval Scotland, Dunbar's finest poems are neither parochial nor dated, but treat of perennial themes. An intelligent but not a profoundly intellectual poet, he excels in the vividness of his imagination and in the intense energy of his expression. No other poet of his time is so rhythmically adroit or so sensitive to the connotations of a word or a phrase. (For critical studies, see Scott 1966; Reiss 1979; Ross 1981; and Bawcutt 1992a. Articles are listed in the bibliographies by Geddie 1912; Ridley 1973; Scheps and Looney 1986.)

Life and milieu (*c.* 1460–1513)

The precise year of Dunbar's birth, like much else in his life, is obscure, but there are grounds for dating it *c.* 1460. (On his life, see Baxter 1952; Ross 1981: 3–39; McDiarmid 1980; Bawcutt 1992a: 3–8). Dunbar grew up in the reign of James III, a deeply unpopular king, and would have

1

witnessed a series of confrontations between king and powerful
magnates that culminated in the abortive coup of 1482 and the rebellion
of 1488, in which James III was deposed and died (Macdougall 1982:
299–310). Dunbar's parentage is unknown, but he was a Lowlander,
probably from the Lothian region, and spent many years in Edinburgh,
of which he has left two vivid and humorous sketches (in **42** and **54**).
He belonged to the most fertile, prosperous and thickly populated part
of Scotland; and his response to the Highlands and their Gaelic-
speaking inhabitants reveals an antagonism then characteristic of the
Lowlander. Scotland was a small kingdom, remote from the mainland
of Europe but by no means isolated, economically or culturally. Scottish
merchants traded with France, the Baltic and the Low Countries; and
Scottish scholars studied and taught at Paris, Louvain, Cologne and
other continental universities, or travelled even further afield, to Rome,
in order to advance their careers in the church. Diplomatically, there
was a tradition of friendship towards France – the 'auld Alliance' – and
hostility to England; yet, despite political disagreements, England and
Scotland had long been closely linked in language and culture
(Nicholson 1974; Wormald 1981; Macfarlane 1985).

Dunbar is commonly styled 'maister' (cf. **54**. 29), which indicates
that he was a university graduate. He is thought to be the William
Dunbar who attended St Andrews University in the 1470s, and was
listed among the *licentiati*, or masters, in 1479. The St Andrews arts
course, conducted in Latin (as was normal) and modelled on that of
Paris, was dominated by the works of Aristotle and his medieval
commentators. This education, with its stress on logic and metaphysics,
left few obvious traces in Dunbar's poetry, apart from some passing
jokes (**56**. 30) or ironic references to the nullity of learning without
moral virtue (**68**) or in the face of death (**16**. 34–9). There is no evidence
that Dunbar had higher degrees in theology or law. It was common at
this time, however, for educated Scottish laymen to act in the courts on
behalf of litigants, and Dunbar is known to have served as a *procurator*,
or advocate. On 15 February 1502, for instance, he represented a
Fifeshire laird, Sir John Wemyss of Wemyss, in a somewhat acrimoni-
ous suit against members of his own family. Dunbar's poems inter-
estingly reveal a close acquaintance with the practice and terminology
of the law courts: some instances are a joke about the 'breif of richt' (**36**.
108) and references to the laws concerning property and inheritance (**3**.
344) or to lawyers and their clients (**2** and **62**). Such familiarity with the
law was not uncommon in Scottish poets (cf. Henryson's fable of *The
Sheep and the Dog*, and Douglas's *Palice of Honour*, 664–702).

Between 1479 and 1500 there is no evidence as to where Dunbar was
or what he was doing. But this void has been amply filled with
conjecture. Earlier scholars, who read one of his poems (**65**) over-
literally, assumed that he became a novice in the Franciscan order of

friars; others have suggested that he participated in an embassy sent to France in 1491, or might have been a member of the Scots Guard, which had the duty of protecting the French king. The absence of Scottish references to Dunbar during this period makes it plausible that he may have been abroad. One of his poems mentions a sea voyage (**54**. 90–96), and others refer to foreign countries or imply that he had the chance of serving a foreign master (**7**, **55**). *The Flyting* (**54**) also evokes very strongly the cosmopolitan world that was then open to Latin-speaking scholars.

It seems possible that some of Dunbar's many undated poems belong to this blank period of his youth. Yet the few that can be dated with precision, such as those on Bernard Stewart (**18**, **45**), all belong to the years between 1500 and 1513, which form by far the best documented period in his life. In 1500 Dunbar was awarded a royal 'pensioun', or annual salary, of £10; in 1507 this was increased to £20, and in 1510 it was raised again to £80. The last mention of Dunbar in *The Treasurer's Accounts*, a valuable source of information about the Scottish court, is dated 14 May 1513; only a few months later James IV invaded England and died, together with his leading nobles and a large part of his army, at the battle of Flodden. It is not impossible that Dunbar survived into the reign of James V, given the fragmentary nature of the records, but there is no evidence that he did so. As a member of the royal household Dunbar would receive not only a 'pensioun', but a livery, or twice-yearly allowance of clothing (cf. **55**), and other occasional fees. We do not know what precisely Dunbar's duties were: he speaks of himself as 'makar' (**58**) and clerk (**57**), often mentions that his service has been long, yet also disparages it as 'lycht' (**57**. **51**). It seems unlikely that Dunbar was rewarded primarily for writing poems; probably, like the contemporary poets he mentions in **16**, Stobo and Patrick Johnston, he served in the household as a scribe, secretary or envoy. He is known to have been in England in 1501, and this is usually taken to mean that he had been on a diplomatic mission, perhaps associated with the marriage between James IV and Margaret Tudor. His own reference to 'wrytting' (**7**. 73) is ambiguous; it might mean either verse or activity as an official scribe.

It was common for those educated at university to enter the church. Gavin Douglas, for instance, became provost of the collegiate church of St Giles, Edinburgh, and ultimately bishop of Dunkeld. Dunbar's poems imply that he too would have liked such a career in the Church: a half-humorous reference to his youthful expectation of a bishopric (**57**. 62) mingles with less specific requests for a benefice, and the still humbler plea for a 'kirk scant coverit with hadder [heather]' (**66**. 85–6). Yet Dunbar is not known to have received a benefice; he was apparently in minor orders till 1504, when on 17 March he celebrated his first mass, having presumably been ordained as priest on the preceding day. By 1509, if not earlier, he was a chaplain, and possibly served either in one of the chapels of St Giles or in the household of the king or queen. Dunbar perhaps failed to obtain promotion in the church because – unlike Douglas – he did not come from a wealthy or noble family. This was a time when nepotism and pluralism were widespread, in Scotland as throughout Europe; ecclesiastical revenues were often employed to provide salaries for the high officers of state, and sometimes put to more scandalous use. James IV appointed one of his illegitimate sons, at the age of 11, to be archbishop of St Andrews, and made John Damian (see 4) head of an abbey that he appears never to have visited.

The turning-point of Dunbar's career at court seems to have been the year 1507: until that date his pension was considerably smaller than those received by masons, gunners, falconers and many other members of the royal household, whose reward – as one poem (56) makes clear – he contrasted with his own. In 1507, however, it was doubled, and in 1510 raised to what was then the very high sum of £80 a year. Although Dunbar's petitionary poems cannot be precisely dated, it is arguable that those that reveal a particularly strong sense of grievance (e.g. 55, 56 and 57) belong to the years shortly before 1507.

There is no doubt as to the importance of the court to Dunbar. It provided him with not only a livelihood but an audience; many of his poems are addressed to the king, the queen or fellow-courtiers. It also provided much, though not all, of his subject matter. He writes of small ephemeral incidents, and also of grander festive occasions, such as James IV's wedding in 1503 (41) or the queen's visit to Aberdeen in 1511 (6). He puts members of the household into his poems, devising lampoons about fools, alchemists and knights. A dance at court is the subject of one poem (58), and provides the metaphoric structure for another (36). The word 'court' itself often occurs, casually but tellingly (e.g. in 7, 21, 44, 55, 57 and 67). In one poem Dunbar claims to describe what he sees 'Daylie in court befoir myn e [eye]' (56. 72), and what we are shown is a place peopled with fools and ruled by 'blind effectioun', or partiality (63). Such a stance, of course, had a long literary history, it was traditional for satirists to find courts venal and corrupt. Yet Dunbar's view of the court is not uniformly bleak; the feudal and hierarchical ideals that inform 41 provide an instructive contrast.

There is a tendency among some Scottish historians to glamorize James IV and his 'brilliant Renaissance court' (Lynch 1992: 160). But James had neither the wealth nor the cultural interests of the Medici. He was dynamic and charismatic, and an effective ruler; but there is little evidence that he was an intellectual, or set out consciously to be an enlightened patron of poets. An energetic extrovert, he enjoyed aristocratic sports, such as falconry and hunting, and lavishly rewarded fiddlers, harpers, luters, minstrels and other entertainers. But the arts that he most promoted were those of war – tournaments, artillery contests and the building up of a great navy. The Scottish court was no rarefied elite, either socially or intellectually. Edinburgh was a small and comparatively democratic place, in which courtiers and burgesses seem to have intermingled easily. Dunbar includes craftsmen, such as masons and shipwrights, along with knights among the 'servitouris' at court, and James is noted for his easy accessibility to people of all classes. The king was certainly important to Dunbar, and figures obliquely in many of his poems; James's affability is also implicit in Dunbar's readiness to tease or chide him. It seems likely, however, that the greatest literary and intellectual stimulus for Dunbar came not from the king but from other members of the household with an education similar to his own – churchmen, clerks, lawyers and fellow-poets. (On James IV, see Mackie 1958; Macdougall 1989 and 1991; Lyall 1991.)

Literary inheritance

Dunbar was an educated but not a bookish poet. He rarely parades his learning in the manner of Douglas; nor does he use a book, like Chaucer and Henryson, as the starting-point for a poem of his own. Despite token references to Homer and Cicero (in **47**), there is little trace of indebtedness to classical writers. The Latin tradition that mattered most to Dunbar was that associated with the church – its hymns, liturgy, and the Scriptures – and with those churchmen who wrote the witty and irreverent poems termed 'Goliardic'. Like most medieval poets, he owed a great debt to the literature of France, and particularly to the tradition of dream poetry that originated in the thirteenth century with *Le Roman de la Rose* of Guillaume de Lorris and Jean de Meun. Yet Dunbar shows no awareness of his French contemporaries, such as Jean Molinet or Octavien de Saint-Gelais, and there is little to substantiate suggestions that he should be viewed as the Scottish equivalent of these 'grands rhétoriqueurs' (Smith 1934; Norman 1989b.)

The poetry that was most important to Dunbar was written in his own tongue, to which he gave the name 'Inglisch' (**47**). Dunbar paid little heed to the political frontier between England and Scotland, and recognized a single language-community, transcending local ones. He unequivocally embraced the poetic traditions associated with Chaucer, addressing a glowing tribute to Chaucer, Lydgate and Gower in **47**, and placing the same trio at the head of the 'makaris' in **16**. The importance of Chaucer – and, to a lesser extent, of Lydgate – to Dunbar and other fifteenth-century Scottish poets is incontrovertible. Chaucer was re-garded as the master of poetic modes and genres that greatly appealed to the late middle ages – dream allegories, such as *The Parliament of Fowls*, and stories of love and chivalry, such as *Troilus and Criseyde*. He introduced new and complex stanza forms, in particular rhyme royal (which Dunbar uses for several poems) and the nine-line stanza adopted for **47**. Above all, Chaucer was admired for the subtlety of his style and diction; he had *illuminated* the language of poetry (Fox 1966; Kratzmann 1980).

Yet it is commonly believed that Dunbar, although he praised Chaucer, was not profoundly influenced by him. What Dunbar praised, however, was not Chaucer's genius as philosopher or story-teller, but his powers of expression. This admiration is reflected in Dunbar's own style, in small allusions or verbal echoes. Many of these are employed with literary tact and decorum, when Dunbar is employing a mode used earlier by Chaucer. When he mentions a fellow-poet and -clerk, he thus alludes to the portrait of the Clerk in the Prologue to *The Canterbury Tales* (**16**. 75); and when he commends a great soldier, Bernard Stewart, he recalls a phrase that Criseyde applied to Troilus (**45**. 82). (Similarly discreet allusion or borrowing occurs in **34** and **47**). Elsewhere, however, Dunbar is more inventive, playfully appropriating Chaucer to his own poetic ends. Sometimes he mixes kinds and genres, adapting a simile from the section on lechery in *The Parson's Tale* to a new use in an alliterative diatribe against a senile old husband (**3**. 186–7). Elsewhere he rewrites a striking passage from *The Merchant's Tale* (**3**. 107), and embeds a sententia from Pandarus in a new and humorous context (**70**. 85–90).

Yet Dunbar clearly had a keen sense of Scotland's own distinctive literary tradition; in **16** he mentions twenty-one poets from 'this cuntre', ranging from the fourteenth century to his own age. Literary historians sometimes call the reign of James IV a 'Golden Age', but the term might be better applied to the fifteenth century as a whole, since it witnessed a remarkable flowering of vernacular poetry in Scotland (see Kratzmann 1980; Jack 1988; Mapstone 1991). The greatness of Robert Henryson is widely acknowledged, but he was by no means a solitary or isolated genius. Many other interesting poets flourished in this century: the names of some are known, such as James I, poet of *The Kingis Quair*, Richard Holland, Gilbert Hay and Walter Kennedy, but several excellent works, such as *Rauf Coilyear* or *The Freiris of Berwick*, are now sadly anonymous. Much has probably been lost – the Scottish Reformers disliked works that smacked of 'papistry' (MacDonald 1983); yet what survives is remarkable both for its diversity of subject and genre – chronicles, dream poems, romances, beast fables – and for its stylistic and metrical skill. We owe the preservation of many of these works to a number of sixteenth-century collectors, who compiled the important manuscript miscellanies that bear their names: the Asloan Manuscript (*c.* 1513–30), the Bannatyne Manuscript (*c.* 1568) and the Maitland Folio (*c.* 1570–86).

It was these fifteenth-century Scottish poets who furnished Dunbar's immediate literary heritage. But not all of them were equally important or congenial to him. He was certainly acquainted with the

Scottish tradition of historical verse, mentioning its leading exponents, John Barbour, Andrew Wyntoun and Blind Hary (16); yet he reveals no trace of the strident anglophobia that informs Hary's *Wallace*. More important to him was a body of didactic writing concerned with good government, known as the *speculum principis*, or 'advice to princes', tradition; some important Scottish examples are Hay's *Gouernaunce of Princis*, *The Thre Prestis of Peblis* and *De Regimine Principum* (Lyall 1976a; Mapstone 1986). The central section of 41 clearly belongs to this tradition of offering forthright advice to kings and their counsellors. Dunbar also knew and admired his greatest predecessor, Henryson. His own beast fable (64) may lack Henryson's moral seriousness, yet shows that he had read *The Fables* attentively. There are other affinities to Henryson, evident in the political symbolism of the Lion in 41 and the lively argumentative birds of 19. Perhaps the greatest native influence upon Dunbar, however, was that of Richard Holland's *Buke of the Howlat* (*c.* 1455). This tale of an owl who became discontented with his ugly plumage mixes witty bird lore with politics, and comedy with instruction. It was popular in Dunbar's time, and its influence can be detected in the style and phrasing of 4, the depiction of the goddess Nature in 41, and the avian court of 57.

Holland's medium was the elaborate thirteen-line alliterative stanza, a form employed by several Scottish poets in this period (Turville-Petre 1977; Riddy 1988). Dunbar owed an enormous debt to the traditions of alliterative poetry written in both England and Scotland; his style and diction were influenced not only by *The Howlat*, but by two anonymous Scottish romances, *Rauf Coilyear* and *Golagros and Gawane*. This is most obvious in 3, but also in poems such as 36 and 54. Equally important to Dunbar was a small but highly distinctive body of comic Scottish verse, mostly anonymous and often characterized by burlesque, or diablerie. Not all the works can be dated with precision, but Dunbar mentions some, such as *Colkelbie Sow* (56), and others are known to have been printed in his lifetime. Dunbar's nightmarish dream poems (e.g. 4, 24, 36 and 65) often treat diabolic themes, and are indebted to this tradition (Bawcutt 1992a: 257–92). It should be noted that Dunbar includes no Gaelic poets among his 'makaris' (16), and – unlike Douglas – does not refer to heroes of Irish myth. In *The Flyting* he speaks scornfully of 'sic eloquence as thay in Erschry use', and humorously but firmly dissociates himself from the traditions of Gaelic-speaking Scotland (on which see Gillies 1988).

'Ballatis under the byrkis'

Dunbar's favourite term for his own writings is *ballatis* (see 50, 57 and 61), a somewhat elastic term that connoted poems that were usually short and lyrical. Dunbar indeed stands out from his contemporaries not just for the brevity of his poems, but for their succinctness and compression. He also speaks of his verse as *making* (53) and calls himself a *makar* (58, 63); these traditional terms do not seem to have such lofty associations as *poetry* and *poet*, and lay stress on the poem as artefact, and the poet as a skilled craftsman. (On Dunbar's attitude to poetry, see Fox 1959; Ebin 1988; Bawcutt 1992a: 16–38.) Dunbar has a versatility that is characteristic of Scottish poetry in this period. He employs many different medieval genres, such as the beast fable (64), the testament (14), the debate (19) and the elegy (18); and there are several, very varied, examples of the dream poem, the petition and the courtly panegyric. Not all his poems, however, can be so easily classified; genres are often subverted or put to new uses, and some poems modulate and radically change as they proceed. One (44) begins as a satiric complaint on the evils of the times, and ends with a vision of the Last Judgment. Much of the pleasure of *The Twa Mariit Wemen and the Wedo* (3) derives from its intertextuality. On the surface it is a framed story-collection, in which each of three women recounts her 'taill', or experience, of marriage. But Dunbar wittily alludes to other genres, such as the *chanson de mal mariée*, the gossips' meeting, and the social pastime of the *demande d'amours*. Even the saint's legend is burlesqued, as the Widow reminds us, when she concludes: 'This is the legeand of my lyf'.

Dunbar, as Auden noted, is a superb and varied metrist. He ranges from alliterative verse (3) to long and complex stanza forms such as rhyme royal (26, 33, 40 and 41), the nine-line 'Anelida' stanza (47) and a very demanding twelve-line stanza with internal rhyme (11). Dunbar also uses more popular forms, such as the carol (30, 55) and different types of tail-rhyme (4, 31 and 36). The stanzas that seem most congenial to him, however, are shorter and simpler: arranged in varying patterns of four or five lines, and often accompanied with a refrain. (For the principal types, see headnotes to 9, 15, 16 and 24.) These refrains are drawn from varied sources – especially proverbial wisdom and the liturgy – and skilfully establish a poem's tone and theme.

Dunbar's style is remarkably flexible and varied, more so than all critics have recognized. At one extreme is the jewelled, aureate 'high style', characteristic of *The Goldyn Targe* and other courtly poems; at the other is a low style, characteristic of *The Flyting* and other invectives, which draws on the most colloquial registers of the language. Both of these are flamboyant, and tend to be associated with complex verse forms. But some of Dunbar's finest poems have an unobtrusive style; thoughtful and melancholy in tone, they are plain in diction and simple in syntax. These poems (e.g. 9, 15, 16 and 21) are probably the easiest to understand, and most accessible to the modern reader. (See Bawcutt 1992a: 347–82.)

In a brief introduction it is impossible to do full justice to Dunbar's artistry. It may be more helpful therefore to call attention to his chief strengths as a poet. These, it seems to me, do not lie in the traditional field of the court poet, compliment and eulogy; Dunbar's poems of this kind, such as the two poems on Bernard Stewart (**18**, **45**), or those addressed to the queen (**6**, **10**), are competent but not distinctive. Where Dunbar particularly excels is in the petitions, the religious verse, and a group of richly varied comic-sardonic poems.

The petitions form a striking and interesting body of poetry, yet have received curiously little critical attention. The pejorative label 'begging-poems' fails to take account of the social system from which they spring. (See, however, Green 1980; Burrow 1981; and Bawcutt 1992a: 103–115.) They are essentially verse letters, conveying a request, or occasionally an apology, to persons of higher rank than the poet. A few are addressed to the queen (**60**, **61**), but most, usually those that begin with 'Schir', are addressed to the king (see **5**, **7**, **50–53**, **55–57**, **63** and **66**). Stylistically and metrically they have much in common, but their range of tone is wide. Some, such as **29** and **52**, sound like comparatively light-hearted *jeux d'esprit*, but most are reflective, and some are sombre and deeply melancholy. Dunbar's self-depiction is often comic and undignified – as a hawk with moulting plumage (**57**), for instance, or an old horse (**55**), or a man obliged to miss his breakfast because his purse is empty (**50**). But he also conveys very powerfully his fear of poverty and old age, and a sense of rejection or exclusion from the king's favour. Critics have differed as to the degree of self-expression in Dunbar; these poems, though undoubtedly containing conventional elements, seem to me the most intimate and introspective in his oeuvre.

Dunbar also wrote several impressive religious poems. Some of these are concerned with the central themes of Christianity – a devout meditation on the Crucifixion (**1**), and jubilant hymn-like celebrations of the Virgin (**11**), the Nativity (**48**) and the Resurrection (**8**); see also **19**, **30**, **49** and **69**. Past editors have labelled other poems as 'moralities' (**16**, **21**, **25**, **34**, **38**, **40** and **44**); but in Dunbar morality can rarely be divorced from religious feeling. These poems give counsel concerning the good life, but many are penitential in tone, and dominated by the fear of death and judgment. Some belong to well-established genres: impersonal in tone and conventional in expression, they are designed for the instruction of *homo*, or Everyman. Two (**16** and **21**), however, are exceptional. In them the poet speaks both as the representative of humanity and as an individual, remembering his dead friends and contemplating his own mortality.

Dunbar's most original poems all contain some strain of comedy. His tone ranges from genial or flippant banter to the black and sardonic mockery for which he is best known. His targets are varied: sometimes he ridicules traditional butts, such as friars, tailors and fools; but he often makes fun of himself (**50**, **55**) or high-ranking courtiers (**58**).

Certain modes seem particularly congenial. Dunbar is a master of satire and invective – he demonstrates this not only in *The Flyting* (54), a literary quarrel with another poet, Kennedy, but in a number of shorter lampoons, such as 58 and 60. He also excels in parody and burlesque. Some poems are parodic in the wider sense, in that they subvert our first expectations as to a poem's literary kind – a pious vision thus turns into a diabolic nightmare (65). Some, such as 31 and 36, contain mock-chivalric elements. Others are parodic in a stricter sense, and spring from the central tradition of medieval Latin parody (14 and 70). Particularly striking is a group of blackly comic dream poems, varied in metrical form and structure, yet similar in tone and a strain of 'eldritch' fantasy (4, 24, 36, 37, 65).

Dunbar is a witty poet; his wit, however, is not easily isolable in the form of neat epigrams, but is allusive and contextual. His comic armoury includes puns and word-play (see 55, 60 and 61); amusing and unexpected rhymes (60. 21–2); and grotesque and reductive imagery. His images are often highly visual, and many come from the animal world (as in 3, 54 and 58) or from unexpected, low and 'unpoetic' sources – a choked gutter (3. 99), soap and a tar barrel (23), and a smith's pincers (36). A constant feature of his style is irony, sometimes sporadic and intermittent, but often sustained throughout a whole poem (37, 62, 64 and 65). The framework of 3 is richly ironic: the women speak indiscreetly because they think they are alone, while the eavesdropping poet-narrator hears nothing but evil of his own sex. Dunbar's comedy is frequently disturbing, and often exploits areas of social tension, between men and women, or between Highlanders and Lowlanders. Poem 3 ends with a playful question to the imagined audience; and others are equivocal, leaving the reader in doubt as to the tone, or exact degree of seriousness. Some indeed, as Dunbar says in 61, are 'bourdes', or jests, designed chiefly to entertain; others, such as 3 and 36, explore extremely contentious issues.

Texts

Dunbar's poems survive scattered in prints and manuscripts of widely different character, whose dates range from the early sixteenth to the seventeenth century. In approximately chronological order these are:

The Aberdeen Burgh Sasine Register (Town House, Aberdeen).
This legal work, in several volumes, dating from June 1484 onwards, contains a number of blank pages into which – as was not uncommon – vernacular poems have been transcribed. Three of these, in proximity to entries dated 1505 and 1511, are attributed to Dunbar; two are included in the present edition (10 and 46).

The Prints (National Library of Scotland, Edinburgh).
A few of Dunbar's most famous poems were printed in his own lifetime by Scotland's first printers, Walter Chepman and Andro Myllar. In 1507 they received a patent from the king, authorizing them to print lawbooks, chronicles, missals and breviaries 'eftir our awin Scottis use'; and in 1508 appeared the first known products of their press, nine small booklets containing a number of vernacular works, including poems by Dunbar (see **45** and **47**). Another undated print, possibly produced by Myllar *c*. 1507, contains three of Dunbar's poems (**3**, **14** and **16**). (See Introduction to *Chepman and Myllar Prints*.)

The Asloan Manuscript (National Library of Scotland, MS 16500).
This important miscellany, containing prose and verse, was compiled by John Asloan, a notary active in Edinburgh between 1497 and 1530. Although sections of the manuscript are now missing, the original table of contents survives and shows that it once included several poems by Dunbar; of these only four remain, one of which is fragmentary (**1**, **4**, **11** and **36**). (See Introduction to *Asloan Manuscript*; and Cunningham 1994.)

The Arundel Manuscript (British Library, MS Arundel 285).
This devotional manuscript, compiled *c*. 1540, largely consists of prayers and meditations on the Passion, in verse and prose, and forms an important guide to devotional practices in Scotland at this time. It contains three poems attributed to Dunbar (**1**, **33** and **69**), and provides a valuable context for his other religious verse. (See Introduction to *Devotional Pieces in Verse and Prose*.)

The Bannatyne Manuscript (National Library of Scotland, MS Adv. 1. 1. 6).
This famous poetic miscellany was compiled *c*. 1568 by George Bannatyne, at a time of plague in Edinburgh. It is notable not only for the quantity and diversity of verse that it contains, but for Bannatyne's ambitious attempt at a thematic arrangement in five sections: 'ballatis of theoligie'; 'ballatis of moralitie'; 'ballettis mirry'; 'ballatis of luve'; and 'fabillis'. In addition to the Main Manuscript there exists an earlier 'Draft'; comparison of these provides evidence as to Bannatyne's methods and accuracy as a copyist. This manuscript contains forty-five poems attributed to Dunbar; it provides the copy-texts for twenty poems in this edition. (See Introductions to *Bannatyne Facsimile* and *Bannatyne Manuscript*.)

The Maitland Folio (Pepys Library, Magdalene College, Cambridge, MS 2553).
Written in a number of hands, and compiled between 1570 and 1586, this manuscript belonged to the family of Sir Richard Maitland of Lethington. By far the most important repository of Dunbar's poems,

· it contains over sixty poems now believed to be his, and supplies copy-texts for thirty-two poems in this edition. (See *Maitland Folio Manuscript*.)

The Reidpeth Manuscript (Cambridge University Library, MS L1. 5. 10).
This is a partial transcript of the Maitland Folio, when that manuscript was more complete than it now is. Fifty of its eighty-five items are attributed to Dunbar, and it contains eight unique copies of poems by Dunbar, from a missing section of the Maitland Folio. The manuscript was written by John Reidpeth, who began it on 7 December 1622, presumably for Christopher Cockburn, who owned it in 1623.

Many of Dunbar's poems exist in multiple copies, but there is no clear-cut relationship between the witnesses, except in the case of the Reidpeth Manuscript's obvious dependence upon the Maitland Folio. No manuscript is written in Dunbar's hand, or has claim to overriding authority. The prints were produced in Dunbar's lifetime, yet contain elementary typographical errors and are unlikely to have been supervised or checked by him. The Asloan manuscript is valuable as a witness, from its early date, but unfortunately is now imperfect, as indeed are some of the prints. Most of Dunbar's poems are thus preserved in late witnesses, the Bannatyne and Maitland manuscripts, which were compiled long after he had died, in a time of great cultural change and religious upheaval. Both are valuable, yet show signs of the 'editing' of Dunbar's texts: some vocabulary that may have seemed archaic has been modernized, and passages in religious poems have been modified to suit Protestant susceptibilities. The chronological spread of the witnesses is a major reason for the strikingly varied orthography of Dunbar's poems. This is well illustrated in the markedly different spellings in the poems on Bernard Stewart (18, 45), written in the same year yet preserved in witnesses over a century apart. (For fuller information and discussion, see Baxter 1952: 216–21; Bawcutt 1981 and 1991.)

Language

In Dunbar's time several languages were used in Scotland: Latin, which was chiefly employed in the church and for education; Gaelic, or *Erse*, which was spoken in the Highlands and Galloway; and Scots, which was the native tongue of Lowlanders, such as Dunbar. Lowland Scots was closely related to the northern dialects of Middle English, although it possessed many distinctive features of phonology, orthography, grammar and vocabulary. Dunbar and other medieval Scottish writers called their language 'Inglis' or 'Inglisch'; the term 'Scottis' was not applied to the vernacular of the Lowlands until the 1490s, and 'Inglis' continued in this sense until the seventeenth century. Although there existed a literary standard, a great variety of usage was tolerated. In poetry this variety was largely determined by considerations of style. Comic verse, for instance, was much more distinctively Scottish in its diction, and drew on the vulgar and colloquial registers of the language. It was also characterized by attempts to show recent developments in Scottish pronunciation, such as the vocalization of /l/ in *aw*, 'all', and *fow*, 'full'. Such shortened forms were particularly characteristic of comic verse, though not confined to it. By contrast, poets who sought a more elevated style tended to imitate the practice of Chaucer and other courtly English poets; their diction was correspondingly anglicized. One feature is the use of rhymes that require southern-English rather than Scots pronunciations; so *more* and *sore* (11. 49, 53), rather than the usual Scots forms with *a* (*mare*, *sare*). Another obvious marker of this style concerns verbal forms: the use of *bene* in the senses 'is' and 'are'; the archaic infinitive ending in *-n* (e.g. 'sene', 41. 88; 'sayn', 47. 198); and the past participle with prefixed *y* (e.g. 'ybent', 47. 110). These usages, along with certain lexical items, such as *lyte*, 'little', or *morowing*, 'morning', were not characteristic of Scottish prose. (The best discussion is in Aitken 1971 and 1983.)

The following brief notes are intended as a preliminary aid to readers. For further information on the language in this period, see Aitken 1977; the *Concise Scots Dictionary*, which contains a brief 'History of Scots'; the entries 'Inglis', 'Scots' and 'Scottish English' in McArthur 1992; Macafee 1992–93; and Murison 1974.

Orthography

1. The spelling system of Scots is extremely variable, and English spellings exist side-by-side with Scots ones.
2. The letters *i* and *y* are used interchangeably.
3. Regular equivalences exist between some Scots spellings and English ones. Thus Scots *-ang* corresponds to English *-ong* (*sang*, *lang*); *-ald* to English *-old* (*ald*, *bald*); *-cht* to English *-ght* (*licht*, *richt*); *quh-* to English *wh-* (see Glossary below); *ei* commonly corresponds either to English *ee* (*feit*, *cheikis*) or *ea* (*cleir*, *pleis*). *Sch* represents English *sh*. Note, however, *schir*, 'sir'.
4. Final *-e* is normally unsounded, but sometimes has syllabic value, chiefly in words of French origin, such as *bewte*, 'beauty', *pete*, 'pity', *trigide*, 'tragedy'. Sometimes it is an orthographic marker of a preceding long vowel (*kene*, 'keen').
5. The variant spellings of some words indicate new developments in pronunciation. Vocalization of /l/ after back vowels is indicated in spellings such as *aw*, beside *all* (54. 95), and *fow*, beside *full* (51. 8). Note also *sell*, 'self' (refrain to 12).

Grammar

6. *A* and *ane* represent both the numeral 'one' and the indefinite article 'a', 'an'. *Ane* is used before consonants as well as vowels: *ane cloister* (**1**. 1).

7. Nouns: the usual plural and genitive ending is *-is* (*-ys*), but endings in *-(e)s* also occur. Note *ene*, 'eyes', and the uninflected plurals, *hors*, *thing*.

8. The pronoun system is close to that in modern English. But the following forms should be noted: *his* = 'its' as well as 'his' (as in **59**. 14); *scho*, 'she'; *thai* and *thay* represent the personal pronoun 'they', and also the demonstrative 'those'; *thir*, 'these'; *thow*, 'thou'; *the*, 'thee'; *ye*, *yow*, 'you', with both singular and plural senses (cf. **3**. 41 and 50). Relative pronouns include *that*, and the reduced form *at*; *quhilk* has the senses 'which' and 'who'. Dunbar occasionally uses relative clauses of the 'zero' type, without an introductory relative pronoun: 'Is no man thair [that] trowis ane udir' (**2**. 11). *That* sometimes signifies 'that which' (**21**. 27; **37**. 10).

9. Verbs: in the present tense *-is* is the regular ending of the 2nd- and 3rd-person singular. But *-is* also occurs with other persons, chiefly when the verb does not have a personal pronoun as its subject, or is separated from the pronoun: *The divillis trymmillis* (**8**. 5), 'the devils tremble'; *I blenk by my buke and blynis* (**3**. 428), 'I look away from my book and cease'.

10. The present participle regularly ends in *-and*, but forms with *-ing* and *-in* also occur.

11. The imperative is usually uninflected, but the plural may end in *-is*: *lythis* (**31**. 1). Sometimes it is accompanied by the appropriate pronoun, e.g. 'thow pres' (**25**. 3).

12. The usual preterite ending of weak verbs is *-it*. On the forms of strong verbs, see Macafee 1992–93.

13. It was common to form present and past tenses by using periphrastic constructions with *do* and *did* + infinitive. Scottish poets extended this practice to form compound present and past participles. Some examples are: *doing . . . fleit* (**41**. 49), 'flowing'; *Doing . . . chace* (**41**. 56), 'chasing'; *has done roune* (**16**. 81), 'has whispered'; *is done ceis* (**8**. 33), 'is finished'.

14. Other periphrastic forms of the preterite occur. In narrative the construction *cowd* (or *culd*) + infinitive is equivalent to the simple past tense (e.g. **54**. 93).

15. Double negatives are used, as in English, for emphasis. Cf. 'I can not leif in no degre' (**13**. 3) and also **67**. 5–6.

16. Word order in verse is flexible, and does not necessarily follow the patterns usual in prose. Inversions are common – e.g *quhome on*, 'on whom' (**54**. 25) – and this sometimes leads to ambiguity. Cf. **11**. 77–8; **44**. 21.

Vocabulary

17. Some common conjunctions and prepositions have senses additional to those familiar in modern English: *and*, 'if'; *but*, 'without'; *in to*, 'in'; *nor*, 'than'; *till*, 'to'.

18. Dunbar, like other medieval poets, uses set phrases and tags to fill out the verse line or supply rhymes: *eik, iwis, ay, but dreid, in erd*, etc.

Glossary of common words

aboif, abone	above	*dar*	dare
agane	again	*de, deit*	die, died
aganis	against, in	*deid*, a.	dead
	preparation for	*deid*, n.	(1) death; (2) deed
al(l)	all, every	*deir*	dear
ald, auld	old	*doun*	down
alkin	every kind of	*durst*	dared
allace	alas		
allane	alone	*e, ene*	eye, eyes
als	also	*efter*	after
als . . . as	as . . . as	*eik*	also
amang	among	*eird, erd(e)*	earth
ane	a(n), one	*ellis*	else
anis	once	*erdlie*	earthly
apon, apone	upon		
at(t)our	over, above	*fals*	false
awalk	awake	*fane*	glad, gladly
awin	own	*fang*	take
ay	ever, always	*fer*	far
		fle, flaw	fly, fled
baith	both	*foryet*	forget
be, prep., conj.	by, when	*fra, fro*	from, after
befoir	before	*fule, fuill*	fool
begowthe	began	*furth*	forth
bene	be, is, are, been		
betwene	between	*ga*	go, walk
betwix	between	*gaif*	gave
bot	but, only	*gang*	go, walk
but	without	*gar* + infin.	cause (to)
		gart	caused
cleir, clere	clear, bright	*gif(e)*, conj.	if
come	came	*gif(e), geif*, v.	give
couth, culd	could, knew how to	*greit, grit*	great
cum	come	*gud(e), guid*	good, goods

haif	have	*narrest*	nearest
haill, a., adv.	healthy, whole, wholly	*nether*	neither
		nixt	next
hald, hauld	hold	*nocht, nought*	not, nothing
hame	home	*nor*	than
hard	heard	*nowder*	neither
he, heich	high, loud		
hecht	vowed	*o(u)cht*	anything
heir	here	*on(e)*	on, in
hie, hye	high, loud	*ony, onie*	any
hes	has	*or*	(1) or; (2) before
hew	hue, colour	*our*	over
hir	her		
		pur(e)	poor
ilk, ilka	each, same		
in to	in, into, within	*quha*	who
		quhais	whose
keip	keep	*quham(e)*	whom
ken	know, teach	*quhar, quhair*	where
kest	cast	*quhat*	what
kirk	church	*quhen*	when
knaw	know	*quhy*	why
		quhilk	which, who
lang	long	*quhill*	(1) until; (2) while
lat(t)	(1) let, allow; (2) prevent	*quhite, quhyt*	white
		quho	who
law	low	*quhois*	whose
le	tell lies	*quhom(e)*	whom
leif	(1) leave; (2) live	*quhone*	when
lyk	like	*quhow*	how
luf(f), luve	love	*quyk*	living
luk(e), luik	look	*quod*	said
lusty	joyful, pleasant		
		riale, riall	royal
ma, mo	more	*rin, ryn*	run
mair, mare	more	*ring*, n., v.	reign
maist	most	*richt*, adv.	very
mak	make		
man, mon	must	*sa*	so
mekill, meikill	much, large	*sair*	sad, grievous
mony	many	*sall*	shall
mot	may	*sam*	same
		sang	song
na	no, nor, than	*schaw*	show
nan(e)	none, no	*schene*	bright, beautiful

schir	sir	*togidder*	together
scho	she	*tother, tuther*	the other
se	see	*trew*	true
sen	since	*trow*	believe
sic	such	*tuik, tuke*	took
sone, n.	(1) son; (2) sun	*twa*	two
sone, adv.	soon		
suld, sould	should	*udir, uther*	other
sum	some, one		
suppois	although	*wait(t)*	know, knows
swa	so	*wald*	would, wished
syn(e)	then	*walk, walkin*	wake, awake
		war, adv.	worse
ta	the one	*war,* v.	were
ta(i)k	take	*warld*	world
tane	taken	*weill, wele*	well
tha(y), thai	(1) they; (2) those	*weir,* n.	(1) war; (2) doubt
thaim	them	*weir,* v.	wear
thair, pron.	their	*wene*	think, suppose
thair, adv.	there	*wicht*	person
than	then	*wirk*	work, make
the	thee	*wode(e), woid*	mad
think, thinkis	seem, seems	*wrocht*	made
thir	these		
thocht, conj.	although	*yeid, yuid*	went
thocht, n., v.	thought	*ying*	young
throw	through	*yit*	yet, still
till	to, until	*yon(e)*	that
to	too		

THE POEMS

1

This meditation on the Passion takes the form of a visionary experience upon Good Friday (see stanzas 1 and 18). The dream itself has two sections, each introduced by 'Methocht' (lines 9 and 97), and each having its own distinctive refrain. The first part is narrative in mode, the second allegorical and introspective. The process of recalling the Crucifixion (cf. 'memorie', line 5) evokes in the dreamer orthodox emotions of compassion and contrition. The poem's ultimate source is the Gospels (especially Matthew 26–7 and Luke 22–3). It resembles the English mystery plays, and many other late-medieval accounts of the Crucifixion, both in the stress laid on the physical suffering of Jesus and in the emotive, penitential tone of the dreamer's response; for contemporary Scottish parallels, see Kennedy's *The Passioun of Crist* and other works included in *Devotional Pieces in Verse and Prose*. This poem, however, is characteristic of Dunbar in its brevity, structural neatness and subtle handling of personification allegory. The stanza, *ababbcbC⁴*, is also employed in 25 and 48.

Text: MF, pp. 203–7; collated with A, ff. 290ᵛ–292ʳ (1–96 only), and Ar, ff. 168ʳ–170ʳ.
3. knelit] A; kneling MF.
19. ruge] A, Ar; rage MF.
59. hyd] A; syde MF.
70. him] Ar; at him MF. nakit] Ar; nathing MF.
79. tak] A; mak MF.
94. marter] Ar; martirdome MF.
103. bludy] Ar; ane MF.
117. The lord] Ar; That schort MF.
129. Grace] Ar; Grudge MF.

Authorship: 'Quod Dunbar' in MF and A. Anonymous in Ar.

Title: Untitled in MF; A has a rubric, 'Heir begynnis the passioun of Ihesu', and in the contents list is entitled 'Ane ballet of the passioun'; Ar has the title: 'The Passioun of Crist'.

21

Further reading: On the devotional background, see Woolf 1968: 183–238, esp. 233–4. For a hostile response, see Scott 1966: 284–8 ('brutal and crude in its insistence on the physical details of the Crucifixion'); for more sympathetic accounts, see Bennett 1982: 121–7, and Bawcutt 1992a: 167–71.

1

Amang thir freiris within ane cloister
I enterit in ane oritorie,
And knelit doun with ane *pater noster*
Befoir the michtie king of glorie,
Haveing his passioun in memorie;   5
Syn to his mother I did inclyne,
Hir halsing with ane *gaude flore*,
And sudandlie I sleipit syne.

2

Methocht Judas with mony ane Jow
Tuik blissit Jesu our salvatour,   10
And schot him furth with mony ane schow,
With schamefull wourdis of dishonour,
And lyk ane theif or ane tratour
Thay leid that hevinlie prince most hie,
With manassing attour messour,   15
O mankynd, for the luif of the.

3

Falslie condamnit befoir ane juge,
Thay spittit in his visage fayr,

1. *thir freiris]* These friars.
2. *oritorie]* Chapel.
3. *knelit]* Knelt.
5. *passioun]* Suffering.
6. *Syn]* Then.
7. *halsing]* Greeting.
8. *sleipit]* Slept.
9. *Methocht]* It seemed to me. *Jow]* Jew.
10. *Tuik]* Took. *blissit]* Blessed. *salvatour* Saviour.
11. *schot]* Drove. *schow]* Shove, thrust.
13. *theif]* Thief.
14. *leid]* Led. *hie]* Noble.
15. *manassing]* Threats. *attour messour]* Excessive.
16. *luif]* Love.
17. *condamnit]* Condemned. *juge* Judge.

And as lyounis with awfull ruge
In yre thay hurlit him heir and thair,   20
And gaif him mony buffat sair
That it wes sorow for to se.
Of all his claythis thay tirvit him bair,
O mankynd, for the luif of the.

4

Thay terandis, to revenge thair tein,   25
For scorne thai cled him in to quhyt,
And hid his blythfull glorious ene,
To se quham angellis had delyt;
Dispituouslie syn did him smyt,
Saying, 'Gif sone of God thow be,   30
Quha straik the now thow tell us tyt',
O mankynd, for the luif of the.

5

In tene thay tirvit him agane,
And till ane pillar thai him band.
Quhill blude birst out at everie vane,   35
Thay scurgit him bayth fut and hand.
At everie straik ran furth ane strand
Quhilk mycht have ransonit warldis thre.
He baid in stour quhill he mycht stand,
O mankynd, for the luif of the.   40

---

19. *awfull ruge]* Terrifying roar.
20. *hurlit]* Threw violently.
21. *buffat sair]* Painful blow.
22. *se]* See.
23. *claythis]* Clothes. *tirvit]* Stripped.
25. *Thay terandis]* Those villains. *revenge . . . tein]* Vent their anger.
26. *cled]* Clad. *quhyt]* White.
27. *blythfull]* Joyful. *ene]* Eyes.
28. *delyt]* Delight.
29. *Dispituouslie]* Without pity. *smyt]* Strike.
30. *Gif]* If. *sone]* Son.
31. *straik]* Struck. *tyt]* At once.
34. *band]* Bound.
35. *Quhill]* Till. *blude]* Blood. *birst]* Burst. *vane]* Vein.
36. *scurgit]* Scourged. *fut]* Foot.
37. *straik]* Stroke. *strand]* Stream.
38. *ransonit]* Redeemed.
39. *baid]* Endured. *stour]* Battle. *quhill]* While.

6

Nixt all in purpyr thay him cled,
And syn with thornis scharp and kene
His saikles blude agane thay sched,
Persing his heid with pykis grene.
Unneis with lyf he micht sustene   45
That croun on thrungin with crueltie,
Quhill flude of blude blindit his ene,
O mankynd, for the luif of the.

7

Ane croce that wes bayth large and lang,
To beir thay gaif this blissit lord,   50
Syn fullelie as theif to hang
Thay harlit him furth with raip and corde.
With bluid and sweit was all deflorde
His face, the fude of angellis fre,
His feit with stanis was revin and scorde,   55
O mankynd, for the luif of the.

8

Agane thay tirvit him bak and syd,
Als brim as ony baris woid.
The clayth that claif to his cleir hyd
Thay raif away with ruggis rude,   60
Quhill fersly followit flesche and blude,
That it was pietie for to se.
Na kynd of torment he ganestude,
O mankynd, for the luif of the.

---

41. Nixt] Next. *purpyr]* Purple clothing.
43. saikles] Innocent.
44. Persing] Piercing. *pykis]* Spikes.
45. Unneis] Scarcely. *lyf]* Life.
46. thrungin] Thrust, pressed.
52. harlit] Dragged. *raip]* Rope.
53. sweit] Sweat. *deflorde]* Disfigured.
54. fude] Food. *fre]* Noble.
55. stanis] Stones. *revin]* Torn. *scorde]* Lacerated.
58. brim] Fierce. *baris woid]* Savage boars.
59. claif] Adhered. *cleir hyd]* Fair skin.
60. raif] Tore. *ruggis rude]* Rough tugs.
61. fersly] Cruelly.
62. pietie] Pity.
63. ganestude] Resisted.

9

On to the crose of breid and lenth   65
To gar his lymmis langar wax,
Thay straitit him with all thair strenth,
Quhill to the rude thay gart him rax,
Syn tyit him on with greit irne takkis,
And him all nakit on the tre,   70
Thay raissit on loft be houris sax,
O mankynd, for the luif of the.

10

Quhen he was bendit so on breid,
Quhill all his vanis brist and brak,
To gar his cruell pane exceid   75
Thay leit him fall doun with ane swak,
Quhill cors and corps and all did crak.
Agane thay rasit him on hie,
Reddie may turmentis for to tak,
O mankynd, for the luif of the.   80

11

Betwix two theiffis the spreit he gaif
On to the fader most of micht.
The erde did trimmill, the stanis claif,
The sone obscurit of his licht,
The day wox dirk as ony nicht,   85

---

65. *breid*] Width. *lenth*] Length.
66. *gar*] Cause. *wax*] Grow.
67. *straitit*] Forcibly extended.
68. *rude*] Cross. *rax*] Stretch.
69. *tyit*] Tied. *irne takkis*] Nails of iron.
70. *tre*] Cross (lit. tree).
71. *on loft*] On high.
73. *bendit . . . breid*] Stretched to the fullest extent.
74. *brist*] Burst. *brak*] Broke.
75. *pane*] Suffering. *exceid*] Increase.
76. *swak*] Violent blow.
77. *cors*] Cross. *corps*] Body.
79. *may*] More. *tak*] Endure.
81. *spreit . . . gaif*] Gave up his spirit.
82. *micht*] Power.
83. *erde*] Earth. *trimmill*] Tremble. *claif*] Split apart.
84. *sone*] Sun.
85. *wox*] Became. *dirk*] Dark.

Deid bodies rais in the cite.
Goddis deir sone all thus was dicht,
O mankynd, for the luif of the.

12

In weir that he wes yit on lyf
Thay rane ane rude speir in his syde,   90
And did his precious body ryff
Quhill blude and watter did furth glyde.
Thus Jesus with his woundis wyde
Ane marter sufferit for to de,
And tholit to be crucifyid,   95
O mankynd, for the luif of the.

13

Methocht Compassioun, wode of feiris,
Than straik at me with mony ane stound,
And soir Contritioun, bathit in teiris,
My visage all in watter drownit,   100
And Reuth in to my eir ay rounde:
'For schame allace, behald, man, how
Beft is with mony bludy wound
Thy blissit salvatour Jesu.'

14

Than rudlie come Remembrance,   105
Ay rugging me withouttin rest,
Quhilk crose and nalis, scharp scurge and lance,
And bludy crowne befoir me kest.

---

86. *rais*] Rose.
87. *dicht*] Treated.
89. *weir*] Doubt. *on lyf*] Alive.
90. *rane*] Thrust. *rude*] rough.
91. *ryff*] Split.
94. *marter*] Agony. *de*] Die.
95. *tholit*] Suffered.
97. *wode*] Angry. *feiris*] Behaviour.
98. *stound*] Pang (of grief).
101. *Reuth*] Pity. *rounde*] Whispered.
102. *behald*] Behold.
103. *Beft*] Struck.
105. *rudlie*] Roughly. *come*] Came.
106. *rugging*] Tugging. *rest*] Pause.
107. *scurge*] Scourge.
108. *kest*] Threw.

Than Pane with passioun me opprest,
And evir did Petie on me pow, 110
Saying, 'Behald how Jowis hes drest
Thy blissit salvatour Chryst Jesu.'

15

With greiting glaid be than come Grace,
With wourdis sweit saying to me,
'Ordane for him ane resting place, 115
That is so werie wrocht for the.
The lord within thir dayis thre
Sall law undir thy lyntell bow,
And in thy hous sall herbrit be
Thy blissit salvatour Chryst Jesu.' 120

16

Than swyth Contritioun wes on steir,
And did eftir Confessioun ryn,
And Conscience me accusit heir
And kest out mony cankerit syn.
To rys Repentence did begin, 125
And out at the yettis did schow.
Pennance did walk the hous within,
Byding our salvitour Chryst Jesu.

17

Grace become gyd and governour
To keip the hous in sicker stait, 130
Ay reddie till our salvatour,
Quhill that he come, air or lait.

110. *pow*] Pull.
111. *drest*] Treated.
115. *Ordane*] Prepare.
116. *werie*] Weary. *wrocht*] Made.
117. *thir*] These.
118. *law*] Low. *bow*] Stoop.
119. *herbrit*] Lodged.
121. *swyth*] Swiftly. *on steir*] In motion.
122. *ryn*] Run.
124. *cankerit*] Malignant.
126. *yettis*] Gates. *schow*] Push forward.
128. *Byding*] Awaiting.
129. *gyd*] Guide.
130. *sicker*] Secure, safe.
132. *air*] Early.

Repentence ay with cheikis wait
No pane nor pennence did eschew,
The hous within evir to debait,   135
Onlie for luif of sweit Jesu.

18

For grit terrour of Chrystis deid
The erde did trymmill quhair I lay,
Quhairthrow I waiknit in that steid,
With spreit halflingis in effray.   140
Than wrayt I all without delay,
Richt heir as I have schawin to yow,
Quhat me befell on Gud Fryday
Befoir the crose of sweit Jesu.

133. cheikis wait] Wet cheeks.
134. eschew] Avoid.
135. debait] Protect.
137. deid] Death.
139. waiknit] Woke up. *steid]* Place.
140. spreit] Spirit. *halflingis]* Half. *effray]* Fear.
141. wrayt] Wrote.
142. schawin] Shown.

2

This poem belongs to a common medieval genre, being largely devoted to satirizing the corruption of lawyers and their clients. Dunbar localizes it, however, referring specifically to Edinburgh and employing Scottish legal terminology. He also sharpens the irony by placing it in the mouth of a naive countryman, for whom such evils are not commonplace but new and shocking 'tythingis' (see line 3 and refrain). The poem has a catalogue structure, employing anaphora on *sum*; it should be noted that this indefinite pronoun is sometimes singular in sense ('one'), sometimes plural ('some'). The device was popular with Dunbar; for other uses, see 3. 480–5; and 5. The stanza, *aabbcbC⁴*, is regularly used by Dunbar for humorous or satiric purposes; see also **20**, **53**, **58** and **64**.

Text: MF, pp. 314–15; collated with B, ff. 59ʳ–59ᵛ, and R, ff. 37ʳ–38ʳ.

Authorship: 'Quod Dumbar' in MF, B and R.

Further reading: Little attention has been paid to this poem. See, however, Baxter 1952: 106–10; Reiss 1979: 62–3; Bawcutt 1992a: 214.

1

Ane murelandis man of uplandis mak
At hame thus to his nychtbour spak:
'Quhat tythingis, gossope, peace or weir?'
The uther roundit in his eir:
'I tell yow this, undir confessioun.   5

---

1. murelandis] From the moor. *uplandis mak]* Rustic appearance.
2. hame] Home. *nychtbour]* Neighbour. *spak]* Spoke.
3. tythingis] News. *gossope]* Friend (lit. godfather). *weir]* War.
4. roundit] Whispered. *eir]* Ear.

29

Bot laitlie lychtit of my meir,
I come of Edinburch fra the Sessioun.'

2

'Quhat tythingis herd ye thair, I pray yow?'
The tuther answerit, 'I sall say yow.
Keip this in secreit, gentill brudir.   10
Is no man thair, trowis ane udir.
A commoun doar of transgressioun
Of innocent folkis prevenis a·fuider.
Sic tythandis hard I at the Sessioun.

3

'Sum withe his fallow rownys him to pleis,   15
That wald for anger byt of his neis.
His fa sum be the oxtar ledis.
Sum pattiris with his mouthe on beidis
That hes his mynd all on oppressioun.
Sum bekis full laich and schawis bair heidis,   20
Wald luke full heich war not the Sessioun.

4

'Sum bydand law layis land in wed,
Sum superspendit gois to his bed,
Sum spedis for he in court hes meynis,

6] Only recently dismounted from my mare.
7. come] Came.
8. herd] Heard.
9. tuther] Other. *say]* Tell.
10. brudir] Brother.
11. trowis] Trusts. *udir]* Other.
12. doar of transgressioun] Wrongdoer.
13. prevenis] Gets the advantage of. *fuider]* Great number.
14. Sic] Such.
15. Sum] One. *fallow]* Companion. *rownys]* Whispers. *pleis]* Please.
16. byt of] Bite off. *neis]* Nose.
17. fa] Enemy. *oxtar]* Arm (lit. armpit). *ledis]* Leads.
18] One mutters aloud in prayers.
19. oppressioun] Violent behaviour.
20] Some are obsequious to their superiors, bowing low and doffing their hats.
21] Would aspire very high, were it not for the courts.
22] One awaiting his case's hearing must grant a security over his land.
23. superspendit] Bankrupt.
24. spedis] Succeeds. *meynis]* Intermediaries.

Of parcialite sum complenis, 25
How feid and favour fleymis discretioun.
Sum speikis full fair and falslie feynis.
Sic tythandis herd I at the Sessioun.

5

'Sum castis summondis and sum exceppis,
Sum standis besyd and skayld law keppis, 30
Sum is continewit, sum wynnis, sum tynis.
Sum makis thame myrre at the wynis,
And sum putt out of his possessioun,
Sum hyrreit and on credence dynis.
Sic tythingis hard I at the Sessioun. 35

6

'Sum sweiris and sum forsaikis God,
Sum in ane lamb skyn is a tod,
Sum on his toung his kyndnes tursis,
Sum kervis throittis and sum cuttis pursis.
To gallows sum gais with processioun, 40
Sum sanis the Sait, and sum thame cursis.
Sic tythingis herd I at the Sessioun.

7

'Religious men of dyvers places
Cumis thair to wow and se fair faces.
Baith Carmeletis and Coirdeleiris 45
Cumis thair to gener and get freirris,

25. *parcialite]* Favouritism. *complenis]* Complains.
26. *feid]* Hatred. *fleymis]* Banish. *discretioun]* Judgment.
27. *fair]* Pleasantly. *feynis]* Deceives.
30. *besyd]* Nearby.
31. *continewit]* Granted a respite. *tynis]* Loses.
32. *myrre]* Merry. *wynis]* Wine-drinking.
33. *possessioun]* Property.
34. *hyrreit]* Impoverished. *credence]* Credit.
36. *sweiris]* Swears. *forsaikis]* Renounces.
37. *tod]* Fox.
38. *on]* In. *tursis]* Wraps up.
39. *kervis]* Slits.
40. *gais]* Goes.
41. *sanis]* Blesses. *Sait]* Court.
43. *Religious men]* Men in religious orders. *places]* Houses.
44. *Cumis]* Come. *wow]* Woo.
46. *gener]* Engender. *get]* Beget. *freirris]* Friars.

As is the use of thair professioun.
The youngar at the elder leiris.
Sic tythingis herd I at the Sessioun.

8

'Thair cumis young monkis of het complexioun,   50
Of devoit mynd, lufe and affectioun,
And in the courte thair proud flesche dantis,
Full fadirlyk, with pechis and pantis.
Thai ar so humill of intercessioun,
All mercyfull women thair errand grantis.   55
Sic tythingis hard I at the Sessioun.'

47. *use]* Custom. *professioun]* Religious order.
48. *leiris]* Learns.
50. *het complexioun]* Hot constitution.
51. *devoit]* Devout.
52. *proud]* Lascivious. *dantis]* Tame.
53. *fadirlyk]* Fatherly. *pechis]* Puffs.
54. *humill]* Humble. *intercessioun]* Entreaty.

3

The Tretis of the Twa Mariit Wemen and the Wedo

Dunbar's longest and most ambitious work is a *tretis*, or story, of three women, talking uninhibitedly of sex, men and marriage, within an incongruously beautiful landscape. Dunbar was clearly familiar with the literature of medieval anti-feminism, yet the few specific debts that can be detected are to Chaucer, notably to the Wife of Bath's Prologue and *The Merchant's Tale*. The poem draws on several literary genres: its frame resembles the *chanson de mal mariée*, in which a wandering poet chances to hear the complaint of an unhappy wife; and the women's dialogue at times recalls another type of work, sometimes called 'the gossips' meeting' (see **46**). Even more important is the tradition of the *demande d'amour*, playful discussion of love in the form of questions and answers. This was a social pastime, often mentioned in courtly literature, and it provides the chief structural pattern of Dunbar's poem. The dialogue is initiated by the Widow's questions to the two Wives (41–8), and the work ends with the poet's own teasing question to his immediate audience. The poem was intended to be controversial, and it still provokes debate among modern critics over many issues, ranging from its tone to the role of the narrator.

Stylistically, the poem is striking for its use of antithesis and other rhetorical devices, designed to expose the stupidity of men and the dissimulation of women; the discrepancy between seeming and being is a constant theme. There is a pervasive but shifting irony, largely but not invariably directed against the women. The Widow is consciously sarcastic when she speaks of the 'blist band' of marriage (47), but the many references to her own wit and wisdom imply moral blindness. The narrator's tone is similar to that in **2** and **62**. The imagery is rich in implications. The women are as beautiful as the flowers that surround them, or the birds that they explicitly envy (e.g. 27–9, 243, 379, 382). But they have the ferocity of tigers and dragons (261, 263). The husbands, by contrast, are degraded to insects, reptiles and animals of the lowest kind (89–92, 107);

33

often they are beasts of burden, sick or diseased (79, 85, 186, 273, 331, 387). The reversal of male–female roles is twice conveyed by such imagery, succinctly in 326, more elaborately in 348–57. The poem is written in unrhymed alliterative verse, by this period a somewhat archaic form. But Dunbar's use is assured, and richly ornamental; many successive lines are often bound together by the same alliterating sound. The diction blends colloquialisms, more characteristic of flyting, with the archaic diction and poetic formulae inherited from the alliterative tradition.

Date: There is no clue as to date, except that the print is conjecturally dated *c*. 1507.

Text: P; collated with MF, pp. 81–96. Since P is imperfect, lacking the first two leaves, lines 1–103 derive from MF, as do the title and Latin rubrics. Many obvious misprints and occasional peculiarities of spelling in P are corrected.
2. in] *Not in* MF.
62–72] *MS stained and difficult to read.*
66. feiris] freiris MF.
157. suth] MF; south P.
184. semis] MF; sunys P.
275. claw] MF; keyth P.
421. I] MF; *not in* P.
451. wemen] MF; men P.
480. rownis] MF; rowis P.
520. and] MF; *not in* P.

Further reading: On medieval anti-feminist writing, see Utley 1970 and Blamires 1992. On alliterative poetry see Turville-Petre 1977 and Riddy 1988; on Dunbar's debt to the alliterative tradition, see Singh 1974 and Bawcutt 1992a: 370–79. Roth 1981 surveys the diversity of critical approaches to the poem up to 1980. For more recent studies of its theme, language and genre, see Pearcy 1980; Spearing 1985: 215–23; Bitterling 1986; Burness 1986; Bawcutt 1992a: 324–46 and 1992b.

Apon the midsummer evin, mirriest of nichtis,
I muvit furth allane In meid as midnicht wes past,
Besyd ane gudlie grein garth, full of gay flouris,
Hegeit of ane huge hicht with hawthorne treis,
Quhairon ane bird on ane bransche so birst out hir notis   5
That never ane blythfullar bird was on the beuche hard.

1. evin] Eve. *mirriest]* Merriest.
2. muvit] Moved. *allane]* Alone. *meid]* Meadow.
3. gudlie] Beautiful. *garth]* Garden. *gay]* Brightly coloured.
4. Hegeit] Hedged. *hicht]* Height.
5. birst] Poured (lit. burst).
6. blythfullar] More joyful. *beuche]* Bough. *hard]* Heard.

Quhat throw the sugurat sound of hir sang glaid,
And throw the savour sanative of the sweit flouris,
I drew in derne to the dyk to dirkin efter mirthis.
The dew donkit the daill, and dynnit the feulis.　　10
I hard, under ane holyn hevinlie grein hewit,
Ane hie speiche at my hand with hautand wourdis.
With that in haist to the hege so hard I inthrang
That I was heildit with hawthorne and with heynd leveis.
Throw pykis of the plet thorne I presandlie luikit,　　15
Gif ony persoun wald approche within that plesand garding.
I saw thre gay ladeis sit in ane grein arbeir,
All grathit in to garlandis of fresche gudlie flouris.
So glitterit as the gold wer thair glorius gilt tressis,
Quhill all the gressis did gleme of the glaid hewis.　　20
Kemmit war thair cleir hair and curiouslie sched,
Attour thair schulderis doun schyre schyning full bricht,
With curches cassin thair abone of kirsp cleir and thin.
Thair mantillis grein war as the gres that grew in May sessoun,
Fetrit with thair quhyt fingaris about thair fair sydis.　　25
Of ferlifull fyne favour war thair faceis meik,
All full of flurist fairheid as flouris in June –
Quhyt, seimlie and soft as the sweit lillies,
Now upspred upon spray as new spynist rose,

7. *Quhat]* Somewhat, partly. *sugurat]* Sweet (as sugar).
8. *sanative]* Health-giving.
9. *derne]* Quietly. *dyk]* Wall. *dirkin]* Rest. *mirthis]* Revelry.
10. *donkit]* Moistened. *daill]* Dale. *dynnit]* Clamoured. *feulis]* Birds.
11. *holyn]* Holly tree. *hewit]* Hued, coloured.
12. *hie]* Loud. *hautand]* Haughty.
13. *hege]* hedge. *inthrang]* Pushed in.
14. *heildit]* Concealed. *heynd]* Pleasant.
15. *pykis]* Prickles. *plet]* Plaited, interwoven. *presandlie]* Presently.
16. *Gif]* If. *garding]* Garden.
17. *arbeir]* Arbour.
18. *grathit]* Arrayed.
19. *glitterit]* Glittering.
20. *gressis]* Green plants. *gleme]* Gleam. *hewis]* Hues.
21. *Kemmit]* Well-combed. *curiouslie sched]* Carefully parted.
22. *Attour]* Over. *schulderis]* Shoulders. *doun schyre]* Straight down.
23. *curches]* Kerchiefs, head-coverings. *cassin]* Thrown. *kirsp]* delicate fabric.
25. *Fetrit]* Fastened. *quhyt]* White.
26. *ferlifull]* Wonderfully. *favour]* Appearance.
27. *flurist fairheid]* Blossoming beauty.
28. *seimlie]* Seemly, fine.
29. *new spynist]* Newly opened.

Arrayit ryallie about with mony riche vardour   30
That Nature full nobillie annamalit with flouris,
Of alkin hewis under hevin that ony heynd knew,
Fragrant, all full of fresche odour fynest of smell.
Ane cumlie tabil coverit wes befoir tha cleir ladyis,
With ryalle cowpis apon rawis, full of ryche wynis.   35
And of thir fair wlonkes twa weddit war with lordis,
Ane was ane wedow, iwis, wantoun of laitis.
And as thai talk at the tabill of mony taill sindry,
Thay wauchtit at the wicht wyne and waris out wourdis,
And syn thai spak more spedelie and sparit no matiris.   40

Aude viduam iam cum interrogatione sua

'Bewrie,' said the wedo, 'Ye woddit wemen ying,
Quhat mirth ye fand in maryage sen ye war menis wyffis.
Reveill gif ye rewit that rakles conditioun,
Or gif that ever ye luffit leyd upone lyf mair
Nor thame that ye your fayth hes festinit for ever,   45
Or gif ye think, had ye chois, that ye wald cheis better.
Think ye it nocht ane blist band that bindis so fast,
That none undo it a deill may bot the deith ane?'

---

30. *ryallie]* Richly. *vardour]* Green plants.
31. *annamalit]* Enameled.
32. *alkin]* Every kind of. *heynd]* Courteous person.
34. *coverit]* Covered with a cloth. *tha]* Those *cleir]* Fair.
35. *cowpis]* Goblets, *apon rawis]* In rows.
36. *thir]* These. *wlonkes]* Splendid creatures.
37. *Ane]* One. *wedow]* Widow. *iwis]* Indeed. *laitis]* Manners.
38. *sindry]* Different.
39. *wauchtit at]* Drank deeply of. *wicht]* Strong. *waris]* Utter.
40. *syn]* Then. *spak]* Spoke. *spedelie]* Quickly.
40a] Now hear the widow together with her question.
41. *Bewrie]* Reveal. *woddit]* Wedded. *ying]* Young.
42. *fand]* Found. *sen]* Since.
43. *rewit]* Regretted. *rakles]* Ill-advised. *conditioun]* Contract.
44. *gif]* If. *leyd upone lyf]* Living man.
45] Than those to whom you have pledged your faith forever.
46. *cheis]* Choose.
47. *blist]* Blessed. *band]* Bond.
48. *a deill]* In the smallest part. *bot the deith ane]* But death alone.

Responsio prime uxoris ad viduam

Than spak ane lusty belyf with lustie effeiris:
'It that ye call the blist band that bindis so fast   50
Is bair of blis and bailfull, and greit barrat wirkis.
Ye speir, had I fre chois, gif I wald cheis bettir?
Chenyeis ay ar to eschew and changeis ar sweit.
Sic cursit chance till eschew, had I my chois anis,
Out of the cheinyeis of ane churle I chaip suld for evir.   55
God gif matrimony wer made to mell for ane yeir!
It war bot merrens to be mair bot gif our myndis pleisit.
It is agane the law of luf, of kynd, and of nature,
Togidder hartis to strene that stryveis with uther.
Birdis hes ane better law na bernis be meikill,   60
That ilk yeir with new joy joyis ane maik
And fangis thame ane fresche feyr, unfulyeit and constant,
And lattis thair fulyeit feiris flie quhair thai pleis.
Cryst gif sic ane consuetude war in this kith haldin!
Than weill war us wemen that evir we war born.   65
We suld have feiris as fresche to fang quhen us likit
And gif all larbaris thair leveis quhen thai lak curage.
My self suld be full semlie in silkis arrayit,
Gymp, jolie and gent, richt joyus and gent.
I suld at fairis be found new faceis to se,   70
At playis and at preichingis and pilgrimages greit,

48a] The reply of the first wife to the widow.
49. lusty] Beautiful woman. belyf] At once. effeiris] Expression.
51. bailfull] Wretched. barrat] Strife. wirkis] Causes.
52. speir] Ask.
53. Chenyeis] Chains. eschew] Be avoided.
54. Sic] Such. anis] For once.
55. churle] Boor. chaip] Escape.
56. gif] Grant. mell] Mingle, copulate.
57. merrens] Vexation. bot gif] Except if.
58. agane] Against. kynd] Nature.
59. Togidder] Together. strene] Force. stryveis] Strive.
60. na bernis] Than men. be meikill] By far.
61. joyis] Enjoy. maik] Mate.
62. fangis] Take. feyr] Mate. unfulyeit] Unwearied.
63. fulyeit] Wearied.
64] God grant such a custom were observed in this country.
65. weill war] It would be well for.
66. fang] Take. us likit] It pleased us.
67] And dismiss all impotent men when they lack desire.
69. Gymp] Graceful. jolie] Merry. gent] Elegant.

To schaw my renone royaly quhair preis was of folk,
To manifest my makdome to multitude of pepill
And blaw my bewtie on breid quhair bernis war mony,
That I micht cheis and be chosin and change quhen me lykit. 75
Than suld I waill ane full weill our all the wyd realme
That suld my womanheid weild the lang winter nicht,
And quhen I gottin had ane grome ganest of uther,
Yaip and ying, in the yok ane yeir for to draw,
Fra I had preveit his pith the first plesand moneth, 80
Than suld I cast me to keik in kirk and in markat,
And all the cuntre about, kyngis court and uther,
Quhair I ane galland micht get aganis the nixt yeir
For to perfurneis furth the werk quhen failyeit the tother:
A forky fure, ay furthwart and forsy in draucht, 85
Nother febill nor fant nor fulyeit in labour,
Bot als fresche of his forme as flouris in May.
For all the fruit suld I fang, thocht he the flour burgeoun.'

Aude ut dicet de viro suo

'I have ane wallidrag, ane worme, ane auld wobat carle,
A waistit wolroun na worth bot wourdis to clatter, 90
Ane bumbart, ane dronbee, ane bag full of flewme,
Ane scabbit skarth, ane scorpioun, ane scutarde behind.

---

72. *schaw]* Show. *renone]* Dignified state. *preis]* Crowd.
73. *makdome]* Elegance.
74. *blaw . . . breid]* Display abroad.
76. *waill]* Choose. *ane full weill]* One of good quality.
77. *womanheid]* Womanliness. *weild]* Possess.
78. *grome]* Man. *ganest of uther]* Fitter than any other.
79. *Yaip]* Keen. *yok]* Yoke.
80. *Fra]* After. *preveit]* Tested. *pith]* Vigour. *moneth]* Month.
81. *keik]* Look around. *kirk]* Church.
82. *cuntre]* Country.
83. *galland]* Young man. *aganis]* In readiness for. *nixt]* Next.
84. *perfurneis furth]* Perform. *failyeit]* Weakened.
85. *forky fure] See note. furthwart]* To the fore. *forsy in draucht]* Strong at pulling (of plough-animals).
86. *Nother]* Neither. *fant]* Faint. *fulyeit]* Wearied.
88. *fang]* Get. *burgeoun]* Cause to bud.
88a] Hear how she speaks of her husband.
89. *wallidrag]* Slovenly fellow. *wobat]* Hairy caterpillar. *carle]* Churl.
90. *wolroun]* ?Wild creature. *na worth]* Good for nothing. *clatter]* Chatter.
91. *bumbart]* Lazy fellow. *dronbee]* Drone. *flewme]* Phlegm.
92. *skarth]* Cormorant. *scutarde] See note. behind]* At the back.

To se him scart his awin skyn grit scunner I think.
Quhen kissis me that carybald, than kyndillis all my sorow.
As birs of ane brym bair his berd is als stif,   95
Bot soft and soupill as the silk is his sary lume.
He may weill to the syn assent, bot sakles is his deidis.
With gor his twa grym ene ar gladderit all about,
And gorgeit lyk twa gutaris that war with glar stoppit.
Bot quhen that glowrand gaist grippis me about,   100
Than think I hiddowus Mahowne hes me in armes.
Thair ma na sanyne me save fra that auld Sathane,
For thocht I croce me all cleine fra the croun doun,
He wil my corse all beclip and clap to his breist.
Quhen schaiffyn is that ald schaik with a scharp rasour,   105
He schovis on me his schevill mouth and schendis my lippis,
And with his hard hurcheone scyn sa heklis he my chekis
That as a glemand gleyd glowis my chaftis.
I schrenk for the scharp stound, bot schout dar I nought,
For schore of that auld schrew, schame him betide.   110
The luf blenkis of that bogill fra his blerde ene
(As Belzebub had on me blent) abasit my spreit.
And quhen the smy on me smyrkis with his smake smolet
He fepillis like a farcy aver that flyrit on a gillot.
Quhen that the sound of his saw sinkis in my eris,   115

93. scart] Scratch. *scunner]* Cause for disgust.
94. carybald] Monster.
95. birs] Bristle. *brym bair]* Fierce boar. *berd]* Beard.
96. soupill] Supple. *sary]* Wretched. *lume]* Tool, penis.
97. sakles] Innocent. *is]* Are.
98. gor] Slime. *ene]* Eyes. *gladderit]* Besmeared.
99. gorgeit] Clogged. *glar]* Filth. *stoppit]* Choked.
100. glowrand] Staring. *gaist]* Ghost.
102. ma] May. *sanyne]* Crossing (myself).
103. croce me] Make the sign of the cross. *cleine]* Completely.
104. corse] Body. *beclip]* Embrace. *clap]* Clasp.
105. schaiffyn] Shaved. *schaik]* Fellow.
106. schovis] Thrusts. *schevill]* Distorted. *schendis]* Soils.
107. hurcheone] Hedgehog. *scyn]* Skin. *heklis]* Scratches.
108. gleyd] Live coal. *chaftis]* Jaws.
109. schrenk] Cower. *stound]* Pain.
110. schore] Threatening. *schrew]* Wretch. *betide]* Befall.
111. blenkis] Glances. *bogill]* Hobgoblin. *blerde]* Bleary.
112. blent] Looked. *abasit]* Dismayed. *spreit]* Spirit.
113. smy] Wretch.
114] He sticks out his lower lip like a diseased old horse leering at a filly.
115. saw] Speech.

Than ay renewis my noy or he be neir cumand.
Quhen I heir nemmyt his name than mak I nyne crocis
To keip me fra the cummerans of that carll mangit,
That full of eldnyng is and anger and all evill thewis.
I dar nought luke to my luf, for that lene gib.   120
He is sa full of jelusy and engyne fals,
Ever ymagynyng in mynd materis of evill,
Compasand and castand cacis a thousand,
How he sall tak me with a trawe attrist of ane othir.
I dar nought keik to the knaip that the cop fillis,   125
For eldnyng of that ald schrew that ever on evill thynkis.
For he is waistit and worne fra Venus werkis,
And may nought beit worth a bene in bed of my mystirs.
He trowis that young folk I yerne yeild for he gane is,
Bot I may yuke all this yer, or his yerd help.   130
Ay quhen that caribald carll wald clym on my wambe,
Than am I dangerus and daine and dour of my will.
Yit leit I never that larbar my leggis ga betwene,
To fyle my flesche na fummyll me without a fee gret,
And thoght his pen purly me payis in bed,   135
His purse pays richely in recompense efter.
For or he clym on my corse, that carybald forlane,
I have condition of a curche, of kersp allther fynest,
A goun of engranyt claith right gaily furrit,

116. *noy]* Irritation. *or]* Before.
117. *nemmyt]* Mentioned. *crocis]* Signs of the cross.
118. *cummerans]* Annoyance. *carll]* Man, fellow. *mangit]* Crazed.
119. *eldnyng]* Jealousy. *thewis]* Qualities.
120. *gib]* Tomcat.
121. *engyne]* Ingenuity.
123. *castand]* Devising. *cacis]* Tricks.
124. *trawe]* Trick. *attrist]* At a rendezvous.
125. *keik]* Peep. *knaip]* Boy. *cop]* Cup.
127. *Venus werkis]* Acts of love.
129] *See note.*
130. *yuke]* Itch. *yerd]* Rod, penis.
131. *caribald]* Monstrous. *clym]* Climb. *wame]* Belly.
132. *dangerus]* Disdainful. *daine]* Haughty. *dour]* Stubborn.
133. *larbar]* Impotent man.
134. *fyle]* Defile. *na]* Nor. *fummyll]* Fumble with.
135. *pen]* Penis. *purly]* Poorly. *payis]* Gratifies.
137. *forlane]* Worthless.
138] I make it a condition that I get a kerchief of the finest fabric.
139. *engranyt]* Dyed scarlet. *furrit]* Fur-trimmed.

A ring with a ryall stane or other riche jowell,   140
Or rest of his rousty raid, thoght he wer rede wod.
For all the buddis of Johne Blunt, quhen he abone clymis
Me think the baid deir aboucht, sa bawch ar his werkis –
And thus I sell him solace, thoght I it sour think.
Fra sic a syre God yow saif, my sweit sisteris deir!'   145
Quhen that the semely had said hir sentence to end,
Than all thai leuch apon loft with latis full mery
And raucht the cop round about, full of riche wynis,
And ralyeit lang, or thai wald rest, with ryatus speche.

Hic bibent et inde vidua interrogat alteram mulierem
et illa respondet ut sequitur

The wedo to the tothir wlonk warpit thir wordis: 150
'Now, fair sister, fallis yow but fenying to tell.
Sen man ferst with matrimony yow menskit in kirk,
How haif ye farne? Be your faith, confese us the treuth.
That band to blise or to ban, quhilk yow best thinkis,
Or how ye like lif to leid in to lell spousage?   155
And syne my self ye exem on the samyn wise,
And I sall say furth the suth, dissymyland no word.'
The plesand said, 'I protest, the treuth gif I schaw,
That of your toungis ye be traist.' The tothir twa grantit.

---

140. ryall] Costly. *jowell]* Jewel.
141. rest] Cease. *rousty]* Clumsy. *rede wod]* Furious.
142. buddis] Bribes.
143. baid] Delay. *aboucht]* Paid for. *bawch]* Feeble. *werkis]* Acts.
145. syre] Man.
146. semely] Fair woman. *sentence]* Speech.
147. leuch] Laughed. *apon loft]* Loudly. *latis]* Manners.
148. raucht] Handed.
149. ralyeit] Jested. *ryatus]* Licentious.
149a] Here they drink and the widow questions the second wife and she replies
as follows
150. wlonk] Fair one. *warpit]* Uttered. *thir]* These.
151. fallis] It befalls. *but fenying]* Without deceit.
152. menskit] Honoured.
153. farne] Fared. *confese]* Confess.
154. blise] Bless. *ban]* Curse. *thinkis]* Seems.
155. lell] Lawful.
156. exem] Examine. *samyn]* Same.
157. suth] Truth. *dissymyland]* Dissembling.
158. plesand] Agreeable woman. *gif]* If.
159. traist] Trustworthy. *grantit]* Consented.

With that sprang up hir spreit be a span hechar.   160
'To speik', quod scho, 'I sall nought spar, ther is no spy neir.
I sall a ragment reveil fra rute of my hert,
A roust that is sa rankild quhill risis my stomok.
Now sall the byle all out brist, that beild has so lang.
For it to beir on my breist wes berdin our hevy.   165
I sall the venome devoid with a vent large,
And me assuage of the swalme that swellit wes gret.
My husband wes a hur maister, the hugeast in erd.
Tharfor I hait him with my hert, sa help me our Lord.
He is a young man ryght yaip, bot nought in youth flouris,   170
For he is fadit full far and feblit of strenth.
He wes as flurising fresche within this few yeris,
Bot he is falyeid full far and fulyeid in labour.
He has bene lychour so lang quhill lost is his natur,
His lume is waxit larbar and lyis in to swoune.   175
Wes never sugeorne wer set na on that snaill tyrit,
For efter sevin oulkis rest it will nought rap anys.
He has bene waistit apon wemen or he me wif chesit,
And in adultre in my tyme I haif him tane oft;
And yit he is als brankand with bonet on syde,   180
And blenkand to the brichtest that in the burgh dwellis,
Alse curtly of his clething and kemmyng of his haris,
As he that is mare valyeand in Venus chalmer.

160. *spreit]* Spirits. *hechar]* Higher.
161. *spar]* Refrain.
162. *ragment]* Long catalogue (of woes). *rute]* Root.
163. *roust]* Rancour. *rankild]* Painful, festering.
164. *byle]* Boil. *brist]* Burst. *beild]* Suppurated.
165. *breist]* Breast. *berdin]* Burden. *our]* Over.
166. *devoid]* Cast out. *vent]* Discharge.
167. *swalme]* Swelling.
168. *hur maister]* Frequenter of whores. *in erd]* On earth.
170. *yaip]* Nimble.
172. *flurising]* Flower. *this]* These.
173. *falyeid]* Enfeebled. *fulyeid]* Exhausted.
174. *lychour]* Lecherous. *natur]* Sexual power.
175. *waxit]* Become. *larbar]* Impotent. *swoune]* Swoon.
176. *sugeorne]* Rest. *wer]* Worse. *set]* Expended. *na]* Than. *snaill]* Slug.
177. *oulkis]* Weeks'. *anys]* Once.
178. *chesit]* Chose.
180. *brankand]* Proud. *on syde]* To one side.
181. *blenkand]* Casting glances. *brichtest]* Prettiest girls.
182. *Alse]* As. *curtly]* Courtly. *kemmyng]* Combing.

He semis to be sumthing worth, that syphyr in bour,
He lukis as he wald luffit be, thoght he be litill of valour.   185
He dois as dotit dog that damys on all bussis,
And liftis his leg apon loft thoght he nought list pische.
He has a luke without lust and lif without curage.
He has a forme without force and fesson but vertu,
And fair wordis but effect, all fruster of dedis.   190
He is for ladyis in luf a right lusty schadow,
Bot in to derne at the deid he salbe drup fundin.
He ralis and makes repet with ryatus wordis,
Ay rusing him of his radis and rageing in chalmer.
Bot God wait quhat I think, quhen he so thra spekis   195
And – how it settis him! – so syde to sege of sic materis.
Bot gif him self of sum evin mycht ane say amang thaim,
Bot he nought ane is, bot nane of naturis possessoris.
Scho that has ane auld man nought all is begylit;
He is at Venus werkis na war na he semys.   200
I wend I josit a gem, and I haif geit gottin.
He had the glemyng of gold and wes bot glase fundin.
Thought men be ferse, wele I fynd (fra falye ther curage)
Thar is bot eldnyng and anger ther hertis within.
Ye speik of berdis on bewch – of blise may thai sing,   205
That on sanct Valentynis day ar vacandis ilk yer.
Hed I that plesand prevelege, to part quhen me likit,
To change and ay to cheise agane, than chastite adew!

184. syphyr] Cipher, nonentity. *bour]* Chamber.
186. dotit] Stupid. *damys]* Makes water. *bussis]* Bushes.
189. forme] Fair shape. *fesson]* Appearance. *but vertu]* Without force.
190. but effect] Without efficacy. *fruster]* Vain.
191. schadow] Delusive appearance.
192. derne] Private. *at the deid]* In the act. *drup]* Feeble. *fundin]* Found.
193. ralis] Jests. *repet]* Noisy outcry.
194. rusing] Boasting. *rageing]* Sexual activity.
195. wait] Knows. *thra]* Boldly.
196] And (how it befits him!) so widely to men of such matters.
199. all] Entirely.
200. na war na] No worse than.
201. wend] Believed. *josit]* Possessed. *geit]* Jet.
202. glase] Glass.
203. ferse] Bold. *fra]* After. *falye]* Fail.
204. eldnyng] Jealousy.
205. berdis] Birds. *bewch]* Bough.
206. vacandis] Free to take mates. *ilk]* Each.
207. prevelege] Privilege. *part]* Depart.
208. cheise] Choose. *adew]* Farewell.

Than suld I haif a fresch feir to fang in myn armys.
To hald a freke quhill he faynt may foly be calit.   210
Apone sic materis I mus at mydnyght full oft
And murnys so in my mynd, I murdris my selfin.
Than ly I walkand for wa and walteris about,
Wariand oft my wekit kyn that me away cast,
To sic a craudoune but curage that knyt my cler bewte,   215
And ther so mony kene knyghtis this kenrik within.
Than think I on a semelyar, the suth for to tell,
Na is our syre be sic sevin. With that I syth oft.
Than he ful tenderly dois turne to me his tume person,
And with a yoldin yerd dois yolk me in armys,   220
And sais, "My soverane sweit thing, quhy sleip ye no betir?
Me think ther haldis yow a hete, as ye sum harme alyt."
Quod I, "My hony, hald abak and handill me nought sair.
A hache is happinnit hastely at my hert rut."
With that I seme for to swoune, thought I na swerf tak,   225
And thus beswik I that swane with my sweit wordis.
I cast on him a crabit e quhen cleir day is cummyn,
And lettis it is a luf blenk quhen he about glemys.
I turne it in a tender luke that I in tene warit,
And him behaldis hamely with hertly smyling.   230
I wald a tender peronall that myght na put thole,

209. *feir]* Mate. *fang]* Clasp.
210. *freke]* Man. *faynt]* Grow weary.
211. *mus]* Meditate.
212. *murnys]* Mourn. *murdris]* Torment. *selfin]* Self.
213. *walkand]* Waking. *wa]* Grief. *walteris]* Toss.
214. *Wariand]* Cursing. *wekit]* Wicked.
215] Who bound my bright beauty to such an impotent coward.
216. *And ther]* There being. *kenrik]* Kingdom.
217–18] Then – to tell the truth – I think of someone seven times more handsome than my husband. At this I sigh often.
219. *tume]* Empty, feeble.
220. *yoldin]* Exhausted. *yerd]* See 130. *yolk]* Clasp.
222. *hete]* Fever. *as ... alyt]* As if you suffered sickness.
223. *sair]* Painfully.
224. *hache]* Ache, pain.
225. *na swerf tak]* Do not faint.
226. *beswik]* Deceive. *swane]* Man.
227. *crabit]* Bad-tempered. *e]* Eye, look.
228. *lettis]* Feign. *luf blenk]* Amorous glance. *glemys]* Looks.
229. *tene]* Anger. *warit]* Expended.
230. *hamely]* Intimately. *hertly]* Heartfelt.
231. *wald]* Wish. *peronall]* Girl. *put]* Thrust. *thole]* Endure.

That hatit men with hard geir for hurting of flesch,
Had my gud man to hir gest, for I dar God swer,
Scho suld not stert for his straik a stray breid of erd.
And syne I wald that ilk band that ye so blist call   235
Had bund him so to that bryght quhill his bak werkit,
And I wer in a beid broght with berne that me likit.
I trow that bird of my blis suld a bourd want.'
Onone quhen this amyable had endit hir speche,
Loud lauchand, the laif allowit hir mekle.   240
Thir gay wiffis maid gam amang the grene leiffis,
Thai drank and did away dule under derne bewis,
Thai swapit of the sweit wyne, thai swan-quhit of hewis,
Bot all the pertlyar, in plane, thai put out ther vocis.

*Nunc bibent et inde prime due interrogant viduam et de sua
responsione et quomodo erat*

Than said the weido: 'Iwis, ther is no way othir.   245
Now tydis me for to talk, my taill it is nixt.
God my spreit now inspir and my speche quykkin,
And send me sentence to say substantious and noble,
Sa that my preching may pers your perverst hertis,
And mak yow mekar to men in maneris and conditiounis.   250
I schaw yow, sister, in schrift, I wes a schrew ever,

232. *geir]* (Sexual) equipment.
233. *gud man]* Husband. *gest]* Lover.
234] She should not flinch, at his stroke, a straw's breadth of ground.
236. *bund]* Bound. *werkit]* Ached.
237. *beid]* Bed. *berne]* Man.
238. *trow]* Believe. *bird]* Girl.
239. *Onone]* At once.
240. *laif]* Others. *allowit]* Praised. *mekle]* Much.
241. *gam]* Sport.
242. *did away]* Cast off. *dule]* Sorrow. *derne]* Shady.
243. *swapit of]* Drank off quickly. *thai swan-quhit]* Those ladies white as swans.
244. pertlyar] More boldly. *in plane]* Plainly.
244a] Now they drink and then the first two question the widow, and concerning her reply and how it was.
245. *Iwis]* Indeed.
246. *tydis]* Behoves.
247. *quykkin]* Give life to.
248. *sentence]* Utterance. *substantious]* Weighty.
249. *pers]* Pierce. *perverst]* Perverse.
250. *conditiounis]* Dispositions.
251. *schrift]* Confession. *schrew]* Evil creature.

Bot I wes schene in my schrowd and schew me innocent;
And thought I dour wes and dane, dispitois and bald,
I wes dissymblit suttelly in a sanctis liknes.
I semyt sober and sweit and sempill without fraud,   255
Bot I couth sexty dissaif that suttillar wer haldin.
Unto my lesson ye lyth and leir at me wit,
Gif you nought list be forleit with losingeris untrew:
Be constant in your governance and counterfeit gud maneris,
Thought ye be kene, inconstant and cruell of mynd.   260
Thought ye as tygris be terne, be tretable in luf,
And be as turtoris in your talk, thought ye haif talis brukill.
Be dragonis baith and dowis ay in double forme,
And quhen it nedis yow, onone note baith ther stranthis.
Be amyable with humble face, as angellis apperand,   265
And with a terrebill tail be stangand as edderis.
Be of your luke like innocentis, thoght ye haif evill myndis.
Be courtly ay in clething and costly arrayit –
That hurtis yow nought worth a hen, yowr husband pays for all.
Twa husbandis haif I had, thai held me baith deir.   270
Thought I dispytit thaim agane, thai spyt it na thing.
Ane wes a hair hogeart that hostit out flewme.
I hatit him like a hund, thought I it hid preve.
With kissing and with clapping I gert the carill fon,
Weill couth I claw his cruke bak and kemm his kewt noddill,   275
And with a bukky in my cheik bo on him behind,

252. *schene]* Fair. *schrowd]* Gown. *schew]* Showed.
253. *dour]* Stubborn. *dane]* Haughty] *dispitois]* Contemptuous. *bald]* Bold.
254. *dissymblit]* Disguised. *suttelly]* Cunningly.
255. *sober]* Mild. *sempill]* Simple.
256. *dissaif]* Deceive.
257. *lyth]* Listen. *leir]* Learn.
258. *list]* Wish. *forleit]* Abandoned. *losingeris]* Deceivers.
259. *governance]* Behaviour.
261. *terne]* Ferocious. *tretable]* Compliant.
262. *turtoris]* Turtle doves. *talis]* Tails. *brukill]* Frail.
263. *dowis]* Doves.
264. *note]* Employ. *stranthis]* Strengths.
265. *apperand]* Appearing.
266. *stangand]* Stinging. *edderis]* Adders.
271. *dispytit]* Despised. *agane]* In return. *spyt]* Spied.
272. *hair hogeart]* Grey-haired old man. *hostit]* Coughed. *flewme]* Phlegm.
273. *hund]* Cur. *preve]* Secretly.
274. *clapping]* Fondling. *gert]* Caused. *carill]* Boor. *fon]* Grow besotted.
275. *claw]* Scratch gently. *kemm]* Comb. *kewt noddill]* Cropped head.
276. *bukky]* Swelling. *bo]* Make a face.

And with a bek gang about and bler his ald e,
And with a kynd contynance kys his crynd chekis,
In to my mynd makand mokis at that mad fader.
Trowand me with trew lufe to treit him so fair.   280
This couth I do without dule and na dises tak,
Bot ay be mery in my mynd and myrthfull of cher.
I had a lufsummar leid my lust for to slokyn,
That couth be secrete and sure and ay saif my honour,
And sew bot at certane tymes and in sicir placis.   285
Ay quhen the ald did me anger with akword wordis,
Apon the galland for to goif it gladit me agane.
I had sic wit that for wo weipit I litill,
Bot leit the sweit ay the sour to gud sesone bring.
Quhen that the chuf wald me chid with girnand chaftis,   290
I wald him chuk, cheik and chyn, and cheris him so mekill
That his cheif chymys he had chevist to my sone,
Suppos the churll wes gane chaist or the child wes gottin.
As wis woman ay I wrought and not as wod fule,
For mar with wylis I wan na wichtnes of handis.   295

'Syne maryt I a merchand, myghti of gudis.
He wes a man of myd eld and of mene statur;
Bot we na fallowis wer in frendschip or blud,
In fredome na furth bering na fairnes of persoune –

277. *bek]* Gesture of respect. *gang about]* Go in front. *bler . . . e]* Deceive him.
278. *contynance]* Countenance. *crynd]* Shrivelled.
279. *mokis]* Derisive gestures.
281. *couth]* Could. *dule]* Sorrow. *dises]* Distress.
282. *cher]* Mood.
283. *lufsummar]* More lovable. *leid]* Man. *slokyn]* Satisfy.
284. *sure]* Dependable.
285. *sew]* Attend. *sicir]* Safe.
286. *akword]* Ill-tempered.
287. *galland]* Young man. *goif]* Gaze.
289. *sesone]* Relish, flavour.
290. *chuf]* Boor. *chid]* Chide. *girnand chaftis]* Snarling jaws.
291. *chuk]* Fondle. *cheris]* Cherish. *mekill]* Much.
292. *chymys]* Manor house. *chevist]* Assigned.
293. *Suppos]* Although. *gane]* Gone. *gottin]* Begotten.
294. *wod fule]* Mad fool.
295. *wan]* Won. *na]* Than. *wichtnes]* Strength.
296. *maryt]* Married. *myghti]* Wealthy.
297. *myd eld]* Middle age. *mene]* Moderate.
298. *fallowis]* Equals. *frendschip]* Kindred.
299. *fredome]* Generosity. *furth bering]* Conduct.

Quhilk ay the fule did foryet for febilnes of knawlege. 300
Bot I sa oft thoght him on, quhill angrit his hert,
And quhilum I put furth my voce and "peddir" him callit.
I wald ryght tuichandly talk, be I wes twyse maryit,
For endit wes my innocence with my ald husband.
I wes apperand to be pert within perfit eild: 305
Sa sais the curat of our kirk, that knew me full ying.
He is our famous to be fals, that fair worthy prelot.
I salbe laith to lat him le quhill I may luke furth.
I gert the buthman obey – ther wes no bute ellis –
He maid me ryght hie reuerens fra he my rycht knew, 310
For (thocht I say it my self) the severance wes mekle
Betwix his bastard blude and my birth noble.
That page wes never of sic price for to presome anys
Unto my persone to be peir, had pete nought grantit.
Bot mercy in to womanheid is a mekle vertu, 315
For never bot in a gentill hert is generit ony ruth.
I held ay grene in to his mynd that I of grace tuk him,
And that he couth ken him self I curtasly him lerit.
He durst not sit anys my summondis, for or the secund charge
He wes ay redy for to ryn, so rad he wes for blame. 320
Bot ay my will wes the war of womanly natur,
The mair he loutit for my luf, the les of him I rakit,
And eik – this is a ferly thing – or I him faith gaif

---

300. foryet] Forget.
301. thoght him on] Caused him to think of it.
302. quhilum] Sometimes. *peddir]* Pedlar.
303. tuichandly] Cuttingly. *be]* After.
305] I was likely to be clever on reaching maturity.
306. curat] Priest. *ying]* Young.
307. our famous] Over reputable *prelot]* Church dignitary.
308. laith] Reluctant. *le]* Tell lies. *luke furth]* Look around.
309. buthman] Stall-keeper. *bute]* Remedy.
310] He showed me respect, when he knew what were my dues.
311. severance] Difference.
313. page] Boor. *price]* Worth. *presome]* Presume.
314. peir] Equal. *pete]* Pity.
316. generit] Engendered. *ruth]* Pity.
317. held . . . grene] Kept fresh. *tuk]* Accepted.
318. ken] Teach. *lerit]* Instructed.
319. durst] Dared. *anys]* Once. *or]* Before. *charge]* Command.
320. ryn] Run. *rad]* Afraid.
321] From female perversity my feelings to him were the worse.
322. loutit] Was subservient. *rakit]* Esteemed.
323. ferly] Strange. *or]* Before.

I had sic favour to that freke, and feid syne for ever.
Quhen I the cure had all clene and him ourcummyn haill,   325
I crew abone that craudone as cok that wer victour.
Quhen I him saw subject and sett at myn bydding,
Than I him lichtlyit as a lowne and lathit his maneris.
Than woxe I sa ummerciable, to martir him I thought,
For as a best I broddit him to all boyis laubour.   330
I wald haif riddin him to Rome with raip in his heid,
Wer not ruffill of my renoune and rumour of pepill.
And yit hatrent I hid within my hert all,
Bot quhilis it hepit so huge quhill it behud out.
Yit tuk I never the wosp clene out of my wyde throte,   335
Quhill I ought wantit of my will or quhat I wald desir.
Bot quhen I severit had that syre of substance in erd,
And gottin his biggingis to my barne and hie burrow landis,
Than with a stew stert out the stoppell of my hals,
That he all stunyst throu the stound as of a stele wappin.   340
Than wald I efter lang first sa fane haif bene wrokin
That I to flyte wes als fers as a fell dragoun.
I had for flattering of that fule fenyeit so lang,
Mi evidentis of heritagis or thai wer all selit,
My breist that wes gret beild bowdyn wes sa huge,   345

324. *freke*] Man. *feid*] Hatred.
325. *cure*] Control. *clene*] Completely. *ourcummyn*] Overcome. *haill*] Wholly.
326. *crew*] Crowed. *craudone*] Coward.
327. *subject*] Submissive.
328. *lichtlyit*] Despised. *lowne*] Boor. *lathit*] Loathed.
329. *unmerciable*] Pitiless. *martir*] Torment.
330. *best*] Animal. *broddit*] Goaded. *boyis*] Menial.
331. *raip*] Rope.
332. *ruffill*] Impairment. *renoune*] Reputation.
333. *hatrent*] Hatred.
334. *quhilis*] At times. *behud out*] Behoved to issue out.
335. *wosp*] Stopper.
336. *wantit*] Lacked.
337. *severit*] Deprived. *substance*] Property.
338. *biggingis*] Buildings. *barne*] Child. *hie burrow landis*] High tenements in the burgh.
339. *stew*] Stench. *stert*] Started. *stoppell*] Stopper. *hals*] Throat.
340. *stunyst*] Was stunned. *stound*] Shock. *wappin*] Weapon.
341. *first*] Delay. *fane*] Gladly. *wrokin*] Avenged.
342. *flyte*] Scold. *fers*] Fierce. *fell*] Cruel.
343. *fenyeit*] Feigned.
344] Until the documents securing my inheritance of the property were all sealed.
345. *beild*] Inflamed. *bowdyn*] Swollen.

That neir my baret out birst or the band makin.
Bot quhen my billis and my bauchles wes all braid selit,
I wald na langar beir on bridill bot braid up my heid.
Thar mygyht na molet mak me moy na hald my mouth in.
I gert the renyeis rak and rif in to sondir,   350
I maid that wif carll to werk all womenis werkis,
And laid all manly materis and mensk in this eird.
Than said I to my cummaris in counsall about,
"Se how I cabeld yone cout with a kene brydill.
The cappill that the crelis kest in the caf mydding   355
Sa curtasly the cart drawis and kennis na plungeing.
He is nought skeich na yit sker na scippis nought on syd."
And thus the scorne and the scaith scapit he nothir.
He wes no glaidsum gest for a gay lady,
Tharfor I gat him a gam that ganyt him bettir.   360
He wes a gret goldit man and of gudis riche.
I leit him be my lumbart to lous me all misteris,
And he wes fane for to fang fra me that fair office,
And thoght my favoris to fynd throw his feill giftis.
He grathit me in a gay silk and gudly arrayis,   365
In gownis of engranyt claith and gret goldin chenyeis,
In ringis ryally set with riche ruby stonis,
Quhill hely raise my renoune amang the rude peple.

346] That my anger nearly burst out before the drawing up of the contract.
347. *billis]* Legal documents. *braid selit]* Provided with a large seal.
348. *on bridill]* A bridle. *braid]* Tossed.
349. *molet]* Bit (of a bridle). *moy]* Quiet.
350] I caused the reins to strain and break apart.
351. *wif carll]* Womanish man. *werk]* Perform.
352. *laid]* (He) laid aside. *mensk]* Dignity.
353. *cummaris]* Gossips, friends.
354. *cabeld]* Tied up. *cout]* Colt.
355. *cappill]* Horse. *crelis]* Creels. *caf mydding]* Dung heap.
356. *plungeing]* Violent leaping forward.
357. *skeich]* Inclined to shy. *sker]* Restive.
358. *scaith]* Humiliation. *scapit]* Escaped. *nothir]* Neither.
359. *gest]* Lover.
360. *gat]* Got. *gam]* Sport. *ganyt]* Suited.
361. *gret goldit]* Possessed of much gold.
362. *lumbart]* Banker (lit. Lombard). *lous . . . misteris]* Free me from business.
363. *fane]* Glad. *fang]* Take.
364. *feill]* Many.
365. *grathit]* Adorned. *silk]* Silk garment. *arrayis]* Clothing.
366. *engranyt]* Dyed scarlet. *chenyeis]* Chains.
368. *hely]* Greatly. *renoune]* Reputation. *rude]* Lower-class.

Bot I full craftely did keip thai courtly wedis
Quhill efter dede of that drupe that docht nought in chalmir.　370
Thought he of all my clathis maid cost and expense,
Ane othir sall the worschip haif that weildis me eftir.
And thoght I likit him bot litill, yit for luf of othris
I wald me prunya plesandly in precius wedis,
That luffaris mycht apon me luke and ying lusty gallandis,　375
That I held more in daynte and derer be ful mekill
Ne him that dressit me so dink – full dotit wes his heyd!
Quhen he wes heryit out of hand to hie up my honoris,
And payntit me as pako, proudest of fedderis,
I him miskennyt, be Crist, and cukkald him maid.　380
I him forleit as a lad and lathlyit him mekle.
I thoght myself a papingay and him a plukit herle.
All thus enforsit he his fa and fortifyit in strenth,
And maid a stalwart staff to strik him selfe doune.
Bot of ane bowrd in to bed I sall yow breif yit:　385
Quhen he ane hal year wes hanyt and him behuffit rage,
And I wes laith to be loppin with sic a lob avoir,
Alse lang as he wes on loft I lukit on him never,
Na leit never enter in my thoght that he my thing persit.
Bot ay in mynd ane othir man ymagynit that I haid,　390
Or ellis had I never mery bene at that myrthles raid.
Quhen I that grome geldit had of gudis and of natur,
Me thoght him gracelese on to goif, sa me God help.

369. *thai*] Those. *wedis*] Garments.
370. *dede*] Death. *drupe*] Feeble fellow. *docht nought*] Was useless.
372. *worschip*] Honour. *weildis*] Possesses.
374. *prunya*] Adorn.
375. *luffaris*] Lovers, suitors.
376. *daynte*] Esteem. *derer*] Dearer.
377. *Ne*] Than. *dink*] Finely. *dotit*] Stupid.
378. *heryit*] Plundered. *out of hand*] Excessively. *hie up*] Raise up. *honoris*]
Signs of rank.
379. *pako*] Peacock.
380. *miskennyt*] Disregarded. *cukkald*] Cuckold.
381. *forleit*] Rejected *lad*] Servant. *lathlyit*] Loathed.
382. *papingay*] Parrot. *plukit herle*] Plucked heron.
383. *enforsit*] Gave strength to.
385. *bowrd*] Jest. *breif*] Tell.
386. *hal*] Whole. *hanyt*] Restrained. *rage*] Take sexual pleasure.
387. *laith*] Reluctant. *loppin*] Mounted. *lob avoir*] Clumsy old horse.
392. *grome*] Man. *natur*] Potency.
393. *gracelese ... goif*] Unattractive to look at.

Quhen he had warit all on me his welth and his substance,
Me thoght his wit wes all went away with the laif.   395
And so I did him dispise, I spittit quhen I saw
That superspendit evill spreit spulyeit of all vertu.
For weill ye wait, wiffis, that he that wantis riches
And valyeandnes in Venus play is ful vile haldin.
Full fruster is his fresch array and fairnes of persoune,   400
All is bot frutlese his effeir and falyeis at the upwith.
I buskit up my barnis like baronis sonnis,
And maid bot fulis of the fry of his first wif.
I banyst fra my boundis his brethir ilkane,
His frendis as my fais I heid at feid evir.   405
Be this ye beleif may, I luffit nought him self,
For never I likit a leid that langit till his blude.
And yit thir wismen, thai wait that all wiffis evill
Ar kend with ther conditionis and knawin with the samin.

'Deid is now that dyour and dollin in erd.   410
With him deit all my dule and my drery thoghtis.
Now done is my dolly nyght, my day is upsprungin.
Adew, dolour, adew, my daynte now begynis.
Now am I a wedow, iwise, and weill am at ese.
I weip as I wer woful bot wel is me for ever.   415
I busk as I wer bailfull bot blith is my hert.
My mouth it makis murnyng and my mynd lauchis.

394. warit] Expended.
395. laif] Rest.
397. superspendit] Bankrupt. *spulyeit]* Robbed. *vertu]* Manly qualities.
398. wait] Know. *wantis]* Lacks.
399. valyeandnes] Strength. *Venus play]* The sport of Venus.
400. fruster] Vain.
401. effeir] Fine appearance. *falyeis]* Fails. *upwith]* Sexual climax.
402. buskit] Dressed.
403. fry] Offspring.
404. banyst] Danished. *boundis]* Property. *ilkane]* Every one.
405. fais] Foes. *heid at feid]* Despised.
407. leid] Person. *langit]* Belonged.
409. kend] Recognised. *conditionis]* Dispositions.
410. dyour] Bankrupt. *dollin]* Buried.
411. deit] Died.
412. dolly] Mournful.
413. daynte] Delight.
414. iwise] Indeed.
416. busk] Dress. *bailfull]* Sorrowful.

My clokis thai ar caerfull in colour of sabill,
Bot courtly and ryght curyus my corse is ther undir.
I drup with a ded luke in my dule habit,   420
As with manis daill I had done for dayis of my lif.
Quhen that I go to the kirk cled in cair weid,
As foxe in a lambis fleise fenye I my cheir.
Than lay I furth my bright buke on breid on my kne,
With mony lusty letter ellummynit with gold,   425
And drawis my clok forthwart our my face quhit,
That I may spy unaspyit a space me beside.
Full oft I blenk by my buke and blynis of devotion,
To se quhat berne is best brand or bredest in schulderis,
Or forgeit is maist forcely to furnyse a bancat   430
In Venus chalmer valyeandly withoutin vane ruse.
And as the new mone all pale oppressit with change
Kythis quhilis her cleir face throw cluddis of sable,
So keik I throw my clokis and castis kynd lukis
To knychtis and to cleirkis and cortly personis.   435
Quhen frendis of my husbandis behaldis me on fer,
I haif a watter spunge for wa within my wyde clokis.
Than wring I it full wylely and wetis my chekis.
With that watteris myn ene and welteris doune teris.
Than say thai all that sittis about, "Se ye nought, allace, 440
Yone lustlese led, so lelely scho luffit hir husband.

418. *caerfull*] Showing signs of mourning.
419. *curyus*] Beautiful.
420. *drup*] Droop. *ded*] Funereal. *dule habit*] Mourning clothes.
421. *manis daill*] Sexual intercourse.
422. *cair weid*] Mourning clothes.
423. *fleise*] Fleece. *fenye*] Feign.
424. *on breid*] Wide open. *kne*] Knee.
425. *ellummynit*] Illuminated.
426. *forthwart*] Forward.
428. *blenk by*] Glance away from. *blynis*] Cease.
429. *berne*] Man. *brand*] Muscled. *bredest*] Broadest.
430. *forcely*] Vigorously. *furnyse*] Furnish. *bancat*] Banquet.
431. *ruse*] Boast.
433. *Kythis*] Shows. *cluddis*] Clouds.
434. *keik*] Peep.
436. *on fer*] From afar.
437. *spunge*] Sponge. *wa*] Grief.
438. *wylely*] In a wily manner.
439. *welteris*] Roll.
441. *lustlese*] Joyless. *led*] Creature. *lelely*] Faithfully.

Yone is a pete to enprent in a princis hert,
That sic a perle of plesance suld yone pane dre."
I sane me as I war ane sanct and semys ane angell,
At langage of lichory I leit as I war crabit.   445
I sith without sair hert or seiknes in body,
According to my sable weid I mon haif sad maneris,
Or thai will se all the suth; for certis we wemen
We set us all for the syght, to syle men of treuth.
We dule for na evill deid, sa it be derne haldin.   450
Wise wemen has wayis and wonderfull gydingis
With gret engyne to bejaip ther jolyus husbandis,
And quyetly with sic craft convoyis our materis,
That under Crist no creatur kennis of our doingis.
Bot folk a cury may miscuke that knawlege wantis,   455
And has na colouris for to cover ther awne kindly fautis;
As dois thir damysellis for derne dotit lufe,
That dogonis haldis in dainte and delis with thaim so lang,
Quhill al the cuntre knaw ther kyndnes and faith.
Faith has a fair name bot falsheid faris beittir.   460
Fy on hir that can nought feyne, her fame for to saif!
Yit am I wise in sic werk and wes all my tyme.
Thoght I want wit in warldlynes I wylis haif in luf,
As ony happy woman has that is of hie blude.
Hutit be the halok lase a hunder yeir of eild!   465
I have ane secrete servand, rycht sovir of his toung,

---

442. *pete]* Pitiable sight. *enprent]* Imprint.
443. *dre]* Suffer.
444. *sane me]* Cross myself.
445. *lichory]* Lechery. *leit]* Behave. *crabit]* Offended.
446. *sith]* Sigh. *sair]* Unhappy.
447. *According to]* In accordance with. *mon]* Must. *sad]* Serious.
448. *certis]* Certainly.
449. *syle]* Deceive.
450. *dule]* Grieve. *derne]* Secret.
451. *gydingis]* Ways of acting.
452. *engyne]* Ingenuity. *bejaip]* Befool. *jolyus]* Jealous.
453. *convoyis . . . materis]* Conduct our business.
455. *cury]* Dish. *miscuke]* Spoil in cooking.
456. *colouris]* Deceptions. *kindly]* Natural.
458. *dogonis]* Worthless men. *dainte]* Favour.
461. *fame]* Reputation.
463. *want]* Lack. *warldlynes]* Worldly matters.
464. *happy]* Fortunate. *hie]* Noble.
466. *sovir]* Trustworthy.

That me supportis of sic nedis quhen I a syne mak.
Thoght he be sympill to the sicht he has a tong sickir,
Full mony semelyar sege wer service dois mak.
Thoght I haif cair under cloke the cleir day quhill nyght,   470
Yit haif I solace under serk quhill the sone ryse.
Yit am I haldin a haly wif our all the haill schyre.
I am sa peteouse to the pur, quhen ther person is mony.
In passing of pilgrymage I pride me full mekle,
Mair for the prese of peple na ony pardon wynyng.   475
Bot yit me think the best bourd quhen baronis and knychtis
And othir bachilleris blith, blumyng in youth,
And all my luffaris lele my luging persewis,
And fyllis me wyne wantonly with weilfair and joy.
Sum rownis and sum ralyeis and sum redis ballatis,   480
Sum raiffis furth rudly with riatus speche,
Sum plenis and sum prayis, sum prasis mi bewte,
Sum kissis me, sum clappis me, sum kyndnes me proferis.
Sum kerffis to me curtasli, sum me the cop giffis,
Sum stalwardly steppis ben with a stout curage,   485
And a stif standand thing staiffis in mi neiff,
And mony blenkis ben our, that but full fer sittis,
That mai for the thik thrang nought thrif as thai wald.
Bot with my fair calling I comfort thaim all:
For he that sittis me nixt I nip on his finger,   490

467. *syne]* Sign.
468. *sickir]* Secure.
469. *semelyar sege]* More handsome man. *wer]* Worse.
471. *serk]* Undergarment.
472. *haill]* Whole. *schyre]* District.
473. *peteouse]* Compassionate. *pur]* Poor. *person is mony]* There are many people.
475. *prese]* Crowd.
477. *bachilleris]* Young knights.
478. *luging]* Dwelling. *persewis]* Visit often.
479. *fyllis me wyne]* Pours out wine for me.
480] One whispers and one jests and one read poems.
481. *raiffis]* Talks loudly. *rudly]* Roughly. *riatus]* Dissolute.
482. *plenis]* Complains. *prasis]* Praises.
483. *clappis]* Embraces.
484. *kerffis]* Acts as carver.
485. *stalwardly]* Boldly. *ben]* Within.
486. *standand]* Erect. *staiffis]* Thrusts. *neiff]* Fist.
487] Many glance inside that sit far outside.
488. *thrang]* Crowd. *thrif]* Succeed.
489. *fair calling]* Warm welcome.

I serf him on the tothir syde on the samin fasson,
And he that behind me sittis I hard on him lene,
And him befor with my fut fast on his I stramp,
And to the bernis far but sweit blenkis I cast.
To every man in speciall speke I sum wordis,   495
So wisly and so womanly quhill warmys ther hertis.
Thar is no liffand leid so law of degre
That sall me luf unluffit, I am so loik hertit.
And gif his lust so be lent in to my lyre quhit
That he be lost or with me lak, his lif sall not danger.   500
I am so mercifull in mynd, and menys all wichtis,
My sely saull salbe saif quhen sabot all jugis.
Ladyis, leir thir lessonis and be no lassis fundin.
This is the legeand of my lif, thought Latyne it be nane.'

Quhen endit had hir ornat speche this eloquent wedow,   505
Lowd thai lewch all the laif and loffit hir mekle,
And said thai suld exampill tak of her soverane teching
And wirk efter hir wordis, that woman wes so prudent.
Than culit thai ther mouthis with confortable drinkis,
And carpit full cummerlik, with cop going round.   510
Thus draif thai our that deir nyght with danceis full noble,
Quhill that the day did up daw and dew donkit flouris.
The morow myld wes and meik the mavis did sing,
And all remuffit the myst and the meid smellit.
Silver schouris doune schuke as the schene cristall,   515

491. *samin]* Same.
493. *stramp]* Stamp.
494. *but]* Outside. *blenkis]* Glances.
497. *liffand leid]* Living man *low]* Low. *degre]* Rank.
498. *loik hertit]* Warm-hearted.
499. *lent]* Inclined. *lyre]* Skin.
500. *lak]* Play, sport. *danger]* Be endangered.
501. *menys]* Take pity on. *wichtis]* Persons.
502. *sely saull]* Pitiable soul.
503. *leir]* Learn.
506. *lewch]* Laughed. *laif]* Rest. *loffit]* Praised.
509. *culit]* Refreshed.
510. *carpit]* Talked. *cummerlik]* Intimately.
511. *draif ... our]* Passed.
512. *up daw]* Dawn. *donkit]* Moistened.
513. *morow]* Morning. *mavis]* Thrush.
514. *remuffit]* Vanished.
515. *schuke]* Fell.

And berdis shoutit in schaw with ther schill notis.
The goldin glitterand gleme so gladit ther hertis,
Thai maid a glorius gle amang the grene bewis.
The soft sowch of the swyr and soune of the stremys,
The sweit savour of the sward and singing of foulis   520
Myght confort ony creatur of the kyn of Adam,
And kindill agane his curage, thoght it wer cald sloknyt.
Than rais thir ryall rosis in ther riche wedis,
And rakit hame to ther rest throw the rise blumys;
And I all prevely past to a plesand arber,   525
And with my pen did report ther pastance most mery.
Ye auditoris most honorable that eris has gevin
Onto this uncouth aventur quhilk airly me happinnit,
Of thir thre wanton wiffis that I haif writtin heir,
Quhilk wald ye waill to your wif, gif ye suld wed one?   530

516. *berdis]* Birds. *schaw]* Wood. *schill]* Shrill.
518. *gle]* Music.
519. *sowch]* Murmur. *swyr]* Valley. *soune]* Sound.
522. *sloknyt]* Extinguished.
523. *rais]* Arose.
524. *rakit]* Went. *rise]* Brushwood. *blumys]* Blossoms.
525. *prevely]* Secretly.
527. *gevin]* Given.
528. *uncouth]* Strange. *airly]* In the early hours.
530. *waill]* Choose.

4

A Ballat of the Abbot of Tungland

The subject of this poem (and also of 24) is John Damian, abbot of *Tungland*, or Tongland, in Galloway (1504–09). This picturesque figure played many roles at the Scottish court – friend and entertainer of James IV, physician and, above all, alchemist. From 1503 to 1508 the king lavishly financed his alchemical experiments; payments for cakes of glass, saltpetre, coals for the furnace and other apparatus are recorded in *The Treasurer's Accounts*. The king was motivated not solely by scientific interest but by a desire to replenish his finances (see Read 1938–46; Holmyard 1957: 211–32). Dunbar's mockery of Damian in this poem has some relationship to reality – he was a man of dubious foreign origin, who dabbled in medicine and alchemy – but there is a curious lack of contemporary evidence for the climactic and ill-fated attempt to fly. There is only one other mention, written long after the event (*c.* 1570), by John Leslie (p. 76):

> This tyme thair wes ane Italiane with the King, quha wes maid Abbott of Tungland, and wes of curious ingyne [cunning]. He causet the King believe that he, be multiplyinge and utheris his inventiouns, wold make fine golde of uther mettall, quhilk science he callit the quintassence; quhairupon the King maid greit cost, bot all in vaine. This Abbott tuik in hand to flie with wingis, and to be in Fraunce befoir the saidis ambassadouris; and to that effect he causet mak ane pair of wingis of fedderis, quhilkis beand fessinit apoun him, he flew of the castell wall of Striveling, bot shortlie he fell to the ground and brak his thee bane [thigh bone]; bot the wyt [blame] thairof he asscryvit to that thair was sum hen fedderis in the wingis, quhilk yarnit [desired] and covet the mydding [dunghill] and not the skyis.

Dunbar's poem is a fiction, a nightmarish dream, and it has a generic resemblance to other tales of disastrous attempts to fly: the legend of Daedalus and Icarus (see 65); Bladud, father of King Lear, who broke his neck in an attempted flight (Geoffrey of Monmouth, I. 10); and a similar story, told of Oliver of Malmesbury by Higden (*Polychronicon*, VII, 222). Such stories

58

illustrate the consequences of human pride and folly, and are often associated with sorcery. Dunbar's poem likewise mocks and humiliates someone who has over-reached himself. It is striking, stylistically, for the wide range of literary allusion. Dunbar burlesques the diction of medieval romance, and finds comic analogues to the abbot in classical myth (65–7). He also wittily embroiders an ancient poetic topos, the bird catalogue (69ff.), echoing similar lists of birds in Chaucer's *Parliament of Fowls* and Holland's *Howlat*. The latter influenced the highly alliterative diction. The poem is written in eight-line tail-rhyme, pairs of stanzas being linked by a common rhyme on the 'tail'. This is a less common type of tail-rhyme than that used in 31 (a six-line stanza) and 36 (twelve-line). It is also used in *The Crying of ane Play*, which follows immediately in B.

Date: The poem is traditionally dated *c*. 1507, largely because of Leslie's account of the incident (Baxter 1952: 168). But the phrase 'new maid channoun' (53) tallies closely with a reference, in March 1504, to 'maister Johne, the Franch medicinar, new maid Abbot of Tungland' (*TA*, II, 423). I think it likely that the poem was composed about this time.

Text: B, ff. 117ʳ–118ᵛ; collated with A, ff. 211ᵛ–212ᵛ (1–69 only).

Title: B has a doggerel title unlikely to be Dunbar's: 'Ane ballat of the fenyeit freir of Tungland / How he fell in the myre fleand to Turkiland'. A's title is 'Off the fenyeit fals frer of tungland'. Although B and A call the protagonist a friar, Dunbar does not use this style in 4 and 24; these term him, more accurately, canon (4. 53) or abbot (24. 23 and 50). The title of A's table of contents seems best: 'a ballat of the abbot of tungland'.

Further reading: Hay 1973–74; Parkinson 1986; Bawcutt 1992a: 274–9.

1

As yung Awrora with cristall haile
In orient schew hir visage paile,
A swevyng swyth did me assaile
    Of sonis of Sathanis seid.
Me thocht a Turk of Tartary   5
Come throw the boundis of Barbary
And lay forloppin in Lumbardy
    Full lang in waithman weid.

1. haile] ? Dew drops.
2. orient] Eastern part of the sky. *schew]* Showed.
3. swevyng] Vision. *swyth]* Swiftly.
4. sonis] Sons. *Sathanis seid]* Satan's descendants.
5. Me thocht] It seemed to me.
6. Come] Came. *boundis]* Lands. *Barbary]* The pagan world.
7. lay forloppin] Remained as a vagabond.
8. waithman weid] Outlaw's dress.

2

Fra baptasing for to eschew,
Thair a religious man he slew   10
And cled him in his abeit new,
    For he cowth wryte and reid.
Quhen kend was his dissimulance
And all his cursit govirnance,
For feir he fled and come in France,   15
    With littill of Lumbard leid.

3

To be a leiche he fenyt him thair,
Quhilk mony a man micht rew evirmair,
For he left nowthir seik nor sair
    Unslane, or he hyne yeid.   20
Vane organis he full clenely carvit.
Quhen of his straik so mony starvit,
Dreid he had gottin that he desarvit
    He fled away gud speid.

4

In Scotland than the narrest way   25
He come his cunnyng till assay.
To sum man thair it was no play,
    The preving of his sciens.

9] To avoid baptism.
10. *religious]* Belonging to a religious order.
11. *cled]* Clad. *abeit]* Religious robe.
12. *cowth]* Knew how to.
13. *kend]* Perceived.
14. *govirnance]* Behaviour.
16. *leid]* Language.
17. *leiche]* Physician. *fenyt him]* Pretended.
18. *rew]* Regret.
19. *seik]* Sick. *sair]* Diseased.
20] Unmurdered before he went away.
21. *Vane organis]* Jugular veins. *carvit]* Slit.
22. *straik]* Stroke. *starvit]* Died.
23] Fearful that he would have got what he deserved (i.e. punishment).
24. *gud speid]* Rapidly.
25. *narrest]* Nearest, shortest.
26] He came to try out his (1) skill, (2) craftiness.
27. *play]* Sport.
28. *preving]* Demonstration. *sciens]* Wisdom.

In pottingry he wrocht grit pyne,
He murdreist in to medecyne.   30
The Jow was of a grit engyne,
And generit was of gyans.

5

In leichecraft he was homecyd.
He wald haif, for a nycht to byd,
A haiknay and the hurt manis hyd,   35
So meikle he was of myance.
His yrnis was rude as ony rawchtir.
Quhair he leit blude, it was no lawchtir.
Full mony instrument for slawchtir
Was in his gardevyance.   40

6

He cowth gif cure for laxatyve,
To gar a wicht hors want his lyve.
Quha evir assay wald, man or wyve,
Thair hippis yeid hiddy giddy.
His practikis nevir war put to preif,   45
Bot suddane deid or grit mischeif.
He had purgatioun to mak a theif
To dee withowt a widdy.

29] He caused great suffering through his pharmacy.
31. engyne] Ingenuity.
32. generit] Engendered. *gyans]* Giants.
33. leichecraft] Medical skill. *homecyd]* Homicidal.
34–5] In return for a night's stay he would get a horse and the skin of the sick man.
36. meikle] Great. *myance]* Resources.
37. yrnis] Surgical instruments. *rude]* Rough. *rawchtir]* Rafter, roof-beam.
38. leit blude] Let blood. *lawchtir]* Laughing matter.
39. slawchtir] Slaughter.
40. gardevyance] Trunks for transporting valuables.
41. laxatyve] Looseness, diarrhoea.
42. wicht] Strong. *Want]* Lose.
43. assay] Try (it). *wyve]* Woman.
44. yeid hiddy giddy] Went helter-skelter.
45. preif] Proof.
46] Without sudden death or great harm.
47. purgatioun] Laxatives.
48. dee] Die. *widdy]* Hangman's noose.

7

Unto no mes pressit this prelat,
For sound of sacring bell nor skellat.   50
As blaksmyth bruikit was his pallatt,
    For battering at the study.
Thocht he come hame a new maid channoun,
He had dispensit with matynnis channoun.
On him come nowther stole nor fannoun,   55
    For smowking of the smydy.

8

Me thocht seir fassonis he assailyeit
To mak the quintessance and failyeit,
And quhen he saw that nocht availyeit
    A fedrem on he tuke,   60
And schupe in Turky for to fle.
And quhen that he did mont on he,
All fowill ferleit quhat he sowld be,
    That evir did on him luke.

9

Sum held he had bene Dedalus,   65
Sum the Menatair marvelus,
Sum Martis blaksmyth, Vulcanus,
    And sum Saturnus kuke.
And evir the tuschettis at him tuggit,
The rukis him rent, the ravynis him druggit,   70

---

49. *mes*] Mass. *pressit*] Hastened. *prelat*] High-ranking churchman.
50. *sacring bell*] Bell rung at the consecration of the eucharist. *skellat*] Hand bell.
51. *bruikit*] Blackened. *pallatt*] Head.
52. *study*] Stiddy, anvil.
55. *stole, fannoun*] Ecclesiastical vestments.
56] For fear of getting soiled by the smoke from the smithy.
57. *seir*] Various. *fassonis*] Methods. *assailyeit*] Tried.
58. *failyeit*] Failed.
59. *nocht availyeit*] Nothing succeeded.
60] He put on a feather coat.
61. *schupe*] Prepared. *fle*] Fly.
62. *mont*] Mount. *he*] High.
63. *fowill*] Bird. *ferleit*] Marvelled.
64. *luke*] Look.
68. *kuke*] Cook.
69. *tuschettis*] Lapwings.
70. *rukis*] Rooks. *rent*] Tore apart. *ravynis*] Ravens. *druggit*] Dragged.

The hudit crawis his hair furth ruggit,
The hevin he micht not bruke.

10

The myttane and Sanct Martynis fowle
Wend he had bene the hornit howle,
Thay set aupone him with a yowle,   75
    And gaif him dynt for dynt.
The golk, the gormaw and the gled
Beft him with buffettis quhill he bled,
The sparhalk to the spring him sped,
    Als fers as fyre of flynt.   80

11

The tarsall gaif him tug for tug,
A stanchell hang in ilka lug,
The pyot furth his pennis did rug,
    The stork straik ay but stynt.
The bissart, bissy but rebuik,   85
Scho was so cleverus of hir cluik
His bawis he micht not langer bruik
    Scho held thame at ane hint.

---

71. hudit crawis] Hooded crows. *ruggit]* Pulled, tugged.

72. bruke] Enjoy.

73. myttane] Unidentified bird of prey.

74. Wend] Believed. *hornit howle]* Horned owl.

75. yowle] Howl.

76. gaif] Gave. *dynt]* Blow.

77. golk] Cuckoo. *gormaw]* Cormorant. *gled]* Kite.

78. Beft] Hit.

79. sparhalk] Sparrow hawk. *spring]* Pounce. *him sped]* Hastened.

80. fers] Fierce.

81. tarsall] Tercel, male hawk.

82. stanchell] Kestrel. *hang]* Hung. *ilka lug]* Each ear.

83] The magpie pulled out his feathers.

84. straik] Struck. *but stynt]* Without stopping.

85. bissart] Buzzard. *but rebuik]* Without reprimand.

86. cleverus] ? Clutching, grasping. *cluik]* Claw, talon.

87. bawis] Testicles. *langer]* Longer. *bruik]* Possess.

88. ane hint] One grasp.

12

Thik was the clud of kayis and crawis,
Of marleyonis, mittanis and of mawis,   90
That bikkrit at his berd with blawis,
 In battell him abowt.
Thay nybbillit him with noyis and cry,
The rerd of thame rais to the sky,
And evir he cryit on Fortoun, 'Fy'!   95
 His lyfe was in to dowt.

13

The ja him skrippit with a skryke
And skornit him, as it was lyk.
The egill strong at him did stryke
 And rawcht him mony a rowt.   100
For feir uncunnandly he cawkit,
Quhill all his pennis war drownd and drawkit.
He maid a hundreth nolt all hawkit
 Beneth him with a spowt.

14

He schewre his feddreme, that was schene,   105
And slippit owt of it full clene,
And in a myre up to the ene
 Amang the glar did glyd.
The fowlis all at the fedrem dang,
As at a monster thame amang,   110

---

89. *clud*] Cloud. *kayis*] Jackdaws. *crawis*] Crows.
90. *marleyonis*] Merlins (small falcons). *mawis*] Gulls.
91. *bikkrit*] Made skirmishing attack. *berd*] Beard. *blawis*] Blows.
93. *nybbillit*] Nibbled.
94. *rerd*] Clamour. *rais*] Rose.
96. *in to dowt*] At risk.
97. *ja*] Jay. *skrippit*] Mocked. *skryke*] Shriek.
98. *skornit*] Derided. *was lyk*] Seemed.
100. *rawcht*] Gave. *rowt*] Blow.
101. *feir*] Fear. *Uncunnandly*] Clumsily. *cawkit*] Defecated.
102. *pennis*] Feathers. *drawkit*] Drenched.
103. *nolt*] Cattle. *hawkit*] Streaked with white.
104. *a spowt*] One spurt.
105. *schewre*] Slit. *feddreme*] Feather coat. *schene*] Fair.
107. *myre*] Bog. *ene*] Eyes.
108. *glar*] Mud. *glyd*] Glide.
109. *dang*] Struck.

Quhill all the pennis of it owtsprang
    In till the air full wyde.

15

And he lay at the plunge evirmair,
Sa lang as any ravin did rair.
The crawis him socht with cryis of cair   115
    In every schaw besyde.
Had he reveild bene to the ruikis,
Thay had him revin all with thair cluikis.
Thre dayis in dub amang the dukis
    He did with dirt him hyde.   120

16

The air was dirkit with the fowlis,
That come with yawmeris and with yowlis,
With skryking, skrymming and with scowlis,
    To tak him in the tyde.
I walknit with the noyis and schowte   125
So hiddowis beir was me abowte.
Sensyne I curs that cankerit rowte,
    Quhair evir I go or ryde.

---

111. owtsprang] Flew out.
113. at the plunge] Immersed.
114. rair] Cry raucously.
115. socht] Searched for. *cair]* Lamentation.
116. schaw] Wood.
117–18] If he had been revealed to the rooks, they would have torn him apart with their claws.
119. dub] Pond. *dukis]* Ducks.
121. dirkit] Darkened.
122. yawmeris] Yells.
123. skryking] Shrieking. *skrymming]* Darting about. *scowlis]* Ugly looks.
124. tyde] Appointed time.
125. walknit] Awoke.
126. hiddowis beir] Appalling din.
127. Sensyne] Since then. *cankerit]* Evil. *rowte]* Crowd.
128. go] Walk.

5

Dunbar has embedded a petition to the king in this lightly satiric picture of the court. It resembles **7** and **56** in technique and verse form, although the tone is less savage. The poem has a catalogue structure, effected by the itemizing use of the pronoun *sum*, 'one, some'; for other uses of the device, see **2**. The same metre, four-stress couplets, is also used in **7** and **56**. There is no firm evidence as to date, although a slight clue may be afforded by the reference to a morris dance (**8** and note); in view of Dunbar's animosity to John Damian (see **4**), this might suggest composition around 1504.

Text: MF, p. 8 (MFa); collated with MF, p. 316 (MFb), and R, f. 10ʳ.
6. Quhill] MFb; Quhilk MFa.

Authorship: 'Quod Dumbar' in MFa and R; 'Quod Dumbar aganis the solistaris in court' in MFb.

Further reading: Scott 1966: 92–3 ('an example of the guile [Dunbar] disclaims having'); Reiss 1979: 63–4; Ross 1981: 137–8; Bawcutt 1992a: 106.

> Be divers wyis and operatiounes
> Men makis in court thair solistationes:
> Sum be service and diligence,
> Sum be continuall residence.
> Sum on his substance dois abyd,   5
> Quhill fortoune do for him provyd.
> Sum singis, sum dances, sum tellis storyis,

1] By different methods and activities.
2. solistationes] Petitions for advancement.
4. residence] Attendance (at court).
5] One gets by on his own resources.

Sum lait at evin bringis in the moryis.
Sum flirdis, sum fenyeis and sum flatteris,
Sum playis the fuill and all owt clatteris. 10
Sum man musand be the waw
Luikis as he mycht nocht do with aw.
Sum standis in a nuk and rownes,
For covetyce ane uthair neir swownes.
Sum beris as he wald ga wud, 15
For hait desyr of warldis gud.
Sum at the mes leves all devocion,
And besy labouris for premocione.
Sum hes thair advocattis in chalmir,
And takis thame selff thairof no glawmir. 20
My sempillnes, amang the laiff,
Wait of na way, sa God me saiff,
Bot with ane hummble cheir and face
Refferis me to the kyngis grace.
Methink his graciows countenance 25
In ryches is my sufficiance.

8. *at evin]* In the evening. *moryis]* Morris dance.
9. *flirdis]* Jeers. *fenyeis]* Dissimulates.
10. *all owt clatteris]* Gabbles out everything.
11. *musand]* Reflecting. *be the waw]* Beside the wall.
13. *nuk]* Corner. *rownes]* Whispers.
14. *covetyce]* Greed. *neir swownes]* Nearly faints.
15. *beris]* Behaves. *ga wud]* Go mad.
16. *hait]* Burning. *warldis gud]* Worldly wealth.
17. *mes]* Service of mass. *devocion]* Spiritual feeling.
18. *besy]* Busily. *premocione]* Promotion.
19. *advocattis]* Advocates, intercessors. *in chalmir]* In private.
20] And they themselves suffer no scandal because of it.
21. *sempillnes]* Simplicity. *laiff]* Rest (of the court).
22. *Wait]* Knows.
23. *cheir]* Expression.
24. *Refferis me]* Entrust myself.
25. *Methink]* It seems to me.
26] Is for me sufficiency of wealth.

6

This poem was occasioned by the visit of Queen Margaret to Aberdeen in May 1511. Some of the advance preparations of the citizens – the cleansing of streets and the decoration of houses with flowers and tapestries (cf. 49) – are documented in the Aberdeen Burgh Records for May 1511. But Dunbar provides the sole account of the pageantry devised to greet the queen. Such royal entries were common throughout western Europe, and were often highly spectacular entertainments. This poem mingles description with two apostrophes: to Aberdeen itself (as in the refrain and the *thow* of lines 25 and 34); and to the queen in the final stanza (up till then she is spoken of in the third person). Possibly the poem was designed for recitation, shortly after the pageantry had ended, when queen, burgesses and poet were together at a banquet. Dunbar's style is uncharacteristically weak and repetitive – note 'Gryt was' (15, 50 and 56) – which may be due to rapidity of composition, and also to faulty transmission. The stanza, *ababbcbC⁵*, is also employed in 8, 18, 19, 34, 45, 67, 68 and 69. In the fifteenth century it was popular for didactic and religious verse.

Text: R, ff. 7ʳ–7ᵛ. The gaps in the text suggest that the exemplar was difficult to read.

43. gold] cold R
44. bravelie] brav R
47. halsand] husband R
54. schene] *Not in* R

Authorship: 'Quod Dumbar' R.

Further reading: Scott 1966: 165–7 ('of little value except as social history'); Reiss 1979: 51 ('epideictic rhetoric'); Bawcutt 1992a: 89–92 (on the occasion, and 'twofold structure'). On civic pageantry in medieval Scotland, see Mill 1927.

1

Blyth Aberdeane, thow beriall of all tounis,
The lamp of bewtie, bountie and blythnes,
Unto the heaven . . . thy renoun is,
Of vertew, wisdome and of worthines
He nottit is thy name of nobilnes.   5
Into the cuming of oure lustie quein,
The wall of welth, guid cheir and mirrines,
Be blyth and blisfull, burgh of Aberdein.

2

And first hir mett the burges of the toun,
Richelie arrayit, as become thame to be;   10
Of quhom they cheset four men of renoun,
In gounes of velvot, young, abill and lustie,
To beir the paill of velves cramase
Abone hir heid, as the custome hes bein.
Gryt was the sound of the artelyie: 15
Be blyth and blisfull, burgh of Aberdein.

3

Ane fair processioun mett hir at the port,
In a cap of gold and silk full pleasantlie,
Syne at hir entrie with many fair disport
Ressaveit hir on streittis lustilie;   20
Quhair first the salutatioun honorabilly

1. *Blyth]* Glad, joyful. *beriall]* Beryl (fig. paragon).
2. *bountie]* Goodness.
3. *renoun]* Renown.
4. *vertew]* Virtue.
5. *He]* Highly. *nottit]* Celebrated.
6. *lustie]* Beautiful.
7] The source (lit. well) of wealth, good cheer and merriness.
9. *burges]* Burgesses.
10. *become]* Befitted.
11. *cheset]* Chose.
12. *velvot]* Velvet. *lustie]* Vigorous.
13. *paill]* Canopy. *velves cramase]* Crimson velvet.
14. *Abone]* Above.
15. *Gryt]* Great. *artelyie]* Artillery.
17. *port]* Gate, entrance to the town.
18. *cap]* Cape.
19. *Syne]* Then. *disport]* Entertainment.
20. *Ressaveit]* Received.

Of the sweitt Virgin guidlie mycht be seine,
The sound of menstrallis blawing to the sky:
Be blyth and blisfull, burgh of Aberdein.

4

And syne thow gart the orient kingis thrie   25
Offer to Chryst with benyng reverence
Gold, sence and mir with all humilitie,
Schawand him king with most magnificence;
Syne quhow the angill, with sword of violence,
Furth of the joy of paradice putt clein   30
Adame and Ev for innobedience:
Be blyth and blisfull, burch of Aberdein.

5

And syne the Bruce that evir was bold in stor
Thow gart as roy cum rydand under croun,
Richt awfull, strang and large of portratour,   35
As nobill, dreidfull, michtie campioun.
The . . . syne of great renoun
Thow gart upspring with branches new and greine,
Sa gloriouslie quhill glaidid all the toun:
Be blyth and blisfull, burch of Aberdein.   40

6

Syne come thair four and twentie madinis ying,
All claid in greine, of mervelous bewtie,
With hair detressit, as threidis of gold did hing,

---

22. *guidlie]* Fittingly.
23. *menstrallis]* Minstrels. *blawing]* Sounding trumpets or other wind instruments.
25. *orient]* Eastern. *gart]* Caused.
26. *benyng]* Gracious.
27. *sence]* Incense. *mir]* Myrrh.
30. *putt]* Drove. *clein]* Completely.
31. *innobedience]* Disobedience.
33. *stor]* Battle.
34. *roy]* King.
35. *awfull]* Awe-inspiring. *portratour]* Stature.
36. *dreidfull]* Causing fear. *campioun]* Champion.
39. *quhill]* Till. *Glaidid]* Rejoiced.
41. *come]* Came. *ying]* Young.
42. *claid]* Clothed.
43. *detressit]* Hanging loose. *hing]* Hang.

With quhyt hattis all browderit rycht bravelie,
Playand on timberallis and singand rycht sweitlie.　　45
That seimlie sort in ordour weill besein
Did meit the quein, hir halsand reverentlie:
Be blyth and blisfull, burch of Aberdein.

7

The streittis war all hung with tapestrie,
Greit was the pres of peopill, dwelt about,　　50
And pleasant padgeanes playit prattelie.
The legeis all did to thair lady loutt,
Quha was convoyed with ane royall routt
Of gryt barrounes and lustie ladyis schene.
'Welcum, our quein!', the commones gaif ane schout:　　55
Be blyth and blisfull, burch of Aberdein.

8

At hir cuming great was the mirth and joy,
For at thair Croce aboundantlie rane wyne.
Untill hir ludgeing the toun did hir convoy,
Hir for to treit thai sett thair haill ingyne.　　60
Ane riche present thai did till hir propyne,
Ane costlie coup that large thing wald contene,
Coverit and full of cunyeit gold rycht fyne:
Be blyth and blisfull, burch of Aberdein.

---

44. *quhyt]* White. *browderit]* Embroidered. *bravelie]* Finely.
45. *timberallis]* Tymbrals, percussion instruments.
46. *seimlie sort]* Handsome company. *besein]* Arrayed.
47. *halsand]* Greeting.
50. *pres]* Crowd. *dwelt about]* Who lived nearby.
51. *padgeanes]* Plays. *prattelie]* Skilfully.
52. *legeis]* Lieges, subjects. *loutt]* Bow deferentially.
53. *convoyed]* Escorted. *routt]* Retinue.
54. *barrounes]* Barons. *schene]* Beautiful.
55. *commones]* Common people.
58. *Croce]* Market Cross. *rane]* Flowed.
59. *ludgeing]* Lodging.
60. *treit]* Entertain. *haill ingyne]* Whole mind.
61. *propyne]* Offer.
62. *coup]* Goblet. *contene]* Contain.
63. *Coverit]* With an ornamental lid. *cunyeit]* Coined.

9

O potent princes, pleasant and preclair,   65
Great caus thow hes to thank this nobill toun,
That for to do the honnour did not spair
Thair geir, riches, substance and persoun,
The to ressave on maist fair fasoun.
The for to pleis thai socht all way and mein.   70
Thairfoir sa lang as quein thow beiris croun,
Be thankfull to this burch of Aberdein.

65. *potent]* Mighty. *preclair]* Renowned.
68. *geir]* Possessions. *substance]* Wealth.
69. *ressave]* Receive. *fasoun]* Fashion.
70] They tried in every way to please you.

7

Dunbar at first veils this petition to James IV in a general complaint on the wrongs suffered by noble and virtuous persons, but the personal implications become explicit in his envoi-like conclusion (67–76). The vivid diatribe against social climbers may well be aimed at specific individuals. Dunbar inherited a medieval belief in the iniquity of rising above one's natural station in life (cf. the reference to Nature in line 58). Criticism of upstarts for presumption, ignorance, and hostility to their social superiors (cf. 64–6) was very common. There is a similar attack on churchmen of lowly origins in *Pierce the Ploughman's Crede*, 744–55. In sixteenth-century Scotland it was believed that James III's low-born favourites were responsible for his fall (see Lindsay, *Papyngo*, 446–71; and Macdougall 1982: 275–80). This poem employs the same metre as 5 and 56, which it resembles in technique and theme. It is striking for its flyting style and reductive images, many drawn from the world of the poor labourer (23–5, 55–60). These both ridicule the physical appearance of upstarts and imply the tasks for which they are best fitted.

Text: MF, pp. 16–18; collated with R, ff. 13ᵛ–14ʳ. MF is badly faded in some passages, but R assists their decipherment.
43. ald] R; all MF.
56. bere] R; be MF.
64. Nobles] And nobles MF, R.

Authorship: 'Quod Dumbar' in MF and R.

Further reading: Bawcutt 1992a: 241–2.

> Complane I wald, wist I quhome till
> Or unto quhome darect my bill:
> Quhidder to God that all thing steiris,

1–2] I should like to complain, if I knew someone suitable, or to whom I should direct my petition.
3. Quhidder] Whether. *steiris]* Governs.

73

All thing seis and all thing heiris,
And all thing wrocht in dayis seveyne,   5
Or till his moder, quein of heveyne,
Or unto wardlie prince heir downe,
That dois for justice weir a crownne –
Of wrangis and of gryt injuris
That nobillis in thar dayis induris,   10
And men of vertew and cuning,
Of wit and wysdome in gydding,
That nocht cane in this cowrt conquys
For lawte, luiff nor lang servys.
Bot fowll jow jowrdane-hedit jevellis,   15
Cowkin kenseis and culroun kevellis,
Stuffettis, strekouris and stafische strummellis,
Wyld haschbaldis, haggarbaldis and hummellis,
Druncartis, dysouris, dyowris, drevellis,
Misgydit memberis of the devellis,   20
Mismad mandragis of mastis strynd,
Crawdones, couhirttis and theiffis of kynd,
Blait-mouit bladyeanes with bledder cheikis,
Clubfacet clucanes, with clutit breikis,
Chuff midding-churllis, cuming of cart-fillaris,   25
Gryt glaschewe-hedit gorge-millaris,

---

4. *seis]* Sees.
5. *wrocht]* Created.
6. *moder]* Mother.
7. *wardlie]* Worldly. *heir downe]* On earth.
9. *wrangis]* Wrongs. *injuris]* Injustices.
10. *dayis]* Lifetimes. *induris]* Endure.
11. *vertew]* Virtue. *cuning]* Learning.
12. *wit]* Intelligence. *gydding]* Conduct.
13. *nocht]* Nothing. *conquys]* Obtain.
14. *lawte]* Loyalty.
15–16] Foul, infidel (*jow*) rascals, with heads shaped like chamber-pots, beggarly ruffians and base knaves.
17. *Stuffettis]* ? Grooms. *stafische]* Stubborn.
19. *dysouris]* Gamblers. *dyowris]* Bankrupts. *drevellis]* Drudges.
20] Badly-behaved agents (lit. limbs) of the devil.
21] Misshapen mandrakes sprung of mastiffs.
22] Cravens, cowards and born thieves.
23. *Blait-mouit]* Weak-mouthed. *bladyeanes]* Obscure. *bledder]* Bladder.
24. *Clubfacet]* With faces like clubs. *clucanes]* ? Yokels. *clutit breikis]* Patched breeches.
25] Rustic dunghill peasants, descended from cart-fillers.
26] *See note.*

Evill, horrible monsteris, fals and fowll –
Sum causles clekis till him ane cowll,
Ane gryt convent fra syne to tys,
And he him self exampill of vys,   30
Enterand for geir and no devocioun.
The devill is glaid of his promocioun.
Sum ramyis ane rokkat fra the roy,
And dois ane dastart destroy,
And sum that gaittis ane personage   35
Thinkis it a present for a page,
And on no wayis content is he
'My lord' quhill that he callit be.
Bot quhow is he content or nocht,
Dem ye abowt in to yowr thocht?   40
The lerit sone of erle or lord,
Upone this ruffie to remord,
That with ald castingis hes him cled,
His erandis for to ryne and red
(And he is maister native borne   45
And all his eldaris him beforne,
And mekle mair cuning, be sic thre,
Hes to posseid ane dignite),
Saying his odius ignorance
Panting ane prelottis countenance,   50
Sa far above him set at tabell,

28] One without justification grabs himself a cowl.
29. *convent]* Monastery. *syne]* Sin. *tys]* Draw away.
30. *vys]* Vice.
31. *geir]* Money. *devocioun]* Spiritual feeling.
33. *ramyis]* Clamours for. *rokkat]* Bishop's vestment. *roy]* King.
35. *gaittis]* Gets. *personage]* Parson's benefice.
36. *page]* Boy.
37. *On no wayis]* In no way.
38. *quhill]* Until.
40. *Dem]* Judge. *abowt]* Around.
41. *lerit sone]* Learned son.
42. *ruffie]* Villain. *remord]* Meditate bitterly.
43. *ald castingis]* Old cast-off clothing. *cled]* Clad.
44. *ryne]* Run. *red]* Perform.
45. *maister]* University graduate.
46. *eldaris]* Ancestors. *beforne]* Before.
47–8] And is much more entitled – being three times as learned – to have high ecclesiastical office.
49. *Saying]* See note.
50. *Panting]* Putting on. *prelottis countenance]* Prelate's manner.

That wont was for to muk the stabell:
Ane pykthank in a prelottis clais,
With his wawill feit and wirrok tais,
With hoppir hippis and henches narrow,   55
And bausy handis to bere a barrow,
With lut schulderis and luttard bak,
Quhilk Natur maid to beir a pak,
With gredy mynd and glaschane gane,
Mell-hedit lyk ane mortar stane,   60
Fenyeing the feris of ane lord
(And he ane strumbell, I stand ford)
And ever moir as he dois rys,
Nobles of bluid he dois dispys
And helpis for to hald thame downe   65
That thay rys never to his renowne.
Thairfoir, O prince maist honorable,
Be in this meter merciabill
And to thy auld servandis haff e,
That lang hes lipinit into the.   70
Gif I be ane of tha my sell,
Throw all regiones hes bein hard tell,
Of quhilk my wrytting witnes beris.
And yete thy danger ay me deris.
Bot efter danger cumis grace,   75
As hes bein herd in mony plece.

---

53. *pykthank]* Sycophant. *clais]* Clothes.
54. *wawill]* Deformed. *wirrok tais]* Toes covered with corns.
55. *henches]* Haunches.
56. *bausy]* ? Clumsy, *barrow]* Hand barrow.
57. *lut]* Bowed. *luttard]* Bent.
58. *pak]* Peddlar's pack.
59. *glaschane]* ? Fishlike. *gane]* Face.
60] See note.
61. *Fenyeing]* Aping. *feris]* Manners.
64. *of bluid]* By birth.
65. *hald]* Keep.
68. *meter]* Matter, issue. *merciabill]* Compassionate.
69. *haff e]* Be considerate.
70. *lipinit]* Trusted.
71] If I myself be one of those.
72. *regiones]* Countries. *hard]* Heard.
74. *danger]* Displeasure. *deris]* Hurts.
76. *herd]* Heard. *plece]* Place.

8

This is one of a number of Scottish poems on the Resurrection, preserved by Bannatyne among his 'ballatis of theoligie'; there survive curiously few medieval English lyrics on the theme. The poem is an affirmation of faith; it embodies an ancient view of the Redemption as a struggle between God and the devil, in which Christ, 'Our campioun', is the heroic champion of humanity. The theme of the Resurrection merges with that of the 'Harrowing of Hell', the legend (first narrated in the apocryphal Gospel of Nicodemus, and dramatized in the mystery plays) that in the interval between his death and resurrection Christ descended into hell and released the souls of the righteous, who had died before his coming. This poem resembles **48** in its exultant tone. Its phrasing and imagery are influenced by the Easter liturgy and the Latin hymns and sequences of the church. The syntax, simple yet bold, is characterized by end-stopped lines, much use of inversion, and the chiasmic patterning of words. On the stanza, see **6**.

Text: B, f. 35^r.

20. a] *Not in* B.

Authorship: 'Quod Dunbar' in B.

Further reading: On the theological background, see Aulén 1970. The Latin hymns mentioned in the notes are available, with translation, in *The Penguin Book of Latin Verse*. For criticism, see Hill 1978; Reiss 1979: 93–4; Bawcutt 1992a: 178–84.

1

Done is a battell on the dragon blak,
Our campioun Chryst confoundit hes his force,

---

1. *Done]* Completed.
2. *campioun]* Champion. *confoundit]* Overthrown.

The yettis of hell ar brokin with a crak,
The signe triumphall rasit is of the croce.
The divillis trymmillis with hiddous voce,   5
The saulis ar borrowit and to the blis can go.
Chryst with his blud our ransonis dois indoce:
Surrexit dominus de sepulchro.

2

Dungin is the deidly dragon, Lucifer,
The crewall serpent with the mortall stang,   10
The auld kene tegir, with his teith on char,
Quhilk in a wait hes lyne for us so lang,
Thinking to grip us in his clowis strang.
The mercifull lord wald nocht that it wer so.
He maid him for to felye of that fang: 15
Surrexit dominus de sepulchro.

3

He for our saik that sufferit to be slane
And lyk a lamb in sacrifice wes dicht,
Is lyk a lyone rissin up agane
And as a gyane raxit him on hicht.   20
Sprungin is Aurora, radius and bricht,
On loft is gone the glorius Appollo,
The blisfull day departit fro the nycht:
Surrexit dominus de sepulchro.

---

3. *yettis]* Gates. *crak]* Explosion.
5. *divillis]* Devils. *trymmillis]* Tremble. *voce]* Voice.
6. *saulis]* Souls. *borrowit]* Redeemed
7. *ransonis]* Ransoms. *indoce]* Endorse.
8] The lord has risen from the tomb.
9. *Dungin]* Beaten.
10. *Crewall]* Cruel. *mortall stang]* Deadly sting.
11. *kene tegir]* Fierce tiger. *on char]* Bared.
12. *wait]* Ambush. *lyne]* Lain.
13. *clowis]* Claws.
14. *wald nocht]* Did not wish.
15. *felye . . . fang]* Be deprived of that prey.
18. *dicht]* Prepared.
20] And as a giant stretched himself on high.
21. *Sprungin]* Risen. *radius]* Radiant.
22. *On loft]* On high.
23. *departit]* Separated.

4

The grit victour agane is rissin on hicht,	25
That for our querrell to the deth wes woundit.	
The sone that wox all paill now schynis bricht,	
And, dirknes clerit, our fayth is now refoundit.	
The knell of mercy fra the hevin is soundit,	
The Cristin ar deliverit of thair wo,	30
The Jowis and thair errour ar confoundit:	
Surrexit dominus de sepulchro.	

5

The fo is chasit, the battell is done ceis,	
The presone brokin, the jevellouris fleit and flemit,	
The weir is gon, confermit is the peis,	35
The fetteris lowsit and the dungeoun temit,	
The ransoun maid, the presoneris redemit,	
The feild is win, ourcumin is the fo,	
Dispulit of the tresur that he yemit:	
Surrexit dominus de sepulchro.	40

26. *querrell]* Cause.
27. *sone]* Sun. *wox]* Grew.
28. *dirknes clerit]* Darkness cleared away. *refoundit]* Re-established.
29. *knell]* Peal of bells.
30. *Cristin]* Christians.
31. *Jowis]* Jews. *errour]* Erroneous belief.
33. *done ceis]* Finished.
34. *jevellouris]* Gaolers. *fleit]* Terrified. *flemit]* Put to flight.
35. *weir]* War. *gon]* Ended. *confermit]* Formally ratified. *peis]* Peace.
36. *lowsit]* Loosened. *temit]* Emptied.
37. *redemit]* Redeemed.
38. *feild]* Battle. *win]* Won. *ourcumin]* Overcome.
39] Deprived of the treasure that he guarded.

9

Dunbar here employs familiar moral commonplaces, such as the mutability of life and Fortune's ever-turning wheel; yet his overall theme is not *contemptus mundi*, or contempt for 'this warld', but a resolution to be content (cf. the theme of **43**), and to have a temperate enjoyment of earthly goods (21–5). The refrain sums up this resolve to make the best of things. The poem is included in Bannatyne's 'ballettis mirry'. The stanza, *aabaB⁴*, is very popular with Dunbar; for his other uses, see **12, 13, 23, 35, 43, 44, 46, 50** and **57**.

Text: MF, p. 337; collated with B, f. 98ᵛ; and R, ff. 43ʳ–43ᵛ.
16–20] B; *not in* MF.
22. man] B; men MF.
33. fro] B; for MF.

Authorship: 'Quod Dumbar' in MF and B.

Further reading: Ross 1981: 159–60; Bawcutt 1992a: 149–50 (the syntactic twists and turns suggest a mind 'in thocht').

1

Full oft I muse and hes in thocht
How this fals warld is ay on flocht,
Quhair no thing ferme is nor degest;
And quhone I have my mynd all socht,
For to be blythe me think it best.   5

1. muse] Reflect. *hes in thocht]* Have in contemplation.
2. on flocht] In uncertainty.
3. ferme] Fixed. *degest]* Settled.
4. quhone] When. *socht]* Searched.

2

This warld dois ever chynge and varie.
Fortoun so fast the quhele dois carie,
No tyme in turning can it tak rest,
For quhois fals chynge sould none be sarie.
For to be blythe me think it best.   10

3

Wauld man in mynd considdir weill,
Or Fortoun turnit on him the quheill,
That erdlie honour may not lest,
His fall les paynfull sould he feill.
For to be blythe me think it best.   15

4

Quha with this warld dois warsill and stryfe
And dois his dayis in dolour dryfe,
Thocht he in lordschip be possest,
He levis bot ane wrechit lyfe.
For to be blyth me think it best.   20

5

Of wardlie guddis and grit riches
Quhat frute hes man but merynes?
Thocht he this warld had, eist and west,
All is bot povertie but glaidnes.
For to be blythe me think it best.   25

6. *chynge]* Change.
7–8] Fortune drives the wheel so fast that at no time in its rotation can it stop.
9. *sarie]* Unhappy.
11. *Wauld man]* If man would.
12. *Or]* Before.
13. *erdlie]* Earthly. *lest]* Last.
16. *Quha]* Whoever. *warsill]* Wrestle.
17. *dolour]* Sadness. *dryfe]* Spend.
18. *Thocht]* Although. *lordschip]* Landed property.
19. *levis]* Lives. *bot]* Only.
21. *wardlie]* Worldly.
22. *frute]* Benefit. *but]* Without.
24. *but glaidnes]* Without gladness.

6

Quha sould for tynsall drowp or de
Of thing that is bot vanite,
Sen to the lyfe that ever sall lest
Heir is bot twynkling of ane e?
For to be blythe me think it best.   30

7

Hed I for warldlie onkyndnes
In hart tane ony havynes,
Or fro my plesance bene opprest,
I had bene deid lang syne doutles.
For to be blythe me think it best.   35

8

How ever this warld dois chynge and varie,
Let us no moir in hart be sarie,
Bot ay be reddie and addrest
To pas out of this fraudfull farie.
For to be blyth me think it best.   40

---

26. *tynsall]* Loss. *Drowp]* Droop. *de]* Die.
28. *Sen]* Since. *to]* Compared to.
29. *twynkling]* Blink. *e]* Eye.
31. *Hed I]* If I had.
32. *tane]* Felt. *havynes]* Despondency.
33] Or been depressed and so deprived of pleasure.
34] I should have been dead long since, no doubt.
38. *addrest]* Prepared.
39. *fraudfull]* Deceitful. *farie]* World (lit. illusion).

10

This is a compliment to Margaret, daughter of Henry VII, who married James IV in August 1503 (see also **6**, **41** and **52**). The poem was probably composed in the period between 1503 and February 1507, when their first child was born. Margaret was only 13 when she arrived in Scotland, and the references to her youth and prettiness (2–3, 26–7) are not mere convention. The style, which abounds in hyperbole, anaphora and other figures of rhetoric, is characteristic of courtly panegyric. The image of the rose (6 and 25) was common in love poetry, but alludes also to the heraldic badge of the Tudors. Margaret's name – Latin *margarita*, 'pearl' – serves as a focus for the striking lapidary symbolism (4–5, 35–40). On the stanza, see **6**.

Text: Ab, II, p. 460.

Authorship: A single ascription, 'quod Dunbar', appears to refer both to this poem and to **46**, but some scholars consider that it refers only to **46**. Dunbar's authorship is therefore debatable, but seems highly plausible.

Further reading: Historians have treated Margaret unsympathetically; for a recent biography, see Buchanan 1985. On the style and genre, see Bawcutt 1992a: 87–9 and 1992b; on the authorship, see Baxter 1952: 222–3.

1

> Gladethe, thoue queyne of Scottis regioun,
> Ying tendir plaunt of plesand pulcritude,
> Fresche flour of youthe, new germyng to burgeoun,

1. Gladethe] Rejoice. *Scottis]* Scots'. *regioun]* Kingdom.
2. Ying] Young.
3. germyng to burgeoun] Breaking into bud.

Our perle of price, our princes fair and gud,
Our charbunkle chosin of hye imperiale blud,   5
Our rois riale most reverent under croune,
Joy be and grace onto thi selcitud,
Gladethe, thoue queyne of Scottis regioun.

2

O hye triumphing peradis of joy,
Lodsteir and lamp of every lustines,   10
Of port surmounting Pollexen of Troy,
Dochtir to Pallas in angillik brichtnes,
Mastres of nurtur and of nobilnes,
Of fresch depictour princes and patroun,
O hevin in erthe of ferlifull swetnes,   15
Gladethe, thou queyne of Scottis regione.

3

Of thi fair fegour Natur micht rejoys,
That so the kervit with ale hir cuir and slicht.
Sche has the maid this verray warldis chois,
Schawing one the hir craftis and hir micht,   20
To se quhow fair sche couthe depaint a wicht,
Quhow gud, how noble of ale condicioun,
Quhow womanly in every mannis sicht.
Gladethe, thoue queyne of Scottis regioun.

---

4. *perle]* Pearl. *price]* Great value.
5. *charbunkle]* Carbuncle, or ruby. *blud]* Lineage.
6. *riale]* Royal *reverent]* Respected.
7. *selcitud]* Majesty.
9. *peradis]* Paradise.
10. *Lodsteir]* Lodestar. *lustines]* Beauty.
11. *port]* Bearing.
12. *Dochtir]* Daughter. *angillik]* Angelic.
13. *Mastres]* Mistress. *nurtur]* Good manners.
14. *depictour]* Painting. *patroun]* Pattern, exemplar.
15. *ferlifull]* Wondrous.
17. *fegour]* Form. *rejoys]* Rejoice.
18. *kervit]* Fashioned. *ale]* All. *cuir]* Care. *slicht]* Artistry.
19. *this verray warldis chois]* The very finest person in this world.
20. *Schawing one]* Revealing in. *craftis]* Skills.
21. *depaint]* Depict. *wicht]* Person.
22. *condicioun]* Characteristic.

4

Rois red and quhit, resplendent of colour,   25
New of thi knop, at morrow fresche atyrit,
One stalk yet grene, O yong and tendir flour,
That with thi luff has ale this regioun firit,
Gret Gode us graunt that we have lang desirit,
A plaunt to spring of thi successioun,   30
Syne with ale grace his spreit to be inspirit.
Gladethe, thoue queyne of Scottis regioun.

5

O precius Margreit, plesand, cleir and quhit,
Mor blith and bricht na is the beriale schene,
Moir deir na is the diamaunt of delit,   35
Mor semly na is the sapheir one to seyne,
Mor gudely eik na is the emerant greyne,
Moir riche na is the ruby of renoune,
Fair gem of joy, Margreit, of the I meyne:
Gladethe, thoue queyne of Scottis regioun.   40

25. *quhit]* White. *resplendent]* Bright.
26. *New of thi knop]* Newly budding. *morrow]* Morning.
29] May God grant us what we have long desired.
31. *Syne]* Then. *spreit]* Spirit.
34. *blith]* Glad. *na]* Than. *beriale schene]* Shining crystal.
35. *deir]* Precious. *diamaunt]* Diamond.
36] More beautiful to look at (*one to seyne*) than the sapphire.
37. *gudely]* Attractive. *emerant]* Emerald.
39. *of the I meyne]* I speak of you.

11

This poem in honour of the Virgin Mary is based upon the Angelic salutation (Luke 1: 28) *Ave, Maria, gracia plena*, 'Hail, Mary, full of grace', which forms an internal refrain. It combines praise with prayer, since the Virgin was regarded as the supreme intercessor with her son (cf. 47–8, 67). The diction, symbolic imagery, and rhyme patterns are highly traditional, and show the influence of Latin hymns to the Virgin and of the many vernacular poems modelled on them. For some Scottish analogues, see the anonymous 'Ros Mary' and Walter Kennedy's 'Closter of Crist', which precede this poem in the Asloan Manuscript; 'Obsecro' and 'Ave Gloriosa' in MS Arundel 285 (*Devotional Pieces*, pp. 290–98); and the inset praises of the Virgin in Holland's *Howlat*, 716–54, and in *Lancelot*, 2085–2112. There are many similar English pieces in *CB XV*, pp. 22–76. This poem has an intricate twelve-line stanza, which contains much alliteration, anaphora on 'Hail', and triple internal rhyme in the *a*-lines. Such metrical ingenuity was characteristic of late-medieval Marian lyrics. There is no evidence as to date, although lines 59–60 suggest that the poem belongs to Dunbar's youth.

Text: A, ff. 303^r–304^v.

Authorship: 'Quod Dunbar' in A.

Further reading: On the European background to religious lyrics, see Diehl 1985; on English poems in honour of the Virgin, see Woolf 1968: 114–58, and Gray 1972: 75–94. On this poem, see Hyde 1956; and Dawcutt 1992a: 354–8 ('the supreme example of Dunbar's aureate style').

1

Hale, sterne superne, hale, in eterne
  In Godis sicht to schyne,
Lucerne in derne for to discerne,
  Be glory and grace devyne.
Hodiern, modern, sempitern,   5
  Angelicall regyne,
Our tern inferne for to dispern,
  Helpe, rialest rosyne.
Ave, Maria, gracia plena.
  Haile, fresche flour femynyne,   10
Yerne, us guberne, virgin matern,
  Of reuth baith rute and ryne.

2

Haile, yhyng benyng fresche flurising,
  Haile, Alphais habitakle.
Thy dyng ofspring maid us to syng   15
  Befor his tabernakle.
All thing maling we doune thring
  Be sicht of his signakle,
Quhilk king us bring unto his ryng
  Fro dethis dirk umbrakle.   20
Ave, Maria, gracia plena.
  Haile, moder and maide but makle,
Bricht syng, gladyng our languissing
  Be micht of thi mirakle.

1. sterne superne] Star on high. *eterne]* Eternity.
3] Lamp in darkness by which to see.
5] For this day, the present age, and all eternity.
6. regyne] Queen.
7. tern inferne] Hellish gloom. *dispern]* Drive away.
8. rialest rosyne] Most royal rose.
11. yerne] Have compassion. *guberne]* Govern. *matern]* Maternal.
12] A perfect example of pity.
13. yhyng] Young. *benyng]* Blessed. *flurising]* Flower.
14. Alphais habitakle] The dwelling of God.
15. dyng] Worthy.
17. maling] Evil. *thring]* thrust.
19. ryng] Kingdom.
20] From the dark shadow of death.
22. moder] Mother. *but makle]* Without blemish.
23. syng] Sign. *gladyng]* Gladdening. *languissing]* Suffering.

3

Haile, bricht be sicht in hevyn on hicht,   25
    Haile, day sterne orientale,
Our licht most richt in clud of nycht,
    Our dirknes for to scale.
Hale, wicht in ficht, puttar to flicht
    Of fendis in battale,   30
Haile, plicht but sicht, hale, mekle of mycht,
    Haile, glorius virgin, hale
Ave, Maria, gracia plena.
    Haile, gentill nychttingale,
Way stricht, cler dicht, to wilsome wicht   35
    That irke bene in travale.

4

Hale, qwene serene, hale, most amene,
    Haile, hevinlie hie emprys,
Haile, schene, unseyne with carnale eyne,
    Haile, ros of paradys,   40
Haile, clene bedene ay till conteyne,
    Haile, fair fresche flour delyce,
Haile, grene daseyne, hale fro the splene,
    Of Jhesu genitrice.
Ave, Maria, gracia plena.   45
    Thow bair the prince of prys,
Our teyne to meyne and ga betweyne,
    As humile oratrice.

25. *be sicht]* In appearance. *hicht]* High.
26] Hail, day star in the east.
27. *richt]* True. *clud]* Cloud
29 *rrale]* Disperse.
29. *wicht]* Courageous.
30. *fendis]* Fiends.
31. *plicht]* Main anchor. *but sicht]* Unseen *mekle]* Great.
35] Straight path, clearly marked, for the lost traveller.
36. *irke bene]* Is weary. *travale]* Journeying.
37. *amene]* Kindly.
38. *emprys]* Empress.
39. *schene]* Beautiful. *eyne]* Eyes.
41. *clene bedene]* Wholly pure. *conteyne]* Continue.
43. *grene daseyne]* Young daisy. *fro the splene]* Whole-heartedly.
44. *genitrice]* Mother.
46. *bair]* Bore. *prys]* Glory.
47–8] To take pity on our suffering, and intercede as a humble advocate.

5

Hale, more decore than of before
    And swetar be sic sevyne,   50
Our glore forlore for to restor
    Sen thow art qwene of hevyn.
Memore of sore, stern in aurore,
    Lovit with angellis stevyne,
Implore, adore, thow indeflore,   55
    To mak our oddis evyne.
Ave, Maria, gracia plena.
    With lovingis lowde ellevyn,
Quhill store and hore my youth devor,
    Thy name I sall ay nevyne.   60

6

Empryce of prys, imperatrice,
    Bricht polist precious stane,
Victrice of vyce, hie genitrice
    Of Jhesu, lord soverayne,
Our wys pavys fro enemys,   65
    Agane the feyndis trayne,
Oratrice, mediatrice, salvatrice,
    To God gret suffragane.
Ave, Maria, gracia plena.
    Haile, sterne meridiane,   70
Spyce, flour delice of paradys,
    That bair the gloryus grayne.

49. *decore*] Beautiful. *of before*] Before.
50. *be sic sevyne*] Seven times.
51. *glore*] Glory. *forlore*] Lost.
53] Mindful of our grief, star at dawn.
54. *Lovit*] Praised. *stevyne*] Voice.
55. *indeflore*] Undeflowered virgin.
58. *lovingis*] Praises.
59. *store*] Adversity. *hore*] Old age. *devor*] Devour.
60. *nevyne*] Recite.
61. *imperatrice*] Empress.
63. *Victrice*] Conqueror.
65. *pavys*] Shield.
66. *trayne*] Deception.
67. *mediatrice*] Mediator. *salvatrice*] Saviour.
68. *suffragane*] Assistant.
70. *meridiane*] Of midday.
72. *grayne*] Seed.

7

Imperiall wall, place palestrall
   Of peirles pulcritud,
Tryumphale hall, hie trone regall   75
   Of Godis celsitud,
Hospitall riall, the lord of all
   Thy closet did include,
Bricht ball cristall, ros virginall,
   Fulfillit of angell fude.   80
Ave, Maria, gracia plena.
   Thy birth has with his blude
Fra fall mortall originall
   Us raunsound on the rude.

73. *place palestrall]* Palatial dwelling.
74. *peirles]* Unequalled.
75. *trone]* Throne.
76. *celsitud]* Loftiness.
77. *Hospitall]* Place of refuge.
78. *closet]* Chamber. *include]* Enclose.
82. *birth]* Child.
84. *raunsound]* Redeemed. *rude]* Cross.

12

This sardonic comment on human stupidity, which is placed among Banna-tyne's 'ballettis mirry', is far from an orthodox 'morality'. If the poem is indeed by Dunbar, there may be veiled references to James IV in stanzas 3 and 4; and stanza 3 would imply composition in the period after the king's marriage. On the stanza, see 9.

Text: B, ff. 115ᵛ–116ʳ; collated with MF, pp. 212–13.

Authorship: This rests on B's 'Quod Dumbar'; the piece is anonymous in MF, but is characteristic of Dunbar in metrical form and in the audacity of the last stanza.

Further reading: Reiss 1979: 146 ('an ironic statement of human perversity'); Ross 1981: 160–61; Bawcutt 1992a: 185–6 ('the tone is amused, rather than indignant').

1

He that hes gold and grit riches
And may be into mirrynes,
And dois glaidnes fra him expell
And levis in to wretchitnes,
He wirkis sorrow to him sell.   5

1. grit] Great.
2. mirrynes] Merriness.
4. levis] Lives. *wretchitnes]* Misery.
5. wirkis] Causes. *sell]* Self.

2

He that may be but sturt or stryfe
And leif ane lusty plesand lyfe,
And syne with mariege dois him mell
And bindis him with ane wicket wyfe,
He wirkis sorrow to him sell.   10

3

He that hes for his awin genyie
Ane plesand prop, but mank or menyie,
And schuttis syne at ane uncow schell,
And is forfairn with the fleis of Spenyie,
He wirkis sorrow to him sell.   15

4

And he that with gud lyfe and trewth,
But varians or uder slewth,
Dois evir mair with ane maister dwell,
That nevir of him will haif no rewth,
He wirkis sorrow to him sell.   20

5

Now all this tyme lat us be mirry,
And sett nocht by this warld a chirry.
Now quhill thair is gude wyne to sell,
He that dois on dry breid wirry,
I gif him to the devill of hell!   25

6. *but]* Without. *sturt]* Quarrel. *stryfe]* Strife.
7. *leif]* Live. *lusty]* Cheerful.
8. *syne]* Then. *him mell]* Involve himself.
11. *genyie]* Arrow shaft.
12. *prop]* Butt (in shooting). *mank]* Flaw. *menyie]* Defect.
13. *schuttis]* Shoots. *uncow]* Strange, unknown. *schell]* Target.
14. *forfairn]* Ruined. *fleis of Spenyie]* Syphilis.
16. *trewth]* Loyalty.
17. *varians]* Fickleness. *uder]* Other. *slewth]* Sloth, laziness.
18. *ane maister]* One master.
19. *rewth]* Compassion.
22. *sett . . . by]* Value. *chirry]* Cherry.
24. *wirry]* Choke.
25. *gif]* Consign.

13

It was a common didactic theme that, no matter how one behaved, one's conduct would be criticized. Preachers placed the topic under the sin of envy, and associated it particularly with the sub-branch, malicious slander (see 32–4). In this poem the neat pairs of antithetical stanzas follow a rhetorical pattern employed by other users of the topos: see 'Musing allone this hinder nicht', a poem less certainly attributed to Dunbar (Kinsley, no. 81); a fifteenth-century carol (Greene, *Carols*, no. 349) with the burden 'Lord, how scholde I roule me, / Of al men ipreysed to be?'; and Lydgate, 'A wicked tunge wille seye amys' (*Minor Poems*, II, no. 76). On the stanza, see 9.

Text: B, ff. 65ᵛ–66ᵛ; collated with MF, pp. 323–4, and R, f. 38ʳ. In MF the sequence of stanzas differs from B.

8] MF; that owt of mynd yone man is hie B.
14. deyme] MF; say B.
21. And gif] MF; Gif B.
29. guerdon] MF; reward B.
31. gif] *Ed. conj*; than B.
41. Sen all is jugit] MF; Now juge thay me B.

Authorship: 'Quod Dumbar' in B and MF.

Further reading: On preachers' use of this theme, see Owst 1961: 456–7; on other parallels, Bawcutt 1992a: 139–41.

1

How sowld I rewill me or quhat wyis,
I wald sum wyisman wald devyis.

1. *rewill me]* Rule myself. *quhat wyis]* In what way.
2. *wald]* Wish. *wyisman]* Sage. *devyis]* Pronounce.

I can not leif in no degre,
Bot sum my maneris will dispyis.
Lord God, how sall I governe me?   5

2

Gif I be galland, lusty and blyth,
Than will thay say on me full swyth,
'Yon man, out of his mynd is he,
Or sum hes done him confort kyth.'
Lord God, how sall I governe me?   10

3

Gife I be sorrowfull and sad,
Than will thay say that I am mad,
I do bot drowp, as I wold die.
Thus will thay deyme, baith man and lad.
Lord God, how sall I governe me?   15

4

Gife I be lusty in array,
Than luve I parramouris, thay say,
Or in my hairt is prowd and hie,
Or ellis I haif it sum wrang way.
Lord God, how sall I governe me?   20

5

And gif I be nocht weill besene,
Than twa and twa sayis thame betwene,
That 'Evill he gydis, yone man, trewlie,

---

3 *leif*] Live. *in no degre*] In any fashion.
4. *dispyis*] Scorn.
6. *Gif*] If. *galland*] Courtly. *lusty*] Cheerful. *blyth*] Glad.
7. *swyth*] Rapidly.
8] That man is out of his senses.
9] Or someone has given him encouragement.
13] I do nothing but look despondent, as if about to die.
14. *deyme*] Pass judgment.
16. *lusty*] Fine. *array*] Dress.
17. *luve I parramouris*] I am in love.
18. *hie*] Haughty.
19] Or else I acquired it (the clothing) wrongfully.
21. *besene*] Dressed.
22. *twa and twa*] Couples.
23. *Evill he gydis*] He behaves badly.

Lo, be his claithis it may be sene!'
Lord God, how sall I governe me? 25

6

Gif I be sene in court ovirlang,
Than will thay murmour thame ammang,
My freyndis ar not worth a fle,
That I sa lang but guerdon gang.
Lord God, how sall I governe me? 30

7

In court rewaird gif purches I,
Than haif thay malyce and invy,
And secreitly thay on me lie
And dois me hinder prevely.
Lord God, how sall I governe me? 35

8

I wald my gyding war devysit:
Gif I spend littill I am dispysit,
Gif I be nobill, gentill and fre,
A prodigall man I am so prysit.
Lord God, how sall I governe me? 40

9

Sen all is jugit, baith gude and ill,
And I may no mans tung hald still,
To do the best my mynd salbe.
Latt every man say quhat he will,
The gratious God mot governe me. 45

24. *claithis]* Clothes. *sene]* Seen.
28. *freyndis]* Friends, kinsmen. *fle]* Fly.
29. *but guerdon gang]* Go without recompense.
31. *purches]* Obtain.
32. *invy]* Envy.
34. *hinder]* Speak ill of. *prevely]* Secretly.
36] I wish that my conduct might be prescribed.
37. *dispysit]* Scorned.
38. *fre]* Generous.
39. *prysit]* Appraised.
41. *jugit]* Criticized.
42. *hald still]* Keep quiet.
43. *mynd]* Intention.
44. *Latt]* Let.
45] May God who is merciful govern me.

14

The mock testament is a form with a long and complex history in medieval literature. It was particularly popular in fifteenth-century France – Villon's *Grand Testament* being the most famous example – and in England also. There are several Scottish examples of the genre: the satiric testament that concludes *King Hart*, Lindsay's *Testament of the Papyngo* and *Testament of Squyer Meldrum*, and the anonymous *Testament of Duncan Laideus*. This poem closely follows the pattern of contemporary wills: the opening that establishes the testator's identity; the 'pious bequests' of soul and body in stanzas 3–5; the disposal of property; and the final directions for the funeral. It also employs – and often parodies – the stereotyped phrases and formulae characteristic of actual wills (see lines 9, 15–16, 17, 82, 89 and 97). The poem is striking for its witty juxtaposition of Latin and the vernacular, a style sometimes called 'macaronic'. 'Andro Kennedy' is lightly satirized as a self-confessed drunkard, foolish clerk, and representative of the Kennedy surname; whether he was a real man, however, is not certain (see note to 1). The metre is irregular. The basic pattern is seen in the first stanza – *abababab⁴* – but there is much variety in length of line and rhyme scheme, and the last stanza contains twelve lines.

Date: One possible clue is the reference to the 'maister of Sanct Antane' (see 60–61). If the proposed identification is correct, this would suggest composition in the 1490s, when the controversy was still topical.

Text: P; collated with B, ff. 154ʳ–155ᵛ; MF, pp. 135–8; and R, ff. 24ᵛ–26ʳ.
65. fenyeing] B; fenyening P.

Authorship: The attribution to Dunbar derives from B's colophon: 'Heir endis the tesment of maister Andro Kennedy maid be Dumbar quhen he wes lyk to dy'; in P the poem is anonymous; in MF and R it is ascribed to 'Kennedie', which possibly resulted from an over-literal reading by the scribe. The verbal ingenuity is characteristic of Dunbar, and his authorship is usually accepted, despite some metrical weaknesses (e.g. the repeated use of *me* as a rhyme word in stanza 14).

Further reading: On the tradition of mock wills and testaments, see Rice 1941

96

and Wilson 1994; on macaronic poetry, see Archibald 1992. For criticism specifically of this poem, see Archibald 1981; and Bawcutt 1992a: 194–8, 350–52 ('two languages . . . in witty equilibrium').

1

I maister Andro Kennedy
Curro quando sum vocatus.
Gottin with sum incuby
Or with sum freir *infatuatus,*
In faith I can nought tell redly
Unde aut ubi fui natus.
Bot in treuth I trow trewly
Quod sum dyabolus incarnatus.

5

2

Cum nichill sit cercius morte
We mon all de, man, that is done.
Nescimus quando vel qua sorte
Na blind Allane wait of the mone.
Ego pacior in pectore,
This night I myght not sleip a wink.
Licet eger in corpore,
Yit wald my mouth be wet with drink.

10

15

1. maister] Master (of arts).
2] Run when I am called.
3. Gottin] Begotten. *incuby]* Incubus.
4. freir infatuatus] Foolish friar.
5. redly] For certain.
6] Of whom or where I was born.
7. treuth] Truth. *trow]* Believe.
8] That I am a devil incarnate.
9] Since nothing is more certain than death.
10. Mon] Must. *de]* Die. *done]* ? Determined.
11] We do not know when or by what chance.
12. Na] Any more than. *wait]* Knows. *mone]* Moon.
13] I suffer in my breast.
15] Although ill in body.
16. Yit] Yet.

3

Nunc condo testamentum meum.
I leiff my saull for evirmare,
Per omnipotentem deum,
In to my lordis wyne cellar,   20
Semper ibi ad remanendum
Quhill domisday, without dissever,
Bonum vinum ad bibendum
With sweit Cuthbert that luffit me nevir.

4

Ipse est dulcis ad amandum.   25
He wald oft ban me in his breith,
Det michi modo ad potandum,
And I forgif him laith and wraith,
Quia in cellario cum cervisia
I had lever lye, baith air and lait,   30
Nudus solus in camesia
Na in my lordis bed of stait.

5

A barell bung ay at my bosum,
Of warldis gud I bad na mair.
Corpus meum ebriosum   35
I leif on to the toune of Air,
In a draf mydding for evir and ay,
Ut ibi sepeliri queam,

17] Now I make my testament.
18. leiff] Leave. *saull]* Soul.
19] Through almighty God.
21] There to remain always.
22. Quhill domisday] Until doomsday. *dissever]* Departing.
23] In order to drink good wine.
25] He is sweet for loving.
26. ban] Curse. *breith]* Anger.
27] Let him only give me something to drink.
28. laith] Bad temper. *wraith]* Hatred.
29] Since in the cellar with the beer.
30. lever] Rather. *air]* Early. *lait]* Late.
31] Naked apart from my shirt.
32. Na] Than.
34. warldis gud] Worldly wealth. *bad]* Desired.
35] My drunken body.
37. draf] Malt refuse. *mydding]* Midden, rubbish heap.
38] In order that I may be buried there.

Quhar drink and draff may ilka day
Be cassyne *super faciem meam.* 40

6

I leif my hert that nevir wes sicir
Sed semper variabile,
That nevir mare wald flow nor flicir
Consorti meo Jacobe.
Thought I wald bynd it with a wicir 45
Verum deum renui.
Bot and I hecht to teme a bicker
Hoc pactum semper tenui.

7

Syne leif I the best aucht I bocht
(*Quod est Latinum propter caupe*) 50
To hede of kyn; bot I wait nought
Quis est ille, than I schrew my scawpe.
I callit my lord my heid, but hiddill,
Sed nulli alii hoc dixerunt.
We weir als sib as seve and riddill, 55
In una silva que creverunt.

8

Omnia mea solacia
(Thai wer bot lesingis, all and ane)

---

39. *ilka]* Every.
40] Be thrown over my face.
41. *sicir]* Faithful.
42] But always fickle.
43. *flow]* Waver. *flicir]* Quiver.
44] To my partner Jacoba.
45. *Thought]* Although. *wicir]* Pliant twig of willow.
46] I denied the true God.
47] But if I vowed to empty a beaker (wooden drinking-vessel).
48] I always kept this promise.
49. *Syne]* Then. *aucht]* Possession. *bocht]* Acquired.
50] Which is Latin for *caupe* (?).
51–2] If I do not know who he is, then I curse myself (lit. my scalp).
53. *but hiddill]* Without concealment, openly.
54] But no others said this.
55. *sib]* Closely related. *seve]* Sieve. *riddill]* Riddle.
56] That grew in the same wood.
57] All my pleasures.
58. *lesingis]* Deceptions.

Cum omni fraude et fallacia
I leif the maister of Sanct Antane,   60
Willelmo Gray, sine gratia,
Myne awne deir cusing, as I wene,
Qui nunquam fabricat mendatia
Bot quhen the holyne growis grene.

9

My fenyeing and my fals wynyng   65
Relinquo falsis fratribus,
For that is Goddis awne bidding:
Dispersit, dedit pauperibus.
For menis saulis thai say thai sing,
Mencientes pro muneribus.   70
Now God gif thaim ane evill ending
Pro suis pravis operibus.

10

To Jok Fule my foly fre
Lego post corpus sepultum.
In faith I am mair fule than he,   75
Licet ostendit bonum vultum.
Of corne and catall, gold and fe
Ipse habet valde multum,
And yit he bleris my lordis e
Fingendo eum fore stultum.   80

59] With every kind of fraud and trickery.
61. sine gratia] Without grace.
62. awne] Own. cusing] Cousin. wene] Think.
63] Who never invents lies.
64. Bot] Except. holyne] Holly.
65. fenyeing] Deceiving. wynyng] Money-making.
66] I leave to the false friars.
68] He distributed, he gave to the poor.
69. menis saulis] Men's souls.
70] Lying in order to get gifts.
71. gif] Grant.
72] In return for their wicked deeds.
73. Fule] Fool. foly] Folly. fre] Generously.
74] I bequeath after the burial of my body.
76] Although he shows a good appearance (appears a fool?).
77. fe] Property.
78] He himself has very much.
79. bleris] Blinds e] Eye.
80] By pretending to be a fool.

11

To master Johne Clerk syne
Do et lego intime
Goddis malisone and myne.
Ipse est causa mortis mee.
War I a dog and he a swyne   85
Multi mirantur super me,
Bot I suld ger that lurdane quhryne
Scribendo dentes sine de.

12

Residuum omnium bonorum
For to dispone my lord sall haif,   90
Cum tutela puerorum,
Ade, Kytte and all the laif.
In faith I will na langar raif.
Pro sepultura ordino
On the new gys, sa God me saif,   95
Non sicut more solito.

13

In die mee sepulture
I will nane haif bot our aune gyng,
Et duos rusticos de rure
Berand a barell on a styng,   100
Drynkand and playand cop out evin,

82] I give and bequeath cordially.
83. malisone] Curse.
84] He is the cause of my death.
86] Many marvel at me.
87. ger] Cause. *lurdane]* Rascal. *quhryne]* Squeal.
89] The residue of my property.
90. dispone] Dispose of.
91] With the wardship of my children.
92. Ade] Adam. *Kytte]* Short form of Katherine. *laif]* Others.
93. raif] Ramble in speech.
94] I arrange for my burial.
95. gys] Fashion.
96] Not according to the usual custom.
97] On the day of my burial.
98. gyng] Group (of friends).
99] And two peasants from the country.
100. styng] Pole.
101. playand cop out] Competing at draining the cup. *evin]* Fully.

Sicut egomet solebam.
Singand and gretand with hie stevin,
Potum meum cum fletu miscebam.

14

I will na preistis for me sing: 105
Dies illa, dies ire,
Na yit na bellis for me ring
Sicut semper solet fieri,
Bot a bag pipe to play a spryng
Et unum ail wosp *ante me;*   110
In stayd of baneris for to bring
Quatuor lagenas cervisie,
Within the graif to set sic thing
In modum crucis juxta me,
To fle the fendis, than hardely sing   115
De terra plasmasti me.

102] Just as I myself was accustomed.
103. gretand] Wailing. *hie stevin]* Loud voice.
105. will] Wish. *preistis]* Priests.
106] That day, the day of wrath.
108] As always is the custom.
109. spryng] Dance tune.
110] And the emblem of an ale house in front of me.
112] Four flagons of beer.
113. graif] Grave. *sic thing]* Such things.
114] In the shape of the cross beside me.
115. fle] Scare away. *fendis]* Fiends. *hardely]* Boldly.
116] Thou hast created me from earth.

15

The tone of this poem on the common medieval theme of mutability is unusually tentative and exploratory. The changeable weather – in which winter and summer seem to co-exist – adroitly symbolizes the nature of 'this warld', and furnishes the evidence for the poet's 'sentence' (5) upon it. Dunbar uses the stanza (*aabba⁴*) elsewhere in **21, 27, 28** and **51**, all of which are brief, personal and reflective poems.

Text: MF, p. 315 (MFb); collated with MF, p. 5 (MFa); and R, ff. 8ᵛ–9ʳ.
11. up] MFa, R; *not in* MFb.
18. dirk] MFa; efter MFb.

Authorship: 'Quod Dumbar' in MFa, MFb and R.

Further reading: Ross 1981: 156; Bawcutt 1992a: 148–9.

1
I seik aboute this warld onstable
To find a sentence conveniable,
Bot I can not in all my witt
Sa trew a sentence find of it,
As say it is dissavable.   5

1. onstable] Unstable, changing.
2. sentence] Saying. *conveniable]* Fitting.
3. witt] Mind.
4. trew] True.
5. dissavable] Deceitful.

2

For yistirday I did declair
How that the sasoun soft and fair
Come in als fresche as pacok feddir.
This day it stangis lyke ane eddir,
Concluding all in my contrair.   10

3

Yistirday fair up sprang the flowris,
This day thai ar all slane with schouris;
And foulis in forrest that sang cleir
Now walkis with ane drerie cheir –
Full caild ar bayth thair beddis and bowris.   15

4

So nixt to symmer wyntir bene,
Nixt eftir confort cairis kene,
Nixt dirk mydnycht the myrthfull morrow,
Nixt eftir joy ay cumis sorrow:
So is this warld and ay hes bene.   20

---

6. *yistirday]* Yesterday.
7. *sasoun]* Season.
8. *Come in]* Began. *pacok feddir]* Peacock feather.
9. *This day]* Today. *stangis]* Stings. *eddir]* Adder.
10. *in my contrair]* In opposition to me.
13. *foulis]* Birds.
14. *walkis]* Awaken. *drerie cheir]* Mournful mood.
15. *caild]* Cold.
16. *nixt]* Next. *symmer]* Summer. *bene]* Is.
17. *confort]* Pleasure. *cairis kene]* Intense sorrows.
18. *morrow]* Dawn.

16

Dunbar meditates on a perennial theme, the inevitability of death. Although the diction is plain and the imagery traditional, the poem has great psychological subtlety, and renders vivid and poignant the ancient commonplace voiced by the refrain, *Timor mortis conturbat me*. Dunbar's tone is melancholy but orthodox; for other treatments of the topic, see **21**, **25**, **34** and **44**. The poem has a simple structure, cataloguing the victims of Death the Leveller; some features in this recall the widespread late-medieval tradition of the Dance of Death. In the second half of the poem one class is considered in greater detail, the 'makaris', or poets, and Dunbar's tone becomes increasingly personal as he moves closer to the present, recalls his brother-poets and contemplates his own death. The poem, untitled in the early witnesses, was first called 'The Lament for the Death of the Makars' by eighteenth-century editors. This title slightly over-stresses the elegiac element; the poem is more than a lament for dead poets, yet nonetheless gives valuable clues to Dunbar's literary environment and his taste in poetry. The stanza, *aabB⁴*, is one of Dunbar's favourite metrical forms, and put to varied uses; see also **17**, **29**, **37**, **38**, **52**, **60**, **61**, and **66**.

Date: The poem is likely to have been composed shortly after July 1505, by which date Stobo was dead (see note to 86).

Text: P; collated with B, ff. 109ʳ–110ʳ, and MF, pp. 189–92.
15. So waveris] B, MF; Wavis P.
26. Takis] B, MF; Tak P.
46. padyanis] B, MF; pageant P.
71. fle] B, MF; *not in* P.

Authorship: 'Quod Dunbar quhen he was sek' in P; 'Quod Dumbar' in B and MF.

Further reading: Drexler 1978 (on the Dance of Death tradition); Baxter 1952: 229–34 (biographical details about the poets); Gray 1972 and Woolf 1968 (the theme of death in medieval verse). For criticism of this poem, see Reiss 1979: 28–31, 70–72; Bawcutt 1992a: 153–7.

1

I that in heill wes and gladnes
Am trublit now with gret seiknes,
And feblit with infermite:
Timor mortis conturbat me.

2

Our plesance heir is all vane glory,   5
This fals warld is bot transitory,
The flesch is brukle, the fend is sle:
Timor mortis conturbat me.

3

The stait of man dois change and vary,
Now sound, now seik, now blith, now sary,   10
Now dansand mery, now like to dee:
Timor mortis conturbat me.

4

No stait in erd heir standis sickir.
As with the wynd wavis the wickir,
So waveris this warldis vanite: 15
Timor mortis conturbat me.

5

On to the ded gois all estatis,
Princis, prelotis and potestatis,
Baith riche and pur of al degre:
Timor mortis conturbat me.   20

---

1. heill] Health.
2. trublit] Afflicted. *seiknes]* Sickness.
3. feblit] Enfeebled. *infermite]* Illness.
5. vane glory] Empty pride.
7. brukle] Frail. *fend]* Devil. *sle]* Cunning.
9. stait] Condition.
10. sound] Healthy. *sary]* Sorrowful.
11. mery] Merrily. *like]* Likely. *dee]* Die.
13. erd] Earth. *sickir]* Assured, permanent.
14. wickir] Willow.
15. waveris] Varies, fluctuates.
17. ded] Death. *estatis]* Ranks of society.
18. prelotis] Prelates. *potestatis]* Rulers.
19. pur] Poor. *degre]* Rank.

6

He takis the knychtis in to feild,
Anarmyt under helme and scheild.
Victour he is at all melle.
Timor mortis conturbat me.

7

That strang unmercifull tyrand   25
Takis on the moderis breist sowkand
The bab full of benignite.
Timor mortis conturbat me.

8

He takis the campion in the stour,
The capitane closit in the tour,   30
The lady in bour full of bewte,
Timor mortis conturbat me.

9

He sparis no lord for his piscence,
Na clerk for his intelligence;
His awfull strak may no man fle: 35
Timor mortis conturbat me.

10

Art-magicianis and astrologgis,
Rethoris, logicianis and theologgis,
Thame helpis no conclusionis sle:
Timor mortis conturbat me.   40

---

21. *in to feild]* On the battlefield.
22. *Anarmyt]* Armed. *helme]* Helmet.
23. *melle]* Combat.
26. *sowkand]* Sucking.
27. *bab]* Baby. *benignite]* Innocence.
29. *campion]* Champion, hero. *stour]* Battle.
30. *capitane]* Governor of a fortress. *closit]* Enclosed.
31. *bour]* Inner room. *bewte]* Beauty.
33. *piscence]* Power.
34. *clerk]* Scholar.
35. *awfull strak]* Fearful stroke. *fle]* Flee.
37. *Art-magicianis]* Magicians. *astrologgis]* Astrologers.
38] Rhetoricians, logicians and theologians.
39. *conclusionis sle]* Subtle arguments.

11

In medicyne the most practicianis,
Lechis, surrigianis and phisicianis,
Thame self fra ded may not supple:
Timor mortis conturbat me.

12

I se that makaris, amang the laif,   45
Playis heir ther padyanis, syne gois to graif.
Sparit is nought ther faculte.
Timor mortis conturbat me.

13

He has done petuously devour
The noble Chaucer, of makaris flour,   50
The monk of Bery and Gower, all thre:
Timor mortis conturbat me.

14

The gud syr Hew of Eglintoun,
And eik Heryot and Wyntoun
He has tane out of this cuntre: 55
Timor mortis conturbat me.

15

That scorpion fell has done infek
Maister Johne Clerk and James Afflek
Fra balat making and trigide:
Timor mortis conturbat me.   60

---

41. most practicianis] Greatest practitioners.
42. Lechis] Doctors. *surrigianis]* Surgeons.
43. supple] Deliver, rescue.
45. makaris] Poets. *laif]* Rest (of humanity).
46. padyanis] Pageants. *graif]* Grave.
47. faculte] Profession.
49. done petuously devour] Devoured, in a manner to rouse pity.
55. tane] Taken. *cuntre]* Country.
57. fell] Cruel. *done infek]* Poisoned.
59. trigide] Tragic narrative.

16

Holland and Barbour he has berevit.
Allace, that he nought with us levit
Schir Mungo Lokert of the Le:
Timor mortis conturbat me.

17

Clerk of Tranent eik he has tane,   65
That maid the anteris of Gawane.
Schir Gilbert Hay endit has he:
Timor mortis conturbat me.

18

He has blind Hary and Sandy Traill
Slaine with his schour of mortall haill,   70
Quhilk Patrik Johnestoun myght nought fle:
Timor mortis conturbat me.

19

He has reft Merseir his endite,
That did in luf so lifly write,
So schort, so quyk, of sentence hie: 75
Timor mortis conturbat me.

20

He has tane Roull of Aberdene
And gentill Roull of Corstophin,
Two better fallowis did no man se:
Timor mortis conturbat me.   80

21

In Dunfermelyne he has done roune
With maister Robert Henrisoun.

---

61. berevit] Snatched away.
62. levit] Left.
66. anteris] Adventures.
70. mortall] Deadly.
73] He has robbed Mersar of his powers of composition.
74. lifly] Vividly.
75. quyk] Lively, energetic. *sentence hie]* Lofty significance.
78. gentill] Noble.
79. fallowis] Companions.
81. done roune] Whispered.

Schir Johne the Ros enbrast has he:
Timor mortis conturbat me.

22

And he has now tane, last of aw, 85
Gud gentill Stobo and Quintyne Schaw,
Of quham all wichtis has pete;
Timor mortis conturbat me.

23

Gud maister Walter Kennedy
In poynt of dede lyis veraly. 90
Gret reuth it wer that so suld be:
Timor mortis conturbat me.

24

Sen he has all my brether tane
He will naught lat me lif alane.
On forse I man his nyxt pray be: 95
Timor mortis conturbat me.

25

Sen for the ded remeid is none,
Best is that we for dede dispone,
Efter our deid that lif may we:
Timor mortis conturbat me. 100

83. *enbrast]* Embraced.
85. *aw]* All.
87. *wichtis]* People. *pete]* Compassion.
90. *veraly]* Certainly.
91. *reuth]* Pity.
93. *Sen]* Since. *brether]* Brothers.
95] Of necessity I must be his next victim.
97. *ded]* Death. *remeid]* Remedy.
98. *dispone]* Make ready.
99. *lif]* Live (eternally)

17

The reference to Dunbar's pension (27) places this poem after 1500; it is usually thought to date after 26 August 1510, when his pension was increased to £80, a large sum that might well justify the epithet 'preclair' (27). It is addressed to the *lord thesaurair*, the important officer of state responsible for both the collection and the administration of various Crown revenues. The treasurer from 1509–10 was George Hepburn, bishop of the Isles; from 1510–12, Andrew Stewart, bishop of Caithness. A high proportion of the treasurer's revenues came from fines imposed at the circuit courts (see 19 and note); his expenditure included the payment of fees and pensions to royal servants, such as Dunbar. Bureaucratic delays were common at medieval courts, and it was often necessary to put pressure on the authorities, to speed up payments. On the stanza, see 16.

Text: R, ff. 5ᵛ–6ʳ.

Authorship: 'Quod Dumbar' in R.

Further reading: Baxter 1952: 181–4 (on Dunbar's pension); Bawcutt 1992a: 106–8 ('the tone is exultant, yet an underlying anxiety is apparent').

1

> I thocht lang quhill sum lord come hame,
> Fra quhom faine kyndnes I wald clame.
> His name of confort I will declair:
> Welcome, my awin lord thesaurair!

1] I felt impatient with longing until a certain lord came home.
2] From whom I desired to claim a favour.
4. awin] Own. *thesaurair]* Treasurer.

2

Befoir all rink of this regioun,   5
Under our roy of most renoun,
Of all my mycht, thocht it war mair,
Welcom, my awin lord thesaurair!

3

Your nobill payment I did assay,
And ye hecht sone, without delay,   10
Againe in Edinburgh till repair:
Welcom, my awin lord thesaurair!

4

Ye keipit tryst so winder weill,
I hald yow trew as ony steill.
Neidis nane your payment till dispair.   15
Welcom, my awin lord thesaurair!

5

Yett in a pairt I was agast,
Or ye the narrest way had past
Fra toun of Stirling to the air.
Welcom, my awin lord thesaurair!   20

6

Thane had my dyt beine all in duill,
Had I my wage wantit quhill Yuill,
Quhair now I sing with heart onsair,
Welcum, my awin lord thesaurair!

5] Taking precedence of every knight in this count[r]y.
6. roy] King.
7] With all my power, even if it were greater.
9. assay] Try to obtain.
10. hecht] Promised. sone] Shortly.
11. Againe ... till repair] To return.
13. tryst] Promise, engagement. winder] Wondrously.
14. hald] Consider. trew] Reliable.
15. Neidis nane] No one needs. dispair] Despair of.
17. in a pairt] To some extent. agast] Anxious.
18] Before you had travelled the shortest route.
19. air] Circuit court.
21. dyt] Poetry. duill] Grief, misery.
22] If I had lacked my wage until Christmas.
23. Quhair] Whereas. onsair] Joyful.

7

Welcum, my benefice and my rent,   25
And all the lyflett to me lent,
Welcum, my pensioun most preclair!
Welcum, my awin lord thesaurair!

8

Welcum als heartlie as I can,
My awin dear maister, to your man   30
And to your servand singulair!
Welcum, my awin lord thesaurair!

25. *rent]* Income.
26. *lyflett]* Livelihood. *lent]* Granted.
27. *preclair]* Splendid.
29. *heartlie]* Sincerely.
30. *man]* Feudal retainer.
31. *singulair]* Special.

18

The formal funeral lament was a common poetic genre in the late Middle Ages.
Numerous examples survive, particularly from fifteenth-century France and
Burgundy, where the *regretz*, *complaintes* and *déplorations* of the *Grands
Rhétoriqueurs* have a bad reputation for cliché and flattery. The earliest extant
Scottish vernacular example is the 'plaint' for the dauphine Margaret, who died
in 1445 (see Bawcutt 1988a); other funeral laments, however, are embedded in
longer works: cf. Henryson, *Orpheus and Eurydice*, 134–83, and Hary, *Wallace*,
XII. 1109–28. Dunbar's short poem employs highly conventional figures and
phrasing, but has little in common with the full-blown *déploration*. It is closer
to earlier French complaints, such as Christine de Pisan's *ballade* on Philip the
Bold and Eustache Deschamps's laments for Guillaume de Machaut and
Bertrand du Guesclin; or to contemporary English pieces, such as Skelton's
elegy on the earl of Northumberland (1489) and the anonymous lament for
Henry VII (see Scammell and Rogers 1957). The subject of this elegy is Bernard
Stewart, who died in Scotland on 11 June 1508; Dunbar celebrated his arrival
in **45**, a poem that closely resembles this one in style and metrical form. For
details of Stewart's career, see headnote to **45**; and on the stanza, see **6**.

Text: R, ff. 6ᵛ–7ʳ.
J. Stewart] Stewar R.

Authorship: 'Quod Dumbar' in R.

Further reading: On the literary and social background, see Gray 1972: 201–6;
and Martineau-Génieys 1978. See also Ross 1981: 152–3; and Bawcutt
1992a: 84–7.

114

1

Illuster Lodovick, of France most cristin king,
Thow may complain with sighis lamentable
The death of Bernard Stewart, nobill and ding,
In deid of armes most anterous and abill,
Most mychti, wyse, worthie and confortable   5
Thy men of weir to governe and to gy.
For him, allace, now may thow weir the sabill,
Sen he is gon, the flour of chevelrie.

2

Complaine sould everie noble valiant knycht
The death of him that douchtie was in deid,   10
That many ane fo in feild hes put to flight,
In weris wicht be wisdome and manheid.
To the Turk sey all land did his name dreid,
Quhois force all France in fame did magnifie.
Of so hie price sall nane his place posseid,   15
For he is gon, the flour of chevilrie.

3

O duilfull death, O dragon dolorous,
Quhy hes thow done so dulfullie devoir
The prince of knychtheid, nobill and chevilrous,
The witt of weiris, of armes and honour,   20
The crop of curage, the strenth of armes in stoir,
The fame of France, the fame of Lumbardy,

1. *Illuster]* Illustrious. *cristin]* Christian.
2. *complain]* Lament.
3. *ding]* Of high worth.
4. *deid of armes]* Warfare. *anterous]* Adventurous. *abill]* Skilled.
5. *confortable]* Giving strength.
6. *weir]* War. *gy]* Guide.
7. *weir]* Wear. *sabill]* Mourning garments.
8. *gon]* Gone (i.e. dead).
10. *douchtie]* Courageous. *deid]* Deed.
12. *In weris wicht]* Fierce in battle. *manheid]* Manhood.
13. *Turk]* Turkish.
14] Whose strength made greater the fame of France.
15] Of such great merit [that] no one will replace him.
17. *duilfull]* Causing sorrow.
18. *done . . . devoir]* So unkindly devoured.
19. *knychtheid]* Knighthood.
20. *witt of weiris]* One who had great talent in war.
21. *crop]* Paragon. *curage]* Courage. *stoir]* Combat.

The schois of chiftanes, most awfull in airmour,
The charbuckell cheif of every chevelrie?

4

Pray now for him all that him loveit heir,   25
And for his saull mak intercessioun
Unto the lord that hes him bocht so deir,
To gif him mercie and remissioun;
And namelie we of Scottis natioun,
Intill his lyff quhom most he did affy,   30
Foryett we nevir into our orisoun
To pray for him, the flour of chavelrie.

23. *schois]* Choicest example. *awfull]* Awe-inspiring.
24. *charbuckell]* Carbuncle, or ruby.
26. *saull]* Soul.
27. *bocht]* Redeemed. *deir]* For a high price.
28. *remissioun]* Pardon.
29. *namelie]* Especially. *Scottis]* Scottish.
30. *Intill]* During. *affy]* Trust.
31. *orisoun]* Prayer.

19

Two contrasted ideals of love are juxtaposed in this poem, which is thematically close to 30. Human love is shown as vain and 'frustir' (90, 98), in comparison with the true, perfect (79) love whose object is God. In form it is a debate, an extremely popular genre throughout the Middle Ages. The poem has a highly patterned structure: the two bird-speakers are allocated alternate stanzas, which have refrains that sum up their contrasted viewpoints. This use of an alternating refrain, in conjunction with a stanza rhyming *ababbcbc*, occurs in a number of late-medieval verse debates, such as *Mercy and Righteousness* and *Nurture and Kynd* (ed. Conlee 1991), and Henryson's *Ressoning betuix Age and Youth*. Dunbar was clearly familiar with the specific tradition of bird debates, many of which took love as their theme and had a nightingale as one of the speakers. (Several are included in Conlee 1991.) He certainly knew Chaucer's *Parliament of Fowls*, Holland's *Buke of the Howlat*, and the lively discussion between argumentative beasts in Henryson's *Fables*. The nightingale, long famous for the beauty of its song, was viewed in the Middle Ages as pre-eminently the bird of love. Most commonly it symbolized passionate human love – in lyrics it is often the confidant or messenger of the lover, and in Sir John Clanvowe's popular debate poem, *The Boke of Cupide*, it defends such love against the cynical cuckoo. Here, however, Dunbar draws on a counter-tradition, best illustrated by the *Philomena* of John Peckham (d. 1292) and the translations of this work into English by Lydgate and another anonymous poet. In these the nightingale has a spiritual significance, singing the praise of God or representing divine love. The merle, or blackbird, sometimes figures in descriptions of spring, but is not otherwise prominent in poetry; Dunbar gives it the role, more often played by the nightingale, of defending human love.

Text: B, ff. 283^r^–284^v^; collated with MF, pp. 165–8.
35. faill] MF; fable B.
72. lufes] lufe B; luffis MF.
74. Ane . . . tak] MF; Man may tak in his lady B.
75. bewtie] MF; vertew B.
90. Sic] MF; sir B.
108. hes maid] MF; maid B.

115. in to] MF; yit maid B.
116. in rest and] MF; restand B.

Authorship: 'Quod Dunbar' in B and MF.

Further reading: On English debate poems, see Utley 1972 and Conlee 1991; and on the Latin tradition, Walther 1920; 1984. For a brief survey of bird poetry, see Davenport 1991; on the medieval traditions of the nightingale, Pfeffer 1985. On this poem, see Reiss 1979: 112–14; and Bawcutt 1992a: 315–22 ('an undervalued poem').

1

In May as that Aurora did up spring,
With cristall ene chasing the cluddis sable,
I hard a merle with mirry notis sing
A sang of lufe with voce rycht confortable,
Agane the orient bemis amiable,   5
Upone a blisfull brenche of lawry grene.
This wes hir sentens sweit and delectable:
'A lusty lyfe in luves service bene.'

2

Undir this brench ran doun a revir bricht,
Of balmy liquour cristallyne of hew,   10
Agane the hevinly aisur skyis licht,
Quhair did upone the tother syd persew
A nychtingall with suggurit notis new,
Quhois angell fedderis as the pacok schone.
This wes hir song and of a sentens trew: 15
'All luve is lost bot upone God allone.'

2. *ene*] Eyes. *cluddis sable*] Black clouds.
3. *hard*] Heard. *merle*] Blackbird. *mirry*] Joyful.
4. *voce*] Voice. *confortable*] Pleasing.
5. *Agane*] Facing. *orient*] In the east. *amiable*] Attractive.
6. *brenche*] Branch. *lawry*] Laurel.
7. *sentens*] Theme, significance.
8] It is a pleasant life in the service of love.
9. *revir*] River.
10. *balmy*] Sweet-smelling. *liquour*] Water, liquid.
11. *aisur*] Azure-blue.
12. *tother*] Other. *persew*] Speak in opposition.
13. *suggurit*] Sweet-sounding.
14. *fedderis*] Feathers. *pacok*] Peacock. *schone*] Shone.

3

With notis glaid and glorius armony
This joyfull merle so salust scho the day,
Quhill rong the widdis of hir melody,
Saying, 'Awalk, ye luvaris, o this May!   20
Lo, fresche Flora hes flurest every spray,
As Natur hes hir taucht, the noble quene.
The feild bene clothit in a new array.
A lusty lyfe in luvis service bene.'

4

Nevir swetar noys wes hard with levand man   25
Na maid this mirry gentill nychtingaill.
Hir sound went with the rever as it ran,
Outthrow the fresche and flureist lusty vaill.
'O merle,' quod scho, 'O fule, stynt of thy taill,
For in thy song gud sentens is thair none;   30
For boith is tynt the tyme and the travaill
Of every luve bot upone God allone.'

5

'Seis', quod the merle, 'thy preching, nychtingale!
Sall folk thair yewth spend in to holines?
Of yung sanctis growis auld feyndis, but faill.   35
Fy, ypocreit in yeiris tendirnes,
Agane the law of kynd thow gois expres,
That crukit aige makis on with yewth serene,

17. *armony*] Music.
18. *salust*] Greeted.
19. *rong*] Resounded. *widdis*] Woods.
20 *Awalk*] Awake. *o*] In.
21. *flurest*] Adorned with flowers. *spray*] Twig.
23. *bene*] Is.
25. *levand*] Living.
26. *Na*] Than.
27. *went with*] Accompanied.
28. *Outthrow*] Throughout. *flureist*] Flowering.
29. *fule*] Fool. *quod*] Said. *stynt*] Cease. *taill*] Speech.
31. *tynt*] Lost. *travaill*] Labour.
33. *Seis*] Cease.
34. *yewth*] Youth.
35] Young saints turn into old devils, without doubt.
36. *Fy*] Shame. *ypocreit*] Hypocrite.
37. *Agane*] In opposition to. *kynd*] Nature. *expres*] Directly.
38. *crukit*] Crooked. *on*] One. *serene*] Untroubled.

Quhome Natur of conditionis maid dyvers.
A lusty lyfe in luves service bene.'   40

6

The nychtingaill said, 'Fule, remembir the
That both in yewth and eild and every hour
The luve of God most deir to man suld be,
That him of nocht wrocht lyk his awin figour,
And deit him self, fro deid him to succour.   45
O quhithir wes kythit thair trew lufe or none?
He is most trew and steidfast paramour.
All luve is lost bot upone him allone.'

7

The merle said, 'Quhy put God so grit bewte
In ladeis with sic womanly having,   50
Bot gife he wald that thay suld luvit be?
To luve eik Natur gaif thame inclynnyng,
And he, of Natur that wirker wes and king,
Wald no thing frustir put nor lat be sene
In to his creature of his awin making.   55
A lusty lyfe in luves service bene.'

8

The nychtingall said, 'Nocht to that behufe
Put God sic bewty in a ladeis face
That scho suld haif the thank thairfoir or lufe,
Bot he, the wirker, that put in hir sic grace.   60
Of bewty, bontie, riches, tyme or space,

39. conditionis] Dispositions (*or*) Different.
40. eild] Old age.
44. nocht] Nothing. *wrocht]* Created. *figour]* Image.
45. deit] Died. *deid]* Death. *succour]* Rescue.
46. quhithir] Whether. *kythit]* Shown.
47. paramour] Lover.
49. bewte] Beauty.
50. sic] Such. *having]* Behaviour.
51. gife] If.
52. inclynnyng] Inclination.
53. wirker] Creator.
54. frustir] Vain.
57. behufe] Purpose.
59. thank] Praise, credit. *thairfoir]* For it.
61. bontie] Goodness.

And every gudnes that bene to cum or gone,
The thank redoundis to him in every place.
All luve is lost bot upone God allone.'

9

'O nychtingall, it wer a story nyce,   65
That luve suld nocht depend on cherite,
And gife that vertew contrair be to vyce,
Than lufe mon be a vertew, as thinkis me,
For ay to lufe invy mone contrair be.
God bad eik lufe thy nychtbour fro the splene,   70
And quho than ladeis swetar nychtbouris be?
A lusty lyfe in lufes service bene.'

10

The nychingaill said, 'Bird, quhy dois thow raif?
Ane man may in his lady tak sic delyt
Him to foryet that hir sic bewtie gaif,   75
And for his hevin rassaif hir cullour quhyt.
Hir goldin-tressit hairis redomyt,
Lyk to Appollois bemis thocht thay schone,
Suld nocht him blind fro lufe that is perfyt.
All lufe is lost bot upone God allone.'   80

11

The merle said, 'Lufe is caus of honour ay,
Luve makis cowardis manheid to purchas,
Luve makis knychtis hardy at assey,

---

62. bene] Is. *gone]* Go (archaic infin.).
63. redoundis] Pertains.
65. nyce] Foolish.
66. cherite] Charity.
67. vertew] Virtue.
68. mon] Must. *thinkis]* Seems (to).
69. invy] Envy.
70] God also commanded, love thy neighbour from the heart.
73. raif] Rave.
75. foryet] Forget. *gaif]* Gave.
76. rassaif] Receive, accept. *cullour]* Complexion.
77. redomyt] Adorned with a wreath.
78] Even though they shone as bright as the sun.
79. perfyt] Perfect.
82. manheid] Manhood, valour. *purchas]* Acquire.
83. hardy] Bold. *assey]* Attack.

Luve makis wrechis full of lergenes,
Luve makis sweir folkis full of bissines,   85
Luve makis sluggirdis fresche and weill besene,
Luve changis vyce in vertewis nobilnes.
A lusty lyfe in luvis service bene.'

12

The nychtingaill said, 'Trew is the contrary!
Sic frustir luve it blindis men so far,   90
In to thair myndis it makis thame to vary.
In fals vane glory thai so drunkin ar,
Thair wit is went, of wo thai ar nocht war
Quhill that all wirchip away be fro thame gone,
Fame, guddis, and strenth – quhairfoir weill say I dar,   95
All luve is lost bot upone God allone.'

13

Than said the merle, 'Myn errour I confes.
This frustir luve all is bot vanite.
Blind ignorance me gaif sic hardines
To argone so agane the varite.   100
Quhairfoir I counsall every man that he
With lufe nocht in the feindis net be tone,
Bot luve the luve that did for his lufe de.
All lufe is lost bot upone God allone.'

14

Than sang thay both with vocis lowd and cleir.   105
The merle sang, 'Man, lufe God that hes the wrocht',
The nychtingall sang, 'Man, lufe the lord most deir

84. *wrechis]* Misers. *lergenes]* Generosity.
85. *sweir]* Slothful. *bissines]* Diligence.
86. *sluggirdis]* Sluggards. *besene]* Arrayed.
87. *vertewis]* Virtuous.
91. *vary]* Wander, go astray.
93. *went]* Gone. *war]* Aware.
94. *wirchip]* Honour.
95 *guddis]* Possessions. *dar]* Dare.
97. *errour]* Erroneous belief. *confes]* Confess.
98. *vanite]* Vanity.
99. *hardines]* Boldness.
100. *argone]* Argue. *varite]* Verity, truth.
102. *feindis]* Fiend's. *tone]* Captured.
103. *de]* Die.

That the and all this warld hes maid of nocht'.
The merle said, 'Luve him that thy lufe hes socht
Fra hevin to erd and heir tuk flesche and bone'.   110
The nychtingall sang, 'And with his deid the bocht.
All luve is lost bot upone him allone.'

15

Thane flaw thir birdis our the bewis schene,
Singing of lufe amang the levis small,
Quhois ythand pleid in to my thocht is grene,   115
Bothe sleping, walking, in rest and in travall.
Me to reconfort most it dois availl,
Agane for lufe quhen lufe I can find none,
To think how song this merle and nychtingaill:
All lufe is lost bot upone God allone.   120

109. socht] Sought.
110. erd] Earth. *tuk]* Took.
111. deid] Death. *bocht]* Redeemed.
113. flaw] Flew. *bewis]* Boughs. *schene]* Beautiful.
115. ythand] Continual. *pleid]* Dispute.
117. reconfort] Comfort, console. *availl]* Help.
118] When I do not receive love in return for (my) love.
119. song] Sang.

20

The opening lines of this comic and bawdy dialogue between a man and a woman imply that it is a furtive, 'secreit' tryst. There are few hints as to the social status of the lovers (see 10 and 44), who are characterized more by personality and experience. The man has courtly pretensions, but is inexperienced; the woman is bold and self-assured. The genre was popular in sixteenth-century Scotland, and the Bannatyne Manuscript contains a number of examples, extremely varied in tone; these include Henryson's *Robene and Makyne*, and several anonymous pieces: 'Jok and Jinny' (f. 137^r); 'In somer quhen flowris will smell' (f. 141^r); 'I met my lady weil arrayit' (f. 143^r); 'I saw me thocht this hindir nicht' (f. 143^v); and the *Commonyng betuix the mester and the heure* (f. 264^r). The most striking feature of this poem is its exuberant burlesque of the language of endearment. It abounds in pet-names and diminutives, animal images, sexual *double entendres* and reduplicating compounds. Many of these are nonce-formations, and some may be deliberately nonsensical. On the stanza, see 2.

Text: MF, pp. 308 and 311; collated with B, ff. 103^v–104^r, and R, ff. 34^v–35^r.

Authorship: MF and R attribute the poem to Dunbar; in R it is anonymous, with a later attribution to 'Clerk'. Dunbar's claim is supported by the inventive use of language, and by stylistic resemblances to other poems, notably 64.

Further reading: Scott 1966: 63–5; Reiss 1979: 110–12 ('shows courtship and love-making in their humorous essence'); Ross 1981: 166 (satirizes 'the high tradition of the love lyric'); Bawcutt 1992a: 301–3 (on genre), 366–7 (diction).

124

1

In secreit place this hyndir nycht
I hard ane beyrne say till ane bricht:
'My huny, my hart, my hoip, my heill,
I have bene lang your luifar leill
And can of yow get confort nane.   5
How lang will ye with danger deill?
Ye brek my hart, my bony ane.'

2

His bony beird wes kemmit and croppit,
Bot all with cale it was bedroppit,
And he wes townysche, peirt and gukit.   10
He clappit fast, he kist and chukkit,
As with the glaikis he wer ovirgane.
Yit be his feirris he wald have fukkit –
'Ye brek my hart, my bony ane.'

3

Quod he: 'My hairt, sweit as the hunye,   15
Sen that I borne wes of my mynnye,
I never wowit weycht bot yow.
My wambe is of your luif sa fow
That as ane gaist I glour and grane.
I trymble sa, ye will not trow,   20
Ye brek my hart, my bony ane.'

---

1. *hyndir]* Past.
2. *hard]* Heard. *beyrne]* Man. *bricht]* Pretty woman.
3. *huny]* Honey. *hart]* Heart.
4. *luifar leill]* Faithful lover.
5. *confort]* Encouragement.
7. *brek]* Break. *bony]* Attractive.
8. *beird]* Beard. *kemmit]* Combed. *croppit]* Trimmed.
9. *cale]* Broth. *bedroppit]* Bespattered.
10. *townysche]* Having the manners of a townsman. *peirt]* Bold. *gukit]* Foolish.
11. *clappit]* Embraced. *chukkit]* Fondled.
12] As if overpowered by passionate love.
13. *Yit]* Yet. *feirris]* Behaviour.
15. *Quod]* Said.
16. *Sen]* Since. *mynnye]* Mother.
17. *wowit]* Wooed. *weycht]* Anyone.
18. *wambe]* Belly. *fow]* Full.
19. *gaist]* Ghost. *glour]* Stare. *grane]* Groan.
20. *trymble]* Tremble. *trow]* Believe.

4

'Tehe!' quod scho, and gaif ane gawfe.
'Be still, my tuchan and my calfe,
My new spanit howffing fra the sowk,
And all the blythnes of my bowk.   25
My sweit swanking, saif yow allane
Na leyd I luiffit all this owk.
Full leif is me yowr graceles gane.'

5

Quod he: 'My claver and my curldodie,
My huny soppis, my sweit possodie,   30
Be not oure bosteous to your billie,
Be warme hairtit and not evill wille.
Your heylis, quhyt as quhalis bane,
Garris ryis on loft my quhillelille.
Ye brek my hart, my bony ane.'   35

6

Quod scho: 'My clype, my unspaynit gyane,
With moderis mylk yit in your mychane,
My belly huddrun, my swete hurle bawsy,
My huny gukkis, my slawsy gawsy,
Your musing waild perse ane harte of stane. 40
Tak gud confort, my grit heidit slawsy,
Full leif is me your graceles gane.'

---

22. *gawfe]* Guffaw.
23. *tuchan]* See note.
24. *new spanit . . . sowk]* Newly weaned. *howffing]* ? Clumsy person.
25. *bowk]* Body.
26. *swanking]* Fellow. *allane]* Alone.
27. *leyd]* Man. *owk]* Week.
28] Very dear to me is your unattractive face.
29. *claver]* Clover. *curldodie]* Ribwort plantain.
31. *bosteous]* Harsh. *billie]* Friend.
32. *evill wille]* Ill-disposed.
33. *heylis]* Heels. *quhalis bane]* Walrus ivory.
34. *Garris]* Cause. *quhillelille]* Penis.
36. *clype]* Big fellow. *unspaynit]* Unweaned. *gyane]* Giant.
37. *moderis]* Mother's.
38. *belly huddrun]* ? Large-bellied man.
39. *huny gukkis]* Sweet fool.
40. *musing]* Complaining. *perse]* Pierce.
41. *grit heidit]* Big-headed.

7

Quod he: 'My kid, my capirculyoun,
My bony baib with the ruch brylyoun,
My tendir gyrle, my wallie gowdye, 45
My tyrlie myrlie, my crowdie mowdie,
Quhone that oure mouthis dois meit at ane,
My stang dois storkyn with your towdie.
Ye brek my hairt, my bony ane.'

8

Quod scho: 'Now tak me by the hand, 50
Welcum, my golk of Marie land,
My chirrie and my maikles munyoun,
My sowklar, sweit as ony unyoun,
My strumill stirk, yit new to spane.
I am applyit to your opunyoun, 55
I luif rycht weill your graceles gane.'

9

He gaiff to hir ane apill rubye.
Quod scho, 'Gramercye, my sweit cowhubye!'
And thai tway to ane play began,
Quhilk men dois call the dery dan, 60
Quhill that thair myrthis met baythe in ane.
'Wo is me,' quod scho, 'Quhair will ye, man?
Best now I luif that graceles gane.'

43. *kid]* Young goat or roe.
44. *ruch]* Rough.
45. *wallie]* Pretty. *gowdye]* Goldie, ? goldenhead.
47. *at ane]* Together.
48. *storkyn]* Stiffen. *towdie]* Buttocks.
52. *chirrie]* Cherry. *maikles munyoun]* Matchless lover.
53. *sowklar]* Suckling (pig, calf). *unyoun]* Onion.
54. *strumill]* ? Ungainly. *stirk]* Young bullock. *spane]* Weaning.
55] I am well-disposed to your proposal.
58. *Gramercye]* Thanks. *cowhubye]* ? Booby.
59. *thai tway]* The two of them.

21

Dunbar here reflects on the common medieval theme of death and mutability. This fine poem has some affinity with **16**, but its conclusion is less spiritually orthodox. The poet's inner state is correlated with the season; both are dark and gloomy. The melancholy 'thocht', which afflicts Dunbar similarly in other poems (cf. **24** and **57**), is here effectively dramatized in the central stanzas. The use of personification resembles the technique employed in **1** and **63**, and morality plays such as *Everyman*. In structure the poem mirrors the cycle of the year, circling back to its own beginning; 'schort' (46) thus answers 'lenth' (6), and there are other echoes of word and imagery. On the stanza, see **15**.

Text: MF, pp. 318–19; collated with R, f. 1ʳ (1–22), and MF, p. 3 (23–50).

Authorship: 'Quod Dumbar' in MF.

Further reading: Reiss 1979: 133–5 (sees poem as 'ironic', and the narrator as wrong-headed); Macafee 1981 (a stylistic analysis); Bawcutt 1992a: 158–61 ('striking for its bleak, truthful-sounding feeling').

1

In to thir dirk and drublie dayis,
Quhone sabill all the hevin arrayis
With mystie vapouris, cluddis and skyis,

1. *thir]* These. *dirk]* Dark. *drublie]* Gloomy.
2. *Quhone]* When.
3. *cluddis]* Clouds.

128

Nature all curage me denyis
Of sangs, ballattis and of playis.   5

2

Quhone that the nycht dois lenth in houris,
With wind, with haill and havy schouris,
My dule spreit dois lurk for schoir.
My hairt for langour dois forloir,
For laik of Symmer with his flouris.   10

3

I walk, I turne, sleip may I nocht,
I vexit am with havie thocht.
This warld all ovir I cast about,
And ay the mair I am in dout,
The mair that I remeid have socht.   15

4

I am assayit on everie syde.
Despair sayis ay, 'In tyme provyde,
And get sum thing quhairon to leif,
Or with grit trouble and mischeif
Thow sall in to this court abyd.'   20

4. curage] Spirit, inclination. *denyis]* Deprives.
5] For songs, poems and entertainments.
6. lenth] Lengthen.
7. havy] Heavy.
8] My melancholy spirit shrinks at the menacing prospect.
9. hairt] Heart. *langour]* Misery. *forloir]* Grow desolate.
10. laik] Lack, absence. *Symmer]* Summer.
11. walk] Lie awake.
12. havie thocht] Burdensome thought.
13. cast about] Reflect upon.
14. ay] Ever. *dout]* Perplexity.
15. remeid] Remedy. *socht]* Sought.
16. assayit] Assailed.
17. provyde] Be provident.
18. quhairon] On which. *leif]* Live.
19. mischeif] Hardship.
20. abyd] Dwell.

5

Than Patience sayis, 'Be not agast,
Hald hoip and treuthe within the fast,
And lat Fortoun wirk furthe hir rage,
Quhone that no rasoun may assuage,
Quhill that hir glas be run and past.'   25

6

And Prudence in my eir sayis ay,
'Quhy wald thow hald that will away,
Or craif that thow may have no space,
Thow tending to ane uther place,
A journay going everie day?'   30

7

And than sayis Age, 'My freind, cum neir,
And be not strange, I the requeir.
Cum, brodir, by the hand me tak.
Remember thow hes compt to mak
Of all thi tyme thow spendit heir.'   35

8

Syne Deid castis upe his yettis wyd,
Saying, 'Thir oppin sall the abyd;
Albeid that thow wer never sa stout,
Undir this lyntall sall thow lowt.
Thair is nane uther way besyde.'   40

21. *agast*] Afrald.
22. *treuthe*] Truth, loyalty.
23. *wirk furthe*] Work out, exhaust. *rage*] Anger.
27–8*] Why do you wish to retain that which will depart, or desire that which you may not possess for long.
29. *tending*] Travelling.
30. *journay*] Day's journey.
32. *strange*] Aloof. *requeir*] Request.
33. *brodir*] Brother.
34. *compt*] Account. *mak*] Make.
36. *Deid*] Death. *upe*] Up, open. *yettis*] Gates.
37. *oppin*] Open. *abyd*] Await.
38*] No matter how brave you may be.
39. *lyntall*] Lintel (of door). *lowt*] Stoop.

9

For feir of this all day I drowp,
No gold in kist nor wyne in cowp,
No ladeis bewtie nor luiffis blys
May lat me to remember this,
How glaid that ever I dyne or sowp.   45

10

Yit quhone the nycht begynnis to schort
It dois my spreit sum pairt confort,
Of thocht oppressit with the schowris.
Cum, lustie Symmer, with thi flowris,
That I may leif in sum disport.   50

41. *feir]* Fear. *drowp]* Droop.
42. *kist]* Treasure chest. *cowp]* Goblet.
43. *ladeis bewtie]* Lady's beauty.
44. *lat]* Prevent.
45. *glaid]* Gladly. *sowp]* Drink.
46. *Yit]* Yet. *schort]* Shorten.
47. *sum pairt]* To some extent. *confort]* Console.
49. *lustie]* Pleasant.
50. *leif]* Live. *disport]* Delight.

22

This highly polemical and topical poem (cf. *now* in 18 and 24) probably belongs to the autumn of 1506. *Donald Owyr* (19) is identified by most scholars with Donald Dubh (?1490–1545), the focus of a serious revolt in the Highlands between 1503 and 1506; *owyr* is thought to represent Gaelic *odhar*, 'brown', and thus corresponds to the nickname *dubh*, 'black, dark'. Donald was the grandson of John, fourth and last Lord of the Isles, who was forfeited in 1493; the rebellion was linked with an attempt to revive the Lordship on Donald's behalf, but was crushed by October 1506. Donald, although captured, was not executed and lived to lead another revolt in 1545 (for a summary of what is known of him, see Munro and Munro 1986: 313–14). Leading Highlanders, such as Lauchlan MacLean and Torquil MacLeod, were put on trial not only for treason but for robbery and other crimes; nonetheless many were granted respites, or conditional pardons (cf. 3–4, 33). Dunbar's tone is acerbic, and he attacks the king's policy of clemency towards the rebels. Bd's colophon calls the poem an epitaph, but this is mistaken. The stanza, aa^4bbba^2, is uncommon, but is employed in a satiric poem by Maitland (MF, no. xcv); there it is arranged as a quatrain.

Text: Bd, pp. 53–4; collated with MF, pp. 11–12, and R, f. 11^r–11^v.
20. hes] MF; had Bd.
21. Round] MF; rimmiu Bd.
24. Now he dois] MF; yitt dois he Bd.
31. fals] MF; falis Bd.
32. all reffar] MF; every Bd.

Authorship: 'Quod Dumbar for Donald Oure epetaphe' in Bd; 'Quod Dumbar' in MF and R.

Further reading: On the Lordship of the Isles, see Munro 1981; and Munro and Munro 1986. On James IV's policy towards the Highlands, and the rebellion, see Nicholson 1974: 541–9; and Macdougall 1989: 175–95. For criticism of this poem, see Scott 1966: 261–4; Ross 1981: 183; and Bawcutt 1992a: 252–6.

1

In vice most vicius he excellis
That with the vice of tressone mellis.
Thocht he remissioun
Haif for prodissioun,
Schame and susspissioun   5
Ay with him dwellis.

2

And he evir odious as ane owle,
The falt sa filthy is and fowle:
Horrible to natour
Is ane tratour,   10
As feind in fratour
Undir a cowle.

3

Quha is a tratour or ane theif,
Upoun him selff turnis the mischeif.
His frawdfull wylis   15
Him self begylis,
As in the Ilis
Is now a preiff.

4

The fell strong tratour, Donald Owyr,
Mair falsett hes nor udir fowyr,   20
Round ylis and seyis

1. *vicius*] Wicked. *excellis*] Is outstanding.
2. *mellis*] Gets involved.
3. *Thocht*] Although. *remissioun*] Pardon.
4. *prodissioun*] Treachery.
8. *falt*] Crime.
9. *natour*] Nature.
11. *feind*] Devil. *fratour*] Refectory.
13. *theif*] Thief.
14. *mischeif*] Evil.
15. *frawdfull wylis*] Fraudulent tricks.
16. *begylis*] Deceive.
17. *Ilis*] Western Isles.
18. *preiff*] Proof.
19. *fell*] Cruel.
20. *falsett*] Falsehood. *nor*] Than. *fowyr*] Four.
21. *seyis*] Seas.

In his suppleis,
On gallow treis
Now he dois glowir.

5

Falsett no feit hes nor deffence,   25
Be power, practik nor puscence.
   Thocht it fra licht
   Be smord with slicht,
   God schawis the richt
With soir vengence.   30

6

Of the fals fox dissimulatour
Kynd hes all reffar, theiff and tratour:
   Eftir respyt
   To wirk dispyt
   Moir appetyt   35
He hes of natour.

7

War the fox tane a thowsand fawd
And grace him gevin als oft for frawd,
   War he on plane,
   All war in vane,   40
   Frome hennis agane
Micht non him hawd.

22. *suppleis]* Allies, supporters.
23. *gallow treis]* Gibbets.
24. *he]* On high. *glowir]* Grimace.
25. *feit]* ? Standing, base.
26. *practik]* Stratagem. *puscence]* Violence.
28. *smord]* Concealed. *slicht]* Cunning.
29. *schawis]* Reveals. *richt]* Truth.
30. *soir]* Grievous.
31. *dissimulatour]* Dissembling.
32. *Kynd]* Character. *reffar]* Robber.
33. *respyt]* Reprieve.
34. *wirk dispyt]* Commit crime.
37] If the fox were captured a thousand times.
38. *grace]* Pardon. *gevin]* Given.
39. *on plane]* Out in the open.
42. *hawd]* Hold, restrain.

8

The murtherer ay murthour mais,
And evir quhill he be slane he slais.
   Wyvis thus makis mokkis,   45
   Spynnand on rokkis:
   Ay rynnis the fox
   Quhill he fute hais.

---

43. murtherer] Murderer. *mais]* Commits.
44. quhill] Until. *slane]* Killed. *slais]* Kills.
45. Wyvis] Women. *mokkis]* Derisive remarks.
46. rokkis] Distaffs.
47–8] The fox continues to run as long as he has the power of walking.

23

Dunbar's description of a black woman is unsympathetic, but vivid; it should be compared with the more extended portrait of Kennedy in **54**. Dunbar's tone is insulting, but the mockery is directed at not only the woman but also the knights. James IV's household contained a number of Africans, who served chiefly as musicians and entertainers. There is nothing to suggest that they were enslaved or badly treated; they received similar lodgings, clothing and fees to other 'servitouris' of their status. The poem is usually dated 1507–1508, since the last three stanzas seem to allude to the famous Tournament of the Black Lady, first held in June 1507 and repeated in May 1508. The historians Leslie and Pitscottie give brief and not wholly reliable descriptions of these tournaments; they are supplemented by *The Treasurer's Accounts*, which contain many vivid details – such as the Black Lady's gown of 'damask floured with gold' – but unfortunately do not describe the proceedings. James commissioned the tournaments, and participated in them; whether he himself jousted under the name of 'the Black Knight' is less certain. On the stanza, see **9**.

Text: MF, pp. 341–2; collated with R, ff. 45ᵛ–46ʳ.

Authorship: 'Quod Dumbar of an blak moir' in MF and R.

Further reading. On black people in sixteenth-century Scotland, see Fradenburg 1991: 244–64, and Edwards 1992; on the tournaments, see Leslie, p. 78; and Pitscottie, I, 243–4. For discussion of the poem, see Scott 1966: 67–8; Ross 1981: 182–3 (a 'bad joke'); Bawcutt 1992a: 54–5, 249–52.

1

Lang heff I maed of ladyes quhytt.
Nou of an blak I will indytt
That landet furth of the last schippis.
Quhou fain wald I descryve perfytt
My ladye with the mekle lippis.   5

2

Quhou schou is tute mowitt lyk an aep,
And lyk a gangarall onto graep,
And quhou hir schort catt nois up skippis,
And quhou schou schynes lyk ony saep,
My ladye with the mekle lippis.   10

3

Quhen schou is claid in reche apparrall
Schou blinkis als brycht as an tar barrell,
Quhen schou was born the son tholit clippis,
The nycht be fain faucht in hir querrell,
My ladye with the mekle lippis.   15

4

Quhai for hir saek with speir and scheld
Preiffis maest mychtellye in the feld,
Sall kis and withe hir go in grippis
And fra thyne furth hir luff sall weld,
My ladye with the mekle lippis.   20

---

1. *maed*] Made verse. *quhytt*] White.
2. *indytt*] Compose.
3. *furth*] Out.
4. *fain wald*] Would like to. *perfytt*] Perfectly.
5. *mekle*] Large.
6. *tute mowitt*] With projecting lips. *aep*] Ape.
7. *gangarall*] Toad. *graep*] Grasp, touch.
9. *saep*] Soap.
11.*claid*] Clothed. *reche*] Rich.
12. *blinkis*] Gleams.
13. *son*] Sun. *tholit clippis*] Suffered an eclipse.
14. *be fain*] With gladness. *faucht*] Fought. *querrell*] Cause.
16. *Quhai*] Whoever. *saek*] Sake. *scheld*] Shield.
17. *Preiffis*] Turns out. *mychtellye*] Strongly. *feld*] Field (of battle).
18. *go in grippis*] Wrestle.
19. *thyne furth*] Thenceforth. *weld*] Enjoy.

5

And quhai in fedle receaves schaem
And tynis thair his knychtlie naem,
Sall cum behind and kis hir hippis
And nevir to uther confort claem,
My ladye with the mekle lippis.   25

21. fedle] Field. *schaem]* Shame.
22. tynis] Loses. *naem]* Reputation.
24. confort] Pleasure. *claem]* Claim (as one's right).

24

On the subject and likely date of this piece, see the headnote to **4**. Although the two poems on Damian are usually coupled by modern editors, they do not occur together in the manuscripts. MF places this one immediately after **65**, with which it has much in common, including length, metrical form and veiled petitionary purpose (note the reference to a benefice in 22). This, like **65**, is a dream, in which the sleeping poet is admonished by a mysterious and untrustworthy visitant. Fortune's speech is a burlesque prophecy, whose mock-apocalyptic tone and cryptic references to strange events and symbolic animals are characteristic of the genre. Interest in prophecy was widespread in the late Middle Ages. Dunbar derides the flying abbot by depicting him as a diabolic prefiguration of Antichrist (see 28–9); but the poem's mockery is also self-directed, since the dream is delusive. Whatever feats the abbot performed, he did not fly above the moon. The stanza, *aabba*[5], is also used for **59**, **63** and **65**.

Text: MF, pp. 334–5; collated with B, ff. 133^r–134^r, and R, ff. 42^v–43^r.
2. sternis] B; sterris MF.
31. Saturnus] B; Saturnis MF.
35. windir] B; wondrus MF.

Authorship: 'Quod Dumbar' in MF, B and R.

Further reading: On Antichrist and the Apocalyptic tradition, see Emmerson 1981. For criticism, see Hay 1973–74; and Bawcutt 1992a: 279–83.

1

Lucina schyning in silence of the nycht,
The hevyn all being full of sternis bricht,

2. sternis] Stars.

To bed I went, bot thair I tuke no rest.
With havie thocht so sair I wes opprest
That sair I langit eftir the dayis licht.   5

2

Of Fortoun I complenit havalie
That scho to me stude so contrariouslie,
And at the last, quhone I had turnit oft,
For werynes on me a slumer soft
Come with a dreming and a fantasie.   10

3

Me thocht dame Fortoun with a fremmit cheir
Stude me beforne and said on this maneir:
'Thow suffir me to wirk, gif thow do weill,
And preis the not to stryve aganis my quheill,
Quhilk everie warldlie thing dois turne and steir.   15

4

'Full mony ane I set upone the heycht,
And makis mony full law doun to lycht.
Vpone my stagis or that thow do ascend,
Traist wele thi trouble is neir at ane end,
Seing thir takynnis; quhairfoir thow mark thame richt.   20

3. *tuke*] Took.
4. *havie thocht*] Burdensome thought. *sair*] Miserably.
5. *langit*] Longed. *dayis licht*] Daylight.
6. *complenit*] Complained. *havalie*] Mournfully.
7 *stude*] Stood. *contrariouslie*] In opposition.
8. *turnit*] Tossed about.
9. *slumer*] Slumber.
10. *Come*] Came. *fantasie*] Fantastic, visionary experience.
11 *Me thocht*] It seemed to me. *fremmit cheir*] Strange expression.
12. *beforne*] Before.
13] Allow me to act, if you are to do well.
14. *preis the*] Attempt. *quheill*] Wheel.
15. *steir*] Guide.
16. *mony ane*] Many a person. *heycht*] Height.
17] And cause many to descend low down.
18. *stagis*] Steps. *or*] Before.
19. *Traist*] Trust. *neir*] Nearly.
20] When you see these signs; therefore interpret them correctly.

5

'Thy trublit gaist sall never be degest
Nor thow in to no benefice possest;
Quhill that ane abbot him cleythe in eirnis pennys
And fle up in the air amang the crennys,
And as a falcoun fair fro eist to west.   25

6

'He sall ascend as ane horrible griphoun.
Him meit sall in the air ane scho dragoun.
Thir terribill monsturis sall togiddir thrist,
And in the cluddis get the Antechrist,
Quhill all the air infect of thair poysoun.   30

7

'Undir Saturnus fyrie regioun
Symon Magus sall meit him and Mahown,
And Merleyn at the mune sall him be bydand,
And Jonet the wedo on a busum rydand,
Of wytchis with ane windir garesoun.   35

8

'And syne thai sall discend with reik and fyre,
And preiche in eird the Antechristis impyre,
And than it salbe neir the warldis end.'
With that this ladie did schortlie fra me wend.
Sleipand and walkand wes frustrat my desyre.   40

21. *trublit gaist*] Troubled spirit. *degest*] Calm.
22. *in to . . . possest*] Possessed of a benefice.
23] Until an abbot clothe himself in eagle's feathers.
24. *fle*] Fly. *crennys*] Cranes.
25. *fair*] Travel.
26. *griphoun*] Griffin.
27. *scho dragoun*] She-dragon.
28. *togiddir thrist*] Copulate together.
29. *cluddis*] Clouds. *get*] Beget.
30. *infect*] Be infected.
33. *mune*] Moon. *bydand*] Awaiting.
34. *wedo*] Widow. *busum*] Broomstick.
35] With an uncanny troop of witches.
36. *syne*] Then. *reik*] Smoke.
37. *in eird*] On earth. *impyre*] Reign.
39. *wend*] Depart.
40. *walkand*] Waking. *frustrat*] Frustrated.

9

Quhone I awoyk, my dreme it wes so nyce,
Fra everie wicht I hid it as a vyce,
Quhill I hard tell be mony suthfast wy,
Fle wald ane abbot up in to the sky
And all his feddrem maid wes at devyce.   45

10

Within my hert confort I tuke full sone.
'Adew,' quod I, 'My drerie dayis ar done.
Full weill I wist to me wald never cum thrift
Quhill that twa munis were first sene in the lift
Or quhill ane abbot flew abone the moyne.'   50

41. *awoyk]* Woke up. *nyce]* Strange.
42. *wicht]* Person.
43. *hard]* Heard. *suthfast wy]* Truthful person.
45. *feddrem]* Feather coat, plumage. *at devyce]* Skilfully.
47. *drerie]* Sad. *done]* Ended.
48. *wist]* Knew. *thrift]* Prosperity.
49. *munis]* Moons. *lift]* Sky.
50. *abone]* Above.

25

Traditional themes, imagery and diction are deployed in this poem on death, an excellent example of a common kind. There are many comparable pieces in Middle English; for a close Scottish parallel in the Makculloch MS, see 'Man, hef in mynd and mend thi mys', which employs the same stanza and has a Latin refrain, *Memor esto novissima* (*IMEV*, 2057; published in *CB XV*, no. 156). Bannatyne places this poem in the 'ballatis of moralitie', close to another poem by Dunbar (38), and Lichtoun's 'O mortall man remembir nycht and day', which has a similar stanza and the refrain *Memento homo quod cinis es*. All three have associations with Ash Wednesday, and seem designed for penitential meditation in Lent (cf. 37–40). On the stanza, see 1.

Text: B, ff. 47^r–47^v, collated with MF, pp. 193–4.
28. all devouris] MF; *in later hand* B.
44. dryff] MF; *not in* B.

Authorship: B's attribution to Dunbar is usually accepted; in MF the poem is anonymous.

Further reading: Woolf 1968: 309–55 ('Lyrics on death'); Hughes and Ramson 1982: 70–73.

1

> *Memento, homo, quod cinis es*:
> Think, man, thow art bot erd and as.
> Lang heir to dwell na thing thow pres,
> For as thow come sa sall thow pas.

2. *erd*] Earth. *as*] Ash.
3] Strive in no way to remain here long.
4. *come*] Came.

Lyk as ane schaddow in ane glas   5
Hyne glydis all thy tyme that heir is.
Think, thocht thy bodye ware of bras,
Quod tu in cinerem reverteris.

2

Worthye Hector and Hercules,
Forcye Achill and strong Sampsone,   10
Alexander of grit nobilnes,
Meik David and fair Absolone
Hes playit thair pairtis and all are gone,
At will of God, that all thing steiris.
Think, man, exceptioun thair is none,   15
Sed tu in cinerem reverteris.

3

Thocht now thow be maist glaid of cheir,
Fairest and plesandest of port,
Yit may thow be within ane yeir
Ane ugsum, uglye tramort.   20
And sen thow knawis thy tyme is schort,
And in all houre thy lyfe in weir is,
Think, man, amang all uthir sport
Quod tu in cinerem reverteris.

4

Thy lustye bewte and thy youth   25
Sall feid as dois the somer flouris,
Syne sall the swallow with his mouth
The dragone, Death, that all devouris.
No castell sall the keip, nor touris,
Bot he sall seik the with thy feiris   30

---

5. *glas]* Mirror.
6. *Hyne]* Hence, from here.
7. *thocht]* Although.
10. *Forcye]* Powerful.
14. *steiris]* Governs.
17. *cheir]* Mood.
18. *plesandest]* Most pleasing. *port]* Appearance.
20. *ugsum]* Repulsive. *tramort]* Corpse.
22. *weir]* Uncertainty.
25. *lustye bewte]* Fresh beauty.
26. *feid]* Fade.
29. *keip]* Protect.
30. *seik]* Seek. *feiris]* Companions.

Thairfore remembir at all houris
Quod tu in cinerem reverteris.

5

Thocht all this warld thow did posseid,
Nocht eftir death thow sall possess
Nor with the tak, bot thy guid deid,   35
Quhen thow dois fro this warld the dres.
Go speid the, man, and the confes,
With humill hart and sobir teiris,
And sadlye in thy hart inpres
Quod tu in cinerem reverteris.   40

6

Thocht thow be taklit nevir so sure,
Thow sall in deathis port arryve.
Quhair nocht for tempest may indure,
Bot ferslye all to speiris dryff,
Thy ransonner with woundis fyve   45
Mak thy plycht anker and thy steiris,
To hald thy saule with him on lyve,
Cum tu in cinerem reverteris.

---

33. posseid] Own.
36. the dres] Betake yourself.
37] Hasten, man and make confession.
38. humill] Humble. *sobir teiris]* Solemn tears.
39. sadlye] Solemnly. *inpres]* Imprint.
41. taklit] Furnished with rigging (of a ship). *sure]* Safe, secure.
43. nocht] Nothing.
45. ransonner] Redeemer.
46. plycht anker] Chief anchor. *steiris]* Rudder.
47. saule] Soul. *on lyve]* Alive.

26

There are many late-medieval poems of this type: a lover's complaint to his mistress that he will die unless she takes pity on him. The epistolary form, diction, imagery and metre belong to a tradition of courtly love poetry greatly influenced by Chaucer. The ornate style and high-pitched, hyperbolic tone also have close parallels among the 'ballattis of luve' in the Bannatyne Manuscript; see, for instance, 'Fresche fragrent flour of bewty souerane' (f. 219ᵛ); 'Brycht sterne of bewtie and well of Lustines' (f. 222ʳ); Bannatyne's own 'As Phebus bricht in speir merediane' (f. 230ᵛ); and Steill's 'Lanterne of lufe and lady fair of hew' (f. 235ʳ). Many critics take Dunbar's poem to be a parody of the typical love complaint, yet there is little to justify this, apart from MF's colophon: 'Quod Dumbar quhone he list to feyne'. The precise implications of 'feyne' are debatable, but possibly indicate scribal doubts as to the poet's sincerity. The rhyme-royal stanza, *ababbcc⁵*, owed its great popularity to Chaucer's use in *Troilus and Criseyde*. Dunbar uses it not only for poems in the love tradition (here and 41) but also for moral verse (33 and 40).

Text: MF, pp. 322–3.

Further reading: Scott 1966: 59–60 (a 'humorous poem in the tradition of *amour courtois*'); Reiss 1979: 99–100 ('a study in irony'); Ross 1981: 215; Bawcutt 1992a: 299–301 ('a conventional and rather dull poem'). On Scottish love poetry, see MacQueen 1970: xi–lxxv; on the English background, see Stevens 1961; 1979.

1

My hartis tresure and swete assured fo,
The finale endar of my lyfe for ever,

1. hartis] Heart's. *assured fo]* Undoubted enemy.

146

The creuell brekar of my hart in two,
To go to deathe this I deservit never.
O man slayar, quhill saule and life dissever,   5
Stynt of your slauchtir, allace, your man am I,
A thowsand tymes that dois yow mercy cry.

2

Have mercie, luif; have mercie, ladie bricht.
Quhat have I wrocht aganis your womanheid
That ye murdir me, a saikles wicht,   10
Trespassing never to yow in word nor deid?
That ye consent thairto, O God forbid!
Leif creuelte and saif your man, for schame,
Or throucht the warld quyte losit is your name.

3

My deathe chasis my lyfe so besalie   15
That wery is my goist to fle so fast.
Sic deidlie dwawmes so mischeifaislie
Ane hundrithe tymes hes my hairt ovirpast.
Me think my spreit rynnis away full gast,
Beseikand grace on kneis yow befoir,   20
Or that your man be lost for evermoir.

4

Behald my wod intollerabill pane,
For evermoir quhilk salbe my dampnage.

---

3. creuell] Cruel.
4. this] Thus.
5. quhill] Until. *saule]* Soul. *dissever]* Divide.
6. Stynt] Cease.
7. dois yow mercy cry] Appeal to you for mercy.
9. wrocht aganis] Done to harm. *womanheid]* Womanliness.
10. saikles wicht] Innocent person.
13. Leif] Abandon. *creuelte]* Cruelty.
14. quyte losit] Totally destroyed. *name]* Reputation.
15. besalie] Actively.
16. goist] Spirit. *fle]* Flee.
17. Sic deidlie dwawmes] Such deadly fainting-fits. *mischeifaislie]* Harmfully.
18. ovirpast] Affected.
19. spreit] Spirit. *rynnis]* Runs. *gast]* Terrified.
20. Beseikand] Imploring.
21. Or] Before.
22. Behald] Behold. *wod]* Mad.
23. dampnage] Destruction.

Quhy undir traist your man thus have ye slane?
Lo, deithe is in my breist with furious rage,   25
Quhilk may no balme nor tryacle asswage
Bot your mercie, for laik of quhilk I de.
Allace, quhair is your womanlie petie?

5

Behald my deidlie passioun dolorous,
Behald my hiddows hew and wo, allace.   30
Behald my mayne and murning mervalous,
Withe sorrowfull teris falling frome my face.
Rewthe, luif, is nocht, helpe ye not in this cace.
For how sould ony gentill hart indure
To se this sycht on ony creature?   35

6

Quhyte dow, quhair is your sobir humilnes?
Swete gentill turtour, quhair is your pete went?
Quhair is your rewthe, the frute of nobilnes,
Of womanheid the tresour and the rent?
Mercie is never put out of meik intent,   40
Nor out of gentill hart is fundin petie,
Sen mercyles may no weycht nobill be.

7

In to my mynd I sall you mercye cry
Quhone that my toung sall faill me to speik,
And quhill that Nature me my sycht deny,   45

---

24. *traist]* Trust.
26] Which no aromatic ointment or medicine may relieve.
27. *Bot]* Apart from. *laik]* Lack. *de]* Die.
28. *petie]* Pity.
29. *passioun]* Suffering.
30. *hiddows hew]* Hideous colour
31. *mayne]* Grief. *murning]* Mourning. *mervalous]* Extraordinary.
33] Compassion does not exist, unless you help in this matter.
36. *Quhyte dow]* White dove. *sobir humilnes]* Mild humility.
37. *turtour]* Turtle–dove. *went]* Gone.
39. *rent]* Wealth.
40. *put]* Expelled. *intent]* Mind, disposition.
41. *fundin]* Found.
42] Since without mercy no person may be truly noble.
44. *me to speik]* To speak for me.
45. *quhill]* Until.

And quhill my ene for pane incluse and steik,
And quhill the dethe my hart in sowndir breik,
And quhill my mynd may think and toung may steir –
And syne fair weill, my hartis lady deir!

46. *ene]* Eyes. *incluse]* Close up. *steik]* Shut.
47. *in sowndir]* Asunder.
48. *quhill]* As long as. *steir]* Stir.
49. *syne]* Then.

27

This succinct poem has several strands: a vivid description of a headache; an apology addressed to the king (see *schir* in 6), for failing to write some unspecified poem; and a final complaint about a recurrent state of mind, a mental apathy, that hinders the poet from writing. The mood resembles the opening of 21 and 41. 26. On the stanza, see 15.

Text: R, f. 6[r].
11. oft] off R.

Authorship: 'Quod Dumbar' in R.

Further reading: Reiss 1979: 25–8 (a moralized interpretation); Ross 1981: 155–6 (finds in it a sign of 'royal neglect'); Bawcutt 1992a: 115–17 ('voices, simply but poignantly, a sense of literary incapacity').

1

My heid did yak yester nicht,
This day to mak that I na micht.
So sair the magryme dois me menyie,
Perseing my brow as ony ganyie,
That scant I luik may on the licht.   5

1. *heid*] Head. *yak*] Ache. *yester nicht*] Last night.
2] So that today I was unable to write poetry.
3. *sair*] Painfully. *magryme*] Headache, migraine. *menyie*] Afflict.
4. *Perseing*] Piercing. *ganyie*] Arrow.
5. *scant*] Hardly. *luik*] Look.

2

And now, schir, laitlie eftir mes
To dyt thocht I begowthe to dres,
The sentence lay full evill till find,
Unsleipit in my heid behind,
Dullit in dulnes and distres.   10

3

Full oft at morrow I upryse,
Quhen that my curage sleipeing lyis.
For mirth, for menstrallie and play,
For din nor danceing nor deray,
It will not walkin me no wise.   15

6. *schir]* Sir. *laitlie]* Not long since. *mes]* Mass.
7. *dyt]* Compose. *begowthe]* Began. *dres]* Prepare.
8. *sentence]* Theme, topic. *evill]* Difficult.
9. *Unsleipit]* Not having slept. *heid behind]* Back of the head.
10. *Dullit]* Made dull. *dulnes]* Gloominess.
11. *morrow]* Morning.
12. *curage]* Mind, creative power.
13. *menstrallie]* Music-making. *play]* Entertainment.
14. *din]* Noise. *deray]* Revelry.
15. *walkin]* Awaken. *no wise]* In no way.

28

This is a humorous complaint on the emptiness of the poet's purse, resembling **50**. It is addressed to the *lordis of chalker*, or lords auditors of the Exchequer, a small group of officials that usually included the treasurer. Their most important duty was to hold an annual audit, at which those concerned with the royal revenues rendered account of their receipts and disbursements. Dunbar's pension did not come within their scope. On the stanza, see **15**.

Date: Although the year cannot be determined, the poem was probably composed at midsummer, since this was the time at which the audit usually took place.

Text: R, ff. 6ʳ–6ᵛ.
8. clink] clank R.

Authorship: 'Quod Dumbar' in R.

Further reading: Baxter 1952: 95–6; Bawcutt 1992a: 369 (displays 'a mastery of talking in verse').

1

> My lordis of chalker, pleis yow to heir
> My coumpt, I sall it mak yow cleir,
> But ony circumstance or sonyie;

1. chalker] Exchequer. *pleis]* If it please.
2. coumpt] Account.
3. But] Without. *circumstance]* Circumlocution. *sonyie]* Excuse.

For left is nether corce nor cunyie
Of all that I tuik in the yeir. 5

2

For rekkyning of my rentis and roumes
Yie neid not for to tyre your thowmes,
Na for to gar your countaris clink,
Na paper for to spend nor ink,
In the ressaveing of my soumes. 10

3

I tuik fra my lord thesaurair
Ane soume of money for to wair.
I cannot tell yow how it is spendit,
Bot weill I waitt that it is endit,
And that me think ane coumpt our sair. 15

4

I trowit, the tyme quhen that I tuik it,
That lang in burgh I sould have bruikit.
Now the remanes ar eith to turs –
I have na preiff heir bot my purs,
Quhilk wald not lie and it war luikit. 20

4. nether] Neither. *corce]* Coin bearing a cross stamped on it. *cunyie]* Coin.
5. tuik] Received. *yeir]* Year.
6. rekkyning] Reckoning. *roumes]* Landed estates.
7. thowmes] Thumbs.
8. Na] Nor. *gar]* Cause. *countaris]* Counters.
10. ressaveing] Receipt. *soumes]* Sums (of money), or accounts?
11. thesaurair] Treasurer.
12. wair] Expend.
14. waitt] Know.
15] And that seems to me an over-painful account.
16] I believed, at the time when I received it.
17. bruikit] Had possession of it.
18. remanes] remains. *eith]* Easy. *turs]* Put in a bundle.
19. preiff] Proof.
20. and . . . luikit] If it were investigated.

29

Dunbar here conveys a New Year's greeting to the king. It was a widely observed courtly custom, dating from antiquity, to send gifts and poems to friends and patrons at the beginning of the year. Cf. the reference to New Year in 63. 55. For later Scottish examples of the genre, see Alexander Scott's 'New Year Gift to Queen Mary' (1562), which has the refrain: 'God gif the grace aganis this guid new yeir'; and the anonymous 'Excelland michtie prince and king' (MF, no. lx), whose refrain stresses the virtue of 'princely liberality'. Dunbar's poem, like these, blends good wishes with moral exhortation and a final hint that a king should be generous to his servitors. With the *repetitio* on 'God gif', cf. 52. On the stanza, see 16. Although commonly regarded as an early poem, there is no good evidence to date it.

Text: R, ff. 2ᵛ–3ʳ.
16. New] *Not in* R.

Authorship: 'Quod Dumbar' in R.

Further reading: Reiss 1979: 43–4 ('the ideals ... are those to be found in the moralisings'); Bawcutt 1992a: 66, 109.

1
My prince in God gif the guid grace,
Joy, glaidnes, confort and solace,
Play, pleasance, myrth and mirrie cheir,
In hansill of this guid New Yeir.

1. gif] Grant.
2. confort] Pleasure.
3. Play] Sport. *mirrie cheir]* Merry entertainment.
4. In hansill] As a gift.

154

2

God gif to the ane blissed chance,   5
And of all vertew aboundance,
And grace ay for to perseveir,
In hansill of this guid New Yeir.

3

God give the guid prosperitie,
Fair fortoun and felicitie,   10
Evir mair in earth quhill thow ar heir,
In hansell of this guid New Yeir.

4

The heavinlie lord his help the send,
Thy realme to reull and to defend,
In peace and justice it to steir,   15
In hansell of this guid New Yeir.

5

God gif the blis quharevir thow bownes,
And send the many Fraunce crownes,
Hie liberall heart and handis not sweir,
In hansell of this guid New Yeir.   20

---

5. blissed chance] Good (lit. blessed) luck.
6. vertew] Virtue.
7. ay] Always. *perseveir]* Persevere (in virtue).
14. reull] Rule.
15. steir] Govern.
17. bownes] Go, travel.
18. Fraunce] French. *crownes]* Gold coins.
19. Hie] Noble. *sweir]* Slow to give, ungenerous.

30

This religious poem has a double theme: the praise of old age for releasing one from youthful passions; and the orthodox medieval contrast between the love of God, which alone is true and perfect (16), and imperfect human love, which entails misery and deception. Both themes were common in Scottish poetry; for the former, see Henryson's *The Praise of Age*, and Kennedy's 'At matyne houre in midis of the nicht' (B, f. 52ᵛ); the latter is treated elsewhere by Dunbar in 19. This poem, however, has a simpler style than 19, and a different metre. It is a carol (like 55), consisting of a four-line stanza, *aaab⁴*, together with a couplet burden, *bb⁴*. This particular metrical scheme was by far the most popular form in English carols. The burden resembles a refrain, except that it is usually free-standing, syntactically, and placed, as here, at the poem's beginning. This poem cannot be dated, although some scholars, taking it to be autobiographical, placed it late in Dunbar's life. But, despite the first-person narrative and mention of 'experience' (27), the speaker is a fiction, a spokesman for enlightened old age.

Text: B, ff. 284ᵛ–285ᵛ.

Authorship: 'Quod Dumbar' in B.

Further reading: On the medieval carol, see Introduction to Greene, *Carols*. On this poem, see Reiss 1979: 114–15 (who discusses its structure); and Bawcutt 1992a: 315–17.

> Now cumis aige quhair yewth hes bene
> And trew luve rysis fro the splene.

1. *yewth*] Youth.
2. *trew*] True. *splene*] Heart (lit. spleen).

1

Now culit is dame Venus brand,
Trew luvis fyre is ay kindilland,
And I begyn to undirstand   5
In feynit luve quhat foly bene.
Now cumis aige quhair yewth hes bene
And trew luve rysis fro the splene.

2

Quhill Venus fyre be deid and cauld,
Trew luvis fyre nevir birnis bauld.   10
So as the ta lufe waxis auld,
The tothir dois incres moir kene.
Now cumis aige quhair yewth hes bene
And trew lufe rysis fro the splene.

3

No man hes curege for to wryte   15
Quhat plesans is in lufe perfyte,
That hes in fenyeit lufe delyt;
Thair kyndnes is so contrair clene.
Now cumis aige quhair yewth hes bene
And trew lufe rysis fro the splene.   20

4

Full weill is him that may imprent,
Or onywayis his hairt consent
To turne to trew luve his intent,
And still the quarrell to sustene.

---

3. culit] Cooled. *Venus brand]* Venus's firebrand.
6. feynit] False, deceptive. *foly]* Folly. *bene]* Is.
9. Quhill] Until. *deid]* Dead, extinct.
10. birnis] Burns. *bauld]* Strongly.
11. ta] One. *waxis]* Becomes.
12. tothir] Other. *incres]* Grow. *kene]* Fervent.
15. curege] Mental ability.
16. perfyte] Perfect.
17. fenyeit] False. *delyt]* Delight.
18] Their natures are so utterly contrasted.
21. imprent] Keep in mind.
22. onywayis] In any way. *consent]* ? Induce.
23. intent] Mind.
24] See note.

Now cumis aige quhair yewth hes bene   25
And trew lufe rysis fro the splene.

5

I haif experience by my sell.
In luvis court anis did I dwell,
Bot quhair I of a joy cowth tell,
I culd of truble tell fyftene.   30
Now cumis aige quhair yewth hes bene
And trew lufe rysis fro the splene.

6

Befoir quhair that I wes in dreid,
Now haif I confort for to speid;
Quhair I had maugre to my meid,   35
I trest rewaird and thankis betwene.
Now cumis aige quhair yewth hes bene
And trew lufe rysis fro the splene.

7

Quhair lufe wes wont me to displeis,
Now find I in to lufe grit eis;   40
Quhair I had denger and diseis,
My breist all confort dois contene.
Now cumis aige quhair yewth hes bene
And trew lufe rysis fro the splene.

8

Quhair I wes hurt with jelosy   45
And wald no luver wer bot I,
Now quhair I lufe I wald all wy

---

27. sell] Self.
28. anis] Once.
29. quhair] Where, whereas. *a]* One.
30. dreid] Fear.
34. confort] Encouragement. *speid]* Succeed.
35. maugre] Hostility. *meid]* Reward.
36] I expect reward and kindness as well.
39. displeis] Distress.
40. eis] Ease, content.
41. denger] Danger. *diseis]* Hardship.
42. contene] Contain.
46] And wished no lover but I existed.
47. wy] Creature.

Als weill as I luvit, I wene.
Now cumis aige quhair yewth hes bene
And trew lufe rysis fro the splene.   50

9

Befoir quhair I durst nocht for schame
My lufe discure nor tell hir name,
Now think I wirschep wer and fame
To all the warld that it war sene.
Now cumis aige quhair yewth hes bene   55
And trew lufe rysis fro the splene.

10

Befoir no wicht I did complene,
So did hir denger me derene,
And now I sett nocht by a bene
Hir bewty nor hir twa fair ene.   60
Now cumis aige quhair yewth hes bene
And trew lufe rysis fro the splene.

11

I haif a luve farar of face,
Quhome in no denger may haif place,
Quhilk will me guerdoun gif and grace,   65
And mercy ay quhen I me mene.
Now cumis aige quhair yewth hes bene
And trew lufe rysis fro the splene.

12

Unquyt I do no thing nor sane,
Nor wairis a luvis thocht in vane.   70

48] Felt as much love as I do, I believe.
51. durst] Dared. *nocht]* Not.
52. discure] Reveal.
53. wirschep] Honour. *wer]* Would be.
54. sene] Seen, plain.
57. no wicht . . . complene] I complained to nobody.
58. denger] Disdain (in love). *derene]* Attack.
59. sett] Value. *bene]* Bean.
60. bewty] Beauty. *ene]* Eyes.
65. guerdoun] Reward.
66. me mene] Lament.
69. Unquyt] Unrewarded. *sane]* Say.
70. wairis] Expend.

I salbe als weill luvit agane,
Thair may no jangler me prevene.
Now cumis aige quhair yewth hes bene
And trew luve rysis fro the splene.

13

Ane lufe so fare, so gud, so sweit,   75
So riche, so rewthfull and discreit,
And for the kynd of man so meit
Nevir moir salbe nor yit hes bene.
Now cumis aige quhair yewth hes bene
And trew lufe rysis fro the splene.   80

14

Is none sa trew a luve as he
That for trew lufe of us did de.
He suld be luffit agane, think me,
That wald sa fane our luve obtene.
Now cumis aige quhair yewth hes bene   85
And trew lufe rysis fro the splene.

15

Is non but grace of God, I wis,
That can in yewth considdir this.
This fals, dissavand warldis blis
So gydis man in flouris grene.   90
Now cumis aige quhair yewth hes bene
And trew luve rysis fro the splene.

---

71. *agane]* In return.
72. *jangler]* Detractor. *prevene]* Supplant.
75. *fare]* Fair.
76. *rewthfull]* Compassionate. *discreit]* Wise.
77. *kynd]* Nature. *meit]* Fitting.
82. *de]* Die.
83. *think me]* It seems.
84. *fane]* Gladly. *obtene]* Obtain.
87. *but]* Without. *I wis]* Indeed.
88. *considdir]* Perceive.
89. *dissavand]* Deceitful.
90. *gydis]* Governs.

31

This mock-eulogy of Thomas Norny, a member of James IV's household, employs the metre, style and formulaic diction characteristic of romance and outlaw balladry (see stanzas 5–6). The topics – the hero's mysterious parentage, his martial deeds, and sporting achievements – also belong to a pattern common in romance. The poem's relationship to Chaucer's *Sir Thopas* has long been recognized; but there is no validity in the common belief that the diction is anglicized, as part of a design to remind the reader of *Sir Thopas* (see Bawcutt 1992a: 359–61). Norny's social status is not wholly clear, and has been much debated by scholars. He figures in the court records between 1503 and 1512, receiving costly clothing and accompanying the king on journeys, including one to the north in 1505 (*TA*, III, 166); but he is usually listed with known entertainers, and is explicitly termed a fool on 24 March 1512 (IV, 184). He is commonly styled 'Nornee', but occasionally – and perhaps derisively – receives the title *Schir*, as in 'ane ribane to Schir Thomas Norneis bonet' (III, 155; also III, 166, 375, and IV, 358). It is not impossible that Norny was both knight and fool; but the most attractive hypothesis is that he was knighted in some festivity or mock-investiture. Dunbar's metre is the six-line version of tail-rhyme, also employed by Chaucer in *Sir Thopas*; it was common in romance, and used in several poems that Dunbar mentions, such as *Sir Bevis of Southampton* (35) and *John the Reeve* (57. 33).

Date: The poem was probably composed between 1503, when Thomas Norny first figures in the court records, and June 1506, by which time Curry was dead (see note to 43–8). There may be an allusion to the 1502 disturbances in the north (see note to 16).

Text: MF, pp. 3–5; collated with R, f. 8ʳ–8ᵛ.
8. On] R; Or MF.
10. comin] com MF, R.
37–40] MF *faded and text supplied from* R.

Authorship: 'Quod Dumbar' in MF and R.

Further reading: On the relationship to *Sir Thopas*, see Snyder 1910, Eddy 1971 and Burrow 1983. See also Reiss 1979: 52–4 ('oblique criticism of chivalry'); and Bawcutt 1992a: 58–62 (on fools at court), 207–11, 215–16.

1

Now lythis of ane gentill knycht,
Schir Thomas Norny, wys and wycht,
   And full of chevelry,
Quhais father was ane giand keyne;
His mother was ane farie queyne,   5
   Gottin be sossery.

2

Ane fairar knycht nor he was ane
On ground may nothair ryd nor gane,
   Na beire buklar nor brand;
Or comin in this court, but dreid,   10
He did full mony valyeant deid
   In Rois and Murray land.

3

Full mony catherein hes he chaist,
And cummerid mony Helland gaist
   Amang thay dully glennis.   15
Of the glen Quhettane twenti scoir
He drave as oxin him befoir –
   This deid thocht na man kennis.

1. lythis] Listen. *gentill]* Noble.
2. wycht] Strong.
3. chevelry] Chivalry.
4. giand keyne] Fierce giant.
6. Gottin] Begotten. *sossery]* Sorcery.
7–8] No better knight than he may ride or walk on earth.
9. Na] Nor. *buklar]* Small shield. *brand]* Sword.
10. Or comin] Before coming. *but dreid]* Without doubt.
13. catherein] Highland marauder. *chaist]* Put to flight.
14. cummerid] Harassed. *Helland gaist]* Highland ghost.
15. thay dully] Those gloomy.
16. glen] Clan.
17. drave] Drove.
18] Although no one knows of this deed.

4

At feastis and brydallis upaland
He wan the gre and the garland,   20
    Dansit non so on deis.
He hes att werslingis bein ane hunder,
Yet lay his body never at under.
    He knawis giff this be leis.

5

Was never wyld Robein under bewch   25
Nor yet Roger of Clekniskleuch
    So bauld a berne as he;
Gy of Gysburne na Allan Bell,
Na Simonis sonnes of Quhynfell
    At schot war never so slie.   30

6

This anterous knycht, quhar ever he went,
At justing and at tornament
    Evermor he wan the gre;
Was never of halff so gryt renowne
Schir Bevis the knycht of Southe Hamptowne –   35
    I schrew him giff I le.

7

Thairfoir Quenetyne was bot a lurdane,
That callit him ane full plum jurdane,
    This wyse and worthie knycht.
He callit him fowlar than a full,   40

19. brydallis] Weddings. *upaland]* In the country.
20. wan] Won. *gre]* Prize.
21. deis] Dais, platform.
22. werslingis] Wrestling matches. *hunder]* Hundred.
23. at under] Under that of his opponent.
24. knawis] Knows. *giff]* If. *leis]* Falsehood.
25. bewch] Bough.
27. bauld] Courageous. *berne]* Man.
30. schot] Archery. *slie]* Skilled.
31. anterous] Adventurous.
32. justing] Jousting.
36. schrew] Curse. *le]* Lie.
37. lurdane] Rascal.
38. full] Foul. *plum jurdane]* Chamber-pot.
40. full] Fool.

He said he was ane licherus bull,
    That croynd baith day and nycht.

8

He wald heff maid him Curris kneff.
I pray God better his honour saiff
    Na to be lychtleit swa.   45
Yet this far furth I dar him prais:
He fyld never sadell in his dais,
    And Curry befyld twa.

9

Quhairfoir ever at Pesche and Yull
I cry him lord of evere full   50
    That in this regeone dwellis;
And verralie that war gryt rycht,
For of ane hy renowned knycht
    He wanttis no thing bot bellis.

---

41. *licherus]* Lecherous.
42. *croynd]* Bellowed.
43. *heff]* Have. *kneff]* Boy, attendant.
44. *saiff]* Preserve.
45. *Na]* Than. *lychtleit]* Insulted.
46. *this far furth]* To this extent. *dar]* Dare.
47. *fyld]* Dirtied. *sadell]* saddle. *dais]* Life.
48. *befyld]* Befouled.
49. *Pesche]* Easter. *Yull]* Christmas.
50. *cry]* Proclaim. *evere full]* Every fool.
51. *regeone]* Country.
52. *verralie]* Truly. *war gryt rycht]* Would be wholly just.
53. *hy]* Noble.
54. *wanttis]* Lacks.

32

Dunbar employs standard topics and imagery in this brief, highly conventional contribution to the medieval debate over women. Bannatyne places it in a section called 'ballattis of the prayis of wemen and to the reproche of vicious men', which contains several other defences of women: *The Letter of Cupid* (f. 269^r), here attributed to Chaucer, but in fact translated by Hoccleve from Christine de Pisan; an anonymous English piece, 'All tho that list of wemen evill to speik' (f. 275^r); Stewart's 'For to declair the he magnificens' (f. 277^r); and Weddirburn's 'I think thir men ar verry fals and vane' (f. 279^r). Dunbar's poem is repetitive and stylistically undistinguished, and has not met with critical favour. It is attributed to him, however, in both witnesses. There is no evidence as to the date. The poem is written in five-stress couplets, a metre not otherwise used by Dunbar.

Text: B, f. 278^v; collated with MF, pp. 294–5.
26. fule] MF; *not in* B.

Further reading: For a bibliography and discussion of works illustrating the debate on women, see Utley 1944; 1970. For key texts, including some defences of women, see Blamires 1992. On this poem, see Scott 1966: 56–7 ('a blatant piece of flattery'); Reiss 1979: 115–17 (sees it as ironic); Bawcutt 1992a: 322–4 ('constructed from commonplaces'), 1992b.

Now of wemen this I say, for me:
Of erthly thingis nane may bettir be.
Thay suld haif wirschep and grit honoring

1. *wemen*] Women. *for me*] For my part.
2. *thingis*] Creatures. *nane*] None.
3. *wirschep*] Respect. *grit*] Great.

165

Of men, aboif all uthir erthly thing.
Rycht grit dishonour upoun him self he takkis,   5
In word or deid, quha evir wemen lakkis.
Sen that of wemen cumin all ar we,
Wemen ar wemen and sa will end and de.
Wo wirth the fruct wald put the tre to nocht,
And wo wirth him rycht so that sayis ocht   10
Of womanheid that may be ony lak,
Or sic grit schame upone him for to tak.
Thay us consaif with pane, and be thame fed
Within thair breistis thair we be boun to bed.
Grit pane and wo and murnyng mervellus   15
Into thair birth thay suffir sair for us.
Than meit and drynk to feid us get we nane,
Bot that we sowk out of thair breistis bane.
Thay ar the confort that we all haif heir,
Thair may no man be till us half so deir.   20
Thay ar our verry nest of nurissing –
In lak of thame quha can say ony thing,
That fowll his nest he fylis, and for thy
Exylit he suld be of all gud cumpany.
Thair suld na wyis man gif audience   25
To sic ane fule without intelligence.
Chryst to his fader he had nocht ane man;
Se quhat wirschep wemen suld haif than.
That sone is lord, that sone is king of kingis,

4. *aboif*] Above.
5. *takkis*] Brings.
6. *lakkis*] Censures.
7. *Sen*] Since. *cumin*] Come.
8. *de*] Die.
10. *rycht so*] In the same way. *ocht*] Anything.
11. *womanheid*] Feminity. *lak*] Criticism.
13. *consaif*] Conceive.
14] Upon their breasts we lie as if in bed.
15. *murnyng mervellus*] Extreme suffering.
16. *birth*] Childbirth. *sair*] Painfully.
17. *Than*] Then. *meit*] Food.
18. *sowk*] Suck. *bane*] Hospitable.
21. *verry*] True. *nurissing*] Nourishment.
23. *fowll*] Bird. *fylis*] Befouls. *for thy*] Therefore.
24. *Exylit*] Excluded.
26. *fule*] Fool.
27. *fader*] Father.
29. *sone*] Son.

In hevin and erth his majestie ay ringis.   30
Sen scho hes borne him in hir halines,
And he is well and grund of all gudnes,
All wemen of us suld haif honoring,
Service and luve, aboif all uthir thing.

30. ringis] Reigns.
31. halines] Holiness.
32. well] Source. *grund]* Foundation.

33

The Maner of Passyng to Confessioun

As the MS title implies, this poem was designed to be read in Lent (see 1–2), as penitential preparation before going to confession. In theme it resembles **69**, but the hortatory tone is very different – note the frequent commands and instructions to an impersonal 'man' (1, 8, 64, 67) – and there are close affinities with moral poems, such as **25, 34, 38** and **43**. On the stanza, see **26**.

Text: Ar, ff. 161ʳ–162ᵛ.
8. the] *Not in* Ar.
14. confessour] confessioun Ar.
19. schrift] schift Ar.
30. That] Than Ar.
48. hert] *Not in* Ar.

Authorship: 'Quod Dumbar' in Ar.

Further reading: On the penitential background, see Tentler 1977 and Boyle 1985. For a prose treatise on penance by the contemporary Scottish theologian John Ireland, see Asloan MS, I, 1–80.

1

O synfull man, thir ar the fourty dayis
That every man sulde wilfull pennence dre.
Oure lorde Jesu, as haly writ sayis,
Fastit him self, oure exampill to be.

1. thir] These.
2. wilfull] Voluntary. *dre]* Endure.
3. haly writ] Holy scripture.

Sen sic ane mychty king and lorde as he   5
To fast and pray was so obedient,
We synfull folk sulde be more deligent.

2

I reid the, man, of thi transgressioun
With all thi hert that thou be penitent.
Thow schrive the clene and mak confessioun   10
And se thairto thou be deligent,
With all thi synnis into thi mynde presente,
That every syn be the selfe be schawin,
To thyne confessour it ma be kend and knawin.

3

Apon thi body gif thou hes ane wounde   15
That caussis the gret panis for to feill,
Thair is no leiche ma mak the haill and sounde
Quhill it be sene and clengit every deill;
Rycht swa thi schrift, bot it be schawin weill,
Thow art not abill remissioun for to get,   20
Wittandlie and thou ane syn foryet.

4

Of twenty wonddis and ane be left unhelit,
Quhat avalis the leiching of the laif?
Richt swa thi schrift, and thair be oucht conselit,
It avalis not thi sely saule to saif,   25
Nor yit of God remissioun for to have.

---

7. deligent] Diligent.
8. reid] Counsel. *transgressioun]* Sin.
10. schrive the clene] Confess fully.
11. se] See. *thairto]* In this.
13. be the selfe] By itself. *schawin]* Revealed.
14. ma] May. *kend]* Perceived. *knawin]* Known.
15. gif] If.
16. panis] Pains. *feill]* Feel.
17. leiche] Doctor. *haill]* Healthy.
18. sene] Seen. *clengit]* Cleansed. *deill]* Part.
19. schrift] Confession. *bot]* Unless.
20. remissioun] Pardon.
21] If knowingly you omit (lit. forget) one sin.
22. wonddis] Wounds. *and]* If. *unhelit]* Unhealed.
23. avalis] Profits. *leiching]* Healing. *laif]* Rest.
24. oucht conselit] Anything concealed.
25. sely saule] Wretched soul.

Of syn gif thou wald have deliverance
Thow sulde it tell with all the circumstance.

5

Se that thi confessour be wys and discreit,
That can the discharge of every doute and weir,   30
And power hes of thi synnes compleit.
Gif thou can not schaw furth thi synnes perqueir
And he be blinde and can not at the speir,
Thow ma rycht weill in thi mynde consydder
That ane blynde man is led furth be ane uther.   35

6

And sa I halde that ye ar baith begylde:
He can not speir nor thou can not him tell
Quhen nor how thi conscience thou hes fylde.
Thairfor I reid that thou excus thi sell
And rype thi mynde, how every thing befell,   40
The tyme, the place, and how and in quhat wys,
So that thi confessioun ma thi synnes pryce.

7

Avys the weill, or thou cum to the preist,
Of all thi synnes, and namelie of the maist,
That thai be reddy prentit in thi breist.   45
Thow sulde not cum to schryfe the in haist,
And syne sit doun abasit as ane beist.

28. *circumstance]* Detail.
29. *wys]* Wise. *discreit]* Discerning.
30. *discharge]* Release. *doute]* Doubt. *weir]* Uncertainty.
31. *compleit]* Full.
32. *perqueir]* Accurately (lit. by heart).
33. *at the speir]* Put questions to you.
34. *consydder]* Understand.
36. *halde]* Consider. *begylde]* Deceived.
38. *fylde]* Defiled.
39. *excus thi sell]* Seek to clear yourself.
40. *rype]* Scrutinize.
41. *wys]* Manner.
42. *pryce]* Assess, evaluate.
43. *Avys the]* Reflect. *or]* Before.
44. *namelie]* Especially. *maist]* Greatest.
45. *prentit]* Imprinted.
47. *syne]* Then. *abasit]* Abashed, dumb.

With humyll hert and sad contrycioun
Thow suld cum to thine confessioun.

8

With thine awin mouth thi synnes thou suld tell;   50
Bot sit and heir the preist hes not ado.
Quha kennes thi synnes better na thi sell?
Thairfor I reid the, tak gude tent thairto.
Thow knawis best quhair bindis the thi scho.
Thairfor be wys afor, or thow thair cum,   55
That thou schaw furth thi synnes, all and sum.

9

Quhair seldin compt is tane and hes a hevy charge
And syne is rekles in his governance
And on his conscience he takis all to large
And on the end hes no rememberance –   60
That man is abill to fall ane gret mischance.
The synfull man that all the yeir oursettis,
Fra Pasche to Pasche, rycht mony a thing foryettis.

10

I reid the, man, quhill thou art stark and young,
With pith and strenth into thi yeris grene,   65
Quhill thou art abill baith in mynde and toung,
Repent the, man, and kepe thi conscience clene.
Till byde till age is mony perrell sene:

48. *humyll]* Humble. *sad]* Solemn.
51] The priest has nothing to do but sit and listen.
52. *kennes]* Knows. *na thi sell]* Than yourself.
53. *tak . . . thairto]* Pay heed to this matter.
54. *bindis]* Pinches. *scho]* Shoe.
55. *afor]* In advance. *or]* Before.
56. *all and sum]* One and all.
57. *seldin]* Seldom. *compt]* Reckoning. *charge]* Burden.
58. *rakles]* Heedless. *governance]* Behaviour.
59. *all to large]* ? Too large a weight of sin.
61. *abill]* Likely. *fall]* Meet with. *mischance]* Misfortune.
62. *yeir]* Year. *oursettis]* Procrastinates.
63. *Pasche]* Easter. *foryettis]* Forgets.
64. *stark]* Strong.
65. *pith]* Force. *grene]* Youthful.
66. *abill]* Sound, healthy.
68. *perell sene]* Evident danger.

Small merit is of synnes for to irke
Quhen thou art ald and ma na wrangis wyrke.   70

69. irke] Grow weary.
70. ald] Old. *wrangis wyrke]* Commit sins.

34

Employing the impersonal, admonitory tone of a preacher, Dunbar draws on biblical language and imagery to treat one of the most common medieval themes, human mutability. The poem is striking for its effective rhetorical patterning; there is much *repetitio* throughout, and in the last stanza a particularly intricate patterning of the syntax, using antithesis and chiasmus. On the stanza, see 6.

Text: MF, pp. 195–6.

Authorship: 'Quod Dunbar' in MF.

Further reading: Bawcutt 1992a: 147–8.

1

O wreche, be war, this warld will wend the fro,
Quhilk hes begylit mony greit estait.
Turne to thy freynd, beleif nocht in thy fo.
Sen thow mon go, be grathing to thy gait,
Remeid in tyme and rew nocht all to lait,   5
Provyd thy place, for thow away man pas

1. war] Vigilant. *wend*] Depart.
2. begylit] Deceived. *greit estait*] Person of high rank.
3. freynd] Friend. *beleif*] Trust.
4. mon] Must. *grathing to thy gait*] Preparing for your journey.
5. Remeid] Reform. *rew*] Feel remorse. *lait*] Late.
6. Provyd] Prepare. *man*] Must.

173

Out of this vaill of trubbill and dissait:
Vanitas vanitatum et omnia vanitas.

2

Walk furth, pilgrame, quhill thow hes dayis licht,
Dres fra desert, draw to thy dwelling place.   10
Speid home, for quhy anone cummis the nicht,
Quhilk dois the follow with ane ythand chaise.
Bend up thy saill and win thy port of grace,
For and the deith ourtak the in trespas,
Than may thow say thir wourdis with allace: 15
Vanitas vanitatum et omnia vanitas.

3

Heir nocht abydis, heir standis nothing stabill.
This fals warld ay flittis to and fro:
Now day up bricht, now nycht als blak as sabill,
Now eb, now flude, now freynd, now cruell fo,   20
Now glaid, now said, now weill, now into wo,
Now cled in gold, dissolvit now in as.
So dois this warld transitorie go:
Vanitas vanitatum et omnia vanitas.

---

7. *dissait*] Deceit.
9. *quhill*] As long as.
10. *Dres*] Turn
11. *Speid*] Hasten. *for quhy*] Because. *anone*] Soon.
12. *ythand chaise*] Unceasing pursuit.
13. *Bend*] Draw.
14. *and*] If. *ourtak*] Catch up with. *trespas*] Sin.
15. *allace*] Cry of grief.
18. *flittis*] Shifts, moves.
19. *day up*] Dawn. *sabill*] Sable.
20. *eb*] Ebb tide. *flude*] High tide.
21. *said*] Sad. *weill*] Well. *wo*] Grief.
22. *cled*] Clothed. *as*[Ash, dust.

35

This petition to the king has a similar opening to **51**, and in the first three stanzas uses the same image of a feast to suggest that benefices should be more fairly distributed among churchmen. The tone changes slightly in the second half; becoming less personal, the poem turns into a denunciation of greedy clerics who neglect their parishioners and the fabric of their churches. The witty and ingeniously varied refrain depicts churchmen behaving like thieves and robbers. On the stanza, see **9**.

Text: MF, pp. 321–2 (MFb); collated with MF, pp. 8–9 (MFa), and R, f. 10ʳ.
17. spraidis . . . net] MFa; spendis . . . mett MFb.
26. warryit] MFa; variant MFb.

Authorship: 'Quod Dumbar' in MFb, MFa and R.

Further reading: Bawcutt 1992a: 112–14.

1

Of benefice, sir, at everie feist,
Quha monyast hes makis maist requeist.
Get thai not all, thai think ye wrang thame.
Ay is the ovirword of the geist:
Giff thame the pelffe to pairt amang thame.   5

1. benefice] Benefices.
2] Those who have the most (benefices) are most demanding.
3. Get thai] If they get. *wrang]* Injure.
4. ovirword] Refrain. *geist]* Song.
5. Giff] Give. *pelffe]* Plunder. *pairt]* Share.

175

2

Sum swelleis swan, sum swelleis duke,
And I stand fastand in a nuke,
Quhill the effect of all thai fang thame.
Bot lord! how petewouslie I luke,
Quhone all the pelfe thai pairt amang thame.   10

3

Of sic hie feistis of sanctis in glorie
(Baithe of commoun and propir storie),
Quhair lairdis war patronis, oft I sang thame,
Charitas, pro dei amore;
And yit I gat na thing amang thame.   15

4

This blynd warld ever so payis his dett.
Riche befoir pure spraidis ay thair net.
To fische all watiris dois belang thame.
Quha na thing hes can na thing gett,
Bot ay as syphir set amang thame.   20

5

Swa thai the kirk have in thair cure,
Thai fors bot litill how it fure,
Nor of the buikis or bellis, quha rang thame.
Thai pans not of the prochin pure,
Hed thai the pelfe to pairt amang thame.   25

---

6. *Sum]* One. *swelleis]* Swallows. *duke]* Duck.
7. *nuke]* Corner.
8*]* **While** they seize the greater part for themselves.
9. *petewouslie]* Pitifully.
10. *Quhone]* When.
11. *sic hie]* Such great. *sanctis]* Saints.
14*]* Charity, for the love of God.
15. *gat]* Got.
16. *dett]* Debt, obligation.
17. *pure]* Poor. *spraidis]* Spread.
18. *dois belang thame]* It pertains to them.
20. *syphir]* Cipher.
21. *cure]* Control.
22. *fors]* Care. *fure]* Prospers.
23. *buikis]* Service books.
24. *pans]* Think. *prochin pure]* Poor people of the parish.

6

So warryit is this warldis rent
That men of it ar never content,
Of deathe quhill that the dragoun stang thame.
Quha maist hes than sall maist repent,
With largest compt to pairt amang thame.   30

26. *warryit*] Accursed. *rent*] Wealth.
28] Until death, the dragon, sting them mortally.
30. *compt*] Account.

36

The poem's basic structure is that of a vision of hell: within a 'trance' (3, 223) the poet sees first a dance of the Seven Deadly Sins and then a mock tournament, both devised as diabolic entertainments for 'Fasternis Evin', or Shrove Tuesday. The first part is orthodox, iconographically and doctrinally, and although it has no precise source is clearly indebted to the multifarious medieval traditions concerning hell, and the depiction of the Seven Deadly Sins. Comparable, though fuller, treatments of the theme include *St Patrick's Purgatory*, Chaucer's *Parson's Tale* (386–955), Langland's *Piers Plowman*, B. V. 60–461, and Spenser's *Faerie Queene*, I. iv. In the portrayal of the Sins Dunbar employs brief but suggestive animal symbolism (33, 68, 80), and his style is characteristically dynamic and pictorial. The second part, the tournament of the tailor and soutar, belongs to a type of burlesque verse that had English parallels, such as the fifteenth-century *Tournament of Tottenham*, but was particularly popular in sixteenth-century Scotland. Some examples are Alexander Scott's 'Justing and Debait', the anonymous 'Sym and his Bruder' (both in the Bannatyne Manuscript), and Lindsay's *Justing betuix James Watson and Jhone Barbour*. Neither tailors nor soutars enjoyed social esteem. A tailor's work consisted as much in repairing old clothes as making new ones (Sanderson 1987: 75–90); and soutars were not highly skilled cordwainers but cobblers, or shoe-menders. Both crafts were often the butt of derisive tales and jokes; Bannatyne includes a later work of this kind, possibly influenced by Dunbar: Stewart's *Flyting betwix the Soutar and the Tailyour* (B, f. 140ʳ).

Metre: The verse is arranged in twelve-line stanzas in B, but in six-line stanzas in A, MF and R. The twelve-line form of tail-rhyme – unified by the tail lines – was very common in medieval English romance. Two stanzas (3 and 10) have only six lines, and may be defective, or possibly interpolations, since their presence disturbs not only the metrical but the numerical pattern of the poem. Without them both the *Dance* and the *Turnament* would have the same number of stanzas.

Date: The references to 15 February and 'Fasternis Evin' have been taken by
some scholars to indicate composition in 1507, a year when Shrove Tuesday
occurred on 16 February (Baxter 1952: 154–6). But this interpretation seems
implausible and over-literal. It should be noted that 'Aganis' (8) is a vague
preposition, and means not 'upon' but 'in preparation for'. On 21 February
1507 the queen gave birth to her first child, and there is little evidence of court
revelry in that spring; indeed the year best documented for 'Fasternis Evin'
guisings and tourneying is 1505. I consider the dating symbolic rather than
actual; the poem is carnivalesque in structure, echoing the court pastimes typical
of this season, and also in its prevailing tone of grotesque comedy (Bawcutt
1992a: 69–71).

Text: B, ff. 110^r–112^v; collated with MF, pp. 12–16, 161–5; R, ff. 11^v–13^r; and
A, ff. 210^r–211^v (lines 121–228). All witnesses attribute the poem to Dunbar.
The textual position is complex; for discussion, see Bawcutt 1992a: 288–91.
Only the most important variants are noted.

50. in secreit places] MF; of sindry racis B.
80. Come] MF; *not in* B.
81. Lythenes] MF; ydilnes B.
139. buthman] A; tailyour B.
142. him comfort] A; come furth B.
147. wicht] A; strang B.
149. curage] A, MF; hairt B.
151. And quhen he saw the sowtar] A, MF; quhen to the sowtar he did B.
154] A; In harte he tuke yit sic ane scummer B.
171. Uneis he mycht] A; he mycht nocht rycht B.
187] A, MF; Thay spurrit thair hors on adir syd B.
188] A; Syne thay attour the grund cowd glyd B.
193. birnes] A, MF; harnas B.
201. strenyt] A; stern B.
206. flawe to the] A; he straik till B.
210. forswer] A, MF; mensweir B.
221. thar socht] A, MF; it rocht B.
226] A; For this said justing it befell B.
228. Schirris . . . it] A, MF; Now . . . this B.

Further reading: Bloomfield 1952 (the Seven Deadly Sins); Owen 1970 (medieval
conceptions of hell). On this poem specifically, see Scott 1966: 229–37; Ross 1981:
168–76; Norman 1989a; McKenna 1989; Bawcutt 1992a: 283–91.

1

> Of Februar the fyiftene nycht,
> Full lang befoir the dayis lycht,
>   I lay in till a trance,

1. fyiftene] Fifteenth.
2. dayis lycht] Dawn.
3. in till] Within.

And than I saw baith hevin and hell;
Me thocht amangis the feyndis fell   5
   Mahoun gart cry ane dance
Of schrewis that wer nevir schrevin,
Aganis the feist of Fasternis evin
   To mak thair observance.
He bad gallandis ga graith a gyis   10
And kast up gamountis in the skyis,
   That last came out of France.

2

'Lat se,' quod he, 'Now quha begynnis?'
With that the fowll sevin deidly synnis
   Begowth to leip at anis.   15
And first of all in dance wes Pryd,
With bair wyld bak and bonet on syd,
   Lyk to mak waistie wanis.
And round abowt him, as a quheill,
Hang all in rumpillis to the heill   20
   His kethat for the nanis.
Mony prowd trumpour with him trippit,
Throw skaldand fyre ay as thay skippit
   Thay gyrnd with hiddous granis.

3

Heilie harlottis on hawtane wyis   25
Come in with mony sindrie gyis,

---

5. *Me thocht*] It seemed to me. *feyndis fell*] Cruel fiends.
6. *gart cry*] Had proclaimed.
7. *schrewis*] Sinners. *schrevin*] Shriven, absolved from sin.
8. *Aganis*] In readiness for. *Fasternis evin*] Shrove Tuesday.
9. *observance*] Ritual ceremonies.
10] He ordered young men to prepare a masquerade.
11. *kast*] Cast. *gamountis*] Leaps.
13. *Lat se*] Let us see. *quod*] Said.
15. *Begowth*] Began. *anis*] Once.
17. *bair*] Bare.
18. *Lyk*] Likely. *waistie wanis*] Desolate dwellings.
19. *quheill*] Wheel.
20. *Hang*] Hung. *rumpillis*] Folds, pleats. *heill*] Heel.
21 *kethat*] Large-skirted coat. *for the nanis*] Assuredly (tag).
22. *trumpour*] Deceiver.
24. *gyrnd*] Grimaced. *hiddous granis*] Horrifying groans.
25. *Heilie harlottis*] Proud rascals. *hawtane wyis*] Haughty manner.
26. *Come*] Came. *sindrie*] Varied.

Bot yit luche nevir Mahoun
Quhill preistis come in with bair schevin nekkis.
Than all the feyndis lewche and maid gekkis,
    Blak belly and Bawsy brown.   30

4

Than Yre come in with sturt and stryfe,
His hand wes ay upoun his knyfe,
    He brandeist lyk a beir.
Bostaris, braggaris and barganeris
Eftir him passit in to pairis,   35
    All bodin in feir of weir.
In jakkis and stryppis and bonettis of steill,
Thair leggis wer chenyeit to the heill,
    Frawart wes thair affeir.
Sum vpoun uder with brandis beft,   40
Sum jaggit uthiris to the heft,
    With knyvis that scherp cowd scheir.

5

Nixt in the dance followit Invy,
Fild full of feid and fellony,
    Hid malyce and dispyte.   45
For pryvie hatrent that tratour trymlit.
Him followit mony freik dissymlit,
    With fenyeit wirdis quhyte,

27. *luche]* Laughed.
28. *schevin]* Shaven.
29. *lewche]* Laughed. *gekkis]* Derisive gestures.
31. *sturt]* Quarrelling.
33. *brandeist]* Behaved aggressively. *beir]* Bear.
34. *braggaris]* Braggarts. *barganeris]* Quarrellers.
36] All equipped in warlike manner.
37] In leather jerkins, splints and steel helmets.
38. *chenyeit]* Chained.
39. *Frawart]* Bad-tempered. *affeir]* Manner.
40] Some struck each other with swords.
41. *jaggit]* Stabbed. *heft]* Handle.
42. *scherp]* Sharply. *scheir]* Cut.
43. *Invy]* Envy.
44. *feid]* Hostility. *fellony]* Cruelty.
45. *Hid]* Hidden. *dispyte]* Contempt.
46. *pryvie hatrent]* Secret hatred. *trymlit]* Trembled.
47. *freik]* Man. *dissymlit]* Dissembling.
48. *fenyeit wirdis]* Deceitful words.

And flattereris in to menis facis,
And bakbyttaris in secreit places,   50
   To ley that had delyte,
And rownaris of fals lesingis –
Allace, that courtis of noble kingis
   Of thame can nevir be quyte.

6

Nixt him in dans come Cuvatyce,   55
Rute of all evill and grund of vyce,
   That nevir cowd be content.
Catyvis, wrechis and ockeraris,
Hudpykis, hurdaris and gadderaris
   All with that warlo went.   60
Out of thair throttis thay schot on udder
Hett moltin gold, me thocht a fudder,
   As fyreflawcht maist fervent.
Ay as thay tomit thame of schot,
Feyndis fild thame new up to the thrott,   65
   With gold of allkin prent.

7

Syne Sweirnes at the secound bidding
Come lyk a sow out of a midding.
   Full slepy wes his grunyie.
Mony sweir bumbard belly huddroun,   70

---

51. *ley*] Tell lies.
52. *rownaris*] Whisperers. *lesingis*] Slanders.
54. *quyte*] Free.
55. *Cuvatyce*] Covetousness.
56. *Rute*] Root. *grund*] Foundation.
58] Villains, misers and usurers.
59] Skinflints, hoarders and money-grabbers.
60. *warlo*] Evil creature.
61. *schot*] Vomited. *udder*] Others.
62. *Hett*] Heated. *fudder*] Cartload.
63] As intensely hot as lightning.
64. *tomit thame*] Emptied themselves.
65. *thrott*] Throat.
66. *allkin prent*] Every imprint.
67. *Sweirnes*] Sloth.
68. *midding*] Dunghill.
69. *grunyie*] Grunt.
70. *sweir*] Slothful. *bumbard*] Lazy.

Mony slute daw and slepy duddroun
　　Him servit ay with sounyie.
He drew thame furth in till a chenyie,
And Belliall with a brydill renyie
　　Evir lascht thame on the lunyie. 75
In dance thay war so slaw of feit,
Thay gaif thame in the fyre a heit
　　And maid thame quicker of counyie.

8

Than Lichery, that lathly cors,
Come berand lyk a bagit hors, 80
　　And Lythenes did him leid.
Thair wes with him ane ugly sort,
And mony stynkand fowll tramort
　　That had in syn bene deid.
Quhen thay wer entrit in the dance 85
Thay were full strenge of countenance,
　　Lyk turkas birnand reid.
All led thay uthir by the tersis.
Suppois thay fycket with thair ersis,
　　It mycht be na remeid. 90

71] Many a sluttish slattern and sleepy sloven.
72. sounyie] Excuse (for delay).
73. chenyie] Chain.
74. renyie] Rein.
75. lascht] Whipped. *lunyie]* Loin.
76. slaw] Slow.
77. heit] Heat.
78. of counyie] In the dance.
79. Lichery] Lechery. *lathly cors]* Foul body.
80. berand] Crying. *bagit]* Swollen.
81. Lythenes] Wantonness.
82. sort] Crew.
83. tramort] Corpse.
84. bene deid] Died.
86. strenge] Strange.
87. turkas] Pincers. *birnand]* Glowing.
88. tersis] Penises.
89. Suppois] Although. *fycket]* Fidgeted. *ersis]* Arses.
90. remeid] Remedy.

9

Than the fowll monstir Glutteny,
Of wame unsasiable and gredy,
  To dance he did him dres.
Him followit mony fowll drunckart,
With can and collep, cop and quart,   95
  In surffet and exces.
Full mony a waistles wallydrag
With wamis unweildable did furth wag,
  In creische that did incres.
'Drynk!' ay thay cryit, with mony a gaip.   100
The feyndis gaif thame hait leid to laip,
  Thair lovery wes na les.

10

Na menstrallis playit to thame, but dowt,
For glemen thair wer haldin owt,
  Be day and eik by nycht;   105
Except a menstrall that slew a man,
Swa till his heretage he wan,
  And entirt be breif of richt.

11

Than cryd Mahoun for a heleand padyane.
Syne ran a feynd to feche Makfadyane,   110
  Far northwart in a nuke.
Be he the correnoch had done schout

---

92. *wame]* Belly. *unsasiable]* insatiable.
93. *him dres]* Prepare himself.
95. *collep]* ? Drinking vessel. *cop]* Cup. *quart]* Quart-pot.
96. *surffet]* Surfeit.
97. *waistles]* Without a waist. *wallydrag]* good-for-nothing.
98. *unweildable]* Unwieldy. *wag]* Totter.
99. *creische]* Fat.
100. *gaip]* Gape.
101. *hait leid]* Hot lead. *laip]* Drink.
102. *lovery]* Livery, food allowance. *na les]* No less.
103. *but dowt]* For certain.
104. *glemen]* Minstrels. *haldin]* Kept.
107. *wan]* Won.
108. *breif of richt]* See note.
109. *heleand padyane]* Highland pageant, entertainment.
110. *feche]* Fetch.
111. *nuke]* Nook.
112. *Be]* After. *correnoch]* Loud outcry.

Erschemen so gadderit him abowt,
In hell grit rowme thay tuke.
Thae tarmegantis with tag and tatter   115
Full lowd in Ersche begowth to clatter
And rowp lyk revin and ruke.
The devill sa devit wes with thair yell
That in the depest pot of hell
He smorit thame with smuke.   120

12

Nixt that a turnament wes tryid,
That lang befoir in hell wes cryid
In presens of Mahoun;
Betwix a telyour and ane sowtar,
A pricklous and ane hobbell clowttar,   125
The barres wes maid boun.
The tailyeour baith with speir and scheild
Convoyit wes unto the feild,
With mony lymmar loun:
Of seme byttaris and beist knapparis,   130
Of stomok steillaris and clayth takkaris,
A graceles garisoun.

13

His baner born wes him befoir,
Quhairin wes clowttis ane hundreth scoir,

113. Erschemen] Highlanders.
114. rowme] Space. *tuke]* Took.
115] Those devils in rags and tatters.
116. Ersche] Gaelic. *clatter]* Chatter.
117. rowp] Croak. *revin]* Raven. *ruke]* Rook.
118. devit] Deafened.
119. pot] Pit.
120. smorit] Smothered. *smuke]* Smoke.
121. tryid] Attempted.
122. cryid] Proclaimed.
124. telyour] Tailor. *sowtar]* Cobbler.
125] A louse-stabber and a patcher-up of old shoes.
126. barres] Enclosure, lists. *boun]* Ready.
128. Convoyit] Escorted. *feild]* Field.
129. lymmar loun] Knavish rascal.
130. seme] Seam. *knapparis]* Crackers.
131. stomok] Stomacher. *clayth]* Cloth.
132. graceles garisoun] Unattractive troop.
134. clowttis] Rags. *hundreth scoir]* Twenty hundred.

Ilkane of divers hew;   135
And all stowin out of sindry webbis,
For quhill the Greik sie fillis and ebbis,
    Telyouris will nevir be trew.
The buthman on the barrowis blent.
Allais, he tynt all hardyment,   140
    For feir he chaingit hew.
Mahoun him comfort and maid him knycht,
Na ferly thocht his hart wes licht
    That to sic honour grew.

14

He hecht hely befoir Mahoun   145
That he suld ding the sowtar doun,
    Thocht he wer wicht as mast.
Bot quhen he on the barrowis blenkit
The telyouris curage a littill schrenkit,
    His hairt did all ourcast.   150
And quhen he saw the sowtar cum
Of all sic wirdis he wes full dum,
    So soir he wes agast.
For he in hart tuke sic a scunner
Ane rak of fartis lyk ony thunner   155
    Went fra him, blast for blast.

135. Ilkane] Each one. *hew]* Colour.
136. stowin] Stolen. *webbis]* Whole pieces of cloth.
137. Greik sie] Mediterranean. *fillis]* Flows.
138. trew] Honest.
139. buthman] Stall keeper. *barrowis]* Lists. *blent]* Glanced.
140. tynt] Lost. *hardyment]* Boldness.
141. chaingit hew] Grew pale.
142. comfort] Encouraged.
143, ferly] Wonder. *licht]* Joyful.
145. hecht] Vowed. *hely]* Proudly.
146. ding] Strike.
147. wicht] Strong.
148. blenkit] Gazed.
149. curage] Courage. *schrenkit]* Diminished.
150. ourcast] Grow despondent.
153. soir] Greatly. *agast]* Terrified.
154. tuke sic a scunner] Felt such disgust.
155. rak] Explosion. *thunner]* Thunder.

15

The sowtar to the feild him drest,
He wes convoyid out of the west,
As ane defender stout.
Suppois he had na lusty varlot,   160
He had full mony lowsy harlott
Round rynnand him aboute.
His baner wes a barkit hyd,
Quhairin sanct Girnega did glyd,
Befoir that rebald rowt.   165
Full sowttarlyk he wes of laitis,
For ay betwix the harnes plaitis
The uly birstit out.

16

Apon the telyour quhen he did luke,
His hairt a litill dwamyng tuke.   170
Uneis he mycht upsitt.
In to his stommok was sic ane steir,
Of all his dennar, that cost him deir,
His breist held never a bitt.
To comfort him or he raid forder,   175
The devill of knychtheid gaif him order,
For stynk than he did spitt,
And he about the devillis nek
Did spew agane ane quart of blek.
Thus knychtly he him quitt.   180

---

159. stout] Brave.
160. Suppois] Although. *varlot]* Attendant (on a knight).
161. lowsy harlott] Lice-ridden rascal.
163. barkit hyd] Tanned hide.
165. rebald rowt] Knavish troop.
166. sowttarlyk] Cobbler-like. *laitis]* Manners.
167. harnes plaitis] Plates of armour.
168. uly] Oil. *birstit]* Burst.
170. dwamyng] Faintness.
171. Uneis] With difficulty.
172. steir] Tumult.
173. dennar] Dinner. *deir]* A great deal.
175. raid forder] Rode further.
176. knychtheid] Knighthood.
179. blek] Blacking (for leather).
180. quitt] Paid back.

17

Than fourty tymis the feynd cryd. 'Fy!'
The sowtar rycht effeiritly
   Unto the feild he socht.
Quhen thay wer servit of thair speiris,
Folk had ane feill be thair effeiris,   185
   Thair hairtis wer baith on flocht.
Thai spurrit apon athir syd,
The hors attour the grene did glyd,
   And tham togidder brocht.
The tailyeour was no thing weill sittin,   190
He left his sadill all beschittin,
   And to the grund he socht.

18

His birnes brak and maid ane brattill,
The sowtaris hors start with the rattill
   And round about cowd reill.   195
The beist, that frayit wes rycht evill,
Ran with the sowtar to the devill,
   And he rewardit him weill.
Sum thing frome him the feynd eschewit,
He trowit agane to be bespewit,   200
   So strenyt he wes in steill.
He thocht he wald agane debait him.
He turnd his ers and all bedret him,
   Quyte our from nek till heill.

---

182. effeiritly] Fearfully.
183. socht] Made his way.
185. feill] Perception. *effeiris]* Behaviour.
186. on flocht] In a flutter.
187. spurrit] Spurred their horses. *athir]* Either.
188. hors] Horses. *attour the grene]* Over the grass.
190. sittin] Seated.
191. beschittin] Befouled.
193. birnes] Breastplate. *brak]* Broke. *brattill]* Clatter.
194. start] Bounded.
195. reill] Prance wildly.
196. frayit] Frightened. *evill]* Badly.
199] The devil edged away from him a little.
200. trowit] Expected. *bespewit]* Spewed upon.
201. strenyt] Constricted.
202. debait him] Defend himself.
203. ers] Arse. *bedret]* Befouled.

19

He lowsit it of with sic a reird,   205
Baith hors and man flawe to the eird,
He fart with sic ane feir.
'Now haif I quitt the', quod Mahoun.
The new maid knycht lay in to swoun,
And did all armes forswer.   210
The devill gart thame to dungeoun dryve
And thame of knychtheid cold depryve,
Dischargeing thame of weir;
And maid thame harlottis agane for evir,
Quhilk still to keip thay had fer levir,   215
Nor ony armes beir.

20

I had mair of thair werkis written,
Had nocht the sowtar bene beschittin,
With Belliallis ers unblist.
Bot that sa gud ane bourd me thocht,   220
Sic solace to my hairt thar socht,
For lawchtir neir I brist.
Quhairthrow I walknit of my trance.
To put this in rememberance,
Mycht no man me resist,   225
To dyte how all this thing befell,
Befoir Mahoun, the heir of hell.
Schirris, trow it gif ye list!

---

205. lowsit of] Let loose, fired. *reird]* Din.
206. flawe] Flew. *eird]* Earth.
207. fart] Farted. *sic ane feir]* Such a manner.
210. armes forswer] Renounce warfare.
213. weir] War.
215–16] Which title they had much rather keep than bear arms.
217. werkis] Deeds.
219. unblist] Unblessed, accursed.
220. bourd] Jest.
221. solace] Pleasure. *socht]* Proceeded.
222. neir] Nearly. *brist]* Burst.
223. walknit] Woke up.
224–6] No man might prevent me from committing this to memory, [and] writing how all this business happened.
228. Schirris] Sires. *trow]* Believe. *list]* Please.

37

Dunbar's ironic commendation of tailors and soutars, or cobblers, cast in the form of a dream, is described in both witnesses as an *amendis*, or apology, to the two crafts. B places it as a pendant to **36**, but treats it as a separate poem, with the rubric: 'Followis the amendis ... to the telyouris and sowtaris for the turnament maid on thame'. In MF the poem is wholly independent, with no link to **36**. There is some similarity of tone to the apology addressed to Dog (**61**). But the irony of this poem is more audacious, since Dunbar transforms the craftsmen's skill at concealing the physical deformities of their customers into the power to improve upon the handiwork of God. The poem exploits a number of double-edged words, *blist* (4), *craft* (11), *slie* (31), and *knavis* (39). On the stanza, see **16**.

Text: B, ff. 112ᵛ–113ʳ; collated with MF, p. 317.
25. swayne] MF; man B.
30. gude] MF; gud crafty B.

Authorship: 'Quod Dumbar' in B and MF.

Further reading: Scott 1966: 230 (an attack on 'spiritual dissembling'), Reiss 1979: 83–4; Ross 1981: 176–7; Bawcutt 1992a: 217–19.

1

Betwix twell houris and ellevin
I dremed ane angell came fra hevin,

1. Betwix] Between. *twell]* Twelve. *ellevin]* Eleven.

With plesand stevin sayand on hie:
Telyouris and sowtaris, blist be ye.

2

In hevin hie ordand is your place,   5
Aboif all sanctis in grit solace,
Nixt God grittest in dignitie,
Tailyouris and sowtaris, blist be ye.

3

The caus to yow is nocht unkend;
That God mismakkis ye do amend   10
Be craft and grit agilitie:
Tailyouris and sowtaris, blist be ye.

4

Sowtaris, with schone weill maid and meit,
Ye mend the faltis of ill maid feit,
Quhairfoir to hevin your saulis will fle: 15
Telyouris and sowtaris, blist be ye.

5

Is nocht in all this fair a flyrok
That hes upoun his feit a wyrok,
Knowll tais nor mowlis in no degrie,
Bot ye can hyd thame, blist be ye.   20

---

3. stevin] Voice. *hie]* High.
4. Telyouris] Tailors. *sowtaris]* Cobblers. *blist]* Blessed.
5. ordand] Ordained.
6. solace] Happiness.
7. Nixt] Next to. *grittest]* Greatest. *dignitie]* Honour.
9. unkend] Unknown.
10] That which God makes badly you put right.
11. agilitie] Quickness of mind.
13. schone] Shoes. *meit]* Fitting.
14. faltis] Blemishes.
15. saulis] Souls. *fle]* Fly.
17. flyrok] ? Deformed person.
18. wyrok] Corn.
19. Knowll tais] Toes with swollen joints. *mowlis]* Chilblains. *degrie]* Respect.
20. hyd] Hide.

6

And ye tailyouris, with weil maid clais
Can mend the werst maid man that gais
And mak him semely for to se:
Telyouris and sowtaris, blist be ye.

7

Thocht God mak ane misfassonit swayne,   25
Ye can him all schaip new agane,
And fassoun him bettir, be sic thre:
Telyouris and sowtaris, blist be ye.

8

Thocht a man haif a brokin bak,
Haif he a gude telyour, quhattrak,   30
That can it cuver with craftis slie:
Telyouris and sowtaris, blist be ye.

9

Of God grit kyndnes may ye clame,
That helpis his peple fra cruke and lame,
Supportand faltis with your supple: 35
Tailyouris and sowtaris, blist be ye.

10

In erd ye kyth sic mirakillis heir,
In hevin ye salbe sanctis full cleir,
Thocht ye be knavis in this cuntre:
Telyouris and sowtaris, blist be yie.   40

---

21. *clais*] Clothes.
22. *werst*] Worst. *gais*] Goes.
23. *semely*] Attractive.
25. *Thocht*] though. *misfassonit*] Misshapen. *swayne*] Churl.
26. *schaip*] Form.
27] And make him three times better-looking.
29. *brokin*] Crippled.
30. *Haif he*] If he has. *quhattrak*] What does it matter.
31. *cuver*] Conceal. *slie*] Clever.
34. *cruke*] Deformity. *lame*] Lameness.
35. *Supportand*] Alleviating. *supple*] Assistance.
37. *In erd*] On earth. *kyth*] Display.
38. *cleir*] Shining.
39. *cuntre*] Country.

38

This didactic poem on the theme of mutability is addressed to *man*, or
Everyman, by a bird. Such admonitory birds are common in moral lyrics,
sometimes associated with a *chanson d'aventure* setting. For English examples,
see Greene, *Carols*, nos. 370, 378 and 389; several Scottish examples are placed
close to this one by Bannatyne: 'Furth throw ane forrest as I fure' (f. 44^r); 'Doun
by ane rever as I red' (f. 48^v); and 'Walking allone amang thir levis grene' (f. 53^r).
The bird sometimes symbolizes the voice of conscience, and often has a more
dramatic role than here; see, for instance, Dunbar's use in **19**. The poem is
appropriately set on Ash Wednesday, the first day of Lent; cf. **25**, which is also
designed for penitential contemplation. The style is characterized by a heavy use
of *repetitio* and antithesis. The stanza is one often used by Dunbar; see **16**.

Text: B, f. 48^v; collated with MF, pp. 319–20.
7. revert] MF; return B.
15. for] MF; in B.

Authorship: 'Quod Dumbar' in B and MF.

Further reading: On admonitory birds and the *chanson d'aventure* tradition, see
Sandison 1913: 82–7; on this poem, see Hughes and Ramson 1982: 73–5.

1

> Of Lentren in the first mornyng,
> Airly as did the day up spring,
> Thus sang ane bird with voce up plane:
> 'All erdly joy returnis in pane.

1. Lentren] Lent.
2. Airly] Early.
3. voce] Voice. *plane]* Loudly, clearly.

2

'O man, haif mynd that thow mon pas,   5
Remembir that thow art bot as,
And sall in as revert agane:
All erdly joy returnis in pane.

3

'Haif mynd that eild ay followis yowth,
Deth followis lyfe with gaipand mowth,   10
Devoring fruct and flowring grane:
All erdly joy returnis in pane.

4

'Welth, wardly gloir and riche array
Ar all bot thornis laid in thy way,
Ourcoverd with flouris, laid for a trane: 15
All erdly joy returnis in pane.

5

'Come nevir yit May so fresche and grene,
Bot Januar come als wod and kene,
Wes nevir sic drowth bot anis come rane:
All erdly joy returnis in pane.   20

6

'Evirmair unto this warldis joy
As nerrest air succeidis noy;
Thairfoir quhen joy ma nocht remane,
His verry air succeidis, pane.

5. *haif mynd*] Be conscious. *mon pas*] Must depart.
6. *as*] Ashes, dust.
7. *in as revert*] Turn to dust.
9. *eild*] Old age.
11. *Devoring*] Devouring. *fruct*] Fruit.
13. *wardly gloir*] Worldly glory.
15. *trane*] Trap.
17. *Come*] Came. *yit*] Yet.
18. *als*] Also. *wod*] Violent. *kene*] Fierce.
19] There was never so great a drought but rain followed later.
22. *nerrest air*] Most immediate heir. *noy*] Distress.
23. *ma*] May.
24. *verry*] Rightful.

7

'Heir helth returnis in seiknes,   25
And mirth returnis in havines,
Toun in desert, forrest in plane:
All erdly joy returnis in pane.

8

'Fredome returnis in wrechitnes
And trewth returnis in dowbilnes,   30
With fenyeit wirdis to mak men fane:
All erdly joy returnis in pane.

9

'Vertew returnis in to vyce
And honour in to avaryce.
With cuvatyce is consciens slane: 35
All erdly joy returnis in pane.

10

'Sen erdly joy abydis nevir
Wirk for the joy that lestis evir,
For uder joy is all bot vane:
All erdly joy returnis in pane.'   40

25. *returnis in]* Turns into.
26. *havines]* Melancholy.
27. *plane]* Open, treeless country.
29. *Fredome]* Liberality. *wrechitnes]* Miserliness.
30. *dowbilnes]* Duplicity.
31. *fenyeit wirdis]* Deceitful words. *fane]* Glad.
35. *cuvatyce]* Covetousness.
38. *Wirk]* Work. *lestis]* Lasts.
39. *uder]* Other.

39

Bannatyne placed this first in a group of poems entitled 'the contempt of blyndit luve'. In its ironical tone it resembles Douglas's Fourth Prologue, which depicts love as a paradoxical state, 'Begynnyng with a fenȝeit faynt plesance/ Continewit in lust, and endyt with pennance.' Although there is here no fully developed personification, love is implicitly female ('scho' and 'hir'), and there are similarities to Henryson's portrait of Venus in *The Testament of Cresseid*, 218–38, which also lays great stress on the 'variance' of love. The metrical shape is demanding; there are only two rhymes throughout, on *-ance* and *-ure*. The stanza, $aaa^4b^2aaa^4b^2$, resembles the tail-rhyme stanza of 4 in arrangement of lines, but the 'tail' in this poem is shorter, containing only two beats. A similar stanza is employed in a much-copied moral poem, 'Grund the in patience' (B, f. 74^r), but in the latter the *a*-lines are shorter, with three beats rather than four.

Text: B, f. 281^r.

Authorship: 'Quod Dumbar' in B.

1

Quha will behald of luve the chance
With sweit dissavyng countenance,
In quhais fair dissimulance
    May none assure;
Quhilk is begun with inconstance   5

2. *dissavyng]* Deceitful.
3. *dissimulance]* Dissimulation.
4. *assure]* Trust.
5. *inconstance]* Inconstancy.

And endis nocht but variance.
Scho haldis with continuance
No serviture.

2

Discretioun and considerance
Ar both out of hir govirnance;   10
Quhairfoir of it the schort plesance
    May nocht indure.
Scho is so new of acquentance,
The auld gais fra remembrance.
Thus I gife our the observans   15
    Of luvis cure.

3

It is ane pount of ignorance
To lufe in sic distemperance,
Sen tyme mispendit may avance
    No creature.   20
In luve to keip allegance,
It war als nys an ordinance
As quha wald bid ane deid man dance
    In sepulture.

6. *but variance]* Without changing.
7. *continuance]* Steadfastness.
8. *serviture]* Service.
9. *considerance]* Consideration.
10. *govirnance]* Conduct.
12. *indure]* Last.
13. *acquentance]* Acquaintance.
15. *gife our]* Give up. *observans]* Performance.
16. *luvis cure]* Love's business.
17. *pount]* Sign (lit. point).
18. *distemperance]* Disordered manner.
19. *mispendit]* Ill-spent.
21. *allegance]* Allegiance.
22. *nys]* Foolish. *ordinance]* Order.

40

This is a succinct statement of the homiletic view of life as a time for choice between the stark alternatives of heaven and hell. In form it is a definition, a minor literary topos more common in love poetry. Cf. Henryson's 'Quhat art thou lufe? How sall I the dyffyne?' (*Orpheus*, 401–7); and Bawcutt 1992a: 145–6. On the rhyme-royal stanza, see **26**.

Text: MF, p. 310; collated with B, f. 75ᵛ.

Authorship: The attribution rests on MF's 'Quod Dumbar'; in B it is anonymous. There are some stylistic similarities to other poems of Dunbar (see lines 2 and 5, and notes).

> Quhat is this lyfe bot ane straucht way to deid,
> Quhilk hes a tyme to pas and nane to dwell,
> A slyding quheill us lent to seik remeid,
> A fre chois gevin to paradice or hell,
> A pray to deid, quhome vane is to repull, 5
> A schort torment for infineit glaidnes,
> Als schort ane joy for lestand hevynes.

1. straucht] Straight, direct. *deid]* Death.
2. dwell] Linger.
3. quheill] Wheel. *lent]* Granted. *remeid]* Salvation.
4. fre chois] Free choice. *gevin]* Given.
5. pray] Prey.
6. for] In return for.
7. lestand hevynes] Eternal misery.

198

41

This poem is associated with the wedding of James IV to Margaret Tudor, which took place on 8 August 1503. There is a detailed account of the festivities by the English herald Sir John Young (Leland 1774: IV, 264–300; also Mackie 1958: 90–112). Dunbar depicts Margaret as the Rose 'of cullour reid and quhyt'; this was a common figure for a woman in the courtly tradition of *Le Roman de la Rose* (cf. **59**), but here has a further topical and political significance as the particoloured rose of the Tudors, which symbolized the union of the houses of York and Lancaster. (On the popularity and ubiquity of this Tudor emblem after the accession of Henry VII, and throughout the sixteenth century, see Anglo 1992: 74–97.) James too is depicted heraldically – in triple guise as Lion, Eagle and Thistle – and is far more prominent in the poem. Its three central stanzas (13–15) are devoted to the Lion, the king's most important symbol; and at the midpoint of this highly patterned poem occurs a description of the Royal Arms of Scotland. (On the symbolic importance of the centre as the place for an image of sovereignty, 'both in the arts and in political ceremony', see Fowler 1970: 23ff.) Dunbar is complimentary, but far from sycophantic. The personified figure of Nature crowns both king and queen, but also admonishes, giving instruction in good government. The poem owes much to the tradition of dream allegory, and specifically to Chaucer's *Parliament of Fowls*, also a work possibly linked with a royal wedding. On the rhyme-royal stanza, see **26**.

Date: The poem may have been designed for presentation, or recitation, at the wedding, although there is no external evidence for this. The reference to 9 May may be symbolic rather than factual (see note to 189).

Text: B, ff. 342ᵛ–345ʳ, in the section called 'Fabillis'. Allan Ramsay, who first printed the poem in *The Ever Green* (1724), supplied the title 'The Thistle and the Rose'.
24. lark] lork B.
45. fresche and weill] hestely B.
119. *parcere]* proceir B.
135. hald] thow hald B.

Authorship: 'Quod Dumbar' in B.

Further reading: Scott 1966: 46–52 ('lightweight'); Spearing 1976: 192–7 (the dream separates 'the world of art, or poetic fiction, from the world of reality'); Ross 1981: 239–50; Bawcutt 1986b (on symbolism of lion and thistle); Fradenburg 1991: 134–49; Bawcutt 1992a: 92–103 ('an intensely feudal poem, celebrating hierarchy, rank and degree').

1

Quhen Merche wes with variand windis past,
And Appryll had with hir silver schouris
Tane leif at Nature with ane orient blast,
And lusty May, that muddir is of flouris,
Had maid the birdis to begyn thair houris   5
Amang the tendir odouris reid and quhyt,
Quhois armony to heir it was delyt –

2

In bed at morrow sleiping as I lay,
Me thocht Aurora with hir cristall ene
In at the window lukit by the day   10
And halsit me with visage paill and grene,
On quhois hand a lark sang fro the splene:
'Awalk, luvaris, out of your slomering,
Se how the lusty morrow dois up spring!'

3

Me thocht fresche May befoir my bed upstude,   15
In weid depaynt of mony divers hew,

1. *Merche*] March.
3. *Tane leif*] Taken leave (of). *orient blast*] East wind.
4. *lusty*] Beautiful. *muddir*] Mother.
5. *houris*] Church services at fixed hours.
6. *odouris*] Sweet-smelling flowers.
7. *armony*] Harmony, music.
8. *morrow*] Morning.
9. *ene*] Eyes.
10. *by the day*] At daylight.
11. *halsit*] Greeted. *grene*] Wan.
12. *fro the splene*] In a heartfelt way.
13. *Awalk*] Awake. *slomering*] Slumber.
15. *upstude*] Stood erect.
16. *weid*] Dress. *depaynt*] Coloured. *hew*] Hue.

Sobir, benyng and full of mansuetude,
In brycht atteir of flouris forgit new,
Hevinly of color, quhyt, reid, broun and blew,
Balmit in dew and gilt with Phebus bemys,　　　　20
Quhill all the hous illumynit of hir lemys.

4

'Slugird,' scho said, 'Awalk annone for schame,
And in my honour sum thing thow go wryt.
The lark hes done the mirry day proclame,
To rais up luvaris with confort and delyt,　　　　25
Yit nocht incresis thy curage to indyt,
Quhois hairt sum tyme hes glaid and blisfull bene,
Sangis to mak undir the levis grene.'

5

'Quhairto,' quod I, 'Sall I uprys at morrow?
For in this May few birdis herd I sing.　　　　30
Thai haif moir caus to weip and plane thair sorrow.
Thy air it is nocht holsum nor benyng.
Lord Eolus dois in thy sessone ring.
So busteous ar the blastis of his horne,
Amang thy bewis to walk I haif forborne.'　　　　35

6

With that this lady sobirly did smyll,
And said, 'Uprys and do thy observance.
Thow did promyt, in Mayis lusty quhyle
For to discryve the ros of most plesance.

17. *Sobir]* Mild. *benyng]* Benign. *mansuetude]* Gentleness.
18. *atteir]* Attire. *forgit]* Formed.
19. *broun]* Dark-coloured.
20. *Balmit]* Perfumed. *gilt]* Gilded. *Phebus bemys]* Sunbeams.
21. *illumynit]* Grew bright. *lemys]* Rays of light.
22. *Slugird]* Sluggard. *annone]* At once.
26. *curage]* Desire. *indyt]* Compose.
29. *Quhairto]* Why. *quod]* Said.
31. *plane]* Lament.
32. *holsum]* Healthy.
33. *sessone]* Season. *ring]* Reign.
34. *busteous]* Violent.
35. *bewis]* Branches.
36. *sobirly]* Gently. *smyll]* Smile.
38. *promyt]* Promise. *quhyle]* Season.
39. *discryve]* Describe. *ros]* Rose.

Go se the birdis how thay sing and dance,   40
Illumynit our with orient skyis brycht,
Annamyllit richely with new asur lycht.'

7

Quhen this was said departit scho, this quene,
And enterit in a lusty gairding gent,
And than me thocht, full fresche and weill besene   45
In serk and mantill, full haistely I went
In to this garth, most dulce and redolent
Of herb and flour and tendir plantis sweit,
And grene levis doing of dew doun fleit.

8

The purpour sone with tendir bemys reid   50
In orient bricht as angell did appeir,
Throw goldin skyis putting up his heid,
Quhois gilt tressis schone so wondir cleir
That all the world tuke confort, fer and neir,
To luke upone his fresche and blisfull face,   55
Doing all sable fro the hevynnis chace.

9

And as the blisfull soune of cherarchy
The fowlis song throw confort of the licht.
The birdis did with oppin vocis cry:
'O luvaris fo, away thow dully nycht,   60
And welcum day that confortis every wicht.

---

41. *Illumynit]* Illuminated, made bright. *our]* Above.
42. *Annamyllit]* Enamelled, coloured.
44. *gairding]* Garden. *gent]* Beautiful.
45. *besene]* Arrayed.
46. *serk]* Shirt.
47. *garth]* Garden. *dulce]* Sweet. *redolent]* Fragrant.
49. *doing . . . fleit]* Flowing.
50. *purpour]* Scarlet.
53. *schone]* Shone.
54. *confort]* Pleasure. *fer]* Far.
56. *Doing . . . chace]* Chasing away darkness.
57. *soune]* Sound. *cherarchy]* Angelic hierarchies.
58. *song]* Sang.
59. *oppin]* Open. *vocis]* Mouths (lit. voices).
60. *luvaris fo]* Enemy of lovers. *dully]* Dismal.
61. *wicht]* Creature.

Haill, May, haill, Flora, haill, Aurora schene!
Haill, princes Natur, haill, Venus, luvis quene!'

10

Dame Nature gaif ane inhibitioun thair
To fers Neptunus and Eolus the bawld,   65
Nocht to perturb the wattir nor the air;
And that no schouris nor blastis cawld
Effray suld flouris nor fowlis on the fold,
Scho bad eik Juno, goddas of the sky,
That scho the hevin suld keip amene and dry.   70

11

Scho ordand eik that every bird and beist
Befoir hir hienes suld annone compeir,
And every flour, of vertew most and leist,
And every herb be feild fer and neir,
As thay had wont in May fro yeir to yeir,   75
To hir thair makar to mak obediens,
Full law inclynnand with all dew reverens.

12

With that annone scho send the swyft ro
To bring in beistis of all conditioun.
The restles swallow commandit scho also   80
To feche all fowll of small and greit renown;
And to gar flouris compeir of all fassoun

62. *schene*] Beautiful.
64. *inhibitioun*] Prohibition.
65. *fers*] Fierce. *bawld*] Bold.
66. *perturb*] Throw into confusion.
68. *Effray*] Frighten. *fold*] Earth.
69. *bad*] Commanded. *goddas*] Goddess.
70. *amene*] Pleasant.
71. *ordand*] Decreed.
72. *hienes*] Highness. *compeir*] Appear.
73. *vertew*] Medicinal or magical power. *most and leist*] Greatest and lowest (in esteem).
74. *be feild*] From field.
76. *obediens*] Homage.
77. *law inclynnand*] Bowing low. *dew reverens*] Due respect.
78. *send*] Sent.
79. *conditioun*] Kind.
82. *gar*] Cause. *fassoun*] Fashion, kind.

Full craftely conjurit scho the yarrow,
Quhilk did furth swirk als swift as ony arrow.

13

All present wer in twynkling of ane e,   85
Baith beist and bird and flour befoir the quene.
And first the Lyone, gretast of degre,
Was callit thair, and he most fair to sene,
With a full hardy contenance and kene
Befoir dame Natur come and did inclyne,   90
With visage bawld and curage leonyne.

14

This awfull beist full terrible wes of cheir,
Persing of luke and stout of countenance,
Rycht strong of corpis, of fassoun fair but feir,
Lusty of schaip, lycht of deliverance,   95
Reid of his cullour as is the ruby glance.
On feild of gold he stude full mychtely,
With flour delycis sirculit lustely.

15

This lady liftit up his cluvis cleir,
And leit him listly lene upone hir kne;   100
And crownit him with dyademe full deir,
Of radyous stonis most ryall for to se,
Saying, 'The king of beistis mak I the

---

83. conjurit] Summoned (by magic). *yarrow]* Milfoil.
84. swirk] ? Dart quickly.
87. degre] Rank.
88. sene] See (archaic infin.).
89. hardy] Bold. *kene]* Fierce.
90. come] Came.
91. curage] Spirit.
92. awfull] Awe-inspiring. *cheir]* Expression.
93. Persing] Piercing *stout]* Courageous.
94. corpis] Body. *fassoun]* Build. *but feir]* Without match.
95. deliverance] Deportment.
96. ruby glance] Gleam from a ruby.
97. feild] Field, surface of shield (heraldic).
98. flour delycis] Fleur de lys (heraldic). *sirculit]* Encircled.
99. cluvis] Claws. *cleir]* Bright.
100. leit] Let. *listly]* Gracefully.
101. deir] Precious.
102. radyous] glittering. *ryall]* Royal.

And the cheif protector in woddis and schawis.
Onto thi leigis go furth and keip the lawis.   105

16

'Exerce justice with mercy and conscience,
And lat no small beist suffir skaith na skornis
Of greit beistis that bene of moir piscence.
Do law elyk to aipis and unicornis,
And lat no bowgle with his busteous hornis   110
The meik pluch ox oppres for all his pryd,
Bot in the yok go peciable him besyd.'

17

Quhen this was said, with noyis and soun of joy
All kynd of beistis in to thair degre
At onis cryit lawd: *Vive le roy!*   115
And till his feit fell with humilite,
And all thay maid him homege and fewte;
And he did thame ressaif with princely laitis,
Quhois noble yre is *parcere prostratis.*

18

Syne crownit scho the Egle king of fowlis,   120
And as steill dertis scherpit scho his pennis,
And bawd him be als just to awppis and owlis
As unto pacokkis, papingais or crennis,
And mak a law for wycht fowlis and for wrennis,

---

104. *schawis]* Groves.
105. *leigis]* Lieges, subjects.
106. *Exerce]* Exercise.
107. *skaith na skornis]* Harm nor insults.
108. *piscence]* Strength.
109. *Do law]* Enforce the law. *elyk]* Alike, impartially.
110. *bowgle]* Wild ox. *busteous]* Powerful.
111. *pluch]* Plough.
112. *peciable]* Peacefully.
114. *degre]* Rank.
115. *lawd]* Praise. *Vive le roy]* Long live the king.
117. *fewte]* Fealty.
118. *laitis]* Manners.
121. *dertis]* Spears. *scherpit]* Sharpened. *pennis]* Feathers.
122. *bawd]* Ordered. *awppis]* ? Curlews.
123. *pacokkis]* Peacocks. *papingais]* Parrots. *crennis]* Cranes.
124] And make one law for powerful birds and for weak ones, such as wrens.

And lat no fowll of ravyne do efferay,   125
Nor devoir birdis bot his awin pray.

19

Than callit scho all flouris that grew on feild,
Discirnyng all thair fassionis and effeiris.
Upone the awfull Thrissill scho beheld,
And saw him kepit with a busche of speiris.   130
Concedring him so able for the weiris,
A radius croun of rubeis scho him gaif
And said, 'In feild go furth and fend the laif.

20

'And sen thow art a king, thow be discreit.
Herb without vertew hald nocht of sic pryce   135
As herb of vertew and of odor sweit,
And lat no nettill vyle and full of vyce
Hir fallow to the gudly flour delyce,
Nor latt no wyld weid full of churlichenes
Compair hir till the lilleis nobilnes.   140

21

'Nor hald non udir flour in sic denty
As the fresche Ros of cullour reid and quhyt,
For gife thow dois, hurt is thy honesty,
Conciddering that no flour is so perfyt,
So full of vertew, plesans and delyt,   145
So full of blisfull angeilik bewty,
Imperiall birth, honour and dignite.'

---

125. ravyne] Prey. *do efferay]* Cause an affray.
126. devoir] Devour. *bot]* Except. *awin pray]* Own prey
128. Discirnyng] Examining. *fassionis]* Shapes. *effeiris]* Manners.
130. kepit] Protected. *speiris]* Spears.
131. Concedring] Considering. *able . . . weiris]* Fit for warfare.
133. feild] Battle. *fend]* Defend. *laif]* Rest (of your countrymen).
134. discreit] Prudent.
135. pryce] Value.
138. Hir fallow to] Associate with as an equal.
139. weid] Weed. *churlichenes]* Boorishness.
140. compair] Compare.
141. udir] Other. *denty]* Esteem.
143. gife] If. *honesty]* Honour.
144. perfyt] Perfect.
147. Imperiall] Exalted.

22

Than to the Ros scho turnyt hir visage,
And said, 'O lusty dochtir most benyng,
Aboif the lilly illustare of lynnage,   150
Fro the stok ryell rysing fresche and ying,
But ony spot or macull doing spring,
Cum, blowme of joy, with jemis to be cround,
For our the laif thy bewty is renownd.'

23

A coistly croun with clarefeid stonis brycht   155
This cumly quene did on hir heid inclois,
Quhill all the land illumynit of the licht;
Quhairfoir me thocht all flouris did rejos,
Crying attonis, 'Haill be thow richest Ros,
Haill, hairbis empryce, haill, freschest quene of flouris! 160
To the be glory and honour at all houris.'

24

Thane all the birdis song with voce on hicht,
Quhois mirthfull soun wes mervelus to heir.
The mavys song, 'Haill, Rois most riche and richt
That dois up flureis undir Phebus speir.   165
Haill, plant of yowth, haill, princes dochtir deir,
Haill, blosome breking out of the blud royall
Quhois pretius vertew is imperiall.'

149. *dochtir*] Daughter.
150. *illustare*] Illustrious.
151. *stok*] Stock, ancestry. *ryell*] Royal. *ying*] Young.
152. *But*] Without. *macull*] Blemish.
153. *blowme*] Flower. *jemis*] Gems.
154. *our*] Above. *laif*] Rest (of women).
155. *clarefeid*] Polished.
156. *inclois*] Encircle.
159. *attonis*] Together.
160. *hairbis empryce*] Empress of plants.
162. *song*] Sang.
164. *mavys*] Thrush.
165. *flureis*] Flourish. *Phebus speir*] Sphere of the sun.
166. *princes*] Prince's.
167. *breking*] Springing. *blud*] Race.

25

The merle scho sang, 'Haill, Rois of most delyt,
Haill, of all flouris quene and soverane!'   170
The lark scho song, 'Haill, Rois both reid and quhyt,
Most plesand flour of michty cullouris twane!'
The nychtingaill song, 'Haill, Naturis suffragene,
In bewty, nurtour and every nobilnes,
In riche array, renown and gentilnes.'   175

26

The commoun voce uprais of birdis small,
Apone this wys: 'O blissit be the hour
That thow wes chosin to be our principall.
Welcome to be our princes of honour,
Our perle, our plesans and our paramour,   180
Our peax, our play, our plane felicite.
Chryst the conserf frome all adversite!'

27

Than all the birdis song with sic a schout
That I annone awoilk quhair that I lay,
And with a braid I turnyt me about   185
To se this court, bot all wer went away.
Than up I lenyt halflingis in affrey,
And thus I wret, as ye haif hard toforrow,
Of lusty May upone the nynt morrow.

169. *merle]* Blackbird.
172. *twane]* Two.
173. *suffragene]* Deputy.
174. *nurtour]* Good breeding.
175. *gentilnes]* Nobility.
177. *blissit]* Blessed.
178. *principall]* Ruler.
180. *perle]* Pearl. *paramour]* Beloved.
181. *peax]* Peace. *play]* Delight. *plane]* Full.
182. *conserf]* Protect.
184. *awoilk]* Awoke.
185. *braid]* Start.
186. *went]* Gone.
187. *lenyt]* Rose. *halflingis]* Half. *affrey]* Fear.
188. *wret]* Wrote. *hard]* Heard. *toforrow]* Before.
189. *nynt]* Ninth.

42

This poem contains a wealth of vivid details concerning the noise and squalor in the crowded streets of late-medieval Edinburgh, but its purpose is not primarily descriptive. Hortatory in tone, it calls on the great merchants to reform the administration of their burgh. Dunbar appeals to their civic pride (note the repeated antithesis between *schame* and *name*), their self-interest (e.g. in 62–3) and, above all, to orthodox morality: the private gain of individuals should give way to the good of the community (71–2). The topics and even the phrasing are similar to those employed by the merchants themselves, as preserved in the burgh records of Edinburgh. The poem is rhetorically striking, with much use of *interrogatio* and *repetitio*. The unusual stanza – $aaab^4b^2ab^4$ – has two variable refrains, and is handled with great virtuosity.

Text: R, ff. 1^v–2^v. This is a late and imperfect copy, containing obvious errors, and a lacuna in the final line.
17. foirstairis] foirstair R.
25. Jame] James R.
37. streitis] streit R.
67. proclame] proclameid R.

Authorship: 'Quod Dumbar' in R.

Further reading: On medieval Scottish burghs, see Dickinson 1977: 278–98, and Lynch *et al.* 1988; for Edinburgh, see the first chapter of Lynch 1981. On this poem, see Ross 1981: 139–41; Bawcutt 1992a: 45–7, and 150–53.

1

Quhy will ye, merchantis of renoun,
Lat Edinburgh, your nobill toun,

1. renoun] Repute.
2. Lat] Let.

For laik of reformatioun
The commone proffeitt tyine and fame?
   Think ye not schame   5
That onie uther regioun
Sall with dishonour hurt your name?

2

May nane pas throw your principall gaittis,
For stink of haddockis and of scattis,
For cryis of carlingis and debaittis,   10
For feusum flyttingis of defame.
   Think ye not schame,
Befoir strangeris of all estaittis,
That sic dishonour hurt your name?

3

Your Stinkand Stull, that standis dirk,   15
Haldis the lycht fra your parroche kirk.
Your foirstairis makis your housis mirk,
Lyk na cuntray bot heir at hame.
   Think ye not schame,
Sa litill polesie to work,   20
In hurt and sklander of your name?

4

At your hie Croce, quhar gold and silk
Sould be, thair is bot crudis and milk,

---

3. *laik*] Lack.
4.] Lose the prosperity of the community and its reputation.
5. *Think . . . schame*] Feel shame.
6. *regioun*] Country.
8. *gaittis*] Streets
9. *scattis*] Skate (fish).
10. *carlingis*] Old women. *debaittis*] Quarrels.
11. *feusum*] Foul, offensive. *defame*] Defamation.
13. *estaittis*] Ranks
14. *sic*] Such.
15. *Stull*] *See note. dirk*] Dark.
16. *Haldis*] Keeps. *parroche kirk*] Parish church.
17. *mirk*] Gloomy.
18. *hame*] Home.
20. *polesie*] Improvement.
21. *sklander*] Slander.
22. *hie*] High. *Croce*] Market cross.
23. *crudis*] Curds.

And at your Trone bot cokill and wilk,
Pansches, pudingis of Jok and Jame.   25
   Think ye not schame,
Sen as the world sayis that ilk,
In hurt and sclander of your name?

5

Your commone menstrallis hes no tone
Bot 'Now the day dawis' and 'Into Joun'.   30
Cunningar men man serve sanct Cloun,
And nevir to uther craftis clame.
   Think ye not schame,
To hald sic mowaris on the moyne,
In hurt and sclander of your name?   35

6

Tailyouris, soutteris and craftis vyll
The fairest of your streitis dois fyll,
And merchandis at the Stinkand Styll
Ar hamperit in ane hony came.
   Think ye not schame   40
That ye have nether witt nor wyll,
To win yourselff ane bettir name?

7

Your burgh of beggeris is ane nest,
To schout thai swentyouris will not rest.
All honest folk they do molest,   45
Sa piteuslie thai cry and rame.
   Think ye not schame,
That for the poore hes nothing drest,
In hurt and sclander of your name?

24. *Trone]* *See note.* *cokill]* Cockles. *wilk]* Whelks.
25. *Pansches]* Tripes. *pudingis]* Sausages.
27.] Since the whole world makes the same disgraceful charge.
29. *commone]* Public. *tone]* Tune.
30. *dawis]* Dawns. *Joun]* June.
31. *Cunningar]* More skilled. *man]* Must.
32. *craftis]* Occupations. *clame]* Claim the right.
36. *Tailyouris]* Tailors. *soutteris]* Cobblers. *vyll]* Vile, base.
37. *fyll]* Defile.
39. *hamperit]* Confined. *hony came]* Honeycomb.
41. *witt]* good sense. *wyll]* Guile, subtlety.
44. *thai swentyouris]* Those scoundrels.
46. *piteuslie]* Pitifully. *rame]* Clamour.
48. *nothing drest]* Made no provision.

8

Your proffeit daylie dois incres,   50
Your godlie workis les and les.
Through streittis nane may mak progres,
For cry of cruikit, blind and lame.
    Think ye not schame,
That ye sic substance dois possess,   55
And will not win ane bettir name?

9

Sen for the court and the Sessioun,
The great repair of this regioun
Is in your burgh, thairfoir be boun
To mend all faultis that ar to blame,   60
    And eschew schame.
Gif thai pas to ane uther toun,
Ye will decay and your great name.

10

Thairfoir strangeris and leigis treit,
Tak not over mekill for thair meit,   65
And gar your merchandis be discreit.
That na extortiounes be, proclame
    All fraud and schame.
Keip ordour and poore nighbouris beit,
That ye may gett ane bettir name.   70

50. *incres]* Increase.
51.] Your virtuous deeds are fewer and fewer.
52. *mak progres]* Pass red, move.
53. *cruikit]* Crippled.
55. *substance]* Wealth.
57. *Sessioun]* Court of justice.
58. *repair]* Resort.
59. *boun]* Prepared.
60. *mend]* Amend.
61. *eschew]* Avoid.
62. *Gif]* If.
64. *leigis]* Subjects. *treit]* Welcome.
65. *mekill]* Much. *meit]* Food.
66. *gar]* Cause. *discreit]* Wise.
67–8.] See note.
69. *nighbouris]* Citizens. *beit]* Assist.

11

Singular proffeit so dois yow blind,
The common proffeit gois behind.
I pray that lord remeid to fynd
That deit into Jerusalem,
    And gar yow schame,   75
That sumtyme ressoun may yow bind,
For to . . . yow guid name.

72. *gois behind]* Is disregarded.
73. *remeid]* Remedy.
74. *deit]* Died.
75. *schame]* Feel shame.
76.] That in the future reason may govern you.

43

The praise of content was a common topic for medieval moralists, and often figured in sermons (see Owst 1961: 296ff.). It had the sanction of St Paul (Philippians 4: 11, and I Timothy 6: 6–8), and was a moral theme inherent in the popular fable of the Town Mouse and the Country Mouse, treated by Lydgate and Henryson. Dunbar's tone is hortatory, and his style is strikingly proverbial. On the stanza, see **9**.

Text: MF, p. 307; collated with R, ff. 5^r–5^v.
11. Quhairfoir . . . brother] R; Thairfoir I pray yow bredir MF.
12. Not servit be with] R; Not to delyt in MF.
18. maist sall] R; sall sonast it MF.
28. nane] R; not MF. be lent] R; imprent MF.
33. neidfullest in] R; moist nedy of MF.
34. is his] R; he hes MF.

Authorship: 'Quod Dumbar' in MF and R.

Further reading: Bawcutt 1992a: 142–3.

1

    Quho thinkis that he hes sufficence
    Of gudis hes no indigence.
    Thocht he have nowder land nor rent,

1. Quho] Whoever. *sufficence]* Sufficiency.
2. gudis] Possessions. *indigence]* Poverty.
3. Thocht] Although. *nowder]* Neither. *rent]* Income.

214

Grit mycht nor hie magnificence,
He hes anewch that is content.   5

2

Quho had all riches unto Ynd,
And wer not satefeit in mynd,
With povertie I hald him schent –
Of covatyce sic is the kynd.
He hes anewch that is content.   10

3

Quhairfoir, thocht thow, my brother deir,
Not servit be with daynteis seir,
Thank God of it is to the sent,
And of it glaidlie mak gud cheir.
Anewch he hes that is content.   15

4

Defy the warld, feynyeit and fals,
Withe gall in hart and hunyt hals.
Quha maist it servis maist sall repent;
Of quhais subchettis sour is the sals.
He hes aneuch that is content.   20

5

Giff thow hes mycht, be gentill and fre,
And gif thow standis in povertie,
Of thine awin will to it consent
And riches sall returne to the.
He hes aneuch that is content.   25

4. *mycht]* Wealth. *magnificence]* Pomp.
5. *anewch]* Enough.
6. *Ynd]* India.
7. *satefeit]* Contented.
8. *hald]* Consider. *schent]* Injured.
9. *covatyce]* Covetousness. *sic]* Such. *kynd]* Nature.
12. *servit]* Provided. *daynteis seir]* Various luxuries.
14. *mak gud cheir]* Take great pleasure (in).
16. *Defy]* Renounce. *feynyeit]* Deceitful.
17. *gall]* Rancour. *hunyt]* Honeyed. *hals]* Voice (lit. throat).
19. *sals]* Sauce.
21] If you have the resources, be generous and bountiful.
23] Accept it willingly.

6

And ye and I, my bredir all,
That in this lyfe hes lordschip small,
Lat langour nane in us be lent.
Gif we not clym, we tak no fall.
He hes aneuch that is content.   30

7

For quho in warld moist covatus is
In warld is purast man, I wis,
And neidfullest in his intent.
For of all gudis no thing is his,
That of no thing can be content.   35

---

26. *bredir]* Brothers.
27. *lordschip small]* Little property.
28] Let no unhappiness be present in us.
29. *clym]* Climb.
32. *purast]* Poorest. *I wis]* Indeed.
33. *neidfullest]* Most impoverished. *intent]* Mind.

44

There are several strands in this complex poem. Although not explicitly addressed to the king, a petitionary element is evident in the references to long service (7), unjust bestowal of benefices (24), and princes' lack of compassion (29). This mingles with a more general complaint concerning the evils of the times, and of the court in particular (21); for a similar tone and technique, see 7 and 63. But the second half of this poem, which contemplates the end of 'this warld' and the imminence of the Last Judgment, is apocalyptic in tone, and as devout as 16. What begins, apparently, as a veiled petition to an earthly 'Lord', ends as a solemn prayer for God's mercy. Stylistically, the poem is characterized by effective use of personification, echoes of the liturgy and a striking use of *interrogatio*, or rhetorical questions. On the stanza, see 9.

Text: MF, pp. 331–3; collated with B, ff. 84^r–85^r, and R, ff. 40^v–42^r.
9. bigone] B; bigane MF.
40. this] B; the MF.
54. than] B; *not in* MF.
62. gold gadderit] gadderit gold MF; the gold gatherit B.
81. in] B; the MF.

Authorship: 'Quod Dumbar' in MF and B.

Further reading: Ross 1981: 142–3; Bawcutt 1992a: 161–4.

1

Quhom to sall I compleine my wo
And kythe my cairis, ane or mo?

1. compleine] Lament.
2. kythe] Reveal. *cairis]* Sorrows. *mo]* More.

I knaw not amang riche or pure,
Quha is my freind, quha is my fo,
For in this warld may none assure.   5

2

Lord, how sall I my dayis dispone?
For lang service rewarde is none,
And schort my lyfe may heir indure,
And losit is my tyme bigone:
In to this warld may none assure.   10

3

Oft falsatt rydis with a rowtt,
Quhone treuthe gois on his fute about,
And laik of spending dois him spure.
Thus quhat to do I am in doutt:
In to this warld may none assure.   15

4

Nane heir bot rich men hes renown,
And pure men ar plukit doun,
And nane bot just men tholis injure,
Swa wit is blyndit and ressoun,
For in this warld may none assure.   20

5

Vertew the court hes done dispys.
A rebald to renoun dois rys,
And carlis of nobillis hes the cure,

3. *knaw*] Know. *pure*] Poor.
4. *freind*] Friend.
6. *dispone*] Dispose.
8. *schort*] A short time. *indure*] Last.
9. *losit*] Wasted. *bigone*] Past.
11. *falsatt*] Falsehood. *rowtt*] Retinue.
12. *treuthe*] Truth. *on his fute*] On foot.
13. *laik*] Lack. *spending*] Spending-money. *spure*] Spur.
14. *doutt*] Doubt.
16. *renown*] Honour.
17. *plukit doun*] Humiliated.
18. *tholis*] Suffer. *injure*] Injury.
19. *wit*] Understanding.
21. *Vertew*] Virtue. *done dispys*] Despised.
22. *rebald*] Rascal.
23] And peasants have authority over noblemen.

And bumbardis brukis benefys:
So in this warld may none assure.   25

6

All gentrice and nobilite
Ar passit out of hie degre.
On fredome is led foirfalture,
In princis is thair no petie:
So in this warld may none assure.   30

7

Is none so armit in to plait
That can fra trouble him debait.
May no man lang in welthe indure,
For wo that lyis ever at the wait:
So in this warld may none assure.   35

8

Flattrie weiris ane furrit goun,
And falsate with the lordis dois roun,
And trewthe standis barrit at the dure,
Exylit is honour of the toun:
So in this warld may none assure.   40

9

Fra everie mouthe fair wordis procedis,
In everie harte deceptioun bredis,
Fra everie e gois lukis demure,
Bot fra the handis gois few gud deidis:
Sa in this warld may none assure.   45

24] And indolent louts acquire benefices.
26–7] People no longer manifest the virtues traditionally associated with those of high rank.
28. fredome] Liberality. *led]* Laid. *foirfalture]* Forfeiture.
29. petie] Compassion.
31. plait] Plate armour.
32. debait] Defend.
33. welthe] Prosperity.
34. at the wait] In ambush.
37. roun] Whisper.
38. barrit] Shut out. *dure]* Door.
39. Exylit] Exiled.
41. procedis] Come forth.
42. bredis] Exists.
43. e] Eye. *lukis demure]* Grave looks.

10

Towngis now ar maid of quhite quhale bone,
And hartis ar maid of hard flynt stone,
And eyn ar maid of blew asure,
And handis of adamant, laithe to dispone:
So in this warld may none assure.   50

11

Yit hart and handis and body all
Mon anser Dethe quhone he dois call
To compt befoir the juge future.
Sen all ar deid or than de sall,
Quha sould in to this warld assure?   55

12

No thing bot deithe this schortlie cravis,
Quhair Fortoun ever as fo dissavis,
Withe freyndlie smylingis lyk ane hure,
Quhais fals behechtis as wind hyne wavis:
So in this warld may none assure.   60

13

O quho sall weild the wrang possessioun,
Or gold gadderit with oppressioun,
Quhone the angell blawis his bugill sture,
Quhilk onrestorit, helpis no confessioun?
In to this warld may none assure.   65

---

46. *Towngis]* Tongues. *quhale bone]* Whale bone, walrus ivory.
48. *eyn]* Eyes. *blew asure]* Blue lapis lazuli.
49. *laithe]* Reluctant. *dispone]* Hand over.
52. *Mon anser]* Must answer
53. *compt]* Account. *juge]* Judge.
54. *Sen]* Since. *deid]* Dead. *de]* Die.
57. *dissavis]* Deceives.
58. *smylingis]* Smiles. *hure]* Whore.
59. *behechtis]* Promises. *hyne wavis]* Pass away.
61. *weild]* Enjoy. *wrang possessioun]* Wrongfully acquired goods.
62. *gadderit]* Gathered. *oppressioun]* Extortion.
63. *blawis]* Blows. *bugill]* Trumpet. *sture]* Loudly.
64. *onrestorit]* Unrestored.

14

Quhat help is thair in lordschips sevin,
Quhone na hous is bot hell and hevin,
Palice of lycht or pit obscure,
Quhair yowlis ar with horrible stevin?
In to this warld may none assure.   70

15

Ubi ardentes anime
Semper dicentes sunt, Ve Ve!
Sall cry, allace, that women thame bure.
O quante sunt iste tenebre!
In to this warld may none assure.   75

16

Than quho sall wirk for warldis wrak,
Quhone flude and fyre sall our it frak
And frelie frustir feild and fure,
With tempest keyne and thundir crak?
In to this warld may none assure.   80

17

Lord, sen in tyme sa sone to cum
De terra surrecturus sum,
Rewarde me with na erthlie cure;
Bot me ressave *in regnum tuum*,
Sen in this warld may none assure.   85

---

66. *lordschips]* Landed estates.
67. *hous]* Dwelling.
68. *obscure]* Dark.
69. *yowlis]* Howls. *stevin]* Sound.
73. *bure]* Bore.
76. *wirk]* Toil. *wrak]* Dross (of wealth).
77. *flude]* Flood. *frak]* Move swiftly.
78] And without restraint lay waste field and furrow.
79. *keyne]* Fierce. *crak]* Explosion.
82] I shall rise again from the earth.
83. *cure]* Church living.
84] But receive me into thy kingdom.

45

The Ballade of Barnard Stewart

The subject of this poem is Bernard Stewart (*c.* 1452–1508), third seigneur d'Aubigny, whose grandfather, Sir John Stewart of Darnley, entered the service of the French in 1422 and was rewarded with estates in France. Bernard (in French usually known as *Bérault*) Stewart had a very distinguished military career. He was captain of the Scots Guard, and successively served three French kings, Louis XI, Charles VIII and Louis XII. He assisted Henry VII at the battle of Bosworth (1485), but his most famous exploits were in Italy. He served Charles VIII in the first expedition to Rome and Naples (1494), and was briefly governor of Calabria. Under Louis XII he led an army against Milan in 1499, and another, ultimately disastrous expedition to Naples. Contemporary historians and chroniclers praised Stewart's courage and skill as a commander, and his wisdom as a diplomat.

This poem can be dated precisely since it was composed to welcome Bernard Stewart when he arrived in Scotland in May 1508, on a diplomatic mission. Stewart died shortly after his arrival; for Dunbar's elegy on him, see 18. The complimentary address to a visiting prince or magnate was a type of panegyric very common in the Middle Ages. This piece is characteristic in its use of hyperbole, *repetitio*, and other rhetorical topoi and figures. On the stanza, see 6.

Text: CM.

Further reading: On Bernard Stewart, see Gray 1974; and De Comminges 1976. On the poem, see Ross 1981: 150–52; and Bawcutt 1992a: 82–4 (use of 'eulogistic commonplaces').

The ballade of ane right noble victorius and myghty lord, Barnard Stewart, lord of Aubigny, erle of Beaumont Roger and Bonaffre, consaloure and chamerlane ordinare to the maist hee, maist excellent and maiste crystyn prince Loys, king of France, knyght of his ordoure, capitane of the kepyng of his body, conquereur of Naplis and umquhile

constable general of the same. Compilit be Maistir Willyam Dumbar at
the said lordis cumyng to Edinburghe in Scotland send in ane ryght
excellent embassat fra the said maist crystin king to our maist souverane
lord and victorius prince, James the ferde kyng of Scottis.

1

Renownit, ryall, right reverend and serene,
Lord hie tryumphing in wirschip and valoure,
Fro kyngis downe most cristin knight and kene,
Most wyse, most valyand, moste laureat hie victour,
Onto the sterris upheyt is thyne honour.   5
In Scotland welcum be thyne excellence
To king, queyne, lord, clerk, knight and servatour,
Withe glorie and honour, lawde and reverence.

2

Welcum, in stour most strong, incomparable knight,
The fame of armys and floure of vassalage,   10
Welcum, in were moste worthi, wyse and wight,
Welcum, the soun of Mars of moste curage,
Welcum, moste lusti branche of our linnage,
In every realme oure scheild and our defence,
Welcum, our tendir blude of hie parage,   15
With glorie and honour, lawde and reverence.

3

Welcum, in were the secund Julius,
The prince of knightheyd and flour of chevalry,
Welcum, most valyeant and victorius,
Welcum, invincible victour moste wourthy,   20

Title. umquhile] Formerly. *embassat]* Embassy.
1. ryall] Royal. *reverend]* Revered.
2. wirschip] Honour.
3. downe] Descended. *cristin]* Christian. *kene]* Bold.
4. valyand] Valiant. *laureat]* Worthy of the laurel crown.
5. sterris] Stars. *upheyt]* Exalted.
7. clerk] Scholar. *servatour]* Servant.
8. lawde] Praise.
9. stour] Combat.
10. armys] Warfare. *vassalage]* Military prowess.
11. were] War. *wight]* Courageous.
12. soun] Son.
13. lusti] Vigorous. *linnage]* Lineage.
15. tendir] Closely related. *blude]* Kinsman. *parage]* Rank.
18. knightheyd] Knighthood.

Welcum, our Scottis chiftane most dughti,
With sowne of clarioun, organe, song and sence.
To the atonis, lord, 'Welcum!', all we cry,
With glorie and honour, lawde and reverence.

4

Welcum, oure indeficient adjutorie,   25
That evir our naceoun helpit in thare neyd,
That never saw Scot yit indigent nor sory
Bot thou did hym suport with thi gud deid.
Welcum, therfor, abufe all livand leyd,
Withe us to live and to maik recidence,   30
Quhilk never sall sunye for thi saik to bleid,
To quham be honour, lawde and reverence.

5

Is none of Scotland borne fathfull and kynde,
Bot he of naturall inclinacioune
Dois favour the withe all his hert and mynde,   35
Withe fervent, tendir, trew intencioun
And wald of inwart hie effectioun,
But dreyd of danger, de in thi defence,
Or dethe or schame war done to thi persoun,
To quham be honour, lawde and reverence.   40

6

Welcum, thow knight moste fortunable in feild,
Welcum, in armis moste aunterus and able
Undir the soun that beris helme or scheild,
Welcum, thow campioun in feght unourcumable,

---

21. *Scottis chiftane]* Scottish leader. *dughti]* Doughty.
22. *sowne]* Sound *clarioun]* Trumpet. *sence]* Incense.
23. *the]* thee. *atonis]* In unison.
25. *indeficient adjutorie]* Unfailing assistance.
27. *sory]* In distress.
29. *livand leyd]* Living creature.
30. *maik recidence]* Reside.
31. *sunye]* Hesitate.
37. *inwart]* Heartfelt.
38. *But]* Without. *de]* Die.
39. *Or]* Before.
41. *fortunable]* Successful. *feild]* Battle.
42. *aunterus]* Adventurous. *able]* Skilled.
43. *soun]* sun. *helme]* Helmet.
44. *campioun]* Champion. *unourcumable]* Unbeatable.

Welcum, most dughti, digne and honorable,   45
And moist of lawde and hie magnificence,
Nixt undir kingis to stand incomparable,
To quham be honour, lawde and reverence.

7

Throw Scotland, Ingland, France and Lumbardy
Fleys on weyng thi fame and thi renoune,   50
And our all cuntreis undirnethe the sky,
And our all strandis fro the sterris doune.
In every province, land and regioun
Proclamit is thi name of excellence,
In every cete, village and in toune,   55
Withe gloire and honour, lawd and reverence.

8

O feyrse Achill in furius hie curage,
O strong, invincible Hector undir scheild,
O vailyeant Arthur in knyghtli vassalage,
Agamenon in governance of feild,   60
Bold Henniball in batall to do beild,
Julius in jupert in wisdom and expence,
Most fortunable chiftane bothe in yhouth and eild,
To the be honour, lawde and reverence.

9

At parlament thow suld be hye renownit,   65
That did so mony victoryse opteyn.
Thi cristall helme withe lawry suld be crownyt,
And in thi hand a branche of olyve greyn.
The sweird of conquis and of knyghtheid keyn

---

45. *digne]* Worthy.
50. *Fleys]* Flies. *weyng]* Wing.
51. *our]* Over.
52. *strandis]* Shores.
55. *cete]* City.
57. *feyrse* Fierce. *furius]* Enraged.
60. *governance]* Rule, control.
61. *beild]* Brave deeds.
62. *jupert]* Daring, audacity. *expence]* Expenditure.
63. *eild]* Age.
66. *opteyn]* Obtain.
67. *cristall]* Bright as crystal. *lawry]* Laurel.
69. *conquis]* Conquest.

Be borne suld highe before the in presence,   70
To represent sic man as thou has beyn,
With glorie and honour, lawde and reverence.

10

Hie furius Mars, the god armipotent,
Rong in the hevin at thyne nativite.
Saturnus doune withe fyry eyn did blent   75
Throw bludy visar men manasing to gar de.
On the fresche Venus keist hir amourouse e,
On the Marcurius furtheyet his eloquence.
Fortuna major did turn hir face on the,
Wyth glorie and honour, lawde and reverence.   80

11

Prynce of fredom and flour of gentilnes,
Sweyrd of knightheid and choise of chevalry,
This tyme I lefe, for grete prolixitnes,
To tell quhat feildis thow wan in Pikkardy,
In France, in Bertan, in Naplis and Lumbardy,   85
As I think eftir withe all my diligence,
Or thow departe, at lenthe for to discry,
With glorie and honour, lawd and reverence.

12

B in thi name betaknis batalrus,
A able in feild, R right renoune most hie,   90
N nobilnes and A for aunterus,
R ryall blude, for dughtines is D,
V valyeantnes, S for strenewite:

71] To indicate what sort of man you have been.
74. Rong] Reigned. *nativite]* Birth.
75. eyn] Eyes. *blent]* Glance.
76. visar] Vizard, front of helmet. *manasing]* Threatening.
78. furtheyet] Poured down.
81. fredom] Liberality.
82. choise] Choice, the most excellent.
83. lefe] Cease. *prolixitnes]* Prolixity.
84. wan] Won.
87. Or] Before. *Discry]* Describe.
89. betaknis] Signifies. *batalrus]* Bellicose.
90. right] True.
92. dughtines] Courage.
93. strenewite] Vigour, energy.

Quhoise knyghtli name so schynyng in clemence,
For wourthines in gold suld writtin be,   95
With glorie and honour, lawd and reverence.

94. *clemence]* Clemency.

46

Dunbar depicts two women carousing and making fun of their husbands. There are several English examples of this minor comic genre, of which the best are the fifteenth-century carol 'How, gossip myne, gossip myn, / Whan will we go to the wyne?' (Greene, *Carols*, no. 419), and Skelton's *The Tunning of Elinor Rumming*. By setting the incident on Ash Wednesday Dunbar introduces a further theme, which occurs in sermons: the ingenious quibbles by which people attempt to evade the Lenten fast. The poem is simply but neatly structured. On the stanza, very popular with Dunbar, see **9**.

Text: Ab II, p. 460; collated with B, f. 137^r; MF, pp. 57–8; and R, f. 19^v. Note the spellings characteristic of this text, with otiose final *e*: *one*, 'on' (1, 6), *ande* (4), *Ale*, 'all' (13, 22); *youe*, 'you' (18).
19. husband] B, MF; susband Ab.
22. is] B, MF; Ale Ab.
24. me to] B, MF; to me Ab.

Authorship: 'Quod Dumbar' in Ab, B, MF and R.

Further reading: On the 'gossips' meeting' genre, see Robbins 1969. Critics differ over the poem's seriousness: see Scott 1966; 65–7 ('an irreverent joke'); Reiss 1979: 85–6 ('an ironic statement of the misuse of this time of penance'); Bawcutt 1992a: 214–15 ('the irony is obvious, but deft and amusing').

1

Richt arely one Ask Wedinsday
Drinkande the wyne sat cummaris twa.
The tane couthe to the tothir complene,

1. arely] Early. *one*] On. *Ask*] Ash.
3] The one complained to the other.

228

Granand ande suppand couth sche say:
'This lang Lentrin it makis me lene.'   5

2

One couch befor the fyir sche sat.
God wait gif sche was gret and fat,
Yet to be feble sche did hir fene.
Ay sche said, 'Cummar, lat preif of that,
This lang Lentrin it makis me lene.'   10

3

'My fair swet cummar,' quod the tothir,
'Ye tak that megirnes of your modir.
Ale wyne to tast sche wald disdene
Bot malvasy, and nay drink uthir.
This lang Lentryn it makis me lene.   15

4

'Cummar, be glaid baith evin and morrow,
The gud quhar euere ye beg or borrow.
Fra our lang fasting youe refrene,
And lat your husband dre the sorrow.
This lang Lentryn it makis me lene.'   20

5

'Your counsaile, commar, is gud,' quod sche.
'Ale is to tene him that I do;
In bed he is nocht worth ane bane.
File anis the glas and drink me to.
This lang Lentryn it makis me lene.'   25

---

4. *Granand]* Groaning. *suppand]* Sipping.
5. *Lentrin]* Lent. *lene]* Thin.
7. *wait]* knows. *gret]* Large.
8. *hir fene]* Pretend.
9. *lat preif]* Let us prove the truth.
11. *swet]* Sweet. *quod]* Said.
12. *tak]* Inherit. *megirnes]* Slenderness. *modir]* Mother.
13. *Ale]* All. *disdene]* Disdain.
14. *malvasy]* Malmsey. *nay]* Not.
16. *evin]* Eve. *morrow]* Morning.
17] Wherever and however you obtain the good things of life.
18. *youe refrene]* Abstain.
19. *dre]* Endure.
22. *tene]* Annoy.
23. *bane]* Bean.
24. *File]* Fill. *anis]* Once.

6

Of wyne out of ane chopin stoip
Thai drank twa quartis, bot soip and soip,
Of droucht sic axis did thame strene.
Be thane to mend thai hed gud hoip:
That lang Lentrin suld nocht mak thaim lene.   30

26. *chopin stoip*] Cup holding half a pint.
27] They drank two quarts (four pints), sipping in turn.
28. *droucht*] Thirst. *sic axis*] Such excess. *strene*] Afflict.
29. *thane*] Then. *mend*] Improve in health. *hoip*] Hope.

47

The Goldyn Targe

The Goldyn Targe combines themes and motifs that had been popular in medieval courtly verse for centuries: a dreaming poet, an idyllic May-morning setting, and an allegorical story, in which love overpowers reason. Out of such traditional elements Dunbar made something new and brilliant that much impressed his contemporaries; the poem was printed in his own lifetime, singled out for praise by Lindsay (*Papyngo*, 17–18) and imitated by later sixteenth-century Scottish poets. The allegorical plot is brief and comparatively simple: the dreamer discovers a familiar truth, that love is passionate, painful and anti-rational. He views this paradoxical experience with irony, and wakes with relief, as from a nightmare. What is remarkable about the poem is not simply the jewelled artifice of the opening dawn description, for which it has long been famous, but its intricate structure and subtle interweaving of themes, motifs and imagery. One of these is the use of art terms, such as gold, enamel, 'ourgilt' (27) and 'depaynt' (40); another is the recurrent symbolism of clothing (7, 12, 42, 58–62, 87–90, 139 and 278); even more important is the pervasive imagery of light, which links the first line with the last, and lends force to the climactic parallel between the sun and Chaucer, 'of oure Inglisch all the lycht' (259). This network of metaphor and verbal echoes is more than decorative; it implies a world full of symbolic analogies between nature, love and poetry. The poem contains two important passages that reveal something of Dunbar's attitude to poetry (64–72 and 253–79). The tribute to Chaucer is reinforced by the use of 'southern' forms and words (see Introduction, p. 13); by echoes and allusions to Chaucer's poems (see 15, 18, 39, 76, 77, 120, 262 and 271); and by the elaborate nine-line stanza, *aabaabbab⁵*. This stanza, first used for the complaint in *Anelida and Arcite*, became very popular with Scottish poets in the late fifteenth century, especially for inset complaints (cf. Henryson, *Testament of Cresseid*, 407–69); but Dunbar was probably the first to use it for a complete poem. Poem **41**, which precedes *The Goldyn Targe* in B, has many affinities of style and is similarly indebted to the Chaucerian tradition.

Date: The poem was printed *c.* 1508, but is likely to have been written much earlier. The modesty topos (271–9) may reflect Dunbar's comparative youth.

231

Although the precise date is uncertain, I would conjecturally assign the poem to the 1490s, since Douglas's *Palice of Honour* (*c.* 1501) seems to show its influence.

Text: CM; collated with B, ff. 345^r–348^v; and MF, pp. 64–6, 73–7, and 81.
14. schuke] B, MF; schake CM.
16. Depart] B, MF; To part CM.
19. hoppis] B, MF; happis CM.
32. The] B, MF; That CM.
140. bowis] B, MF; lowis CM.
187. anker] B, MF; ankers CM.
201. assayit] B, MF; assayes CM.
203. Quhill] B, MF; Quhilk CM.
228. tuke] B, MF; take CM.
231. toschuke] B, MF; toschake CM.
254. ane] and CM, B, MF.
274. hes spent] B; may spent CM; may spend MF.

Title: 'Here begynnys ane litil tretie intitulit the goldyn targe compilit be Maister Wilyam Dunbar' in CM. 'Explicit the goldin targe compylit be maister William Dunbar' in MF.

Further reading: The style and significance of this poem have provoked much critical debate. Lewis (1936: 252) finds the allegory of slight importance; Cruttwell (1954) attacks the artifice of the diction; Fox (1959) sees it primarily as 'a poem about poetry'; Lyall (1974a) finds in it a subtle 'moral argument'. See also Ebin 1972; Shuffelton 1975; Ross 1981: 250–69; and Bawcutt 1992a: 307–15.

1

> Ryght as the stern of day begouth to schyne,
> Quhen gone to bed war Vesper and Lucyne,
> I raise and by a rosere did me rest.
> Up sprang the goldyn candill matutyne,
> With clere depurit bemes cristallyne,   5
> Glading the mery foulis in thair nest.
> Or Phebus was in purpur cape revest

1. *Ryght*] Just. *stern*] Star. *begouth*] Began.
3. *raise*] Rose. *rosere*] Rose bush. *me rest*] Pause.
4. *matutyne*] Of the morning.
5. *depurit*] Pure.
6. *Glading*] Gladdening.
7] Before the sun was clothed in a dazzling scarlet robe.

Up raise the lark, the hevyns menstrale fyne,
In May in till a morow myrthfullest.

2

Full angellike thir birdis sang thair houris　　　10
Within thair courtyns grene in to thair bouris,
Apparalit quhite and rede wyth blomes swete;
Anamalit was the felde wyth all colouris.
The perly droppis schuke in silvir schouris,
Quhill all in balme did branch and levis flete.　　　15
Depart fra Phebus did Aurora grete –
Hir cristall teris I saw hyng on the flouris,
Quhilk he for lufe all drank up wyth his hete.

3

For mirth of May wyth skippis and wyth hoppis
The birdis sang upon the tender croppis　　　20
With curiouse note, as Venus chapell clerkis.
The rosis yong, new spreding of thair knopis,
War powderit brycht with hevinly beriall droppis,
Throu bemes rede birnyng as ruby sperkis.
The skyes rang for schoutyng of the larkis,　　　25
The purpur hevyn, ourscailit in silvir sloppis,
Ourgilt the treis branchis, lef and barkis.

8. *menstrale]* Minstrel.
9. *in till]* in. *morow]* Morning.
10. *houris]* Church services.
13. *Anamalit]* Enamelled.
14. *perly]* Pearl-like. *schuke]* Shook, scattered.
15. *flete]* Flow with moisture.
16. *Depart]* Separated. *grete]* Weep.
17. *hyng]* Hang.
18. *hete]* Heat.
20. *croppis]* Upper shoots.
21. *curiouse]* Skilful. *note]* Music.
22. *knopis]* Buds.
23. *powderit]* Sprinkled. *beriall]* Beryl, crystal.
24] Through the sunbeams flaming red like small rubies.
25. *rang]* Resounded.
26. *ourscailit . . . sloppis]* See note.
27. *Ourgilt]* Gilded, tinged with gold. *lef]* Foliage.

4

Doun throu the ryce a ryvir ran wyth stremys,
So lustily agayn thai lykand lemys
That all the lake as lamp did leme of licht, 30
Quhilk schadowit all about wyth twynkling glemis.
The bewis bathit war in secund bemys
Throu the reflex of Phebus visage brycht.
On every syde the hegies raise on hicht,
The bank was grene, the bruke was full of bremys, 35
The stanneris clere as stern in frosty nycht.

5

The cristall air, the sapher firmament,
The ruby skyes of the orient,
Kest beriall bemes on emerant bewis grene.
The rosy garth, depaynt and redolent, 40
With purpur, azure, gold and goulis gent
Arayed was by dame Flora, the quene,
So nobily that joy was for to sene
The roch agayn the rivir resplendent,
As low enlumynit all the leves schene. 45

6

Quhat throu the mery foulys armony
And throu the ryveris soun, rycht ran me by,
On Florais mantill I slepit as I lay;

---

28. *ryce]* Bushes. *stremys]* Currents.
29] So attractively against those pleasing rays.
30. *lake]* Flowing water. *leme]* Gleam.
31. *schadowit]* Was reflected.
32. *bewis]* Boughs.
33. *reflex]* Reflected light.
34. *hegies]* Hedges. *hicht]* High.
35. *bruke]* Brook. *bremys]* Bream, a type of carp.
36. *stanneris]* Pebbles. *stern]* Stars.
37. *sapher]* Sapphire.
38. *orient]* Eastern sky.
39. *Kest]* Cast. *emerant]* Emerald.
40. *garth]* Garden. *depaynt]* Brightly coloured.
41. *goulis]* Gules, heraldic term for red. *gent]* Attractive.
43. *sene]* See (archaic infin.).
44. *roch]* Rocky cliff. *resplendent]* Shining.
45. *low]* Flame. *enlumynit]* Illumined. *schene]* Beautiful.
46. *Quhat]* Partly. *armony]* Harmony.
47. *soun]* Sound. *rycht ... by]* That flowed just by me.

Quhare sone in to my dremes fantasy
I saw approch agayn the orient sky 50
A saill als quhite as blossum upon spray,
Wyth merse of gold brycht as the stern of day,
Quhilk tendit to the land full lustily,
As falcoun swift desyrouse of hir pray.

7

And hard on burd unto the blomyt medis 55
Amang the grene rispis and the redis
Arrivit sche; quharfro anon thare landis
Ane hundreth ladyes, lusty in to wedis,
Als fresch as flouris that in May up spredis,
In kirtillis grene, withoutyn kell or bandis. 60
Thair brycht hairis hang gleting on the strandis,
In tressis clere wyppit wyth goldyn thredis,
With pappis quhite and mydlis small as wandis.

8

Discrive I wald, bot quho coud wele endyte
How all the feldis wyth thai lilies quhite 65
Depaynt war brycht, quhilk to the hevyn did glete?
Noucht thou, Omer, als fair as thou coud wryte,
For all thine ornate stilis so perfyte.
Nor yit thou, Tullius, quhois lippis swete
Of rethorike did in to termes flete. 70

---

52. *merse]* Top-castle.
53. *tendit]* Moved. *lustily]* Vigorously.
54. *pray]* Prey.
55. *hard on burd]* Close at hand. *blomyt medis]* Flowery meadows.
56. *rispis]* Sedge. *redis]* Reeds.
57. *quharfro]* From whom. *anon]* At once.
58. *hundreth]* Hundred. *lusty]* Fair. *wedis]* Dress.
59. *up spredis]* Unfold.
60. *kirtillis]* Gowns. *kell]* Netted cap. *bandis]* Headbands.
61. *gleting]* Gleaming.
62. *wyppit]* Bound.
63. *pappis]* Breasts. *mydlis small]* Waists slender.
64. *Discrive]* Describe. *endyte]* Put into verse.
65. *thai]* Those.
66. *glete]* Gleam.
68. *stilis]* Literary compositions. *perfyte]* Perfect.
70. *termes]* Figures of speech. *flete]* Abound (lit. flow).

Your aureate tongis both bene all to lyte
For to compile that paradise complete.

9

Thare saw I Nature and Venus, quene and quene,
The fresch Aurora and lady Flora schene,
Juno, Appollo and Proserpyna,   75
Dyane, the goddesse chaste of woddis grene,
My lady Cleo, that help of makaris bene,
Thetes, Pallas and prudent Minerva,
Fair feynit Fortune and lemand Lucina.
Thir mychti quenis in crounis mycht be sene,   80
Wyth bemys blith, bricht as Lucifera.

10

Thare saw I May, of myrthfull monethis quene,
Betwix Aprile and June, hir sistir schene,
Within the gardyng walking up and doun,
Quham of the foulis gladdith all bedene.   85
Scho was full tender in hir yeris grene.
Thare saw I Nature present hir a goun,
Rich to behald and nobil of renoun,
Of eviry hew under the hevin that bene,
Depaynt and broud be gude proporcion.   90

11

Full lustily thir ladyes all in fere
Enterit within this park of most plesere,
Quhare that I lay, ourhelit wyth levis ronk.
The mery foulis blisfullest of chere
Salust Nature, me thoucht, on thair manere;   95

---

71. to lyte] Too inadequate.
72. compile] Describe. *complete]* Perfect.
77. makaris] Poets. *bene]* Is.
79. feynit] Deceitful. *lemand]* Shining.
83. sistir] Sisters.
84. gardyng] Garden.
85] Of whom the birds all rejoice greatly.
88. renoun] Repute.
90. broud] Embroidered. *be gude proporcion]* Well proportioned.
91. in fere] Together.
93. ourhelit] Covered over. *ronk]* Thick.
94. chere] Mood.
95. Salust] Greeted.

And eviry blome on branch and eke on bonk
Opnyt and spred thair balmy levis donk,
Full low enclynyng to thair quene so clere,
Quham of thair noble norising thay thonk.

12

Syne to dame Flora on the samyn wyse   100
Thay saluse and thay thank a thousand syse,
And to dame Venus, lufis mychti quene,
Thay sang ballettis in lufe, as was the gyse,
With amourouse notis lusty to devise,
As thay that had lufe in thair hertis grene.   105
Thair hony throtis opnyt fro the splene
With werblis swete did perse the hevinly skyes,
Quhill loud resownyt the firmament serene.

13

Ane othir court thare saw I consequent
Cupide, the king, wyth bow in hand ybent   110
And dredefull arowis grundyn scharp and square.
Thare saw I Mars, the god armypotent,
Aufull and sterne, strong and corpolent.
Thare saw I crabbit Saturn, ald and haire –
His luke was lyke for to perturb the aire.   115

96. *blome]* Flower. *bonk]* Bank.
97. *Opnyt]* Opened. *donk]* Moist.
98. *enclynyng]* Bowing. *clere]* Bright.
99. *norising]* Nourishment. *thonk]* Thank.
100. *samyn wyse]* Same manner.
101. *saluse]* Greet. *syse]* Times.
103. *ballettis]* Poems, songs. *gyse]* Custom.
104. *devise]* Describe.
105. *grene]* Youthful.
106. *splene]* Heart (lit. spleen).
107. *werblis]* Songs.
108. *Quhill]* Until. *resownyt]* Resounded.
109. *consequent]* Following.
110. *ybent]* Bent, drawn.
111. *grundyn]* Sharpened. *square]* Strong.
112. *armypotent]* Mighty in war.
113. *Aufull]* Awe-inspiring. *corpolent]* Large of body.
114. *crabbit]* Bad-tempered. *haire]* Grey-haired.
115. *luke]* Look, aspect (astrol.). *perturb]* Trouble.

Thare was Mercurius, wise and eloquent,
Of rethorike that fand the flouris faire.

14

Thare was the god of gardingis, Priapus,
Thare was the god of wildernes, Phanus,
And Janus, god of entree delytable.   120
Thare was the god of fludis, Neptunus,
Thare was the god of wyndis, Eolus,
With variand luke rycht lyke a lord unstable.
Thare was Bacus, the gladder of the table,
There was Pluto, the elrich incubus,   125
In cloke of grene – his court usit no sable.

15

And eviry one of thir in grene arayit
On harp or lute full merily thai playit,
And sang ballettis with michty notis clere.
Ladyes to dance full sobirly assayit,   130
Endlang the lusty ryvir so thai mayit,
Thair observance rycht hevynly was to here.
Than crap I throu the levis and drew nere,
Quhare that I was rycht sudaynly affrayt,
All throu a luke, quhilk I have boucht full dere.   135

16

And schortly for to speke, be lufis quene
I was aspyit. Scho bad hir archearis kene
Go me arrest, and thay no tyme delayit.
Than ladyes fair lete fall thair mantillis gren,

---

117. fand] Found, invented.
118. gardingis] Gardens.
120. entree] Entry, entering. *delytable]* Delightful.
123. variand] Changeable. *unstable]* Treacherous.
124. gladder] Rejoicer, one who gladdens.
125. elrich] Weird, uncanny.
126. sable] Black clothing.
130. sobirly] Gravely. *assayit]* Proceeded.
131. Endlang] Along. *mayit]* Celebrated May.
133. crap] Crept.
134. affrayt] Frightened.
135. boucht] Paid for. *dere]* Dearly.
137. aspyit] Perceived. *bad]* Ordered.
139. Than] Then.

With bowis big in tressit hairis schene 140
All sudaynly thay had a felde arayit.
And yit rycht gretly was I noucht affrayit,
The party was so plesand for to sene.
A wonder lusty bikkir me assayit.

17

And first of all with bow in hand ybent 145
Come dame Beautee, rycht as scho wald me schent.
Syne folowit all hir dameselis yfere,
With mony diverse aufull instrument.
Unto the pres Fair Having wyth hir went,
Fyne Portrature, Plesance and Lusty Chere. 150
Than come Reson with schelde of gold so clere,
In plate and maille as Mars armypotent.
Defendit me that nobil chevallere.

18

Syne tender Youth come wyth hir virgyns ying,
Grene Innocence and schamefull Abaising, 155
And quaking Drede wyth humble Obedience.
The goldyn targe harmyt thay no thing.
Curage in thame was noucht begonne to spring,
Full sore thay dred to done a violence.
Swete Womanhede I saw cum in presence – 160
Of artilye a warld sche did in bring,
Servit wyth ladyes full of reverence.

---

140. tressit hairis] Braided hair.
141. felde] Armed force. *arayit]* Prepared.
143. party] Hostile force. *sene]* See.
144. wonder] Extraordinarily. *bikkir]* Attack with missiles.
146. Come] Came. *wald me schent]* Would have me harmed.
147. dameselis] Female attendants. *yfere]* Together.
148. instrument] Weapon.
149. pres] Thick of the fight. *Having]* Behaviour.
150. Portrature] Appearance. *Chere]* Expression.
152. plate] Plate armour.
153. chevallere] Knight.
154. ying] Young.
155. schamefull] Modest. *Abaising]* Bashfulness.
158. Curage] Desire.
159. sore] Greatly. *dred]* Feared. *done]* Do (archaic infin.).
160. Womanhede] Womanliness.
161. artilye] Artillery. *warld]* Large quantity.

19

Scho led wyth hir Nurture and Lawlynes,
Contenence, Pacience, Gude Fame and Stedfastnes,
Discrecion, Gentrise and Considerance,   165
Levefull Company and Honest Besynes,
Benigne Luke, Mylde Chere and Sobirnes.
All thir bure ganyeis to do me grevance,
Bot Reson bure the targe wyth sik constance,
Thair scharp assayes mycht do no dures   170
To me, for all thair aufull ordynance.

20

Unto the pres persewit Hie Degree:
Hir folowit ay Estate and Dignitee,
Comparison, Honour and Noble Array,
Will, Wantonnes, Renon and Libertee,   175
Richesse, Fredom and eke Nobilitee.
Wit ye, thay did thair baner hye display.
A cloud of arowis, as hayle schour, lousit thay
And schot quhill wastit was thair artilye,
Syne went abak reboytit of thair pray.   180

21

Quhen Venus had persavit this rebute,
Dissymilance scho bad go mak persute
At all powere to perse the goldyn targe;

163. Nurture] Breeding. *Lawlynes]* Humility.
164. Contenence] Continence.
165. Gentrise] Nobility. *Considerance]* Consideration.
166. Levefull] Lawful. *Besynes]* Diligence.
167. Sobirnes] Gravity.
168. bure] Carried. *ganyeis]* Arrows *grevance]* Harm
170. assayes] Attacks. *dures]* Injury.
171. ordynance] Show of military force.
172. persewit] Advanced. *Degree]* Rank.
173. Estate] Social Standing *Dignitee]* High Status.
175. Will] Desire. *Wantonnes]* Sportiveness.
176. Fredom] Generosity.
177. Wit] Know.
178. lousit] Fired.
179. wastit] Exhausted.
180. went abak] Retreated. *reboytit]* Deprived.
181. persavit] Perceived. *rebute]* Repulse.
182. Dissymilance] Dissimulation. *persute]* Pursuit.
183. At all powere] In full force.

And scho that was of doubilnes the rute
Askit hir choise of archeris in refute. 185
Venus the best bad hir go wale at large.
Scho tuke Presence, plicht anker of the barge,
And Fair Callyng, that wele a flayn coud schute,
And Cherising for to complete hir charge.

22

Dame Hamelynes scho tuke in company, 190
That hardy was and hende in archery,
And broucht dame Beautee to the felde agayn
With all the choise of Venus chevalry.
Thay come and bikkerit unabaisitly,
The schour of arowis rappit on as rayn. 195
Perilouse Presence, that mony syre has slayn,
The bataill broucht on bordour hard us by.
The salt was all the sarar, suth to sayn.

23

Thik was the schote of grundyn dartis kene,
Bot Reson with the scheld of gold so schene 200
Warly defendit, quho so evir assayit.
The aufull stoure he manly did sustene,
Quhill Presence kest a pulder in his ene,
And than as drunkyn man he all forvayit.
Quhen he was blynd the fule wyth him thay playit, 205

184. *doubilnes*] Deceitfulness. *rute*] Source (lit. root).
185. *in refute*] For protection.
186. *wale*] Choose. *at large*] Freely.
187. *barge*] Ship.
188. *Callyng*] Greeting. *flayn*] Arrow. *schute*] Shoot.
189. *Cherising*] Cherishing. *complete*] Achieve. *charge*] Task.
190. *Hamelynes*] Intimacy, Familiarity.
191. *hardy*] Bold. *hende*] Skilled.
193. *choise*] Most excellent. *chevalry*] Fighting force.
194. *bikkerit*] Assaulted. *unabaisitly*] Fearlessly.
196. *syre*] Man.
197. *on bordour*] ? To the edge of the field. *hard*] Close.
198] The assault was much fiercer, to tell the truth.
199. *dartis*] Spears.
201. *Warly*] Prudently.
202. *stoure*] Conflict.
203. *pulder*] Powder. *ene*] Eyes.
204. *forvayit*] Went astray.
205. *fule*] Fool.

And banyst hym amang the bewis grene.
That sory sicht me sudaynly affrayit.

24

Than was I woundit to the deth wele nere
And yoldyn as a wofull prisonnere
To lady Beautee in a moment space.   210
Me thoucht scho semyt lustiar of chere
(Efter that Reson tynt had his eyne clere)
Than of before and lufliare of face.
Quhy was thou blyndit, Reson, quhi, allace?
And gert ane hell my paradise appere,   215
And mercy seme quhare that I fand no grace.

25

Dissymulance was besy me to sile,
And Fair Calling did oft apon me smyle,
And Cherising me fed wyth wordis fair.
New Acquyntance enbracit me a quhile   220
And favouryt me, quhill men mycht go a myle,
Syne tuke hir leve. I saw hir nevir mare.
Than saw I Dangere toward me repair.
I coud eschew hir presence be no wyle,
On syde scho lukit wyth ane fremyt fare.   225

26

And at the last Departing coud hir dresse,
And me delyverit unto Hevynesse
For to remayne, and scho in cure me tuke.

206. *banyst]* Banished. *bewis]* Boughs.
209. *yoldyn]* Surrendered.
211. *lustiar]* More pleasant. *chere]* Expression.
212. *tynt]* Lost.
213. *of before]* Before.
215. *gert]* Caused.
216. *fand]* Found.
217. *besy]* Busy. *sile]* Deceive.
220. *Acquyntance]* Acquaintance.
222. *tuke hir leve]* Departed.
223. *Dangere]* See note.
224. *eschew]* Avoid. *wyle]* Cunning trick.
225. *On syde]* Aside. *fremyt fare]* Hostile expression.
226. *Departing]* Parting. *hir dresse]* Prepare herself.
227. *Hevynesse]* Depression.
228. *in cure me tuke]* Took charge of me.

Be this the lord of wyndis with wodenes
(God Eolus) his bugill blew, I gesse,   230
That with the blast the levis all toschuke.
And sudaynly in the space of a luke
All was hyne went, thare was bot wildernes,
Thare was no more bot birdis, bank and bruke.

27

In twynklyng of ane eye to schip thai went,   235
And swyth up saile unto the top thai stent,
And with swift course atour the flude thai frak.
Thai fyrit gunnis with powder violent,
Till that the reke raise to the firmament.
The rochis all resownyt wyth the rak,   240
For rede it semyt that the raynbow brak.
Wyth spirit affrayde apon my fete I sprent,
Amang the clewis so careful was the crak.

28

And as I did awake of my sweving,
The joyful birdis merily did syng   245
For myrth of Phebus tender bemes schene.
Swete war the vapouris, soft the morowing,
Halesum the vale depaynt wyth flouris ying,
The air attemperit, sobir and amene.
In quhite and rede was all the felde besene,   250

229. *wodenes]* Madness.
230. *gesse]* Believe.
231. *toschuke]* Shook fiercely.
233. *hyne]* Hence.
236. *swyth]* At once. *top]* Masthead. *stent]* Stretched.
237. *atour]* Over. *frak]* Move swiftly.
238. *powder]* Gunpowder.
239. *reke]* Smoke.
240. *rochis]* Cliffs. *rak]* Report of a gun.
241. *rede]* Din. *brak]* Broke.
242. *sprent]* Leapt.
243. *clewis]* Crags. *carefull]* Dismal. *crak]* Explosion.
244. *sweving]* Vision.
247. *morowing]* Morning.
248. *Halesum]* Health-giving. *depaynt]* Coloured.
249. *attemperit]* Temperate. *sobir]* Mild. *amene]* Pleasant.
250. *besene]* Arrayed.

Throu Naturis nobil fresch anamalyng
In mirthfull May of eviry moneth quene.

29

O reverend Chaucere, rose of rethoris all
(As in oure tong ane flour imperiall)
That raise in Britane evir, quho redis rycht,   255
Thou beris of makaris the tryumph riall,
Thy fresch anamalit termes celicall
This mater coud illumynit have full brycht.
Was thou noucht of oure Inglisch all the lycht,
Surmounting eviry tong terrestriall,   260
Alls fer as Mayes morow dois mydnycht?

30

O morall Gower and Ludgate laureate,
Your sugurit lippis and tongis aureate
Bene to oure eris cause of grete delyte.
Your angel mouthis most mellifluate   265
Oure rude langage has clere illumynate
And fair ourgilt oure spech, that imperfyte
Stude or your goldyn pennis schupe to write.
This ile before was bare and desolate
Of rethorike or lusty fresch endyte.   270

31

Thou lytill quair, be evir obedient,
Humble, subject and symple of entent
Before the face of eviry connyng wicht.

---

251. *anamalyng]* Enamelling.
253. *rethoris]* Poets, rhetoricians.
254. *imperiall]* Pre-eminent.
255. *raise]* Flourished. *redis]* Reads.
256. *tryumph riall]* Honour befitting a king.
257. *celicall]* Heavenly.
258. *mater]* Subject. *illumynit]* Adorned.
265. *mellifluate]* Sweet (as honey).
266. *rude]* Crude. *illumynate]* Made bright, adorned.
267. *ourgilt]* Gilded.
268. *Stude]* Existed. *Or]* Before. *schupe]* Prepared.
269. *ile]* Island.
270. *endyte]* Composition, poetry.
271. *quair]* Small book.
272. *subject]* Submissive. *symple]* Modest. *entent]* Mind.
273. *connyng wicht]* Learned person.

I knaw quhat thou of rethorike hes spent.
Of all hir lusty rosis redolent   275
Is non in to thy gerland sett on hicht.
Eschame tharof and draw the out of sicht.
Rude is thy wede, disteynit, bare and rent,
Wele aucht thou be aferit of the licht.

274. *spent]* Expended.
277. *Eschame]* Be ashamed. *draw the]* Withdraw.
278. *Rude]* Coarse. *wede]* Garment. *disteynit]* Dirt-stained.
279. *aucht]* Ought. *aferit]* Fearful.

48

Celebrating the birth of Jesus, Dunbar summons the whole of creation – 'Hevin, erd, se, man, bird and best', in the climactic line 54 – to worship God. This fine poem is one of several 'ballatis of the natiuitie', preserved in the Bannatyne Manuscript (ff. 27ʳ–31ʳ). In phrasing and imagery, jubilant tone, and choice of stanza with a Latin refrain, it has a generic resemblance to these other anonymous poems, but far excels them in lucidity and careful structural patterning. There are echoes and quotations of the *Te Deum*, and of scriptural passages employed in the liturgy for Advent and Christmas (see notes to 1, 5–7 and 8). The pervasive imagery of light (see 3, 5–7, 37–9) is highly characteristic of poems on this theme (cf. Gray 1972: 95–9). On the stanza, see 1.

Text: B, f. 27ʳ–27ᵛ.
8. *puer*] power B.

Authorship: 'Quod Dumbar' in B.

Further reading: On the devotional background and the liturgical imagery, see Hyde 1956, and Woolf 1968: 287–9 and 302–7. On the poem's structure, see Bawcutt 1992a: 174–8.

1

Rorate, celi, desuper!
Hevins, distill your balmy schouris,
For now is rissin the brycht day ster

1] Send down dew from above, you heavens.
2. *distill*] Let fall in drops. *schouris*] Showers.
3. *ster*] Star.

Fro the ros Mary, flour of flouris.
The cleir sone quhome no clud devouris,   5
Surminting Phebus in the est,
Is cumin of his hevinly touris,
Et nobis puer natus est.

2

Archangellis, angellis and dompnationis,
Tronis, potestatis and marteiris seir,   10
And all ye hevinly operationis,
Ster, planeit, firmament and speir,
Fyre, erd, air and watter cleir,
To him gife loving, most and lest,
That come in to so meik maneir   15
Et nobis puer natus est.

3

Synnaris, be glaid and pennance do
And thank your makar hairtfully,
For he that ye mycht nocht cum to
To yow is cumin full humly,   20
Your saulis with his blud to by
And lous yow of the feindis arrest,
And only of his awin mercy,
Pro nobis puer natus est.

4. *Fro]* From.
5. *sone]* Sun. *clud]* Cloud.
6. *Surminting]* Surpassing. *est]* East.
7. *cumin of]* Come from.
8] And unto us a child is born. *See note.*
9. *dompnationis]* Dominations.
10. *Tronis]* Thrones. *potestatis]* Powers. *seir]* Many.
11. *operationis]* Agencies.
12. *speir]* Sphere.
13. *erd]* Earth.
14. *loving]* Praise. *lest]* Least.
15. *come]* Came.
18. *hairtfully]* Whole-heartedly.
19. *cum]* Come.
20. *humly]* In humble manner.
21. *saulis]* Souls. *by]* Buy, redeem.
22. *lous]* Free. *arrest]* Custody.
23. *awin]* Own.

4

All clergy, do to him inclyne   25
And bow unto that barne benyng,
And do your observance devyne
To him that is of kingis king.
Ensence his altar, reid and sing
In haly kirk with mynd degest,   30
Him honouring attour all thing,
Qui nobis puer natus est.

5

Celestiall fowlis in the are,
Sing with your nottis upoun hicht,
In firthis and in forrestis fair   35
Be myrthfull now at all your mycht,
For passit is your dully nycht.
Aurora hes the cluddis perst,
The son is rissin with glaidsum lycht
Et nobis puer natus est.   40

6

Now spring up, flouris, fra the rute,
Revert yow upwart naturaly,
In honour of the blissit frute
That rais up fro the rose Mary.
Lay out your levis lustely,   45
Fro deid tak lyfe now at the lest,

25. *do . . . inclyne]* Bow down.
26. *barne benyng]* Innocent child.
27. *observance devyne]* Religious worship.
29. *Ensence]* Perfume with incense. *reid]* Read (the office).
30. *haly]* Holy. *degest]* Solemn.
31. *attour]* Above.
33. *fowlis]* Birds. *are]* Air.
34. *nottis]* Tunes. *hicht]* High.
35. *firthis]* Woods.
37. *dully]* Gloomy.
38. *perst]* Pierced.
39. *glaidsum]* Joyful.
41. *rute]* Root.
42. *Revert yow]* Turn. *upwart]* Upwards.
43. *blissit]* Blessed.
44. *rais]* Rose.
45. *lustely]* Beautifully.
46. *deid]* Death. *the lest]* Last.

In wirschip of that prince wirthy,
Qui nobis puer natus est.

7

Syng, hevin imperiall most of hicht,
Regions of air, mak armony.   50
All fische in flud and foull of flicht,
Be myrthfull and mak melody.
All, *gloria in excelsis* cry,
Hevin, erd, se, man, bird and best,
He that is crownit abone the sky,   55
Pro nobis puer natus est.

---

47. *wirschip]* Honour. *wirthy]* Worthy.
49. *most of hicht]* Highest.
50. *armony]* Music.
51. *flud]* River. *flicht]* Flight.
54. *se]* Sea.
55. *abone]* Above.

49

This single eight-line stanza, *ababbcbc*, with much alliteration and internal rhyme (6) is a prayer, similar in purpose to the longer, more emotive pieces in verse and prose contained in Manuscript Arundel 285 (see *Devotional Pieces in Verse and Prose*). The latent personification-allegory resembles that developed more fully in the final section of *King Hart*.

Text: MF, p. 326; collated with R, f. 40^r.

Authorship: 'Quod Dumbar' in MF and R.

> Salviour, suppois my sensualite
> Subject to syn hes maid my saule of sys,
> Sum spark of lycht and spiritualite
> Walkynnis my witt, and ressoun biddis me rys.
> My corrupt conscience askis, clips and cryis 5
> First grace, syne space for to amend my mys,
> Substance with honour, doing none suppryis,
> Freyndis, prosperite, heir peax, syne hevynis blys,

1. *Salviour*] Saviour. *suppois*] Although.
2. *saule*] Soul. *of sys*] Often.
4. *Walkynnis*] Awakens.
5. *clips*] Calls loudly. *cryis*] Cries for.
6. *space*] Time. *syne*] Then. *mys*] Sin.
7. *Substance*] Wealth. *none suppryis*] Harm to nobody.
8. *peax*] Peace.

50

Many medieval poets employ an empty purse as the focus for a complaint about poverty. Some English examples are Chaucer's *Complaint to his Purse*, and carols with the proverbial burden, 'Gramercy my own purse' (see Greene, *Carols*, nos. 390 and 391). Dunbar's chief theme is that his empty purse resembles a physical disease: see refrain, and lines 9, 16 and 34. Such imagery was traditional; cf. Hoccleve, *La Male Regle*, 409: 'My body and purs been at ones seeke'; and Lydgate's *Letter to Gloucester* (in *Minor Poems*, II), which develops the conceit very elaborately. The tone of this poem is more light-hearted than petitions such as **56** and **57**, and it is appropriately included in Bannatyne's 'ballettis mirry'. On the stanza, see **9**. There is no clue as to the date of composition.

Text: B, ff. 113ᵛ–114ʳ.

Authorship: 'Quod Dumbar to the king' in B.

Further reading: Reiss 1979: 42–4 (a moral interpretation); Bawcutt 1992a: 110–12 (on the 'allusive humour').

1

Sanct salvatour, send silver sorrow!
It grevis me both evin and morrow,
Chasing fra me all cheritie.

1. Sanct salvatour] Holy saviour.
2. grevis] Distresses. *evin]* Evening. *morrow]* Morning.
3. cheritie] Charity.

It makis me all blythnes to borrow,
My panefull purs so priclis me.   5

2

Quhen I wald blythlie ballattis breif
Langour thairto givis me no leif.
War nocht gud howp my hart uphie,
My verry corpis for cair wald cleif.
My panefull purs so prikillis me.   10

3

Quhen I sett me to sing or dance
Or go to plesand pastance,
Than pansing of penuritie
Revis that fra my remembrance.
My panefull purs so prikillis me.   15

4

Quhen men that hes pursis in tone
Pasis to drynk or to disione,
Than mon I keip ane gravetie
And say that I will fast quhill none.
My panefull purs so priclis me.   20

5

My purs is maid of sic ane skyn,
Thair will na cors byd it within.
Fra it as fra the feynd thay fle.

4] I am forced to borrow money, and also the happiness that accompanies money.
5. priclis] Pricks, causes pain.
6. ballattis breif] Write poems.
7. Langour] Unhappiness. *leif]* Permission.
8] If it were not for good hope to raise my spirits.
9. corpis] Body. *cair]* Grief. *cleif]* Split.
11. sett me] Arrange.
12. pastance] Recreation.
13. pansing] Thinking. *penuritie]* Poverty.
14. Revis] Robs.
16. in tone] In a healthy state (lit. in tune).
17. Pasis] Pass, go. *disione]* Breakfast.
18. mon] Must. *gravetie]* Grave expression.
19. none] Noon.
22. cors] Cross. *byd]* Remain.
23. feynd] Devil. *fle]* Flee.

Quha evir tyne, quha evir win,
My panefull purs so priclis me.   25

6

Had I ane man of ony natioun,
Culd mak on it ane conjuratioun
To gar silver ay in it be,
The devill suld haif no dominatioun
With pyne to gar it prickill me.   30

7

I haif inquyrit in mony a place
For help and confort in this cace,
And all men sayis, my lord, that ye
Can best remeid for this malice,
That with sic panis prickillis me.   35

24. tyne] Lose.
27. conjuratioun] Magic spell.
28. gar] Cause.
30. pyne] Pain.
34. remeid] Provide a remedy. *malice]* Malaise, disease.

51

This witty petition to the king takes the form of an extended metaphor. Dunbar argues for a more equitable distribution of benefices through the analogy of a feast at which guests should be treated equally. There are similarities to 35 in theme and imagery, although the poems differ in tone and metrical form. This employs a five-line stanza, *aabba* (see further, 15); 35 has a different pattern, *aabab*, with refrain. Editors commonly couple the two poems, yet they are not placed together in the manuscripts. Possibly they were composed at much the same time, but there are no clues as to the precise date.

Text: MF, p. 316 (MFb); collated with MF, p. 7 (MFa), and R, f. 9ᵛ. MFa is affected by damp, and barely legible.
1. of] MFa; *not in* MFb.
8. brist] MFa; birst MFb.

Authorship: 'Quod Dumbar quhone mony benefices vakit [were vacant]' in MFb.

1

Schir, at this feist of benefice
Think that small partis makis grit service,
And equale distributioun
Makis thame content that hes ressoun,
And quha hes nane ar plesit na wyis.   5

1. Schir] Sir. *benefice]* Benefices.
2] Consider that you serve a greater number, if they get small portions.
5] And those who lack reason are never satisfied.

254

2

Schir, quhiddir is it mereit mair
To gif him drink that thristis sair,
Or fill a fow man quhill he brist,
And lat his fallow de a-thrist,
Quhilk wyne to drink als worthie war?   10

3

It is no glaid collatioun,
Quhair ane makis myrrie, ane uther lukis doun,
Ane thristis, ane uther playis cop out.
Lat anis the cop ga round about,
And wyn the covanis banesoun.   15

<hr/>

6. *mereit]* Merit. *quhiddir]* Whether.
7. *thristis sair]* Is painfully thirsty.
8. *fow]* Drunk (lit. full). *brist]* Burst.
9. *fallow]* Companion. *de a-thrist]* Die of thirst.
12. *myrrie]* Merry. *lukis doun]* Is downcast.
13. *thristis]* Is thirsty. *cop]* Cup.
14] Let the cup circulate once.
15. *covanis banesoun]* Company's blessing.

52

This poem, ostensibly a pious prayer on the king's behalf (cf. 1–3, 31), is a petition for the poet's own advancement. Its tone is humorous, and verges on impertinence: compliments to the queen, Margaret Tudor, are balanced against the refrain's audacious suggestion that the king should, in effect, be ruled by his wife. On the stanza, one of Dunbar's commonest, see **16**.

Date: The mention of Queen Margaret indicates a date between 1503 and 1513, possibly not long after the composition of **41** (see note to 21–2).

Text: MF, pp. 194–5, with colophon 'Finis quod Dunbar'.

Further reading: Bawcutt 1992a: 109–10 ('the comic effect springs largely from the refrain, which evokes the humdrum world of domineering wives ... It collides incongruously with the fantastic vows of medieval chivalry').

1

Schir, for your grace, bayth nicht and day,
Richt hartlie on my kneis I pray,
With all devotioun that I can:
God gif ye war Johne Thomsounis man.

1. Schir] Sir. *nicht]* Night.
2. hartlie] In a heartfelt way. *kneis]* Knees.
3. devotioun] Devout feeling.
4. gif] Grant.

2

For war it so, than weill war me.   5
But benefice I wald nocht be,
My hard fortoun wer endit than.
God gif ye war Johne Thomsounis man.

3

Than wald sum reuth within yow rest,
For saik of hir, fairest and best   10
In Bartane sen hir tyme began.
God gif ye war Johne Thomsounis man.

4

For it micht hurt in no degre,
That on so fair and gude as sche
Throw hir vertew sic wirschip wan,   15
Als yow to mak Johne Thomsounis man.

5

I wald gif all that ever I have,
To that conditioun, sa God me saif,
That ye had vowit to the Swan,
Ane yeir to be Johne Thomsounis man.   20

6

The mersy of that sweit meik Rose
Suld soft yow, Thirsill, I suppois,
Quhois pykis throw me so reuthles ran.
God gif ye war Johne Thomsounis man.

5] For if it were so, then I would be well-off.
6. *But]* Without.
7. *fortoun]* Fortune.
9. *reuth]* Compassion. *rest]* Be present.
10. *saik]* Sake.
11. *Bartane]* Britain.
13. *degre]* Degree, extent.
14. *on]* One.
15. *vertew]* Virtue. *sic wirschip]* Such honour. *wan]* Won.
17. *gif]* Give.
18. *To that conditioun]* On condition.
20. *Ane yeir]* One year.
22. *soft]* Mollify. *Thirsill]* Thistle. *suppois]* Believe.
23. *pykis]* Spikes. *reuthles]* Pitilessly.

7

My advocat, bayth fair and sweit,   25
The hale rejosing of my spreit,
Wald speid in to my erand than,
And ye war anis Johne Thomsounis man.

8

Ever quhen I think yow harde or dour,
Or mercyles in my succour,   30
Than pray I God and sweit sanct An,
Gif that ye war Johne Thomsounis man.

25. *advocat]* Intercessor.
26. *hale]* Whole. *rejosing]* Cause of joy. *spreit]* Spirit.
27. *speid]* Succeed. *in to my erand]* On my behalf.
28. *And]* If. *anis]* Once.
29. *dour]* Surly.
31. *sanct]* Saint.

53

Dunbar does not here petition for advancement, but complains to the king about an otherwise unknown poet, whom he accuses of tampering with his poetry. Mure has both mutilated Dunbar's work and inserted inferior and slanderous verses of his own. Dunbar here reveals a strong sense of pride in his own 'name' and craftsmanship. The tone is mocking and contemptuous, aided by the violence of the imagery ('magellit', 'dismemberit', 'poysonid', 'bait him lyk a buill'). On the stanza, see 2.

Date: A slight clue is provided by the reference to Cuddy Rug (24), who was associated with the Scottish court from 1504 to 1512.

Text: MF, pp. 10–11; collated with R, f. 11ʳ.
16. awin] *Marginal insertion* MF, R.
18. seasoun] R; *marginal correction from* ressoun MF.

Authorship: 'Quod Dumbar' in MF and R.

Further reading: Baxter 1952: 128 (the tone 'is not that of one who jests'); Reiss 1979: 31–3 ('Dunbar would hardly seem to be serious'); Bawcutt 1992a: 33–4, 242–4 ('the poem itself is the punishment; it . . . achieves the public humiliation of the other poet').

1

Schir, I complane of injuris:
A refing sonne of rakyng Muris
Hes magellit my making throw his malis,

1. Schir] Sir. *complane]* Complain. *injuris]* Injustices.
2. refing] Thieving. *rakyng]* Roaming.
3. magellit] Mutilated. *making]* Verse. *malis]* Malice.

And present it in to yowr palis.
Bot sen he ples with me to pleid,   5
I sall him knawin mak hyne to Calis,
Bot giff yowr henes it remeid.

2

That fulle dismemberit hes my meter
And poysonid it with strang salpeter,
With rycht defamows speiche of lordis,   10
Quhilk with my collouris all discordis,
Quhois crewall sclander servis ded,
And in my name all leis recordis.
Your grace beseik I of remeid.

3

He has indorsit myn indyting   15
With versis of his awin hand wryting,
Quhairin baithe sclander is and tressoun.
Of ane wod fuill, far owt of seasoun,
He wantis nocht bot a rowndit heid,
For he has tynt baith wit and ressoun.   20
Yowr grace beseik I of remeid.

4

Punes him for his deid culpabile,
Or gar deliver him a babile,
That Cuddy Rug, the Drumfres fuill,

---

4. present] Presented. *palis]* Palace.
5] But since he sees fit to dispute with me.
6. knawin] Notorious. *hyne]* From here.
7] Unless your highness find a remedy for it.
8 fulle] Fool. *meter]* Metre.
9. strang salpeter] Strong-smelling saltpetre.
10. rycht defamows] Extremely defamatory.
11. collouris] Figures of speech. *discordis]* Is discordant.
12. sclander] Slander *servis ded]* Deserves the death penalty.
13. leis] Lies. *recordis]* Relates.
14. beseik] Beseech. *remeid]* Redress.
15. indorsit] Endorsed, written on the back of. *indyting]* Poetry.
18. wod] Demented. *owt of seasoun]* At an inopportune time.
19. wantis nocht] Lacks nothing. *rowndit heid]* Cropped head.
20. tynt] Lost.
22. Punes] Punish. *culpabile]* Guilty.
23. gar] Cause. *babile]* Bauble, mock-sceptre.
24. Drumfres] Dumfries.

May him resave agane this Yuill,
All roundit, in to yallow and reid,
That ladis may bait him lyk a buill,
For that to me war sum remeid.

25. *agane]* In readiness for. *Yuill]* Yule.
26. *roundit]* With cropped hair. *yallow]* Yellow. *reid]* Red.
27. *ladis]* Boys. *bait]* Attack. *buill]* Bull.

54

The Flyting of
Dumbar and Kennedie

The Flyting is both a quarrel and a contest in poetic virtuosity. Each poet speaks
as an individual and also as a representative of a group, voicing the mutual
antagonisms of Lowlander and Highlander. Dunbar draws on common
stereotypes of the Highlander in his depiction of Kennedy as a thief and cattle-
robber; as dirty and poverty-stricken; and, above all, as a bard, which among
Lowlanders was a highly pejorative term, applied chiefly to idle, wandering
entertainers (see 17, 49, 63, and passim). The portrait is brilliant but scurrilous:
imagery drawn from animals and rural life assimilates Kennedy to the landscape
in which he is placed. Nonetheless it is largely a comic travesty, as is Kennedy's
own portrait of Dunbar. Walter Kennedy (?1460–?1518) graduated from
Glasgow University in 1478. He was a younger son of Gilbert, first Lord
Kennedy of Dunure, in Ayrshire; his nephew, Sir David Kennedy, became first
Earl of Cassilis in 1509. The Kennedys, a family rising in status and wealth,
were important landowners in Ayrshire and Carrick; cf. Dunbar's mocking
references (112, 134, 211). Walter Kennedy had acquired several properties in
Carrick by 1504; he was still alive in 1510, but had died by 1518, when his heir,
also called Walter, succeeded him as parson of Douglas (*Ailsa Muniments*, no.
241). This part of Scotland was still Gaelic-speaking, hence the gibes directed
at Gaelic by Dunbar (107–112) and its defence by Kennedy himself. (Yet there
is little sign of Gaelic influences on Kennedy's extant verse.) Dunbar mocks
Kennedy's claim to be a poet (97, 107–112), yet speaks warmly of him elsewhere
(16. 89–92).

    The Flyting has a four-part structure: two short passages that serve as
introductory challenges are succeeded by the principal invectives of each poet.
This extract contains the whole of Dunbar's contribution, together with
Kennedy's opening challenge (1–248), but omits the second section of
Kennedy's flyting (249–552). *The Flyting* poses many intractable questions.
Suggestions as to its date range from the early 1490s (McDiarmid 1980: 130–32)
to *c.* 1500–1505 (Kinsley, p. 285). A *terminus ad quem* is provided by a mention
of the poet Stobo (d. 1505), but other topical-sounding allusions are not easy to
date. The tone is also difficult to assess: most critics have seen the work as, in

262

part, a collaborative game between the two poets; yet it clearly voices animosities, personal and cultural.

Metre: Dunbar uses an eight-line stanza, rhyming *ababbccb⁵* in the first section and *ababbcbc⁵* in the second. The diction is densely alliterative, and many lines contain four or more alliterating syllables. He concludes with a virtuoso display of internal rhymes (233–48).

Text: B, ff. 147ʳ–150ᵛ; collated with MF, pp. 53–4, 69–72 (some leaves in MF are displaced); and R, ff. 58ᵛ–64ʳ. The CM fragment lacks this section. Only a few of the numerous variants are noted.

18. richt] MF; for B.
51. Densmen] MF; denseman B.
58. Skitterand . . . scauld] MF; Scarth fra scorpione scaldit B.
83. Ganyelon] MF; glengoir loun B.
88. recry it] MF; recryat B.
92. us] MF; wes B. wind and] MF; woundis B.
95. sey] MF; *not in* B.
102. lauchtane] MF; lathand B.
139. my] thy B, MF.
152. lymmair] MF; lymmerfull B.
169. linkis . . . lenye] MF; lukis . . . lene B.
185. pynhippit] MF; hippit B.
220. brachis] *Ed. conj.*; bichis B; brachattis R.
241. byt] MF; byle B.
242. flay] MF; foule B.

Further reading: On medieval flyting and invective, see Lampe 1979; Bawcutt 1983; Lyall 1983; and Gray 1984. On the text, date and topical allusions, see Baxter 1952: 62–84; McDiarmid 1980; and Kinsley headnote. For critical responses, see Scott 1966: 171–8 (a 'repellent poem'); Ross 1981: 184–92; and Bawcutt 1992a: 220–39 ('quasi-dramatic . . . captures the effect of street-flyting').

The Flyting of Dumbar and Kennedie
Heir efter followis jocound and mirrie

1

Schir Johine the Ros, ane thing thair is compild
In generale be Kennedy and Quinting,
Quhilk hes thame self aboif the sternis styld.

1. *thing]* Document. *compild]* Composed.
2. *generale]* General terms. *be]* By.
3] Who have praised themselves in hyperbolic terms.

Bot had thay maid of mannace ony mynting
In speciall, sic stryfe sould rys but stynting;   5
Howbeit with bost thair breistis wer als bendit
As Lucifer that fra the hevin discendit,
Hell sould nocht hyd thair harnis fra harmis hynting.

2

The erd sould trymbill, the firmament sould schaik,
And all the air in vennaum suddane stink,   10
And all the divillis of hell for redour quaik,
To heir quhat I suld wryt with pen and ynk;
For and I flyt, sum sege for schame sould sink,
The se sould birn, the mone sould thoill ecclippis,
Rochis sould ryfe, the warld sould hald no grippis,   15
Sa loud of cair the commoun bell sould clynk.

3

Bot wondir laith wer I to be ane baird.
Flyting to use richt gritly I eschame.
For it is nowthir wynnyng nor rewaird,
Bot tinsale baith of honour and of fame,   20
Incres of sorrow, sklander and evill name.
Yit mycht thay be sa bald in thair bakbytting,
To gar me ryme and rais the feynd with flytting
And throw all cuntreis and kinrikis thame proclame.

Quod Dumbar to Kennedy

4. *mannace . . . mynting]* Any attempt at threats.
5. *In speciall]* Directed at an individual. *but stynting]* Without stopping.
6. *Bost]* Vaunting speech. *bendit]* Stretched to bursting.
8. *harnis]* Brains. *harmis hynting]* Receiving injury.
9. *erd]* Earth. *trymbill]* Tremble.
10. *vennaum]* Venom. *suddane]* Suddenly.
11. *divillis]* Devils. *redour]* Terror.
13. *and]* If. *sege]* Man.
14. *se]* Sea. *birn]* Burn. *mone]* Moon. *thoill]* Suffer.
15. *Rochis]* Rocks. *ryfe]* Split. *hald no grippis]* Fall apart.
16. *cair]* Distress. *commoun]* Public.
17. *wondir laith]* Extremely reluctant.
18] I am greatly ashamed to engage in flyting.
19. *nowthir]* Neither. *wynnyng]* Material gain.
20. *tinsale]* Loss.
21. *Incres]* Increase. *sklander]* Slander.
22. *bald]* Bold.
23. *gar]* Cause. *feynd]* Fiend.
24. *cuntreis]* Countries. *kinrikis]* Kingdoms. *proclame]* Denounce.

4

Dirtin Dumbar, quhome on blawis thow thy boist,   25
Pretendand the to wryte sic skaldit skrowis,
Ramowd rebald, thow fall doun att the roist,
My laureat lettres at the and I lowis.
Mandrag, mymmerkin, maid maister bot in mows,
Thrys scheild trumpir with ane threidbair goun,   30
Say, '*Deo* mercy', or I cry the doun,
And leif thy ryming, rebald, and thy rowis.

5

Dreid, dirtfast dearch, that thow hes dissobeyit
My cousing Quintene and my commissar.
Fantastik fule, trest weill thow salbe fleyit.   35
Ignorant elf, aip, owll irregular,
Skaldit skaitbird and commoun skamelar,
Wanfukkit funling, that Natour maid ane yrle,
Baith Johine the Ros and thow sall squeill and skirle,
And evir I heir ocht of your making mair.   40

6

Heir I put sylence to the in all pairtis.
Obey and ceis the play that thow pretendis,
Waik walidrag and verlot of the cairtis,

---

25. Dirtin] Filthy. *blawis]* Blows.
26. Pretendand the] Presuming. *skaldit skrowis]* Contemptible writings (lit. scrolls).
27–8] Foul-mouthed rascal, you will fall down at the feast, if I fire at you my eloquent writings.
29] Mandrake, dwarf, given a master's degree only in mockery.
30. Thrys scheild] Thrice exposed. *trumpir]* Impostor.
31] Ask mercy, by God, before I denounce you.
32. leif] Give up. *rowis]* Rolls of parchment, or paper.
33. Dreid] Dread. *dirtfast dearch]* Filthy dwarf.
34. cousing] Cousin.
35. Fantastik] Deluded. *trest]* Trust. *fleyit]* Scared away.
36. aip] Ape. *irregular]* Disorderly.
37. skamelar] Sponger.
38. Wanfukkit funling] Misbegotten foundling. *yrle]* Dwarf.
39. squeill] Squeal. *skirle]* Shriek.
40. And] If. *making]* Making verse.
41. pairtis] Respects.
42. ceis] cease. *play]* Accusation. *pretendis]* Allege.
43. Waik walidrag] Weak good-for-nothing.

Se sone thow mak my commissar amendis
And lat him lay sax leichis on thy lendis,   45
Meikly in recompansing of thi scorne,
Or thow sall ban the tyme that thow wes borne,
For Kennedy to the this cedull sendis.

Quod Kennedy to Dumbar

Juge in the nixt quha gat the war

7

Iersche brybour baird, vyle beggar with thy brattis,
Cuntbittin crawdoun, Kennedy, coward of kynd,   50
Evill farit and dryit, as Densmen on the rattis,
Lyk as the gleddis had on thy gulesnowt dynd,
Mismaid monstour, ilk mone owt of thy mynd,
Renunce, rebald, thy rymyng, thow bot royis.
Thy trechour tung hes tane ane Heland strynd,   55
Ane Lawland ers wald mak a bettir noyis.

8

Revin, raggit ruke, and full of rebaldrie,
Skitterand scorpioun, scauld in scurrilitie,
I se the haltane in thy harlotrie
And in to uthir science no thing slie,   60

---

44. amendis] Compensation.
45. sax leichis] Six strokes (of a rope). *lendis]* Loins.
46. recompansing] Recompense.
47. ban] Curse.
48. cedull] Document
48b] Judge in the next who got the worst.
49] Highland vagabond bard, vile beggar in your ragged clothes.
50. crawdoun] Coward. *of kynd]* By nature.
51] Ugly and dried up, like Danes on the wheels.
52. gleddis] Kites. *gulesnowt]* Yellow nose.
53. Mismaid] Deformed. *ilk mone]* Each moon.
54. Renunce] Give up. *royis]* Raves.
55. trechour] Treacherous. *Heland strynd]* Highland strain.
56. Lawland] Lowland. *ers]* Arse. *noyis]* Noise.
57. Revin] Raven. *ruke]* Rook. *rebaldrie]* Obscenity.
58. Skitterand] Defecating. *scauld]* Scold.
59. haltane] Arrogant. *harlotrie]* Loose living.
60. science] Knowledge. *slie]* Skilled.

Of every vertew voyd, as men may sie.
Quytclame clergie and cleik to the ane club,
Ane baird blasphemar in brybrie ay to be,
For wit and woisdome ane wisp fra the may rub.

9

Thow speiris, dastard, gif I dar with the fecht.   65
Ye, Dagone dowbart, thairof haif thow no dowt.
Quhair evir we meit, thairto my hand I hecht,
To red thy rebald rymyng with a rowt.
Throw all Bretane it salbe blawin owt,
How that thow, poysonit pelour, gat thy paikis.   70
With ane doig leich I schepe to gar the schowt
And nowther to the tak knyfe, swerd nor aix.

10

Thow crop and rute of tratouris tressonable,
The fathir and moder of morthour and mischeif,
Dissaitfull tyrand with serpentis tung unstable,   75
Cukcald, cradoun, cowart and commoun theif,
Thow purpest for to undo our lordis cheif
In Paislay with ane poysone that wes fell,
For quhilk, brybour, yit sall thow thoill a breif.
Pelour, on the I sall it preif my sell.   80

61. *voyd]* Deprived. *sie]* See.
62. *Quytclame clergie]* Renounce learning. *cleik]* Grab.
63. *blasphemar]* Evil speaking. *brybrie]* Beggary.
64] For your (small) wit and wisdom may be brushed away with a handful of straw.
65. *speiris]* Ask. *dastard]* Coward. *fecht]* Fight.
66. *Ye]* Yes. *dowt]* Doubt.
67. *thairto . . . hecht]* I pledge my hand to this.
68. *red]* get rid of. *a rowt]* One blow.
69. *Bretane]* Britain. *blawin owt]* Proclaimed.
70. *poysonit]* Venomous. *pelour]* Robber. *gat]* Got. *paikis]* Thrashing.
71. *doig leich]* Dog leash. *schepe]* Intend.
72. *aix]* Axe.
74. *morthour]* Murder.
75. *Dissaitfull]* Deceitful.
76. *Cukcald]* Cuckold.
77. *purpest]* Planned. *undo]* Destroy. *cheif]* Chief.
78. *fell]* Deadly.
79. *thoill a breif]* Receive a summons.
80. *preif]* Prove. *sell]* Self.

11

Thocht I wald lie, thy frawart phisnomy
Dois manifest thy malice to all men.
Fy, tratour theif, fy, Ganyelon, fy, fy!
Fy, feyndly front far fowlar than ane fen,
My freyindis thow reprovit with thy pen.   85
Thow leis, tratour, quhilk I sall on the preif,
Suppois thy heid war armit tymis ten,
Thow sall recry it, or thy croun sall cleif.

12

Or thow durst move thy mynd malitius,
Thow saw the saill abone my heid up draw.   90
Bot Eolus, full woid, and Neptunus,
Mirk and moneles us met with wind and waw,
And mony hundreth myll hyne cowd us blaw,
By Holland, Seland, Yetland and Northway coist,
In sey desert quahir we wer famist aw.   95
Yit come I hame, fals baird, to lay thy boist.

13

Thow callis the rethore with thy goldin lippis.
Na, glowrand, gaipand fule, thow art begyld.
Thow art bot gluntoch, with thy giltin hippis,
That for thy lounry mony a leisch hes fyld.   100
Wan-visaged widdefow, out of thy wit gane wyld,

81. *frawart*] Ugly. *phisnomy*] Face.
84. *feyndly front*] Fiendish forehead.
85. *reprovit*] Accused.
86. *leis*] Lies.
87. *Suppois*] Although. *heid*] Head.
88. *recry*] Retract. *croun*] Crown (of head). *cleif*] Split.
89] Before you dared put into practice your malicious purpose.
90. *draw*] Raised.
91. *woid*] Angry, stormy.
92. *Mirk*] Dark. *moneles*] Without a moon. *waw*] Wave.
93. *myll*] Mile. *hyne*] Hence. *blaw*] Blow.
95. *sey desert*] Empty sea. *famist aw*] All famished.
96. *come*] Came. *hame*] Home. *lay*] Put a stop to.
97. *rethore*] Rhetorician, poet.
98. *glowrand*] Staring. *fule*] Fool. *begyld*] Deceived.
99. *giltin*] Gilded.
100. *lounry*] Villainy. *leisch*] Leash. *fyld*] Defouled.
101. *widdefow*] Gallows-bird.

Laithly and lowsy, als lauchtane as ane leik,
Sen thow with wirschep wald sa fane be styld,
Haill, soverane senyeour, thy bawis hingis throw thy breik.

14

Forworthin fule, of all the warld reffuse, 105
Quhat ferly is thocht thow rejoys to flyte?
Sic eloquence as thay in Erschry use,
In sic is sett thy thraward appetyte.
Thow hes full littill feill of fair indyte.
I tak on me, ane pair of Lowthiane hippis 110
Sall fairar Inglis mak and mair parfyte
Than thow can blabbar with thy Carrik lippis.

15

Bettir thow ganis to leid ane doig to skomer,
Pynit pykpuris pelour, than with thy maister pingill.
Thow lay full prydles in the peis this somer 115
And fane at evin for to bring hame a single,
Syne rubb it at ane uther auld wyvis ingle.
Bot now in winter for purteth thow art traikit,
Thow hes na breik to latt thy bellokis gyngill,
Beg the ane bratt, or, baird, thow sall go naikit. 120

---

102. *Laithly]* Loathesome. *lauchtane]* Livid. *leik]* Leek.
103] Since you so wish to be addressed with ceremony.
104. *senyeour]* Lord. *bawis]* Testicles. *hingis]* Hang. *breik]* Breeches.
105. *Forworthin]* Deformed. *reffuse]* Rejected.
106. *ferly]* Marvel. *rejoys]* Rejoice.
107. *Erschry]* Gaelic.
108. *sic]* Such. *thraward]* Perverse.
109. *feill]* Understanding. *indyte]* Writing.
110. *tak on me]* Vow.
111. *Inglis]* English. *parfyte]* Perfect.
113. *ganis]* Are suited. *skomer]* Defecate.
114. *Pynit pykpuris]* Emaciated pickpurse. *pingill]* Contend.
115. *prydles]* Without pride. *peis]* Peas.
116. *evin]* Evening. *single]* Bundle of gleaned corn.
117. *rubb]* Rub between hands. *ingle]* Hearth.
118. *purteth]* Poverty. *traikit]* Worn out.
119. *latt]* Prevent. *bellokis]* Testicles.
120. *bratt]* Ragged cloak.

16

Lene, larbar loungeour, lowsy in lisk and lonye,
Fy, skolderit skyn, thow art bot skyre and skrumple:
For he that rostit Lawrance had thy grunye.
And he that hid sanct Johnis ene with ane wimple,
And he that dang sanct Augustyne with ane rumple   125
Thy fowll front had, and he that Bartilmo flaid.
The gallowis gaipis eftir thy graceles gruntill,
As thow wald for ane haggeis, hungry gled.

17

Commirwarld crawdoun, na man comptis the ane kers.
Sweir swappit swanky, swynekeper ay for swaittis,   130
Thy commissar, Quintyne, biddis the cum kis his ers.
He luvis nocht sic ane forlane loun of laittis,
He sayis thow skaffis and beggis mair beir and aitis
Nor ony cripill in Karrik land abowt.
Uther pure beggaris and thow for wage debaittis,   135
Decrepit karlingis on Kennedy cryis owt.

18

Mater annuche I haif, I bid not fenyie,
Thocht thow, fowll trumpour, thus upoun me leid.
Corrupt carioun, he sall I cry my senyie.
Thinkis thow nocht, how thow come in grit neid,   140

---

121. larbar loungeour] Feeble layabout. *lisk]* Groin. *lonye]* Loin.
122. skolderit] Tanned. *skyre]* Crease. *skrumple]* Wrinkle.
123. rostit] Roasted. *grunye]* Snout.
124. wimple] Veil.
125. dang] Hit. *rumple]* Tail (of fish).
126. flaid] Flayed.
127. gaipis] Gapes in hunger, *gruntill]* Snout.
128. haggeis] Haggis.
129. comptis] Values. *kers]* Cress.
130] Lazy, drunken fellow, swine-keeper in return for small beer.
131. ers] Arse.
132. forlane loun] Useless rascal. *laittis]* Manners.
133. skaffis] Scrounges. *beir]* Barley. *aitis]* Oats.
134. Nor] Than.
135. pure] Poor. *for wage debaittis]* Struggle for reward.
136. karlingis] Old women. *cryis]* Shout.
137. Mater annuche] Enough material. *bid]* Seek. *fenyie]* Feign.
138. trumpour] Cheat. *leid]* Lied.
139. carioun] Corpse. *he sall I cry my senyie]* I shall shout my war-cry loudly.
140. Thinkis] Recall. *come]* Came.

Greitand in Galloway lyk to ane gallow breid,
Ramand and rolpand, beggand koy and ox.
I saw the thair in to thy wathemanis weid,
Quhilk wes nocht worth ane pair of auld gray sox.

19

Ersch katherene, with thy polk breik and rilling,   145
Thow and thy quene as gredy gleddis ye gang
With polkis to mylne, and beggis baith meill and schilling.
Thair is bot lys and lang nailis yow amang,
Fowll heggirbald, for henis thus will ye hang.
Thow hes ane perrellus face to play with lambis.   150
Ane thowsand kiddis, wer thay in faldis full strang,
Thy lymmair luke wald fle thame and thair damis.

20

In till ane glen thow hes, owt of repair,
Ane laithly luge that wes the lippir menis.
With the ane sowtaris wyfe, of blis als bair,   155
And lyk twa stalkaris steilis in cokis and henis.
Thow plukkis the pultre and scho pullis of the penis.
All Karrik cryis, 'God gif this dowsy be drownd!'
And quhen thow heiris ane guse cry in the glenis,
Thow thinkis it swetar than secrrind bell of sound.   160

21

Thow Lazarus, thow laithly lene tramort,
To all the warld thow may example be,

---

141. Greitand] Weeping.
142. Ramand] Shouting. *rolpand]* Screaming. *koy]* Young cow.
144. sox] Socks.
146. quene] Wench. *gleddis]* Kites. *gang]* Go.
147. polkis] Sacks. *mylne]* Mill. *meill]* Oatmeal. *schilling]* Oat husks.
148. lys] Lice.
149. heggirbald] ? Rascal. *henis]* Hens.
151. kiddis] Young goats. *faldis]* Folds, enclosures.
152. lymmair luke] Evil look. *fle]* Frighten. *damis]* Mothers.
154] A loathsome hut that belonged to the lepers.
155. sowtaris] Cobbler's. *bair]* Devoid.
156. stalkaris] Poachers. *cokis]* Cocks.
157. plukkis] Steals. *pultre]* Poultry. *pullis]* Plucks. *penis]* Feathers.
158. gif] Grant. *dowsy]* Harlot.
159. guse] Goose.
161. tramort] Corpse.

To luk upoun thy gryslie peteous port;
For hiddowis, haw and holkit is thyne ee,
Thy cheikbane bair and blaiknit is thy ble.   165
Thy choip, thy choll garris men for to leif chest,
Thy gane, it garris us think that we mon de.
I conjure the, thow hungert Heland gaist.

22

The larbar linkis of thy lang lenye craig,
Thy pure pynit thrott, peilit and owt of ply,   170
Thy skolderit skin, hewd lyk ane saffrone bag,
Garris men dispyt thar flesche, thow spreit of Gy.
Fy, feyndly front, fy, tykis face, fy, fy!
Ay loungand lyk ane loikman on ane ledder,
With hingit luik, ay wallowand upone wry,   175
Lyk to ane stark theif glowrand in ane tedder.

23

Nyse nagus nipcaik with thy schulderis narrow,
Thow lukis lowsy, loun of lounis aw,
Hard hurcheoun hirpland, hippit as ane harrow,
Thy rigbane rattillis and thy ribbis on raw,   180
Thy hanchis hirklis with hukebanis harth and haw,
Thy laithly lymis ar lene as ony treis.

163. *peteous port]* Deplorable appearance.
164. *hiddowis]* Hideous. *haw]* Livid. *holkit]* Hollow.
165] Your jawbone is fleshless and pallid is your complexion.
166. *choip]* Jaw. *choll]* Jowl. *garris]* Cause. *leif chest]* Live chaste.
167. *gane]* Face. *mon de]* Must die.
168. *hungert]* Starving. *gaist] Ghost.
169. *linkis]* Joints, vertebrae. *lenye craig]* Skinny neck.
170. *pynit thrott]* Scraggy throat. *peilit]* Meagre. *ply]* Condition.
171. *hewd]* Coloured.
172. *dispyt]* Despise. *spreit]* Spirit.
174. *loungand]* Lolling. *loikman]* Hangman. *ledder]* Ladder.
175. *hingit]* Hanged. *wallowand upone wry]* Rolling to one side.
176. *stark]* Utter. *glowrand]* Staring. *tedder]* Noose.
177. *Nyse nagus nipcaik]* Foolish, stingy miser.
178. *loun of lounis aw]* Arch-villain.
179. *hurcheoun]* Hedgehog. *hirpland]* Limping.
180. *rigbane]* Backbone. *raw]* Row.
181] Your haunches crouch, with rough and discoloured hipbones.
182. *lymis]* Limbs.

Obey, theif baird, or I sall brek thy gaw.
Fowll carrybald, cry mercy on thy kneis.

24

Thow pure, pynhippit, ugly averill,   185
With hurkland banis holkand throw thy hyd,
Reistit and crynit as hangitman on hill,
And oft beswakkit with ane ourhie tyd,
Quhilk brewis mekle barret to thy bryd.
Hir cair is all to clenge thy cabroch howis,   190
Quhair thow lyis sawsy in saphron, bak and syd,
Powderit with prymros, savrand all with clovis.

25

Forworthin wirling, I warne the, it is wittin
How, skyttand skarth, thow hes the hurle behind.
Wan wraiglane wasp, ma wormis hes thow beschittin   195
Nor thair is gers on grund or leif on lind.
Thocht thow did first sic foly to me fynd,
Thow sall agane with ma witnes than I.
Thy gulsoch gane dois on thy bak it bind,
Thy hostand hippis lattis nevir thy hos go dry.   200

183. *brek . . . gaw]* Break your spirit (lit. gall).
184. *carrybald]* Monster.
185. *pynhippit]* Narrow-hipped. *averill]* Old horse.
186. *hurkland banis]* Crouching bones. *holkand]* Poking out.
187. *Reistit]* Dried (with smoke). *crynit]* Shrivelled.
188. *beswakkit]* Drenched. *ourhie tyd]* Too high a tide.
189. *brewis]* Causes. *barret]* Trouble. *bryd]* Bride.
190. *clenge]* Cleanse. *cabroch]* Scraggy. *howis]* Houghs.
191. *sawsy]* In a sauce.
192. *savrand]* Scenting. *clovis]* Cloves.
193. *Forworthin wirling]* Deformed wretch. *wittin]* Known.
194. *skyttand skarth]* Shitting cormorant. *hurle behind]* Diarrhoea.
195. *wraiglane]* Wriggling. *beschittin]* Excreted.
196. *gers]* Grass. *lind]* Lime tree.
197. *foly]* Filth. *fynd]* Attribute.
198. *witnes]* Witnesses.
199. *gulsoch]* Jaundice.
200. *hostand]* Coughing. *lattis]* Allow. *hos]* Hose.

26

Thow held the burch lang with ane borrowit goun
And ane caprowsy, barkit all with sweit,
And quhen the laidis saw the sa lyk a loun,
Thay bickerit the with mony bae and bleit.
Now upaland thow leivis on rubbit quheit,   205
Oft for ane caus thy burdclaith neidis no spredding,
For thow hes nowthir for to drink nor eit,
Bot lyk ane berdles baird that had no bedding.

27

Strait Gibbonis air, that nevir ourstred ane hors,
Bla, berfute berne, in bair tyme wes thow borne.   210
Thow bringis the Carrik clay to Edinburgh cors,
Upoun thy botingis hobland, hard as horne.
Stra wispis hingis owt, quhair that the wattis ar worne.
Cum thow agane to skar us with thy strais,
We sall gar scale our sculis all the to scorne,   215
And stane the up the calsay quhair thow gais.

28

Of Edinburgh the boyis as beis owt thrawis,
And cryis owt, 'Hay, heir cumis our awin queir clerk!'
Than fleis thow lyk ane howlat chest with crawis,
Quhill all the brachis at thy botingis dois bark.   220

201. *held]* Frequented.
202. *barkit]* Hardened, tanned. *sweit]* Sweat.
203. *laidis]* Lads.
204. *bickerit]* Attacked. *bae]* Baa (sheep's bleat).
205. *upaland]* In the country. *quheit]* Wheat.
206. *burdclaith]* Tablecloth.
208. *berdles]* Beardless.
209. *Strait]* Skinny. *air]* Heir. *ourstred]* Rode upon.
210. *Bla]* Blue (with cold). *berfute berne]* Bare-footed man. *bair tyme]* Hard times.
211. *cors]* Market cross.
212. *botingis]* Boots. *hobland]* Hobbling.
213. *Stra]* Straw. *hingis]* Hang. *wattis]* Welts.
214. *skar]* Scare. *strais]* Straws.
215] We shall dismiss the schools for the pupils to mock you.
216. *stane]* Stone. *calsay]* Pavement. *gais]* Walk.
217. *boyis]* Lads. *thrawis]* Swarms.
218. *queir clerk]* Rascally scholar.
219. *fleis]* Fly off. *howlat]* Owl. *chest]* Chased. *crawis]* Crows.
220. *brachis]* Hunting hounds.

Than carlingis cryis, 'Keip curches in the merk.
Our gallowis gaipis, lo, quhair ane greceles gais!'
Ane uthir sayis, 'I se him want ane sark,
I reid yow, cummer, tak in your lynning clais.'

29

Than rynis thow doun the gait with gild of boyis,   225
And all the toun tykis hingand in thy heilis.
Of laidis and lownis thair rysis sic ane noyis
Quhill runsyis rynis away with cairt and quheilis
And cager aviris castis bayth coillis and creilis,
For rerd of the and rattling of thy butis.   230
Fische wyvis cryis 'Fy!' and castis doun skillis and skeilis,
Sum claschis the, sum cloddis the on the cutis.

30

Loun, lyk Mahoun, be boun me till obey,
Theif, or in greif mischeif sall the betyd.
Cry grace, tykis face, or I the chece and fley,   235
Oule, rare and yowle, I sall defowll thy pryd,
Peilit gled, baith fed and bred of bichis syd,
And lyk ane tyk, purspyk, quhat man settis by the?
Forflittin, countbittin, beschittin, barkit hyd,
Clym-ledder, fyle-tedder, foule edder, I defy the.   240

---

221. *curches]* Head-dresses. *in the merk]* Out of sight.
222. *gaipis]* Gapes hungrily. *greceles]* Evil man.
223. *want]* Lack. *sark]* Shirt.
224. *reid]* Advise. *cummer]* Gossip. *lynning clais]* Linen clothes.
225. *rynis]* Run. *gait]* Road. *gild]* Clamour.
226. *tykis]* Curs. *heilis]* Heels.
228. *runsyis]* Horses. *cairt]* Cart. *quheilis]* Wheels.
229] And peddlars' nags throw down coals and paniers.
230. *rerd]* Din. *butis]* Boots.
231. *skillis]* Baskets. *skeilis]* Tubs.
232] One strikes you, one pelts your ankles with clods.
233. *Mahoun]* Muhammad. *boun]* Ready.
234. *greif]* Distress. *betyd]* Befall.
235. *Cry grace]* Implore mercy. *chece]* Chase. *fley]* Put to flight.
236. *rare]* Shriek. *yowle]* Howl. *defowll]* Cast down.
237. *Peilit gled]* Plucked kite. *bred]* Nourished.
238. *purspyk]* Pickpocket. *settis by the]* Esteems you.
239] Outdone in flyting, impotent, filthy, like a tanned hide.
240] Ladder-climber, noose-defiler, foul serpent, I defy you.

31

Mauch muttoun, byt buttoun, peilit gluttoun, air to Hilhous,
Rank beggar, ostir-dreger, flay-fleggar in the flet.
Chittirlilling, ruch rilling, lik-schilling in the milhous,
Baird rehator, theif of nator, fals tratour, feyindis gett,
Filling of tauch, rak-sauch, cry crauch, thow art oursett.   245
Muttoun-dryver, girnall-ryver, yadswyvar, fowll fell the!
Herretyk, lunatyk, purspyk, carlingis pet,
Rottin crok, dirtin dok, cry cok, or I sall quell the!

                                            Quod Dumbar to Kennedy

241] Maggotty sheep, button-biter, destitute glutton, heir to Hillhouse.
242] Out-and-out beggar, oyster-dredger, flea-chaser in the hall.
243] Chitterling, rough rilling-wearer, licker-up of husks in the mill.
244] Villainous bard, thief by nature, false traitor, devil's offspring.
245] Lump of tallow, gallows-bird, cry 'defeated', you are conquered.
246] Sheep-stealer, granary-robber, mare-swiver, a curse upon you.
247] Heretic, lunatic, pick-purse, old woman's fart.
248] Diseased ewe, filthy arse, confess defeat, or I shall destroy you.

55

Dunbar here adopts the persona of an old, neglected horse. He asks to be brought in from the cold (6, 11, 17), hinting perhaps at some exclusion from court or loss of the king's favour. He also requests that he should receive his seasonal livery, the allowance of clothing that courtiers regularly received at Whitsuntide and Yule (see 6, 41, 45, 63–6). The poem is striking for its witty word-play, and for its imaginative use of the metaphor of the old horse, through which Dunbar explores his relation not only with the king but with his fellow-men. There is a hierarchy among horses that has parallels in the gradations of human society. Dunbar's tone is rueful and self-mocking. The poem has no known source, although Dunbar would be familiar with the use of the horse in fables and proverbs. He possibly recalled the ageing lover's self-identification with 'olde Grisel' in Gower's *Confessio Amantis*, VIII. 2407, or Chaucer's *Scogan*, 35. In form the poem is a carol, and has the same metrical shape as 30 (see headnote to that poem). Like many carols, it is associated with Christmas, and seems to allude to some lost Yuletide custom or belief (see note to line 2). It has analogues in folk-songs on the 'Poor Old Horse' theme, in which the speaker identifies with a neglected animal, the occasion is convivial, and the season usually Christmas.

Date: The poem was possibly composed in the winter of 1505–06, since on 27 January 1506 Dunbar received a payment of £5 'be the kingis command, for caus he wantit his goun at ȝule' (*TA*, III, 181).

Text: MF, p. 18 (1–32); R, ff. 1ʳ–1ᵛ (33–76); collated with R, ff. 14ʳ–14ᵛ (1–32). MF originally had a copy of the whole poem, but because a quire has been lost, it now contains only the burden and first five stanzas. When R's transcript was made, this quire was still extant, but misplaced; R preserves the whole poem, but in two separate parts of the manuscript.
1. toune] R; toume MF.
5. Strenever] Streneverne MF, R.
36. gnawid] gnawin R.

Authorship: 'Quod Dunbar' (after line 68) in R.

277

Further reading: Baxter 1952: 149–51 (on text and date); Scott 1966: 109–15 ('imaginative paralleling of the life of the poet and that of a horse'); Bawcutt 1986 (on relation to Christmas customs and folk-song); Bawcutt 1992a: 126–30.

Schir, lat it never in toune be tald
That I suld be ane Yowllis yald.

1

Suppois I war ane ald yald aver,
Schott furth our clewch to squische the clever,
And hed the strenthis of all Strenever,   5
I wald at Youll be housit and stald.
Schir, lat it never in toune be tald
That I suld be ane Yowllis yald.

2

I am ane auld hors, as ye knaw,
That ever in duill dois drug and draw.   10
Gryt court hors puttis me fra the staw,
To fang the fog be firthe and fald.
Schir, lat it never in toune be tald
That I suld be ane Yowllis yald.

3

I heff run lang furth in the feild   15
On pastouris that ar plane and peld.
I mycht be now tein in for eild,
My bekis ar spruning he and bald.
Schir, lat it never in toun be tald
That I suld be ane Yowllis yald.   20

1–2] Sir, do not let it ever be proclaimed in public that I should be a 'Yule horse'.
3. Suppois] Even if. *yald aver]* Worn-out draught horse.
4–5] See note.
6. housit and stald] Provided with a horse-cover and a stable.
10. duill] Sorrow. *drug]* Drag.
11. Gryt] Large. *hors]* Horses. *puttis]* Push. *staw]* Stall.
12. fang] Take. *fog]* Withered grass. *firthe]* Wood. *fald]* Enclosed field.
15. heff] Have. *furth]* Outside.
16. pastouris] Pasterns. *plane]* Smooth. *peld]* Worn bare.
17. tein] Taken. *eild]* Old age.
18] See note.

4

My maine is turned in to quhyt,
And thair of ye heff all the wyt.
Quhen uthair hors hed brane to byt,
I gat bot gris, grype giff I wald.
Schir, lat it never in towne be tald   25
That I suld be ane Yowllis yald.

5

I was never dautit in to stabell.
My lyff hes bein so miserabell
My hyd to offer I am abell,
For evill schoud strae that I reiv wald.   30
Schir, lat it never in towne be tald
That I suld be ane Yowllis yald.

6

And yett, suppois my thrift be thyne,
Gif that I die your aucht within
Lat nevir the soutteris have my skin,   35
With uglie gumes to be gnawid.
Schir, lat it nevir in toun be tald
That I sould be ane Yowllis yald.

7

The court hes done my curage cuill
And maid me ane forriddin muill.   40
Yett to weir trapperis at the Yuill,
I wald be spurrit at everie spald.

---

21. *maine]* Mane.
22. *thair of]* For this. *wyt]* Blame.
23. *brane]* Bran. *byt]* Bite.
24] I got nothing but grass, if I would grasp it.
27. *dautit]* Petted.
29–30] I am ready to sell my skin (in advance of death), in return for poor-quality straw that I would devour.
33. *thrift]* Resources. *thyne]* Thin, scanty.
34. *aucht]* Possession.
35. *soutteris]* Cobblers.
36. *gumes]* Gums. *gnawid]* Chewed.
39. *done my curage cuill]* Cooled my high spirits.
40. *forriddin]* Weary from hard riding. *muill]* Mule.
41. *weir]* Wear. *trapperis]* Horse-covers.
42. *spald]* Limb (lit. shoulder).

Schir, lett it nevir in toun be tald
That I sould be ane Yuillis yald.

8

Now lufferis cummis with larges lowd.   45
Quhy sould not palfrayis thane be prowd,
Quhen gillettis wilbe schomd and schroud,
That riddin ar baith with lord and lawd?
Schir, lett it nevir in toun be tald
That I sould be ane Yuillis yald.   50

9

Quhen I was young and into ply
And wald cast gammaldis to the sky,
I had beine bocht in realmes by,
Had I consentit to be sauld.
Schir, lett it nevir in toun be tauld   55
That I sould be ane Yuillis yald.

10

With gentill hors quhen I wald knyp,
Thane is thair laid on me ane quhip.
To colleveris than man I skip,
That scabbit ar, hes cruik and cald.   60
Schir, lett it nevir in toun be tald
That I sould be ane Yuillis yald.

11

Thocht in the stall I be not clappit,
As cursouris that in silk beine trappit,

45. *lufferis]* Liveries. *larges lowd]* Loud cries of largess.
46. *palfrayis]* Riding horses. *prowd]* Fine.
47. *gillettis]* (1) Mares; (2) young women. *schomd]* Adorned. *schroud]* Well dressed.
48. *lawd]* Man of low rank.
51. *ply]* Good health.
52. *gammaldis]* Leaps, capers.
53] I might have been bought in nearby countries.
54. *sauld]* Sold.
57. *gentill]* Noble. *knyp]* Eat.
58. *quhip]* Whip.
59. *colleveris]* Horses that carry coal. *man]* Must.
60. *scabbit]* Scabby. *cruik]* Lameness. *cald]* Respiratory illness.
63. *clappit]* Patted fondly.
64. *cursouris]* Large riding horses. *trappit]* Decked.

With ane new hous I wald be happit   65
Aganis this Crystinmes for the cald.
Schir, lett it nevir in toun be tald
That I sould be ane Yuillis yald.

Respontio regis

Efter our wrettingis, thesaurer,
Tak in this gray hors, auld Dumbar,   70
Quhilk in my aucht with service trew
In lyart changeit is his hew.
Gar hows him new aganis this Yuill
And busk him lyk ane bischopis muill,
For with my hand I have indost   75
To pay quhatevir his trappouris cost.

65. *hous]* Horse-cover. *happit]* Wrapped warmly.
66. *Aganis]* In readiness for.
68a] The King's answer.
69] In accordance with our written instructions, Treasurer.
72. *lyart]* Silvery-grey. *is]* ? Has. *hew]* Colour.
73. *Gar hows]* Have him clothed.
74. *busk]* Dress finely.
75. *indost]* Endorsed, authorized.

56

This is one of the most interesting and carefully composed of Dunbar's petitions. It has four main sections: two longer passages, with a catalogue structure (1–24; 35–60), contrast the king's industrious and 'profitable' servants with those who are not 'sa profitable' (38); juxtaposed with these are two shorter and highly personal passages, each beginning with 'And thocht' (25, 61). In these Dunbar speaks of himself as poet, revealing pride in his craftsmanship, and awareness of his own bent to flyting and the destructive power of his 'pen' (82). In technique there is some resemblance to 7. On the metre, see 5. Some editors date the poem after September 1507 (see note to line 16). It is arguable, however, that this and several other petitions should be dated just before rather than after 1507 (see Introduction, p. 4).

Text: MF, pp. 196–8. The paragraphing is editorial.
85. Or] And MF.

Authorship: 'Quod Dumbar' in MF.

Further reading: Scott 1966: 105–9 ('the most devastating of these poems of complaint'); Bawcutt 1992a: 34–6; 117–18.

Schir, ye have mony servitouris
And officiaris of dyvers curis:
Kirkmen, courtmen and craftismen fyne,
Doctouris in jure and medicyne,
Divinouris, rethoris and philosophouris,   5

1. Schir] Sir. *servitouris]* Servants.
2. officiaris] Officials. *dyvers curis]* Different responsibilities.
3. Kirkmen] Churchmen.
4. Doctouris] Scholars, teachers. *jure]* Law.
5. Divinouris] Soothsayers. *rethoris]* Rhetoricians.

Astrologis, artistis and oratouris,
Men of armes and vailyeand knychtis
And mony uther gudlie wichtis,
Musicianis, menstralis and mirrie singaris,
Chevalouris, cawandaris and flingaris, 10
Cunyouris, carvouris and carpentaris,
Beildaris of barkis and ballingaris,
Masounis lyand upon the land,
And schipwrichtis hewand upone the strand,
Glasing wrichtis, goldsmythis and lapidaris, 15
Pryntouris, payntouris and potingaris;
And all of thair craft cunning,
And all at anis lawboring,
Quhilk pleisand ar and honorable
And to your hienes profitable, 20
And richt convenient for to be
With your hie regale majestie,
Deserving of your grace most ding
Bayth thank, rewarde and cherissing.

And thocht that I amang the laif 25
Unworthy be ane place to have
Or in thair nummer to be tald,
Als lang in mynd my work sall hald,

---

6. *Astrologis]* Astrologers. *artistis]* Men skilled in the learned arts.
7. *vailyeand]* Courageous.
8. *gudlie wichtis]* Excellent people.
9. *menstralis]* Minstrels. *mirrie]* Merry.
10. *chevalouris]* Mounted soldiers.
11. *cunyouris]* Makers of coins. *carvouris]* Carvers.
12. *Beildaris]* Builders. *barkis]* Barques. *ballingaris]* Small ships.
13. *Masounis]* Masons. *lyand]* Dwelling.
14. *hewand]* Cutting wood. *strand]* Shore.
15. *Glasing wrichtis]* Makers of glass. *lapidaris]* Jewellers.
16. *potingaris]* Apothecaries.
17. *cunning]* Skilled.
18. *at anis]* At once, together.
19. *pleisand]* Pleasing.
20. *hienes]* Highness.
21. *richt convenient]* Most fitting.
23. *ding]* Worthy.
24. *thank]* Gratitude. *cherissing]* Support.
25. *thocht]* Although. *laif]* Rest.
27. *nummer]* Number. *tald]* Reckoned.
28. *mynd]* Mind, memory. *hald]* Remain.

Als haill in everie circumstance,
In forme, in mater and substance,   30
But wering or consumptioun,
Roust, canker or corruptioun,
As ony of thair werkis all,
Suppois that my rewarde be small.

Bot ye sa gracious ar and meik,   35
That on your hienes followis eik
Ane uthir sort more miserabill,
Thocht thai be nocht sa profitable:
Fenyeouris, fleichouris and flatteraris,
Cryaris, craikaris and clatteraris,   40
Soukaris, groukaris, gledaris, gunnaris,
Monsouris of France, gud clarat cunnaris,
Inopportoun askaris of Yrland kynd
And meit revaris lyk out of mynd,
Scaffaris and scamleris in the nuke   45
And hall huntaris of draik and duik,
Thrimlaris and thristaris, as thai war woid,
Kokenis, and kennis na man of gude,
Schulderaris and schovaris that hes no schame
And to no cunning that can clame,   50
And can non uthir craft nor curis

29. *haill]* Whole. *circumstance]* Respect.
31. *wering]* Wearing away. *consumptioun]* Decay.
32. *roust]* Rust. *canker]* Cancer.
33. *werkis]* Works.
34. *Suppois]* Even though.
35. *gracious]* Kindly. *meik]* Unassuming.
36. *eik]* Also.
37. *sort]* Company. *miserabill]* Wretched.
39. *Fenyeouris]* Dissemblers. *fleichouris]* Hypocrites.
40. *cryaris]* Shouters. *craikaris]* Clamourers. *clatteraris]* Chatterers.
41. *soukaris]* Parasites. *groukaris]* Obscure. *gledaris]* Obscure. *gunnaris]* Gunners.
42. *Monsouris]* Monsieurs. *cunnaris]* Tasters.
43] Importunate beggars of Irish race.
44] And stealers of food, as if out of their wits.
45. *Scaffaris]* Scroungers. *scamleris]* Spongers. *nuke]* Corner.
46. *draik]* Drake. *duik]* Duck.
47. *Thrimlaris]* Pushers. *thristaris]* Thrusters. *woid]* Mad.
48] And rogues who are unacquainted with any respectable man.
49. *Schulderaris]* Those who shoulder their way forward. *schovaris]* Pushers.
50. *cunning]* Skill. *clame]* Lay claim.
51. *can]* Know. *curis]* Duties.

Bot to mak thrang, schir, in your duris,
And rusche in quhair thay counsale heir
And will at na man nurtir leyr;
In quintiscence eik ingynouris joly,   55
That far can multiplie in folie,
Fantastik fulis, bayth fals and gredy,
Of toung untrew and hand evill-diedie.
Few dar of all this last additioun
Cum in Tolbuyth without remissioun.   60

And thocht this nobill cunning sort
(Quhom of befoir I did report)
Rewardit be, it war bot ressoun;
Thairat suld no man mak enchessoun.
Bot quhen the uther fulis nyce   65
That feistit at Cokelbeis gryce
Ar all rewardit and nocht I,
Than on this fals warld I cry fy!
My hart neir bristis than for teyne,
Quhilk may nocht suffer nor sustene   70
So grit abusioun for to se,
Daylie in court befoir myn e.
And yit more panence wald I have,
Had I rewarde amang the laif.
It wald me sumthing satisfie   75

52. *mak thrang*] Crowd. *duris*] Doors.
53. *counsale*] Private discussion. *heir*] Hear.
54] And will learn good manners from no one.
55. *quintiscence*] Alchemy. *ingynouris joly*] Fine contrivers.
57. *Fantastik fulis*] Deluded fools.
58. *untrew*] Untruthful. *evill-diedie*] Evil-doing.
60. *Tolbuyth*] Tolbooth. *remissioun*] Pardon.
61. *cunning*] Skilled.
62] Of whom I wrote before.
63. *war bot ressoun*] Would be only reasonable.
64. *Thairat*] At that. *enchessoun*] Objection.
65. *nyce*] Absurd.
66. *feistit*] Feasted.
69. *bristis*] Breaks. *teyne*] Vexation.
70. *sustene*] Endure.
71. *grit*] Great. *abusioun*] Abuse.
72. *e*] Eye.
73. *panence*] See note.
75. *sumthing*] Somewhat.

And les of my malancolie,
And gar me mony falt ourse
That now is brayd befoir myn e.
My mind so fer is set to flyt
That of nocht ellis I can endyt.   80
For owther man my hart tobreik
Or with my pen I man me wreik.
And sen the tane most nedis be –
In to malancolie to de
Or lat the vennim ische all out –   85
Be war anone, for it will spout,
Gif that the tryackill cum nocht tyt
To swage the swalme of my dispyt.

76. *les]* Relieve (me). *malancolie]* Melancholy.
77. *gar]* Cause. *ourse]* Overlook.
78. *brayd]* Plain.
79. *set]* Disposed. *flyt]* Flyte, utter abuse.
80. *nocht ellis]* Nothing else. *endyt]* Compose verse.
81] For either must my heart break apart.
82. *man]* Must. *wreik]* Avenge.
83] And since one (of these) must necessarily come about.
84. *de]* Die.
85. *vennim]* Poison. *ische]* Issue.
86. *Be war anone]* Take heed at once.
87. *Gif]* If. *tryackill]* Remedy. *tyt]* Rapidly.
88. *swage]* Heal. *swalme]* Swelling. *dispyt]* Resentment.

57

Although this petition to the king cannot be dated precisely, it may have been written about the same time as 55, with which it has much in common. Dunbar speaks of himself as old (2, 63), and conveys a sense of being excluded from royal favour. There are themes that occur in other petitions, such as the poet's long service and reluctance to flatter; a striking preoccupation with 'degre' (29) and social status; and a richly sustained use of bird symbolism in stanzas 2–6. Dunbar explicitly compares himself to a hawk, a member of the birds of prey that in medieval poetry commonly symbolized the nobility or knightly classes; cf. Chaucer's *Parliament of Fowls* and Holland's *Howlat*. He also implicitly associates himself, as a poet, with the nightingale (17), and, as one who is out of favour, with the owl (24). On the stanza, see 9.

Text: MF, pp. 295–6, 309 (a displaced leaf); collated with B, ff. 94ᵛ–95ᵛ, and R, f. 34ʳ (stanzas 16–17 only).
1. yit] B; ye MF.

Authorship: 'Quod Dumbar' in MF and B.

Further reading: On James IV's interest in falconry, see Gilbert 1979 and Cummins 1988. See also Ross 1981: 146–8; Reiss 1979: 38–40 (questions the poem's unity and Dunbar's 'control over his material'); Bawcutt 1992a: 122–6 (a more favourable evaluation, and discussion of the symbolism).

1

Schir, yit remember as befoir
How that my youthe is done forloir
In your service with pane and greiff.

1. *Schir*] Sir. *befoir*] In the past.
2. *is done forloir*] Has been lost.
3. *greiff*] Grief.

287

Gud conscience cryis reward thairfoir.
Exces of thocht dois me mischief.   5

2

Your clarkis ar servit all aboute
And I do lyke ane rid halk schout,
To cum to lure that hes na leif,
Quhair my plumis begynnis to mowt.
Exces of thocht dois me mischeiff.   10

3

Foryet is ay the falcounis kynd,
Bot ever the myttell is hard in mynd;
Quhone the gled dois the peirtrikis preiff
The gentill goishalk gois undynd.
Exces of thocht dois me mischeiff.   15

4

The pyat withe the pairtie cote
Feynyeis to sing the nychtingale note,
Bot scho can not the corchet cleiff
For hasknes of hir carleche throte.
Exces of thocht dois me mischeiff.   20

5

Ay fairast feddiris hes farrest foulis.
Suppois thai have na sang bot yowlis,
In sylver caiges thai sit but greif.

---

4. *cryis]* Demands. *thairfoir]* For this.
6. *clarkis]* Clergy, scholars. *aboute]* Around.
7. *rid halk]* Red hawk.
8. *leif]* Permission.
9. *Quhair]* When. *plumis]* Feathers. *mowt]* Moult.
11. *Foryet]* Forgotten. *ay]* Always. *kynd]* Species.
12. *hard in mynd]* Remembered.
13] When the kite feeds on partridges.
14. *gentill]* Noble. *goishalk]* Goshawk. *undynd]* Without dinner.
16. *pyat]* Magpie. *pairtie cote]* Particoloured coat.
17. *Feynyeis]* Pretends. *note]* Melody.
18] See note.
19. *hasknes]* Harshness. *carleche]* Rough, boorish.
21] Birds from far-off places ever have the finest feathers.
22. *Suppois]* Although. *sang]* Song. *yowlis]* Yells.
23. *but greif]* Without discomfort.

Kynd native nestis dois clek bot owlis.
Exces of thocht dois me mischeiff.   25

6

O gentill egill, how may this be,
Quhilk of all foulis dois heast fle?
Your leggis quhy do ye not releif
And chirreis thame eftir thair degre?
Exces of thocht dois me mischeiff.   30

7

Quhone servit is all uther man,
Gentill and sempill, of everie clan,
Raf Coilyearis kynd and Johnne the Reif,
No thing I gett nor conqueis can.
Exces of thocht dois me mischeif.   35

8

Thocht I in courte be maid refuse
And have few vertewis for to ruse,
Yit am I cum of Adame and Eve
And fane wald leif as utheris dois.
Exces of thocht dois me mischeif.   40

9

Or I suld leif in sic mischance,
Giff it to God war na grevance,
To be ane pykthank I wald preif,
For thai in warld wantis na plesance.
Exces of thocht dois me mischeif.   45

---

24. *Kynd]* Of this country. *clek]* Hatch. *bot]* Only.
27. *foulis]* Birds. *heast fle]* Fly the highest.
28. *leggis]* Lieges, subjects. *releif]* Assist.
29. *chirreis]* Cherish, foster. *eftir thair degre]* According to their rank.
32. *sempill]* Simple, lowly.
33] *See note.*
34. *conqueis]* Acquire.
37. *ruse]* Boast of.
39. *fane wald leif]* Would like to live.
41. *Or]* Before. *mischance]* Misery.
42. *Giff]* If. *grevance]* Offence.
43. *pykthank]* Sycophant. *preif]* Attempt.
44. *wantis]* Lack.

10

In sum pairt of my selffe I pleinye:
Quhone utheris dois flattir and feynye,
Allace, I can bot ballattis breif.
Sic barnheid leidis my brydill reynye.
Exces of thocht dois me mischeiff.   50

11

I grant my service is bot lycht.
Thairfoir, of mercye and not of rycht,
I ask you, schir, no man to greiff,
Sum medecyne gif that ye mycht.
Exces of thocht dois me mischeiff.   55

12

Nane can remeid my maledie
Sa weill as ye, schir, veralie.
With ane benefice ye may preiff,
And gif I mend not haistalie,
Exces of thocht lat me mischeif.   60

13

I wes in youthe on nureice kne
Cald dandillie, bischop, dandillie.
And quhone that age now dois me greif
A sempill vicar I can not be.
Exces of thocht dois me mischeif.   65

46] To some extent I blame myself
47. *feynye*] Deceive.
48. *bot ballattis breif*] Only write poems.
49. *barnheid*] Childishness. *reynye*] Rein.
51. *grant*] Concede. *lycht*] Slight.
53. *no man to greiff*] Without harming anyone.
54. *gif*] Give.
56. *remeid*] Cure.
57. *veralie*] Truly.
58. *preiff*] Put it to the test.
59. *mend*] Improve in health.
60. *lat*] Allowed.
61. *nureice kne*] Nurse's knee.
63. *greif*] Distress.

14

Jok that wes wont to keip the stirkis
Can now draw him ane cleik of kirkis,
With ane fals cairt in to his sleif,
Worthe all my ballattis under the byrkis.
Exces of thocht dois me mischeif.   70

15

Twa curis or thre hes uplandis Michell,
With dispensationis in ane knitchell,
Thocht he fra nolt had new tane leif.
He playis with totum and I with nychell.
Exces of thocht dois me mischeiff.   75

16

How sould I leif, and I not landit
Nor yit withe benefice am blandit?
I say not, schir, yow to repreiff,
Bot doutles I go rycht neirhand it.
Exces of thocht dois me mischeiff.   80

17

As saule in to purgatorie,
Leifand in pane with hoip of glorie,
So is my selffe, ye may beleiff,
In hoip, schir, of your adjutorie.
Exces of thocht dois me mischeiff.   85

66. *keip]* Look after. *stirkis]* Bullocks.
67. *cleik]* Large number.
68. *cairt]* Playing card. *sleif]* Sleeve.
69. *byrkis]* Birch trees.
71. *curis]* Benefices. *uplandis]* Rustic, boorish.
72. *knitchell]* Small bundle.
73. *nolt]* Cattle. *new tane leif]* Just departed.
74] *See note.*
76. *leif]* Live. *landit]* Possessed of lands.
77. *yit]* Even. *blandit]* Soothed, mollified.
78. *say]* Speak. *repreiff]* Rebuke.
79. *rycht neirhand]* Very close to.
81. *saule]* Soul.
82. *pane]* Pain, punishment.
83. *beleiff]* Believe.
84. *adjutorie]* Assistance.

58

Several courtiers, including the poet himself, are ridiculed in this series of comic sketches. In ironic tone and use of reductive animal imagery, it resembles the descriptions of rustic dances found in Scottish poems such as *Colkelbie Sow*, *Peblis to the Play* (MF, no. xlix) and *Christis Kirk on the Grene* (MF, no. xliii). The type of dance is not specified; there is little to substantiate the notion that it is a morris (Jung 1989), and dances of many kinds were known in Scotland at this time (see the references in *The Complaynt of Scotland*, pp. 51–2). The poem is likely to have been composed close in time to **60** and **61**, probably after 1511, when James Dog (44) is first recorded as one of the queen's servitors. Mistress Musgrave (26ff.) is also prominent in the records between 1511 and 1513. On the stanza, see **2**.

Text: MF, pp. 340–41; collated with R, f. 45^r.

Authorship: 'Quod Dunbar of a dance in the quen[is] chalmer' in MF.

Further reading: On the literary tradition of the 'peasant-brawl', see Jones 1953 and Maclaine 1964. On this poem see Ross 1981: 207–8 (a moralized interpretation); Bawcutt 1992a: 247–9.

1

Sir Jhon Sinclair begowthe to dance,
For he was new cum owt of France.
For ony thing that he do mycht

1. begowthe] Began.
3] No matter what he did.

The an futt yeid ay onrycht,
And to the tother wald nocht gree. 5
Quod an, 'Tak up the quenis knycht!'
A mirrear dance mycht na man see.

2

Than cam in maistir Robert Schau:
He leuket as he culd lern tham a,
Bot ay his an futt did waver. 10
He stackeret lyk an strummall aver
That hopschackellt war aboin the kne.
To seik fra Sterling to Stranaver,
A mirrear daunce mycht na man see.

3

Than cam in the maister almaser, 15
An hommiltye jommeltye juffler.
Lyk a stirk stackarand in the ry,
His hippis gaff mony hoddous cry.
John Bute the fule said, 'Waes me,
He is bedirtin, fye, fy!' 20
A mirrear dance mycht na man se.

4

Than cam in Dunbar the mackar:
On all the flure thair was nan frackar,
And thair he dancet the dirrye dantoun.
He hoppet lyk a pillie wanton, 25

4. an futt] One foot. *yeid]* Went. *onrycht]* Wrong.
5. tother] Other. *gree]* Agree (with).
6. Quod] Said. *an]* One person. *Tak]* Pick.
7. mirrear] Merrier.
8. cam] Came. *maistir]* Master.
9] He looked as if he could teach them all.
11. stackeret] Staggered. *strummall]* ?Ungainly. *aver]* Old horse.
12. hopschackellt] Hobbled. *aboin]* Above. *kne]* Knee.
16. juffler] Shuffler.
17. stirk] Young bullock. *ry]* Rye.
18. gaff] Gave. *hoddous]* Hideous.
19. fule] Fool. *Waes]* Woe is.
20. bedirtin] Befouled.
22. mackar] Poet.
23. flure] Floor. *frackar]* More agile.
24. dirrye dantoun] Name of a dance.
25. pillie wanton] ? Randy person.

For luff of Musgraeffe, men tellis me.
He trippet quhill he tint his panton.
A mirrear dance mycht na man see.

5

Than cam in maesteres Musgraeffe:
Scho mycht heff lernit all the laeffe.   30
Quhen I schau hir sa trimlye dance,
Hir guid convoy and contenance,
Than for hir saek I wissit to be
The grytast erle or duk in France.
A mirrear dance mycht na man see.   35

6

Than cam in dame Dounteboir:
God waett gif that schou louket sowr.
Scho maid sic morgeownis with hir hippis,
For lachtter nain mycht hald thair lippis.
Quhen schou was danceand bisselye   40
An blast of wind son fra hir slippis.
A mirrear dance mycht na man se.

7

Quhen thair was cum in fyve or sax,
The quenis Dog begowthe to rax
And of his band he maid a bred   45
And to the danceing soin he him med.

---

26. *luff*] Love.
27. *trippet*] Danced. *tint*] Lost. *panton*] Slipper.
29. *maesteres*] Mistress.
30. *lernit*] Taught. *laeffe*] Rest.
31. *schau*] Saw.
32. *convoy*] Bearing. *contenance*] Appearance.
33. *saek*] Sake. *wissit*] Wished.
34. *duk*] Duke.
37. *waett*] Knows. *schou*] She. *louket*] Looked.
38. *morgeownis*] Odd movements.
39. *lachtter*] Laughter. *hald*] Hold shut.
40. *bisselye*] Energetically.
41. *son*] Soon.
43. *sax*] Six.
44. *rax*] Stretch.
45. *of his band*] From his tether. *bred*] Sudden movement.
46. *soin*] Soon. *him med*] Made his way.

Quhou mastevlyk abowt yeid he!
He stinckett lyk a tyk, sum saed.
A mirrear dance mycht na man see.

59

Dunbar elegantly compliments a lady on her beauty and virtue, but makes the lover's stock complaint that she is merciless (cf. the theme of 26). He plays wittily with the different senses of 'rew' (10), and with the central image of the 'garthe' (6), a metaphor for the lady's heart. This motif, which derives ultimately from *Le Roman de la Rose*, was very popular in contemporary love poetry. For other Scottish uses, cf. the fragmentary 'In all oure gardyn growis thare na flouris' (*Chepman and Myllar Prints*, 88); and Alexander Scott's 'Sen in your garth the lilly quhyte / May nocht remane amang the laif' (*Poems*, no. vii, 25–6). There is no evidence to support the notion that this poem is a disguised petition to the queen (Baxter 1952: 121). On the stanza, see 24.

Text: MF, p. 320.

Authorship: 'Quod Dumbar'.

Further reading: Scott 1966: 57–9 ('Dunbar's most perfect lyric'); Reiss 1979: 100–102 ('essentially ironic'); Bawcutt 1992a: 297–9 ('witty, and compact as a sonnet').

1

Sweit rois of vertew and of gentilnes,
Delytsum lyllie of everie lustynes,
Richest in bontie and in bewtie cleir
And everie vertew that is deir,
Except onlie that ye ar mercyles.   5

1. vertew] Virtue. *gentilnes]* Nobility.
2. Delytsum] Delightful. *lustynes]* Loveliness.
3. bontie] Goodness. *cleir]* Shining.

2

In to your garthe this day I did persew.
Thair saw I flowris that fresche wer of hew,
Baithe quhyte and rid, moist lusty wer to seyne,
And halsum herbis upone stalkis grene,
Yit leif nor flour fynd could I nane of rew.   10

3

I dout that Merche with his caild blastis keyne
Hes slane this gentill herbe that I of mene,
Quhois petewous deithe dois to my hart sic pane
That I wald mak to plant his rute agane,
So confortand his levis unto me bene.   15

6. *garthe]* Garden. *persew]* Enter.
7. *hew]* Colour.
8. *rid]* Red. *lusty]* Attractive. *seyne]* See (archaic infin.).
9. *halsum]* Health-giving.
10. *rew]* Rue.
11. *dout]* Fear. *caild]* Cold. *keyne]* Fierce.
12. *gentill]* Noble. *that I of mene]* Of which I speak.
13. *petewous]* Piteous. *pane]* Suffering.
14. *mak]* Attempt.
15. *confortand]* Encouraging. *bene]* Are.

60 and 61

These poems form a pair: both are addressed to the queen, Margaret Tudor, and both make fun of James Dog (or Doig), with whose name Dunbar plays humorously. Dog had been a Wardrobe official in James IV's household since the beginning of his reign; in 1494, for instance, he was paid for hanging the king's chamber with arras and other furnishings, and many later references link him specifically with the king. The king and queen had separate households, and Dog is not listed as one of the queen's *servitores* until 1511 (*TA*, IV, 265); this suggests that these poems should be dated between 1511 and 1513. Dunbar himself, as a member of the king's household, was entitled to a twice-yearly clothing allowance, at Whitsun and Christmas (cf. **55**). The complaint in **60** presumably refers to a special gift of clothing, authorized by the queen (see 5 and 9). Poem **60** is remarkable for its witty deployment of canine imagery: Dog barks (6) and snarls (10) at the poet; large and ungainly as a mastiff, he is not suited to be the queen's lapdog, or favourite. Poem **61** is a comic palinode: closely mirroring the preceding poem in length and stanza (on which, see **16**), it apparently retracts the criticism of Dog. But the praise is ironic, and the new unifying image of the lamb presents Dog as a feeble victim.

Text: MF, pp. 339–40; collated with R, f. 44ʳ–ᵛ.

Authorship. 60 has the colophon 'Quod Dunbar of Iames Dog kepair of the quenis wardrep'; **61** has the colophon 'Quod Dunbar of the said Iames quhen he had plesett him'.

Further reading: Reiss 1979; 51–2; Bawcutt 1992a: 244–7.

60

1

The wardraipper of Venus boure,
To giff a doubtlett he is als doure
As it war of an futt-syd frog:
Madame, ye heff a dangerous dog.

2

Quhen that I schawe to him your markis,   5
He turnis to me again and barkis,
As he war wirriand an hog:
Madame, ye heff a dangerous dog.

3

Quhen that I schawe to him your wrytin,
He girnis that I am red for bytin –   10
I wald he had an havye clog:
Madame, ye heff an dangerous dog.

4

Quhen that I speik till him freindlyk,
He barkis lyk an midding tyk,
War chassand cattell throu a bog: 15
Madam, ye heff a dangerous dog.

5

He is an mastive, mekle of mycht,
To keip your wardroippe over nycht
Fra the grytt sowdan Gog Magog:
Madam, ye heff a dangerous dog.   20

1. wardraipper] Officer of the Wardrobe.
2. doublett] Short, close-fitting man's garment. *doure]* Unwilling.
3] As if it were a matter of a foot-length cloak.
4. heff] Have.
5. schawe] Show.
7] As if he were worrying, or mauling, a young sheep.
9. wrytin] Written document.
10. girnis] Snarls. *red for bytin]* Fearful of being bitten.
11. wald] Wish. *havye clog]* Heavy wooden block.
13. freindlyk] In a friendly way.
14. midding tyk] Dunghill cur.
17. mastive] Mastiff. *mekle]* Great.
18. keip] Guard. *wardroippe]* Wardrobe.
19. Fra] From. *sowdan]* Pagan ruler.

6

He is over mekle to be your messan.
Madam, I red you, get a less an.
His gang garris all your chalmeris schog.
Madam, ye heff a dangerous dog.

61

1

O gracious princes guid and fair,
Do weill to James, your wardraipair,
Quhais faythfull bruder maist freind I am:
He is na dog, he is a lam.

2

Thocht I in ballet did with him bourde,   5
In malice spack I nevir an woord,
Bot all, my dame, to do you gam:
He is na dog, he is a lam.

3

Your hienes can nocht gett an meter
To keip your wardrope, nor discreter   10
To rewle your robbis and dres the sam:
He is na dog, he is a lam.

4

The wyff that he had in his innis,
That with the taingis wald braek his schinnis,

---

21. *messan]* Lapdog.
22. *red]* Advise. *less an]* Smaller one.
23] His tramp causes all your rooms to shake.

3. *bruder]* Brother. *freind]* Friendly.
5] Although I jested with him in verse.
6. *spack]* Spoke.
7. *dame]* Lady. *do you gam]* Entertain you.
9. *hienes]* Highness. *an meter]* A person more fitting.
10. *discreter]* More judicious.
11] To look after your robes and keep them in order.
13. *wyff]* Wife. *innis]* Dwelling.
14. *taingis]* Fire tongs. *braek]* Break.

I wald schou drownet war in a dam: 15
He is na dog, he is a lam.

5

The wyff that wald him kuckald mak,
I wald schou war, bayth syd and back,
Weill batteret with an barrou tram:
He is na dog, he is an lam.   20

6

He hes sa weill doin me obey
In till all thing, thairfoir I pray,
That nevir dolour mak him dram:
He is na dog, he is a lam.

15. wald] Wish. *dam]* Mill-dam.
17. kuckald] Cuckold.
19. batteret] Beaten.
21. doin me obey] Obeyed me.
22. In till] In.
23. dolour] Grief. *dram]* Dejected.

62

This is a mock-commendation of women, who, it is implied, by granting sexual favours enable their husbands to pervert the course of justice. In tone it resembles **2**, also a satire on legal corruptions, and the ironic praise of female wisdom and honesty has parallels in **3**. B includes the poem in a section entitled 'Schort Epegrammis aganis Women' (f. 258ʳ); there it is followed by an anonymous and cruder poem on a similar theme, 'The use of court richt weill I knaw' (f. 261ᵛ). Dunbar's poem is notable for its extended irony, directed against the husbands as well as their wives, and for its word-play that often contains sexual innuendos. He employs an ingenious stanza, characterized by internal rhyme and an alternation of long and short lines: $a^4b^3a^4b^3c^4d^3c^4d^3$. Some of the stanzas employed by Alexander Scott are disposed in similar patterns; cf. 'Happie is he hes hald him fre' (*Poems*, no. xxxv) and 'Ladeis be war that plesand ar' (no. xxix).

Text: MF, pp. 324–5; collated with B, f. 261ʳ–261ᵛ, and R, ff. 38ᵛ–39ʳ.
7. So] B; For MF.
47. Swa] B; Sic MF.

Authorship: 'Quod Dumbar' in MF, B and R.

Further reading: Scott 1966: 70–72 ('the real target is the middle-class landed gentry, the small lairds'); Ebin 1979–80: 278–80 (on the word-play); Bawcutt 1992a: 216–17 ('the tone is one of amused contempt').

1

Thir ladeis fair that maks repair
And in the courte ar kend,
Thre dayis thair thai will do mair,

1. Thir ladeis] These ladies.
1–2. maks repair . . . kend] Attend court often, and are well known there.

Ane mater for to end,
Than thair gudmen will do in ten   5
  For ony craift thai can.
So weill thai ken quhat tyme and quhen
  Thair meynis thai sould mak than.

2

Withe litill noy thai can convoy
  A mater finalie;   10
Yit myld and moy thai keip it coy
  On evynnis quyetlie.
Thai do no mys, bot gif thai kys
  And kepis collatioun,
Quhat rak of this? The mater is   15
  Brocht to conclusioun.

3

Ye may wit weill, thai have grit feill
  A mater to solist.
Traist as the steill, syne never a deill
  Quhone thai cum hame is myst.   20
Thir lairdis ar, me think, rycht far
  Sic ladeis behaldin to,
That sa weill dar go to the bar,
  Quhone thair is ocht ado.

4. mater] Legal case.
6. craift] Skill. *can]* Know.
7. ken] Know.
8. meynis] Complaints. *than]* Then.
9. noy] Fuss. *convoy]* Conduct.
10. finalie] Decisively.
11. moy] Submissive. *coy]* Quiet.
12. evynnis] Evenings.
13. mys] Wrong.
14. kepis] Take.
15. Quhat rak] What does it matter.
17. wit] Understand. *feill]* Perceptiveness.
18. solist] Plead.
19. Traist] True. *deill]* Bit.
20. myst] Missed.
21. lairdis] Minor landowners. *me think]* It seems.
22] Obliged to such ladies.
23. dar] Dare. *bar]* Court of law.
24. ocht ado] Something to be done.

4

Thairfoir, I rid, gif ye have pleid   25
   Or mater in to pley,
To mak remeid, send in your steid
   Your ladeis, grathit up gay.
Thai can defend, evin to the end,
   Ane mater furthe expres.   30
Suppois thai spend, it is onkend,
   Thair geir is not the les.

5

In quyet place, and thai have space,
   Within les nor twa houris,
Thai can, percace, purches sic grace   35
   At the compositouris,
Thair compositioun, without suspitioun,
   Thair finalie is endit,
With expeditioun and full remissioun,
   And selis thairto appendit.   40

6

All haill almoist thai mak the coist
   With sobir recompence,
Rycht litle loist, thai get indoist
   All haill thair evidens.
Sic ladyis wyis ar all to pryis,   45

25. *rid]* Counsel. *pleid]* Law suit.
26. *in to pley]* In progress.
27. *mak remeid]* Get redress. *steid]* Place.
28. *grathit]* Dressed. *gay]* Finely.
30. *furthe]* On its way. *expres]* Plainly.
31. *Suppois]* Although. *onkend]* Unknown.
32. *geir]* Property. *les]* Less.
33. *and]* If. *space]* Opportunity.
34. *les nor]* Less than.
35. *percace]* Perhaps. *purches]* Obtain. *grace]* Concession.
37. *compositioun]* Settlement of a dispute.
38. *endit]* Achieved.
39–40] With speed and full pardon, and seals attached to the document.
41. *haill]* Whole, undamaged. *coist]* Outlay.
43. *indoist]* Endorsed, authenticated.
44. *All haill]* Completely. *evidens]* Documents establishing a legal right.
45. *Sic]* Such. *pryis]* Be esteemed.

To say the verite,
Swa can devyis, and none supprys.
Thame throw thair honeste.

46. *verite]* Truth.
47–8] Who can so contrive, and nobody damage them because of their virtuous
reputation.

63

Dunbar's request for preferment is here expressed obliquely, in the form of an allegorical dream: his melancholy reflections on the corruption of court life and his own lack of success are personified and dramatized. The man whose service has been long, but vain (53, 67), is the poet himself; and the king seems to be addressed indirectly, in the personified figure of Nobleness, who takes a benign interest in the dreamer's welfare (27–30, 42) and may cure his malady (50, 72). Dunbar implicitly calls upon James to display his inherent nobleness, not only of birth but of character. The poem resembles petitions such as 51 and 57 in its criticism of clerical pluralism and the unjust distribution of benefices. On the stanza, see 24. The poem cannot be dated with certainty, but is associated with New Year (55), and the custom of giving presents at that season (see 29). Lines 111–15 possibly refer to an incident in the summer of 1506; if so, the poem's composition would belong to early in 1507.

Text: R, ff. 3ᵛ–5ʳ. This text is poor: there are aberrant spellings (some silently corrected), oddities of syntax, and a few undoubted errors.
14. feindlie] freindlie R.
25. weid] leid R.
50. his] *Not in* R.
62. thow] 30w R.
73. quod] withe R.
75. thow] 30w R.
109. He] 3e R.
110. thow] 30w R.

Authorship: 'Quod Dumbar' in R.

Further reading: Scott 1966: 151–4; Reiss 1979: 86–9; Ross 1981: 154–5; Bawcutt 1992a: 119–22.

306

1

This hinder nycht, half sleiping as I lay,
Me thocht my chalmer in ane new aray
Was all depent with many divers hew
Of all the nobill storyis, ald and new,
Sen oure first father formed was of clay.   5

2

Me thocht the lift all bricht with lampis lycht,
And thairin enterrit many lustie wicht,
Sum young, sum old, in sindry wyse arayit.
Sum sang, sum danceit, on instrumentis sum playit,
Sum maid disportis with hartis glaid and lycht.   10

3

Thane thocht I thus: this is ane felloun phary,
Or ellis my witt rycht woundrouslie dois varie.
This seimes to me ane guidlie companie,
And gif it be ane feindlie fantasie,
Defend me Jhesu and his moder Marie!   15

4

Thair pleasant sang nor yett thair pleasant toun
Nor yett thair joy did to my heart redoun.
Me thocht the drerie damiesall, Distres,
And eik hir sorie sister, Hevines,
Sad as the leid in baid lay me abone.   20

1. hinder] Past.
2. Me thocht] It seemed to me. *chalmer]* Bedroom. *aray]* Furnishing.
3. depent] Decorated. *divers hew]* Varied hue.
5. Sen] Since.
6. lift] Sky. *lampis lycht]* Lamplight.
7. thairin] Inside. *lustie wicht]* Joyful person.
8. sindry wyse] Different fashions.
10. disportis] Entertainments. *lycht]* Joyful.
11. felloun] Great. *phary]* Supernatural experience.
12. ellis] Else. *varie]* Wander.
13. guidlie] Handsome.
14. gif] If. *feindlie]* Diabolic. *fantasie]* Hallucination.
15. moder] Mother.
16. yett] Even. *toun]* Music.
17. redoun] Enter.
18. drerie] Mournful. *Distres]* Grief.
19. sorie] Sorrowful. *Hevines]* Depression.
20. sad] Heavy. *leid]* Lead. *baid]* Bed. *abone]* Above.

5

And Langour satt up at my beddis heid.
With instrument full lamentable and deid
Scho playit sangis, so duilfull to heir,
Me thocht ane houre seimeit ay ane yeir.
Hir hew was wan and wallowed as the weid.   25

6

Thane com the ladyis danceing in ane trace,
And Nobilnes befoir thame come ane space,
Saying withe cheir bening and womanly:
'I se ane heir in bed oppressit ly,
My sisteris, go and help to gett him grace.'   30

7

With that anon did start out of a dance
Twa sisteris callit Confort and Pleasance,
And with twa harpis did begin to sing.
Bot I thairof mycht tak na rejoseing,
My heavines opprest me with sic mischance.   35

8

Thay saw that I not glader wox of cheir,
And thairof had thai winder all, but weir,
And said ane lady that Persaveing hecht,
'Of hevines he fiellis sic a wecht,
Your melody he pleisis not till heir.   40

21. *Langour]* Sadness.
22. *lamentable]* Mournful. *deid]* Funereal.
23. *duilfull]* Doleful.
25. *hew]* Complexion. *wallowed]* Faded. *the weid]* Woods.
26. *com]* Came. *trace]* Processional dance.
28. *cheir]* Expression. *bening]* Kindly.
29. *ane]* Someone. *oppressit]* Afflicted.
31. *anon]* At once.
32. *Confort]* Delight.
34. *thairof]* In this. *rejoseing]* Pleasure.
35. *mischance]* Misery.
36. *not glader wox]* Grew no happier.
37. *winder]* Astonishment. *but weir]* Without doubt.
38. *Persaveing]* Perceptiveness. *hecht]* Was called.
39. *fiellis]* Feels. *wecht]* Weight.

9

'Scho and Distres, hir sister, dois him greve.'
Quod Nobilnes, 'Quhow sall he thame eschew?'
Thane spak Discretioun, ane lady richt bening,
'Wirk eftir me, and I sall gar him sing,
And lang or nicht gar Langar tak hir leve.'   45

10

And then said Witt, 'Gif thai work not be the,
But onie dout thai sall not work be me.'
Discretioun said, 'I knaw his melody.
The strok he feillis of melancholie,
And, Nobilnes, his lecheing lyis in the.   50

11

'Or evir this wicht at heart be haill and feir,
Both thow and I most in the court appeir,
For he hes lang maid service thair in vane.
With sum rewaird we mane him quyt againe,
Now in the honour of this guid New Yeir.'   55

12

'Weill worth the, sister,' said Considerance,
'And I sall help for to mantene the dance.'
Thane spak ane wicht callit Blind Effectioun:
'I sall befoir yow be with myne electioun,
Of all the court I have the governance.'   60

41. *greve]* Harm.
42. *Quod]* Said. *eschew]* Escape.
43. *spak]* Spoke. *Discretioun]* Discernment.
44. *Wirk]* Work. *eftir me]* ? As I do. *gar]* Cause.
45] And long before night cause sadness to depart.
46. *be the]* For you.
47. *But onie dout]* Without any doubt.
48. *melody]* Malady.
49. *strok]* Stroke.
50. *lecheing]* Cure.
51. *Or evir]* Before. *haill]* Healthy. *feir]* Vigorous.
52. *most]* Must.
54. *mane]* Must. *quyt]* Repay.
56. *Weill worth the]* May you prosper. *Considerance]* Consideration.
57. *mantene]* Continue.
58. *Effectioun]* Affection, partiality.
59. *electioun]* Choice (for an office or living).
60. *governance]* Control.

13

Thane spak ane constant wycht callit Ressoun,
And said, 'I grant thow hes beine lord a sessioun
In distributioun, bot now the tyme is gone.
Now I may all distribute myne alone.
Thy wrangous deidis did evir mane enschesoun.   65

14

'For tyme war now that this mane had sumthing,
That lange hes bene ane servand to the king,
And all his tyme nevir flatter couthe nor faine,
Bot humblie into ballat wyse complaine
And patientlie indure his tormenting.   70

15

'I counsall him be mirrie and jocound.
Be Nobilnes his help mon first be found.'
'Weill spokin, Ressoun, my brother', quod Discretioun,
'To sett on dies with lordis at the cessioun
Into this realme thow war worth mony ane pound.'   75

16

Thane spak anone Inoportunitie:
'Ye sall not all gar him speid without me,
For I stand ay befoir the kingis face.
I sall him deiff or ellis my self mak hace,
Bot gif that I befoir him servit be.   80

---

63. *a sessioun*] For a session.
64. *myne alone*] On my own.
65] Every one blamed your evil deeds.
68. *couthe*] Did. *faine*] Deceive.
69. *into ballat wyse*] In the medium of verse.
70. *indure*] Endure.
71. *mirrie*] Merry. *jocound*] Cheerful.
72. *Be*] By the means of.
74. *sett*] Sit. *dies*] Dais, platform. *cessioun*] Law court.
76. *spak*] Spoke. *Inoportunitie*] Importunity, persistent solicitation.
77. *speid*] Succeed.
79. *deiff*] Deafen. *hace*] Hoarse.
80. *servit*] Provided.

17

'Ane besy askar soonner sall he speid
Na sall twa besy servandis, out of dreid;
And he that askis, not tynes bot his word,
Bot for to tyne lang service is no bourd.
Yett thocht I nevir to do sic folie deid.'   85

18

Thane com anon ane callit Schir Johne Kirkpakar,
Of many cures ane michtie undertaker.
Quod he, 'I am possest in kirkis sevin,
And yitt I think thai grow sall till ellevin,
Or he be servit in ane, yone ballet maker.   90

19

'And then, schir, bet the kirk, sa mot I thryff!
I haif of busie servandis foure or fyve,
And all direct unto sindrie steidis,
Ay still awaitting upoun kirkmenes deidis,
Fra quham sum tithingis will I heir belyff.'   95

20

Quod Ressoun than, 'The ballance gois unevin,
That thow, allece, to serff hes kirkis sevin,
And sevin als worth kirk not haifand ane.
With gredines I sie this world ourgane,
And sufficience dwellis nocht bot in heavin.'   100

---

81. *besy]* Busy. *askar]* Petitioner.
82. *Na]* Than. *dreid]* Doubt.
83. *not]* Nothing. *tynes]* Loses.
84. *bourd]* Joke.
85. *thocht]* Intended. *folie]* Foolish.
86. *ane]* One.
87. *cures]* Benefices. *michtie undertaker]* Wealthy collector.
90. *Or]* Before. *servit in]* Provided with. *yone]* That.
93. *direct]* Despatched. *sindrie steidis]* Various places.
94. *kirkmenes deidis]* The deaths of churchmen.
95. *tithingis]* News. *belyff]* Soon.
96. *ballance]* Scales.
97. *allece]* Alas. *serff]* Serve as a priest.
98. *worth]* Deserving of.
99. *sie]* See. *ourgane]* Overwhelmed.
100. *sufficience]* Contentment. *nocht bot]* Only.

21

'I have not wyt thairof,' quod Temperance,
'For thocht I hald him evinlie the ballance,
And but ane cuir full micht till him wey,
Yett will he tak ane uther and gar it swey.
Quha best can rewll wald maist have governance.'   105

22

Patience to me, 'My freind,' said, 'Mak guid cheir,
And on the prince depend with humelie feir.'
For I full weill dois knaw his nobill intent:
He wald not, for ane bischopperikis rent,
That thow war unrewairdit half ane yeir.'   110

23

Than as ane fary thai to duir did frak,
And schot ane gone that did so ruidlie rak
Quhill all the aird did raird the ranebow under.
On Leith sandis me thocht scho brak in sounder,
And I anon did walkin with the crak.   115

---

101. wyn] Dhuu
102. him] For him.
103] And one benefice alone would weigh enough for him.
104. swey] Sway to one side.
105. rewll] Rule
106. Mak gud cheir] Cheer up.
107. depend] (1) Rely; (2) attend. *humelie feir]* Humble bearing.
109. bischopperikis rent] Revenue from a bishopric.
111. duir] Door. *frak]* Rush.
112. gone] Gun. *ruidlie rak]* Violently explode.
113. Quhill] Till. *aird]* Earth. *raird]* Resound.
114. brak] Broke. *in sounder]* Apart.
115. walkin] Wake up. *crak]* Explosion.

64

The first stanza calls attention to this poem's genre: it is a tale of oral origin (2), and of a strange and puzzling nature, as the refrain insistently reminds us. It is also a fable, and the opening reference to Dunfermline, repeated in the last line, may pay oblique tribute to Henryson, the Scottish master of the beast fable (see **16**. 81–2). Dunbar here makes a novel and ironic use of fable stereotypes, such as the innocent lamb and the wily, seductive fox. The poem is traditionally interpreted as referring to some amorous exploit of James IV, a notorious philanderer. The basis for this is B's doggerel rubric: 'Followis the wowing of the king quhen he wes in Dumfermeling'. Yet no such heading occurs in the other witnesses, and B's titles are far from reliable. It was not uncommon for fables to be put to satiric use, but there are various implausibilities in identifying the fox with James, whom Dunbar elsewhere (see **41**, **57**) depicts as lion or eagle. In Scottish tradition it was not kings but unprincipled churchmen or treacherous nobles who were called foxes; cf. the image of the fox in **22**. This poem probably alludes to some real scandal, despite the disclaimer in 43–4; but precisely what it was remains unknown. The stanza is that employed in **2** and **20**, poems with an affinity to this one in style and tone.

Text: B, ff. 116ʳ–116ᵛ; collated with MF, pp. 335–7, and R. f. 58ʳ (1–14 only). 28. that] MF; this B.

Authorship: 'Quod Dumbar' in B and MF.

Further reading: Lyall 1974c (the link with James is 'not proven' nor 'central' to the theme); Ross 1981: 166–8 (sees a moral purpose, 'to awaken shame in the king'); Bawcutt 1992a: 303–7.

1

This hindir nycht in Dumfermeling
To me wes tawld ane windir thing:
That lait ane tod wes with ane lame
And with hir playit and maid gud game,
Syne till his breist did hir imbrace   5
And wald haif riddin hir lyk ane rame,
And that me thocht ane ferly cace.

2

He braisit hir bony body sweit
And halsit hir with fordir feit,
Syne schuk his taill, with quhinge and yelp,   10
And todlit with hir lyk ane quhelp,
Syne lowrit on growfe and askit grace,
And ay the lame cryd, 'Lady, help!'
And that me thocht ane ferly cace.

3

The tod wes nowder lene nor skowry.   15
He wes ane lusty, reid-haird lowry,
Ane lang-taild beist, and grit with all.
The silly lame wes all to small
To sic ane tribbill to hald ane bace.
Scho fled him nocht, fair mot hir fall,   20
And that me thocht ane ferly cace.

1. *hindir*] Past.
2. *tawld*] Told. *windir thing*] Marvel.
3. *lait*] Lately. *tod*] Fox. *lame*] Lamb.
4. *game*] Sport.
5. *imbrace*] Embrace.
6. *riddin*] Mounted sexually. *rame*] Ram.
7] And that seemed to me astonishing.
8. *braisit*] Embraced. *bony*] Attractive.
9. *halsit*] Clasped. *fordir*] Front.
10. *schuk*] Shook. *quhinge*] Whine.
11. *quhelp*] Puppy.
12. *lowrit on growfe*] Crouched low.
15. *nowder*] Neither. *lene*] Thin. *skowry*] Shabby.
16. *lusty*] Vigorous.
17. *lang-taild*] long-tailed. *grit with all*] Large as well.
19. *sic*] Such. *tribbill*] Treble. *bace*] Bass.
20. *fair . . . fall*] May she prosper.

4

The tod wes reid, the lame wes quhyte,
Scho wes ane morsall of delyte.
He lovit na yowis, auld, tuch and sklender –
Becaus this lame wes yung and tender,   25
He ran upoun hir with a race,
And scho schup nevir for till defend hir,
And that me thocht ane ferly cace.

5

He grippit hir abowt the west
And handlit hir, as he had hest.   30
This innocent that nevir trespast
Tuke hert that scho wes handlit fast
And lute him kis hir lusty face.
His girnand gamis hir nocht agast,
And that me thocht ane ferly cace.   35

6

He held hir till him be the hals
And spak full fair, thocht he was fals,
Syne said (and swoir to hir be God)
That he suld nocht tuich hir prenecod.
The silly thing trowd him, allace.   40
The lame gaif creddence to the tod,
And that me thocht ane ferly cace.

24. *yowis]* Ewes. *tuch]* Tough. *sklender]* Scraggy.
26. *race]* Rush, charge.
27. *schup]* Attempted.
29. *west]* Waist.
30. *as]* As if. *hest]* Haste.
31. *trespast]* Sinned.
32. *Tuke hert]* Grew confident. *fast]* Firmly.
33. *lute]* Let. *lusty]* Attractive.
34. *girnand gamis]* Snarling jaws. *agast]* Frightened.
36. *hals]* Neck.
37. *spak]* Spoke. *thocht]* Though.
39. *tuich]* Touch. *prenecod]* Pincushion.
40. *trowd]* Believed.
41. *gaif creddence to]* Had faith in.

7

I will no lesingis put in vers,
Lyk as thir jangleris dois rehers,
Bot be quhat maner thay war mard.   45
Quhen licht wes owt and durris wes bard
I wait nocht gif he gaif hir grace,
Bot all the hollis wes stoppit hard,
And that me thocht ane ferly cace.

8

Quhen men dois fleit in joy maist far,   50
Sone cumis wo or thay be war.
Quhen carpand wer thir two most crows,
The wolf he ombesett the hous,
Upoun the tod to mak ane chace.
The lamb than cheipit lyk a mows,   55
And that me thocht ane ferly cace.

9

Throw hiddowis yowling of the wowf
This wylie tod plat doun on growf,
And in the silly lambis skin
He crap als far as he micht win   60
And hid him thair ane weill lang space.
The yowis besyd thay maid na din,
And that me thocht ane ferly cace.

---

43. *lesingis]* Lies.
44. *jangleris]* Slanderers. *rehers]* Narrate.
46. *durris]* Doors. *bard]* Bolted.
47. *wait]* Know.
48. *hollis]* Holes. *stoppit]* Closed up.
50. *dois fleit]* Are immersed.
51. *war]* Aware.
52. *carpand]* Talking. *crows]* Boldly.
53. *ombesett]* Surrounded.
55. *cheipit]* Squeaked.
57. *yowling]* Howling. *wowf]* Wolf.
58. *wylie]* Cunning. *plat . . . growf]* Fell flat.
60. *crap]* Crept. *win]* Get.
61. *weill lang space]* Very long time.
62. *besyd]* Nearby.

10

Quhen of the tod wes hard no peip,
The wowf went all had bene on sleip,   65
And quhill the tod had strikkin ten
The wowf hes drest him to his den,
Protestand for the secound place.
And this report I with my pen,
How at Dumfermling fell the cace.   70

---

64. hard] Heard.
65. went] Believed.
67. drest him] Betaken himself.
68. Protestand] Making a claim.
70. fell] Befell. *cace]* Event.

65

This poem was once thought to be autobiographical, providing evidence that in his youth Dunbar had been a novice in the Franciscan order. Most scholars now, however, regard the dreamer's self-incriminating confession (31–45) as a fictional device, inherited from the tradition of anti-mendicant satire. Dunbar does not attack St Francis himself but his followers, who had acquired a bad reputation for trickery and flattery, and whose privilege to preach in every part of the country was resented by the secular clergy (cf. 36–40). He satirizes, lightly rather than ferociously, their 'falset'; the religious habit (mentioned in almost every stanza) is a key symbol, implying that their religion is a superficial sham. The poem also burlesques the kind of religious vision often recounted in saints' lives (cf. 21); this one is a diabolic delusion, and the 'saint' who first appears to the dreamer is exposed as a devil. On the stanza, see 24.

Text: B, f. 115^r–115^v; collated with MF, pp. 333–4, and R, f. 42^r–42^v. Mackenzie and Kinsley rearranged the poem, displacing stanza 6 and inserting it between stanzas 3 and 4. But this is unnecessary. The dialogue has two stages: in stanza 3 the apparent saint makes his peremptory request, which is followed by the dreamer's evasive reply (stanzas 4–5); in stanza 6 'Francis' again chides the dreamer, who defends himself by revealing inside knowledge of the friars' duplicity (stanzas 7–9). The reference to 'exclamationis' (30) loses its point if it is misplaced.

Title and authorship: B has a heading, 'Followis how Dumbar wes desyrd to be ane freir'. 'Quod Dumbar' in MF.

Further reading: Baxter 1952: 26–40 (on the poem as autobiographical); Rigg 1963 (a satiric 'fiction'); Lyall 1977 (on its 'intricate ironic patterns'); Bawcutt 1992a: 269–74. On the wider background of anti-mendicant satire, see Williams 1953 and Szittya 1986.

1

This nycht befoir the dawing cleir
Me thocht Sanct Francis did to me appeir,
With ane religious abbeit in his hand,
And said: 'In this go cleith the my servand.
Reffus the warld, for thow mon be a freir.'   5

2

With him and with his abbeit bayth I skarrit,
Lyk to ane man that with a gaist wes marrit.
Me thocht on bed he layid it me abone,
Bot on the flure delyverly and sone
I lap thairfra and nevir wald cum nar it.   10

3

Quoth he, 'Quhy skarris thow with this holy weid?
Cleith the thairin, for weir it thow most neid.
Thow that hes lang done Venus lawis teiche
Sall now be freir and in this abbeit preiche.
Delay it nocht, it mon be done but dreid.'   15

4

Quod I, 'Sanct Francis, loving be the till,
And thankit mot thow be of thy gude will
To me, that of thy clathis ar so kynd,
Bot thame to weir it nevir come in my mynd.
Sweit confessour, thow tak it nocht in ill.   20

1. *dawing cleir]* Bright dawn.
2. *Me thocht]* It seemed to me.
3. *religious abbeit]* Dress of a religious order.
4. *cleith the my servand]* Clothe yourself as my follower.
5. *Reffus]* Reject. *mon]* Must. *freir]* Friar.
6. *skarrit]* Took fright.
7. *gaist]* Ghost. *marrit]* Astounded.
8. *abone]* Above.
9. *flure]* Floor. *delyverly]* Nimbly. *sone]* At once.
10. *lap thairfra]* Leapt away. *nar]* Near.
11. *Quoth]* Said. *weid]* Garment.
12. *weir ... neid]* You must of necessity wear it.
14. *preiche]* Preach.
15. *but dreid]* Without doubt.
16. *Quod]* Said. *loving ... till]* Praise be to you.
17. *mot]* May.
18. *clathis]* Clothes. *kynd]* Generous.
19. *come]* Came.
20. *tak ... ill]* Do not be angry.

5

'In haly legendis haif I hard allevin
Ma sanctis of bischoppis nor freiris be sic sevin.
Of full few freiris that hes bene sanctis I reid;
Quhairfoir ga bring to me ane bischopis weid,
Gife evir thow wald my sawle yeid unto hevin.'   25

6

'My brethir oft hes maid the supplicationis
Be epistillis, sermonis and relationis
To tak the abyte, bot thow did postpone.
But forder proces cum on thairfoir annone,
All sircumstance put by and excusationis.'   30

7

'Gif evir my fortoun wes to be a freir,
The dait thairof is past full mony a yeir;
For into every lusty toun and place
Of all Yngland, frome Berwick to Kalice,
I haif in to thy habeit maid gud cheir.   35

8

'In freiris weid full fairly haif I fleichit.
In it I haif in pulpet gon and preichit,
In Derntoun kirk and eik in Canterberry,
In it I past at Dover our the ferry
Throw Piccardy, and thair the peple teichit.   40

---

21. *haly legendis*] Holy saints' lives. *hard*] Heard.
23. *reid*] Read.
24. *Quhairfoir*] Therefore. *weid*] Vestments.
25. *Gife*] If. *wald*] Wished. *sawle*] Soul. *yeid*] Went.
26. *brethir*] Brethren (i.e. friars).
27. *epistillis*] Formal letters. *relationis*] Tales.
29] Without more ado get on with the business at once.
30] Put aside all evasive language and excuses.
32. *dait thairof*] Time for it.
33. *lusty*] Pleasant. *place*] Mansion.
35. *maid gud cheir*] Enjoyed myself.
36. *fleichit*] Flattered.
39. *our*] Over, on.
40. *teichit*] Taught.

9

'Als lang as I did beir the freiris style,
In me, God wait, wes mony wrink and wyle.
In me was falset with every wicht to flatter,
Quhilk micht be flemit with na haly watter.
I wes ay reddy all men to begyle.'   45

10

This freir that did Sanct Francis thair appeir,
Ane fieind he wes in liknes of ane freir.
He vaneist away with stynk and fyrie smowk.
With him, me thocht, all the hous end he towk,
And I awoik as wy that wes in weir.   50

---

41. freiris style] Title of friar.
42. wait] Knows. *wrink]* Trick. *wyle]* Deceit.
43. falset] Falsehood. *wicht]* Person.
44. flemit] Dispelled.
45. ay] Always. *begyle]* Cheat.
46. appeir] Appear to be.
47. fieind] Devil.
48. vaneist] Vanished. *smowk]* Smoke.
49. end] End wall. *towk]* Took.
50. awoik] Awoke. *wy]* Man. *weir]* Perplexity.

66

Dunbar at first veils the petitionary element in this poem; complaints on the lack of reward for those who give loyal service (e.g. 3, 13–16) mingle with conventional reflections on the mutability of the world. Approximately half-way through, however, Dunbar's tone becomes more personal and his petition more explicit. He wittily develops the analogy between his longing for a benefice and the anxiety of a merchant awaiting the return of a rich cargo from distant lands. The sense of the refrain also changes slightly as the poem proceeds: in the early stanzas the 'pane' is impersonal, the sort of emotion likely to be evoked in any reflective person; but from line 48 onwards it signifies the private misery of the speaker, and in the final line is explicitly 'my pane'. On the stanza, one of Dunbar's favourites, see 16. The poem cannot be dated precisely: the geographical allusions (62–71), when identifiable, are chiefly to places that were known to Europeans long before the Great Discoveries. The reference to king and queen (57), however, is usually taken to refer to James IV and Queen Margaret; if so, the poem would date after 1503.

Text: MF, pp. 178–81; collated with R, ff. 27ʳ–28ᵛ.
13. labour] liell labour MF, R.
81. it] *Not in* MF, R.

Authorship: 'Quod Dumbar' in MF and R.

Further reading: See MacDonald 1987 (on geographical allusions); and Bawcutt 1992a: 40–43 ('the poem breaks the conventional mould').

1

This waverand warldis wretchidnes,
The failyeand and frutles bissines,

2. *failyeand]* Failing, unsuccessful. *frutles]* Fruitless.

The mispent tyme, the service vane,
For to considder is ane pane.

2

The slydand joy, the glaidnes schort,   5
The feynyeid luif, the fals confort,
The sweit abayd, the slichtfull trane,
For to considder is ane pane.

3

The sugurit mouthis with myndis thairfra,
The figurit speiche with faceis twa,   10
The plesand toungis with hartis unplane,
For to considder is ane pane.

4

The labour lost and liell service,
The lang availl on humill wyse,
And the lytill rewarde agane,   15
For to considder is ane pane.

5

Nocht I say all be this cuntre,
France, Ingland, Ireland, Almanie,
Bot als be Italie and Spane,
Quhilk to considder is ane pane.   20

6

The change of warld fro weill to wo,
The honorable use, is all ago,

4. pane] Pain, misery.
5. slydand] Fleeting.
6. feynyeid] False. *confort]* Delight.
7. abayd] Delay. *slichtfull trane]* Cunning stratagem.
9. sugurit] Sweet-sounding. *thairfra]* Distant, different.
10. figurit] Rhetorically figured.
11. unplane] Dishonest.
13. liell] Loyal.
14. availl] Assistance. *humill wyse]* Humble manner.
15. agane] In return.
17] I do not speak solely of this country.
18. Almanie] Germany.
19. als] Also.
21. weill] Happiness.
22. use] Mode of life. *ago]* Gone.

In hall and bour, in burgh and plane,
For to considder is ane pane.

7

Belief dois liep, traist dois nocht tarie,   25
Office dois flit and courtis dois vary,
Purpos dois change as wynd or rane,
Quhilk to considder is ane pane.

8

Gud rewle is banist our the Bordour,
And rangat ringis but ony ordour,   30
With reird of rebaldis and of swane,
Quhilk to considder is ane pane.

9

The pepill so wickit ar of feiris,
The frutles erde all witnes beiris,
The ayr infectit and prophane,   35
Quhilk to considder is ane pane.

10

The temporale stait to gryp and gather,
The sone disheris wald the father,
And as ane dyvour wald him demane,
Quhilk to considder is ane pane.   40

11

Kirkmen so halie ar and gude
That on thair conscience, rowme and rude,

23. *bour]* Private chamber. *plane]* Open country.
25. *Beleif]* Belief (in others), *liep]* Run away. *traist]* Trust. *tarie]* Linger.
26. *Office]* Official position, status. *flit]* Depart. *vary]* Change.
27. *rane]* Rain.
29. *rewle]* Rule. *banist]* Banished. *our]* Over.
30. *rangat]* Riot. *ringis]* Reigns. *but]* Without.
31. *reird]* Clamour. *rebaldis]* Rogues. *swane]* Peasants.
33. *feiris]* Behaviour.
34. *frutles erde]* Infertile soil.
35. *prophane]* Polluted.
37. *temporale]* Earthly. *gryp]* Seize.
38. *disheris]* Dispossess.
39. *dyvour]* Bankrupt. *demane]* Treat (harshly).
41. *Kirkmen]* Churchmen. *halie]* Holy.
42. *rowme]* Spacious. *rude]* Rough.

May turne aucht oxin and ane wane,
Quhilk to considder is ane pane.

12

I knaw nocht how the kirk is gydit,   45
Bot beneficis ar nocht leill devydit.
Sum men hes sevin and I nocht ane,
Quhilk to considder is ane pane.

13

And sum unworthy to browk ane stall
Wald clym to be ane cardinall.   50
Ane bischoprik may nocht him gane,
Quhilk to considder is ane pane.

14

Unwourthy I, amang the laif,
Ane kirk dois craif and nane can have.
Sum with ane thraif playis passage plane,   55
Quhilk to considder is ane pane.

15

It cumis be king, it cumis be quene,
Bot ay sic space is us betwene,
That nane can schut it with ane flane,
Quhilk to considder is ane pane.   60

16

It micht have cuming in schortar quhyll
Fra Calyecot and the new fund yle,

43. *aucht]* Eight. *wane]* Waggon.
45. *gydit]* Governed.
46. *leill]* Fairly. *devydit]* Distributed.
47. *ane]* One.
49. *sum]* One. *browk]* Possess.
50. *clym]* Climb.
51. *gane]* Be adequate for.
53. *laif]* Rest.
54. *Ane]* One. *craif]* Desire.
55. *thraif]* Large quantity. *passage]* Dice. *plane]* Openly.
57. *be]* By means of.
58. *sic]* Such.
59. *schut]* Shoot. *flane]* Arrow.
61. *cuming]* Come. *quhyll]* Time.
62. *Calyecot]* Calicut. *new fund yle]* Newly discovered island.

The partis of transmeridiane,
Quhilk to considder is ane pane.

17

It micht be this, had it bein kynd,   65
Cuming out of the desertis of Ynde,
Our all the grit se occeane,
Quhilk to considder is ane pane.

18

It micht have cuming out of all ayrtis:
Fra Paris and the orient partis,   70
And fra the ylis of Aphrycane,
Quhilk to consydder is ane pane.

19

It is so lang in cuming me till,
I dreid that it be quyt gane will,
Or bakwart it is turnit agane,   75
Quhilk to considder is ane pane.

20

Upon the heid of it is hecht
Bayth unicornis and crownis of wecht.
Quhen it dois cum, all men dois frane,
Quhilk to considder is ane pane.   80

21

I wait it is for me provydit,
Bot sa done tyrsum it is to byd it,
It breikis my hairt and birstis my brane,
Quhilk to considder is ane pane.

63. *partis]* Regions.
65. *kynd]* normal, natural.
66. *Cuming]* [Have] come. *Ynde]* India.
67. *Our]* Over.
69. *ayrtis]* Directions (lit. points of the compass).
70. *orient partis]* Regions of the east.
71. *Aphrycane]* Africa.
74] I fear that it has gone totally astray.
77. *heid]* Security. *hecht]* Promised.
78. *wecht]* Weight.
79. *frane]* Enquire.
81. *wait]* Know. *provydit]* Pre-arranged.
82. *done]* Utterly. *tyrsum]* Wearisome. *byd]* Wait for.
83. *birstis]* Splits. *brane]* Brain.

22

Greit abbais grayth I nill to gather 85
Bot ane kirk scant coverit with hadder,
For I of lytill wald be fane,
Quhilk to considder is ane pane.

23

And for my curis in sindrie place,
With help, schir, of your nobill grace, 90
My sillie saule sall never be slane,
Na for sic syn to suffer pane.

24

Experience dois me so inspyr,
Of this fals failyeand warld I tyre,
That evermore flytis lyk ane phane, 95
Quhilk to considder is ane pane.

25

The formest hoip yit that I have
In all this warld, sa God me save,
Is in your grace, bayth crop and grayne,
Quhilk is ane lessing of my pane. 100

85] I do not wish to acquire the wealth of great abbeys.
86. ane] One. *scant]* Barely. *hadder]* Heather.
87. fane] Glad.
89. curis] Church livings, benefices. *sindrie]* Different.
91. sillie] Pitiable. *slane]* Punished spiritually.
94. failyeand] Transitory.
95. flytis] Shifts. *phane]* Weather vane.
97. formest] Chief.
99. crop] Shoot. *grayne]* Seed.
100. lessing] (1) Lessening; (2) alleviation.

67

Didactic poems such as this, couched in the form of a father's advice to his son (cf. 6 and 30), formed a common medieval genre. The most famous and influential example was a work much used in schools, the pseudo-Cato's *Disticha de Moribus ad Filium*; for fifteenth-century Scottish examples, see *Ratis Raving* and *The Consail and Teiching at the Vys Man gaif his Sone* (printed in *Ratis Raving*, pp. 66–79). Dunbar's treatment is highly conventional, both in style and choice of topics. On the stanza, see 6.

Text: B, ff. 68ʳ–69ʳ.

Authorship: 'Quod Dumbar' in B.

Further reading: The poem has not been popular with critics; see Scott 1966: 154–5; Reiss 1979: 63; and Bawcutt 1992a: 141–2 (on genre, and later influence).

1

To dwell in court, my freind, gife that thow list,
For gift of fortoun invy thow no degre.
Behold and heir, and lat thy tung tak rest,
In mekle speiche is pairt of vanitie,
And for no malyce preis the nevir to lie.   5

1. *gife]* If. *list]* Desire.
2. *invy]* Envy. *degre]* Person of rank.
3. *lat]* Let.
4. *mekle]* Great. *pairt of]* Some.
5. *preis]* Strive.

328

Als trubill nevir thy self, sone, be no tyd,
Uthiris to reiwll that will not rewlit be:
He rewlis weill that weill him self can gyd.

2

Bewar quhome to thy counsale thow discure,
For trewth dwellis nocht ay for that trewth appeiris. 10
Put not thyne honour into aventeure,
Ane freind may be thy fo, as fortoun steiris.
In cumpany cheis honorable feiris,
And fra vyle folkis draw the far on syd.
The psalme sayis, *cum sancto sanctus eiris*: 15
He rewlis weill that weill him self can gyd.

3

Haif pacience, thocht thow no lordschip posseid,
For hie vertew may stand in law estait.
Be thow content, of mair thow hes no neid,
And be thow nocht, desyre sall mak debait 20
Evirmoir, till Deth say to the than: 'Chakmait!'
Thocht all war thyne this warld within so wyd,
Quha can resist the serpent of dispyt?
He rewlis weill that weill him self can gyd.

4

Fle frome the fallowschip of sic as ar defamit, 25
And fra all fals tungis fulfild with flattry,

6. *Als]* Also. *sone]* Son. *be no tyd]* At any time.
7. *reiwll]* Rule. *rewlit be]* Submit to guidance.
9. *counsale]* Private opinion. *discure]* Reveal.
10] For truth does not always dwell where it appears to do.
11. *into aventeure]* At risk.
12. *fo]* Enemy. *steiris]* Moves (her wheel).
13. *cheis]* Choose. *feiris]* Friends.
14. *draw the]* Withdraw. *on syd]* Away.
17. *thocht]* Although. *lordschip]* Property. *posseid]* Possess.
18. *vertew]* Virtue. *law estait]* Low rank.
19. *Be thow]* If you are.
20. *debait]* Strife.
21. *than]* Then. *Chakmait]* Checkmate.
22. *this ... wyd]* Within this wide world.
23. *dispyt]* Hatred.
25. *Fle]* Flee. *fallowschip]* Company. *sic]* Such. *defamit]* In bad repute.
26. *fulfild]* Filled.

Als fra all schrewis, or ellis thow art eschamit.
Sic art thow callit as is thy cumpany.
Fle parrellus taillis foundit of invy.
With wilfull men, son, argown thow no tyd,   30
Quhome no ressone may seis nor pacify:
He rewlis weill that weill him self can gyd.

5

And be thow not ane roundar in the nuke,
For gif thow be, men will hald the suspect.
Be nocht in countenance ane skornar nor by luke,   35
Bot dowt siclyk sall stryk the in the neck.
Be war also to counsall or coreck
Him that extold hes far him self in pryd,
Quhair parrell is but proffeit or effect:
He rewlis weill that weill him self can gyd.   40

6

And sen thow seyis mony thingis variand,
With all thy hart treit bissines and cure.
Hald God thy freind, evir stabill be him stand,
He will the confort in all misaventeur.
And be no wayis dispytfull to the peure,   45
Nor to no man do wrang at ony tyd.
Quho so dois this, sicker I yow asseure,
He rewlis weill that sa weill him can gyd.

---

27. *schrewis*] Evil people. *ellis*] Else. *eschamit*] Disgraced.
29. *parrellus*] Harmful. *foundit of*] Based on.
30. *wilfull*] Obstinate. *argown*] Argue.
31. *seis*] Stop.
33. *roundar*] Whisperer. *nuke*] Corner.
34. *hald*] Consider. *suspect*] Suspicious.
35–6] Do not be a scorner, in manner or look; something similar will certainly befall you.
37. *coreck*] Chide.
38. *extold*] Elevated.
39. *parrell*] Danger. *but*] Without. *effect*] Result.
41. *sen*] Since. *seyis*] Sees. *variand*] Uncertain.
42. *treit ... cure*] Be busy and industrious.
43. *stabill*] Steadfast.
44. *confort*] Support. *misaventeur*] Misfortune.
45. *no wayis*] In no way. *dispytfull*] Unkind. *peure*] Poor.
46. *wrang*] Wrong.
47. *sicker*] Certainly. *asseure*] Assure.

68

In its admonitory tone and concern with the good life (14), this resembles
Dunbar's other moral poems. It is addressed, however, not to *man* in general but
to *clarkis* in particular (17), scholars or practitioners of the learned disciplines
listed in stanza 2. It criticizes the vanity of learning that is not accompanied by
moral virtue, and calls on scholars to be models to those who are less educated.
It is with the latter, interestingly, that Dunbar associates himself (cf. 'us' and
'our' in 19–20). The mention of 'Oxinfurde' occurs in the colophon of only one
text; although it is not impossible that Dunbar visited or studied at Oxford,
there is no evidence that he did so. On the stanza, see 6.

Text: MF, pp. 317–18 (MFb); collated with MF, pp. 9–10 (MFa), and R, f. 10ᵛ.
7. craft] MFa; craist MFb.
17. grittest] and grittest MFb; grytast MFa, R.

Authorship: 'Quod Dumbar at Oxinfurde' in MFb; 'Quod Dumbar' in MFa and
R.

Further reading: Most comment has concerned the possible biographical
implications; see Baxter 1952: 22; Reiss 1979: 140; Ross 1981: 131 (a challenge,
'to give his art a moral grounding').

1

> To speik of science, craft or sapience,
> Of vertew morall, cunnyng or doctrene,
> Of jure, of wisdome or intelligence,

1. science] Learning. *craft]* Skill. *sapience]* Wisdom.
2. vertew] Virtue. *cunnyng]* Knowledge. *doctrene]* Teaching.
3. jure] Law, jurisprudence.

Of everie study, lair or disciplene –
All is bot tynt or reddie for to tyne,   5
Not using it as it sould usit be,
The craft exerceing, considdering not the fyne:
A paralous seiknes is vane prosperite.

2

The curious probatioun logicall,
The eloquence of ornat rethorie,   10
The naturall science philosophicall,
The dirk apperance of astronomie,
The theologis sermoun, the fablis of poetrie,
Without gud lyfe all in the selfe dois de,
As Maii flouris dois in September dry.   15
A paralous lyfe is vane prosperite.

3

Quhairfoir, ye clarkis grittest of constance,
Fullest of science and of knawlegeing,
To us be myrrouris in your governance
And in our darknes be lamps in schyning,   20
Or than in frustar is your lang leirning.
Giff to your sawis your deidis contrair be,
Your maist accusar salbe your awin cunning.
A paralus seiknes is vane prosperite.

4. *lair]* Lore. *disciplene]* Branch of learning.
5. *tynt]* Wasted. *tyne]* Go to waste.
7. *exerceing]* Exercising. *fyne]* End.
8. *paralous seiknes]* Dangerous illness.
9. *curious]* Subtle. *probatioun]* Proof.
10. *ornat]* Adorned with figures of speech. *rethorie]* Rhetoric.
11] The branch of philosophy that studies natural phenomena
12. *dirk]* Dark, obscure.
13. *theologis sermoun]* Theologian's sermon. *fablis]* Fictions.
14. *all . . . de]* Everything in itself dies.
17. *grittest of constance]* With most devotion (to learning).
18. *knawlegeing]* Erudition.
19. *myrrouris]* Mirrors. *governance]* Behaviour.
21. *than]* Else. *frustar]* Vain.
22] If what you do is the opposite of what you say.
23. *maist accusar]* Greatest accuser.

69

The Tabill of
Confessioun

Dunbar's purpose is penitential: to aid examination of the conscience in preparation for confession to a priest, usually made once a year in Lent. The 'I' represents the voice of a typical sinner, and should not be closely identified with that of the poet. The poem has a numerical structure, listing the five senses, the seven deadly sins, the ten commandments, etc. This scheme was very common in medieval writings on penance, whether in verse or prose. For some English parallels, see *The Winchester Anthology*; for a contemporary Scottish treatise on penance attributed to John Ireland, see Asloan Manuscript (I, 1–80). Dunbar's poem is more than a dry tabulation of sins, and is suffused with emotion, particularly in the refrain and the final prayers. Although resembling 33 in the penitential theme, it is far closer to 1 in its emotive tone and desire to participate imaginatively in the sufferings of Jesus (153–60). On the stanza, see 6.

Text: Ar, ff. 1ʳ–4ᵛ; collated with Bd, pp. 9–11; B, ff. 17ᵛ–19ᵛ; and MF, pp. 199–203. The textual position is complicated. Ar, the earliest witness, preserves a text that is orthodox theologically, but carelessly copied; Bd, B and MF all modify the poem, in order to conform to Protestant dogma (see notes to 42–5, 81–8).
4. schryve] MF; Schir Ar.
30. the deid] Bd, B, MF; I did Ar.
34. ignorantis] Bd, B; the ignorant Ar.
43. eucarist] vnacrist Ar. exellence] exelling Ar.
85–6] *Lines transposed* Ar.
100. hiddous feid] B, MF; having confide Ar.
122–3] *Lines transposed* Ar.
140–42] Bd, B, MF; 141, 142, 140 Ar.
149–50] Bd, B; That seis my hert as thou hir forgaife / Thairfor forgife me as synner penitent Ar.
168. That cryis] Bd, B, MF; I cry Ar.

Title: Ar. Bd, B and MF have no title. MF has a colophon: 'ane confessioun

333

generale compylit be maister Williame Dunbar'.

Further reading: On medieval penitential literature, see Boyle 1985 and Tentler 1977. Criticism of this poem is sparse, but see Reiss 1979: 96–7 (contains 'spiritual truths at the heart of Dunbar's poetry'); and Bawcutt 1992a: 171–4.

1

To the, O marcifull salviour myn, Jesus,
My king, my lord and my redemer sweit,
Befor thy bludy figour dolorus
I schryve me cleyne, with humile spreit and meik,
That ever I did unto this hour compleit,   5
Baith in word, in wark and in entent.
Falling on face full law befor thy feit,
I cry the marcy and laser to repent.

2

To the, my meik sweit salviour, I me schrife,
And dois me in thy marcy maist excelling,   10
Of the wrang spending of my wittis five,
In hering, seing, tuiching, gusting, smelling,
Ganestanding, greving, offending and rebelling
Aganis my lord God omnipotent.
With teris of sorrow fra myn ene distelling,   15
I cry the marcy and laser to repent.

1. the] Thee. *salviour]* Saviour.
2. redemer] Redeemer.
3. bludy figour] Blood-stained image. *dolorus]* Sorrowful.
4. schryve me cleyne] Make a full confession. *humile spreit]* Humble spirit.
5. compleit] Completely.
6. wark] deed. *entent]* Thought.
7. law] Low.
8] I call upon you for mercy and time to repent.
10. dois me] Commit myself. *excelling]* Surpassing.
11. spending] Use. *wittis]* Senses.
12. tuiching] Touch. *gusting]* Taste.
13. Ganestanding] Resisting. *greving]* Distressing.
15. ene] Eyes. *distelling]* Falling in drops.

3

I, wrachit synnar, vile and full of vice,
Of the sevin deidly synnis dois me schrif:
Of prid, invy, of ire and covatice,
Of lichory, gluttony, with sleuth ay till ourdrife,   20
Exercing vicis ever in all my life,
For quhilk, allace, I servit to be schent.
Rew on me, Jesu, for thy woundis five,
I cry the marcy and laser to repent.

4

I schrif me, lord, that I abusit have   25
The sevin deidis of marcy corporall:
The hungry meit, nor thristy drink I gaif,
Vesyit the seik, nor redemit the thrall,
Herbreit the wilsum, nor nakit cled at all,
Nor yit the deid to bery tuke I tent.   30
Thow that put marcy abone thi werkis all,
I cry the marcy and laser to repent.

5

In the sevin deidis of marcy spirituall:
To ignorantis nocht gaif I my teching,
Synneris correctioun, nor distitud consall,   35
Nor unto wofull wrachis conforting,
Nor unto saulis support of my praying,
Nor wes to ask forgevinnes pacient,

---

17. wrachit] Wretched.
18. deidly] Deadly.
19. prid] Pride. *invy]* Envy. *covatice]* Covetousness.
20. lichory] Lechery. *sleuth]* Sloth. *ourdrife]* Waste time.
21. Exercing] Practising.
22. servit] Deserved. *schent]* Punished.
23. Rew] Have mercy.
26. deidis] Acts. *corporall]* Relating to the body.
27–9] I did not give food to the hungry, nor drink to the thirsty; did not visit the sick, nor free the prisoner; gave no shelter to the homeless, nor clothed the naked.
30. deid] Dead. *bery]* Bury. *tuke tent]* Took care.
34. ignorantis] Ignorant persons. *gaif]* Gave.
35. correctioun] Reproof. *distitud]* Destitute. *consall]* Advice.
36. wofull wrachis] The unhappy.
37. saulis] Souls.
38. forgevinnes] Forgiveness.

Nor to forgif my nychtburis offending.
I cry the marcy and laser to repent.   40

6

Lord, I have done full litill reverence
Unto the sacramentis sevin of gret renoun:
To that hie eucarist moist of exellence,
Baptasing, pennence and confirmacioun,
Matremony, ordour and extreme uncioun.   45
Heirof sa fer as I wes necligent,
With hert contrit and teris falling doun,
I cry the marcy and laser to repent.

7

Thy ten commandmentis: a god for to honour,
Nocht tane in vane, na manslaar to be,   50
Fader and moder to worschip at all houre,
To be no theif, the haly day to uphie,
Nychtburis to luf, fals witnes for to fle,
To leif adultre, to covat na manis rent,
In all thir, lord, culpabill knaw I me.   55
I cry the marcy and laser to repent.

8

In the twelf artickillis of the treuth: a god to trow,
The fader that all wrocht and comprehendit,
And in his only sone, blissit Jesu,

39. *nychtburis offending]* Neighbours' crimes.
41. *done]* Shown.
43. *hie eucarist]* Holy eucharist.
44. *Baptasing]* Baptism.
45. *ordour]* Ordination (of priests). *extreme uncioun]* The last rite of anointing the dying
46. *Heirof]* In this. *necligent]* Neglectful.
47. *contrit]* Contrite.
49. *a]* One.
50. *tane in vane]* Treated with contempt. *manslaar]* Murderer.
51. *Fader]* Father. *moder]* Mother.
52. *theif]* Thief. *haly]* Holy. *uphie]* Worship.
53. *luf]* Love. *fle]* Flee.
54. *leif]* Abandon. *adultre]* Adultery. *rent]* Goods.
55. *culpabill]* Guilty. *knaw]* Acknowledge.
57] The twelve clauses of the creed: to believe in one god.
58. *wrocht]* Created. *comprehendit]* Included.
59. *blissit]* Blessed.

Of Mary borne, on croce deid and discendit,   60
The thrid day rais, to the faderis rycht hand ascendit,
Of quik and ded to cum and hald jugement –
Into thir pointis, O lord, quhare I offendit,
I cry the marcy and lasere to repent.

9

I trow into the blissit haly spreit,   65
And in the kirk, to do as it commandis,
And in the day of dome that we sall ris compleit,
And tak oure flesche agane, baith feit and handis,
All to be saif, into the stait of grace that standis.
Plane I revoik in thir quhair I myswent,   70
Befoir the juge and lord of sey and landis.
I cry the marcy and laser to repent.

10

I synnit, lord, nocht being strang as wall
In hope, faith and fervent cherite,
Nocht with the fair foure vertuis cardinall   75
Agins vicis sure anarmyng me;
With fortitud, prudence and temporance, thir thre,
With justice ever in word, werk, and in entent.
To the, Crist Jesu, casting up myn ee,
I cry the marcy and laser to repent.   80

11

In the sevin commandis of the kirk, that is to say,
Thy teind to pay, and cursing to eschew,
To keipe the festuall and the fasting day,

---

60. croce] Cross. *deid]* Died. *discendit]* Descended (to hell)
61. rais] Rose.
62] To come and judge the living and the dead.
63. pointis] Respects.
67. dome] Judgment. *ris compleit]* Rise whole (of body).
69. saif] Saved.
70. Plane] Fully. *revoik]* Recant. *myswent]* Erred.
71. juge] Judge. *sey]* Sea.
74. fervent cherite] Intense love.
75. vertuis cardinall] Principal virtues.
76] Securely arming myself against the sins.
79. ee] Eye.
82. teind] Tithe. *cursing]* Excommunication. *eschew]* Avoid.
83] To observe feastdays and fasts.

The mes on Sonday, the parroche kirk persew,
To proper curat to mak confessioun trew,   85
Anis in the yer to tak the sacrament –
Into thir pointis quhair I have offendit, sair I rew.
I cry the marcy and laser to repent.

12

Of syn also into the haly spreit,
Of schrift postponit, of syn aganis natour,   90
Of incontricioun, of confessour undiscreit,
Of ressait synfull of my salvature,
Of undone pennence and satisfactioun sure,
Of the sevin giftis the haly gaist me sent,
Of *pater noster* and sevin peticionis pure,   95
I cry the marcy and laser to repent.

13

Nocht thankand the of gratitud and grace,
That thou me wrocht and bocht me with thi ded,
Of this schort lyfe remembring nocht the space,
The hevinns blis, the hellis hiddous feid: 100
Bot mor trespas, my synnis to remeid,
Concluding never, all throu myn entent.
Thow quhois blud on rude for me ran reid,
I cry the marcy and laser to repent.

84. mes] Mass. *parroche]* Parish. *persew]* Attend.
85. curat] Priest.
86. Anis] Once. *yer]* Year.
87. sair] Badly. rew] Repent.
90. schrift] Confession. *aganis natour]* Unnatural.
91. incontricioun] Lack of contrition. *undiscreit]* Unfit.
92. ressait] Reception. *salvature]* Saviour.
93] Of failure to perform penance, including its final part, satisfaction, or reparation for sin.
94. gaist] Ghost, spirit.
95. peticionis] Clauses in a prayer.
98. wrocht] Created. *bocht]* Redeemed. *ded]* Death.
100. blis] Joy. *hiddous feid]* Terrifying hatred.
101–2] Never resolving, whole-heartedly, to make amends for my sins without further offence.
103. blud] Blood. *rude]* Cross. *reid]* Red.

14

I knaw me vicius, lord, and rycht culpabill,   105
In aithis, swering, lessingis and blasflemyng,
Of frustrat speiking, in court, in kirk, in tabill,
In word, in will, in wantones expremyng,
Prising my self and evill my nychtburis demyng,
And so in idilnes my dais I have myspent.   110
Thow that wes rent on rude for my redeming,
I cry the marcy and laser to repent.

15

I have synnit in discimilit thochtis joly,
Up to the hevin extollit in myn entencioun,
In hie exaltit arrogance and folly,   115
Imprudence, derisioun, scorne and vilipencioun,
Presumpcioun, inobedience and contempcioun,
In fals vanglore and deidis necligent.
O thow that deit for my redempcioun,
I cry the marcy and laser to repent.   120

16

I have synnit also in reif and opprecioun,
In wrangus gudis taking and posceding,
Contrar my ressoun, conscience and discrecioun,
In prodigall spending, but reuth of pure folkis neding,
In foule descepcioun, in fals invencionis breding,   125

---

105. knaw me] Acknowledge myself.
106] In oaths, swearing, slanders and blasphemy.
107. frustrat] Vain.
108. wantones expremyng] Uttering wanton words.
109] Praising myself and passing malicious judgment on my neighbours.
110. myspent] Wasted.
111. rent] Torn. *redeming]* Redemption.
113. discimilit] Dissembled, deceitful. *joly]* Proud.
114. extollit] Elevated. *entencioun]* Mind.
116. vilipencioun] Contempt of others.
117. contempcioun] Disregard of authority (especially royal).
118. vanglore] Vainglory.
119. deit] Died.
121. reif] Robbery. *opprecioun]* Violence, extortion.
122. wrangus] Wrongful. *posceding]* Possessing.
123. Contrar] Contrary to.
124. but reuth ... neding] without pity for poor people's needs.
125. fals invencionis breding] Making up false tales.

To conqueir honour, tresour, land or rent,
In fleschely lust abone messour exceding.
I cry the marcy and laser to repent.

17

Of mynd dissimilit, lord, I me confes,
Of feid under ane freindlie continance,   130
Of parsiall juging, and perverst wilfulnes,
Of flattering wordis for finyng of substance,
Of fals seling for wrang deliverance,
At counsall, sessioun and at perliament.
Of everilk gilt and wickit governance   135
I cry the marcy and laser to repent.

18

I schrif me of all cursit cumpany,
In all tyme witting and unwiting me,
Of cryminall caus and deid of fellony,
Of tiranny or vengabill cruelte.   140
Of ded or slauchter culpabill gif I be,
In ony wise, deid, counsall or consent,
O deir Jesu that for me deit on tre,
I cry the marcy and laser to repent.

19

Thoucht I have nocht thi precius feit to kis,   145
As had the Magdalyn quhen scho did marcy craife,

126. *conqueir]* Acquire. *rent]* Goods.
127. *abone messour exceding]* Going beyond all bounds.
129. *dissimilit]* Deceitful.
130. *feid]* Hate. *continance]* Appearance.
131. *parsiall juging]* Biased judgment. *perverst]* Stubborn.
132. *finyng]* ? Obtaining. *substance]* Wealth.
133. *seling]* Sealing. *deliverance]* Judgment.
134. *counsall]* Council. *sessioun]* Law court.
135. *everilk gilt]* Every crime. *governance]* Behaviour.
137. *cursit]* Evil.
138. *witting . . . me]* Whether I was aware or unaware of it.
139. *caus]* Fault. *deid]* Act. *fellony]* Cruelty.
140. *tiranny]* Violence. *vengabill]* Vindictive.
141. *ded]* Death. *slauchter]* Manslaughter. *gif]* If.
142. *wise]* Way.
143. *tre]* Tree (i.e. the cross).
145. *Thoucht]* Though.
146. *craife]* Implore.

I sall as scho weipe teris for my mys,
And every morrow seik the at thi graife.
Thairfore forgiff me, as thow hir forgaiff,
That seis my hert as hirris penitent.   150
Thy precius body in breist or I ressaif,
I cry the marcy and laser to repent.

20

Thou mak me, Jesu, unto the to remember.
I ask thy passioun in me so to abound,
Quhill nocht in me unmannyit be a member,   155
Bot felling wo with the of every wound.
At every straik mak throu my hert a stound
That ever did strenye thi fair flesche innocent,
Sa at na part be of my body sound.
I cry the marcy and laser to repent.   160

21

Of all thir synnis that I heir expreme
And hes foryet, to the, lord, I me schrife,
Appelling fra thy justice court extreme
Unto thi court of marcy exultive.
Thou mak my schip in blissit port arrive,   165
That saillis heir in stormes violent,
And saife me, Jesu, for thy woundis five,
That cryis the marcy and laser to repent.

---

147. mys] Sin.
148. morrow] Morning. *graife]* Tomb.
150. hirris] Hers.
151. breist] Breast. *or]* Before. *ressaif]* Receive.
154. passioun] Suffering.
155. unmannyit] Unmangled. *member]* Limb.
156. felling wo] Feeling pain.
157. straik] Stroke. *stound]* Pang.
158. strenye] Torture.
159. at] That. *sound]* Whole, unharmed.
161. thir] These. *expreme]* Declare.
162. foryet] Forgotten.
163. Appelling] Appealing. *extreme]* (1) Final; (2) rigorous.
164. exultive] ? Exultant, joyful.

70

At the core of this poem is the comic contrast between two towns: Stirling, a place of penance, a purgatory, and even a hell (99); and Edinburgh, extolled as a paradise of good living and heavenly bliss, to which the poet prays that the king and those with him may return. Stirling was a place often visited by James IV, for a variety of purposes; in the early years of his reign it was the residence of his mistress, Margaret Drummond; in later years he went there to attend the justice ayre, or circuit court (see 17. 19), to celebrate the feasts of Easter and Yule, and to observe the alchemical experiments of John Damian (see 4). It is commonly believed that Dunbar here refers specifically to James's custom of making a Lenten retreat in the Franciscan friary at Stirling, which he founded in 1494 and supported with generous gifts. This is plausible, yet the joke seems strongly at the expense of Stirling as a town (cf. 45), and some details might suggest composition in the late autumn, possibly in Advent rather than Lent: these are the mention of 'new fresche wyne' (55) and the phrase 'or Yule begyn' (93).

In its humorous use of sacred things, this poem belongs to a distinctive medieval comic tradition; well-known hymns, prayers, or parts of the Scriptures were parodied, and their sense inverted, usually to celebrate the pleasures of eating and drinking. In technique the poem resembles 14, although it is a far more audacious and original work. Structurally, it has two parts: the introductory letter, or *epistell* (8), and the *dirige*, a name then commonly given to part of the Office of the Dead, Matins and Lauds (see note to 23). This solemn office was celebrated in church, both before an actual burial and also in memorial services for the dead; and through its inclusion in books of hours it was read as a devotional exercise by pious members of the laity. Dunbar does not imitate the content of the *lectiones*, or lessons, drawn from the book of Job, but devises three prayers of his own invention; he playfully mimics the striking threefold structure of the service, and the metrical form of the *responsiones* recalls the *repetenda*, or repeated short phrases, common in responsories. The most direct verbal parody occurs in the final passage of Latin prose. The poem is striking for its mixture of Scots and Latin, and for the way four-stress couplets are interspersed with three triolets.

Text: MF, pp. 290–92; collated with B, ff. 102^r–103^v, and R, ff. 55^v–56^v.

14. in to] B; in MF.
46a. *Lectio secunda]* B; *not in* MF.
49. saitt] B; hevinlie court MF.
87. sould ye] B; ye sould MF.
103. *ne*] B; *not in* MF.

Authorship: 'Dumbaris dirige to the king bydand ouir lang in Stirling' in MF.

Further reading: On the medieval Latin parodic tradition, see Lehmann 1963. *The Penguin Book of Latin Verse* contains several hymns, together with their parodic versions. Critical responses to this poem are varied, and some interpretations are moralistic: see Lyall 1974b; Archibald 1981; Norman 1981; Reiss 1979: 65–8; Ross 1981: 162–3; Ting 1987; Bawcutt 1992a: 198–203.

We that ar heir in hevynnis glorie
To you that ar in purgatorie
Commendis us on hartlie wys:
I mene we folk of paradys,
In Edinburgh with all merynes,   5
To yow at Striveling in distres,
Quhair nowdir plesour nor delyt is,
For pietie this epistell wrytis.
O ye heremytis and ankirsadillis,
That takkis your pennance at your tabillis   10
And eitis no meit restorative
Nor drinkis no wyne confortative
Nor aill, bot that is thin and small,
With few coursis in to your hall,
But cumpany of lordis and knychtis   15
Or ony uther gudlie wychtis,
Solitar walking your alone,
Seing no thing bot stok and stone,
Out of your panefull purgatorie,

3. *Commendis]* Recommend. *hartlie wys]* Heartfelt manner.
6. *Striveling]* Stirling.
7. *nowdir]* Neither.
8. *pietie]* Compassion.
9. *heremytis]* Hermits. *ankirsadillis]* Anchorites.
11. *meit]* Food. *restorative]* Able to restore health.
12. *confortative]* Comforting.
13] Nor ale, apart from that which is thin and weak.
15. *But]* Without.
16. *gudlie wychtis]* Fine people.
17. *your alone]* On your own.

To bring yow to the blys and glorie   20
Of Edinburcht, the myrrie town,
We sall begin ane cairfull sown,
Ane dirige, devoit and meik,
The lord of blys doing beseik,
Yow to delyver out of your noy   25
And bring yow sone to Edinburgh joy,
For to be merye amangis us.
The dirige begynnis thus:

Lectio prima

The fader, the sone, the holie gaist,
The blissit Marie, virgen chaist,   30
Of angellis all the ordour nyne,
And all the hevinlie court divyne,
Sone bring yow fra the pyne and wo
Of Striveling, everie court mans foo,
Agane to Edinburchtis joy and blys,   35
Quhair wirschip, welthe and weilfair is,
Play, plesance eik and honestie.
Say ye amen, for chirritie.

Tu autem, domine.

Responsio

Tak consolatioun in your payne,   40
In tribulatioun tak consolatioun,
Out of vexatioun cum hame agayne,
Tak consolatioun in your payne.

Iube, domine etc.

Out of distres of Stirling town   45
To Edinburgh blys God mak yow bown.

---

22. *cairfull]* Sorrowful. *sown]* Melody.
23. *devoit]* Devout.
24. *doing beseik]* Beseeching.
25. *noy]* Distress.
29. *gaist]* Spirit.
30. *blissit]* Blessed.
33. *pyne]* Suffering.
36. *wirschip]* Honour.
37. *honestie]* Good repute.
38. *chirritie]* Charity.
46. *bown]* Ready to go.

Lectio secunda

Patriarchis, prophetis, apostillis deir,
Confessouris, virgynis and martyris cleir
And all the saitt celestiall,
Devoitlie we upone thame call 50
That sone out of your paynis fell
Ye may in hevin heir with us dwell,
To eit swan, cran, peirtrik and pluver,
And everie fische that swowmis in rever,
To drink withe us the new fresche wyne 55
That grew apone the revar of Ryne,
Fresche fragrant claretis out of France,
Of Angeo and of Orliance,
With mony ane cours of grit daynte.
Say ye amen, for chirrite. 60

Tu autem, domine.

Responsio

God and sanct Geill heir yow convoy,
Baythe sone and weill, God and sanct Geill,
To sonce and seill, solace and joy,
God and sanct Geill heir yow convoy. 65

Iube, domine.

Out of Stirling paynis fell
In Edinburgh joy sone mot ye dwell.

Lectio tertia

We pray to all the sanctis in hevin,
That ar abuif the sternis sevin, 70
Yow to delyver out of your pennance:
That ye may sone play, sing and dance

49. *saitt]* Assembly.
51. *fell]* Cruel.
53. *cran]* Crane. *peirtrik]* Partridge. *pluver]* Plover.
54. *swowmis]* Swims. *rever]* River.
56. *revar]* River-bank.
58. *Angeo]* Anjou. *Orliance]* Orleans.
59. *daynte]* Delicacy.
62. *sanct Geill]* St Giles. *convoy]* Conduct.
64. *sonce]* Abundance. *seill]* Prosperity.
68. *mot]* May.
70. *sternis]* Planets.

And in to Edinburgh mak gud cheir,
Quhair welthe and weilfair is, but weir.
And I that dois your paynis discryve 75
Thinkis for to visie yow belyve,
Nocht in desert with yow to dwell
Bot as the angell Gabriell
Dois go betweyne fra hevynis glorie
To thame that ar in purgatorie, 80
And in thair tribulatioun
To gif thame consolatioun,
And schaw thame, quhone thair pane is past,
They sall to hevin cum at the last,
And how nane servis to have sweitnes 85
That never taistit bittirnes.
And thairfoir how sould ye considdir
Of Edinburgh blys quhone ye cum hiddir,
Bot gif ye taistit had befoir
Of Stirling toun the paynis soir? 90
And thairfoir tak in patience
Your pennance and your abstinence,
And ye sall cum, or Yule begyn,
In to the blys that we are in,
Quhilk grant the glorious trinite. 95
Say ye amen, for chirrite.

Tu autem, domine.

Responsio

Cum hame and dwell no mair in Stirling,
Fra hyddows hell cum hame and dwell,
Quhair fische to sell is nane bot spyrling, 100
Cum hame and dwell na mair in Stirling.

Iube, domine.

---

73. *mak gud cheir]* Enjoy yourselves.
74. *but weir]* Without doubt.
75. *discryve]* Describe.
76. *Thinkis]* Intend. *visie]* Visit. *belyve]* Soon.
83. *quhone]* When.
85. *servis]* Deserves.
87. *considdir]* Make appraisal.
88. *hiddir]* Hither.
93. *or]* Before.
99. *hyddows]* Hideous.
100. *spyrling]* Smelt (small fish).

Et ne nos inducas in tentationem de Stirling
Sed libera nos a malo eiusdem.

Requiem Edinburgi dona eis, domine,   105
Et lux ipsius luceat eis.
A porta tristitiae de Stirling
Erue, domine, animas et corpora eorum
Credo gustare vinum Edinburgi
In villa viventium   110
Requiescant statim in Edinburgo. Amen.

Domine, exaudi orationem meam
Et clamor meus ad te veniat.

Oremus.   114

Deus qui iustos et corde humiles ex eorum tribulatione
liberare dignatus es: libera famulos tuos apud villam de
Stirling versantes a penis et tristitiis eiusdem, et ad Edin-
burgi gaudia feliciter perducas. Amen.

103–18] And do not lead us into the temptation of Stirling, but deliver us from
its evil.

Give to them the peace of Edinburgh, Lord, and let its light shine on them.
From Stirling's gate of sadness, Lord, bring forth their souls and bodies. I
believe I shall taste the wine of Edinburgh in the town of the living. May they
shortly be at rest in Edinburgh. Amen.

Lord, hear my prayer and let my cry come to thee.

Let us pray.

God, who deigns to liberate the just and the humble of heart from their
tribulation, liberate thy servants dwelling in the town of Stirling from the pain
and sorrows of that place, and bring them happily to the joys of Edinburgh.
Amen.

Notes

For fuller details of the short-title references in these notes, see the headnotes to the poems and the Bibliography.

1

1–2] The setting is an *oritorie*, or chapel, within a house of friars.

3. pater noster] 'Our father', the first words of the Lord's Prayer.

7. gaude flore] A popular Latin hymn, on the seven heavenly joys of the Virgin, which begins *Gaude flore virginali*, 'Rejoice virginal flower'; it was regularly included in books of hours. For ME translations, see *CB XV*, nos. 35 and 36.

16] The refrain is a reminder of God's love for mankind, and also an appeal for love in return. This stress upon reciprocity was a common theme in the religious lyrics termed 'Appeals from the Cross'.

19–20] The comparison of Christ's tormentors to lions was traditional, and derived from the exegesis of Psalm 17: 12: 'They have taken me, as a lion prepared for the prey'.

26] The white clothing derives from Luke 23: 11 (Vulgate *veste alba*). It was traditionally a sign of derision; cf. Kennedy, *Passioun*, 544–5; and *Devotional Pieces*, p. 220. 'think how king Herod cled him in a quhit claith lik a fule'.

27–8] The blindfolding was taken to imply man's perversity. Cf. *Devotional Pieces*, p. 219: 'Iesu, that tholit thi fair face to be hid, that the angellis desirit to behald'.

39] 'He endured in combat as long as he could stand'. Cf. 47. 202. The heroic passivity of Jesus is implied.

42–8] Medieval commentators stressed the sadistic cruelty of this incident; cf. the prose meditation on the crown of thorns in *Devotional Pieces*, pp. 182–93.

51. fullelie] 'In a foul, ignominious manner'. The word is trisyllabic, as in Henryson, *Bludy Serk*, 93.

54. the fude of angellis] Cf. 11. 80. Scholastic theologians interpreted *panis angelorum*, 'the bread of angels' (Psalm 78: 25), as signifying Christ. A ME poem

348

likewise calls him 'the faire aungels fode' (*CB XIV*, no. 83), and the phrase is used in the liturgy and by devotional writers.

58. brim as ony baris woid] For similar images, cf. Holland, *Howlat*, 775, and *Golagros*, 733, 822; also Whiting, B 390 and 392.

59–60] An apocryphal detail. Kennedy uses similar phrasing; cf. *Passioun*, 1044–6: 'The purpour claithis quhilk claif fast till his hide . . . His tender flesche thai brak fra bak to syid'.

65–9] It was a medieval addition to the Gospel story that Jesus's limbs were cruelly stretched before being nailed to the cross. Cf. *Devotional Pieces*, p. 263: 'Behalde, how with thair rapis teuch / The Iowis fell my lymmes oute dreuch'.

71. be houris sax] 'At the sixth hour' (John 19: 14).

76–80] It was traditional that the cross was allowed to fall, so intensifying Christ's suffering.

81–2] Luke 23: 46.

83. the stanis claif] This translates Matthew 27: 51: *petrae scissae sunt.*

84–5] Luke 23: 45. For the pun on sun/son, cf. 8. 27; 48. 5.

86] Matthew 27: 52–3.

89–92] John 19: 34.

97–112] The dreamer imaginatively participates in the Passion; *straik* (98) and *rugging* (106) recall the physical buffeting of Jesus (31, 37, 60). Dunbar vividly dramatizes the admonitions of moralists; Cf. Kennedy, *Passioun*, 647–8: 'Mak rowme to reuth, a place for piete dycht, / Quhill that thi hert haue perfit compassioun'. The thought also resembles **69**. 157–9.

107–8] It was a devotional exercise to contemplate the 'Instruments of the Passion', such as the cross, nails, scourge, lance and crown of thorns.

115–20] This alludes to the Resurrection, and also to the reception of Christ's body in the eucharist, which was then taken by the laity only at Easter.

118–19] Cf. the Centurion's words, 'Lord, I am not worthy that thou shouldest come under my roof' (Matthew 8: 8); these were included in a prayer then said before communion.

119. thy hous] The image of the body as the soul's dwelling was ancient; cf. II Corinthians 5: 1. There is a contemporary Scottish treatment of the theme in *King Hart.*

123. Conscience me accusit] Conscience accuses the heart similarly in *King Hart*, 572.

126] Only now does Repentance enter the dreamer's soul. The allegory resembles *King Hart*, 578: 'Reassoun and Wit richt at the ʒet thay rang'.

129. gyd and governour] A common alliterative pair. Cf. Hary, *Wallace*, IV. 130: 'The eterne God his gouernour be and gyde'.

131–2] Such spiritual preparedness is the theme of several parables. Cf. 'Watch therefore: for you know not what hour your Lord doth come . . . be ye also ready' (Matthew 24: 42–4).

135. The hous within] The innermost parts of the house, or soul.

138] This echoes line 83. The earthquake at Jesus's death was interpreted as a sign of nature's grief for her creator; here it serves as a model for the dreamer.

140] Cf. the ending of **41**. 187.

2

1] There is a touch of scorn for the simple peasant; cf. Carmichaell, no. 1689: 'Upaland folks hes murelands maners'.

5. undir confessioun] 'As if under the seal of confession, confidentially'. Cf. *in secreit* (10).

7. the Sessioun] The highest court of justice, which consisted of members of the king's council, and held sittings, or sessions, in Edinburgh at the Tollbooth. In the fifteenth century it usually met three times a year, but by 1505 two long sittings were held, from January to Easter and from November to December.

15–21] This stanza is devoted to instances of dissimulation and hypocrisy.

18. pattiris] 'Mutters rapidly'. The verb, which derives from the mechanical repetition of the *pater noster* (cf. 1. 3), is always depreciative.

29. castis summondis] 'Rejects a summons as illegal or improper'. The summons was a writ informing a defendant that an action had been begun against him. *exceppis]* 'Makes an *exceptioun*, or objection, to a claim'.

30. skayld law keppis] The sense is difficult; Kinsley explains as 'picks up the incidental pronouncements of the lawyers'. *DOST* glosses *kep*, v.[2], as 'catch (something falling)'; and *skayld* as 'uttered piecemeal rather than as a coherent statement'.

37] A proverbial image of duplicity. Cf. 3. 423; 64. 59.

38] This implies a kindness expressed only in words, not deeds.

45] The Carmelites were a contemplative and eremitical order of friars, founded on Mount Carmel in the twelfth century; they came to Scotland in 1262, and had established nine houses by the end of the fifteenth century. Franciscan friars were sometimes termed *Coirdeleiris*, from their girdles of knotted cord. This alliterative pairing of Carmelites and Cordeliers occurs in other anti-mendicant satire; cf. Lindsay, *Satyre*, 2615–16.

48] A satiric use of a proverbial-sounding phrase. The closest parallel is in Lindsay, *Satyre*, 28: 'Thocht ʒoung oppressouris at the elder leiris'.

50] It was believed that character was largely determined by the mixture of the four 'humours' in the *complexioun*, or bodily constitution. Cf. Henryson, *Fables*, 2826–9: 'For clerkis sayis the inclinatioun / Off mannis thocht proceidis commounly / Efter the corporall complexioun / To gude or euill'. A hot complexion implied one in which a hot humour was predominant, probably the sanguine, since this disposed to love (cf. *Secular Lyrics*, nos. 76 and 77).

51 5] This passage is highly ironic. Words that commonly have a religious or pious sense, such as *devoit* and *intercessioun*, have further erotic implications. There is a pun on *fadirlyk*, meaning 'venerable, like a father' and also 'able to beget children'.

55. mercyfull] 'Ready to grant sexual favours to men', as also in 3. 501.

3

The Tretis of the Twa Mariit Wemen and the Wedo

1. misdummer evin] Midsummer Eve was celebrated on 23 June, the vigil of the nativity of St John the Baptist, with dancing, bonfires and great revelry. Such practices were condemned by medieval preachers (Bawcutt 1992a: 75–6).

2. allane in meid] The phrase establishes the poet's solitude, in accord with *chanson d'aventure* tradition. Cf. *Wynnere and Wastoure*, 32: 'wandrynge myne one'.

5–7] Although the bird is not identified, the allusion is probably to the nightingale, which sings at night; her song was traditionally regarded as merry, or 'glaid'.

9. dirkin] 'Lie still in the dark'. Cf. *Awntyrs off Arthure*, 53: 'Then durken the dere in the dymme skuwes'.

10. donkit] 'Moistened, sprinkled'. The collocation with *dew* was common, especially in alliterative verse. See 512 below, and cf. *Sir Gawain and the Green Knight*, 519: 'donkand dewe'; and *Parlement of the Thre Ages*, 10: 'The dewe appon dayses donkede full faire'.

11. ane holyn hevinlie grein hewit] Cf. *Tayis Bank*, 11–12: 'Ane holene hevinly hewit grene / Rycht heyndly did me hyd'. The owl in Holland, *Howlat*, 48, is also observed 'under ane holyne'.

14] For the poet who rests beside or beneath a hawthorn, cf. *Wynnere and Wastoure*, 36; and Henryson, *Fables*, 1729.

17. arbeir] Probably a bower, within the garden, similar to those described in *The Floure and the Leafe*, 49–56, or *The Kingis Quair*, 211–24.

19. glitterit] According to *DOST*, this is an idiomatic transitive use of the past participle, 'made glittering'.

21–5] The ladies' dress is rich but decorous; and their hair, though loosened, is partly covered. On the green clothing, see note to 47. 127. Cf. Also 47. 59–60.

27–9] Dunbar employs highly conventional similes – the ladies are as fair as flowers, lilies and roses in particular. In 29 he is more audaciously metaphorical: *upspred upon spray* means 'opening and blossoming'. Cf. the rose metaphor in 523.

27. full of flurist fairheid] Cf. Holland, *Howlat*, 6: 'The feldis flurist ... full of fairhed'.

30. Arrayit ryallie] A traditional collocation; cf. the phrase 'ryall array', used in *Rauf Coilyear*, 480 and passim.

31. annamalit] 'Coloured brightly (lit. enamelled)'. Cf. 47. 13, and 250–51.

32. heynd] 'Courteous person'. The substantival use of adjectives is a feature of alliterative verse; in this poem it is often ironic, as in *wlonkes* (36) and later references to the women (49, 146, 158).

36. wlonkes] 'Fine, splendid (women)'. Dunbar is the last recorded user of this eulogistic word, current in alliterative verse and often applied to women. Cf. *Pistel of Susan*, 186: 'weddet to wif, wlankest in wedes'.

37. wantoun] An ambiguous word, which might be taken innocuously as 'sportive, jesting', but commonly had a pejorative sexual sense, 'lascivious, lewd'. See also 479 and 529.

47. blist band] Cf. *Gude and Godlie Ballatis*, p. 202: 'Marriage is ane blissit band'.

49. lusty . . . lustie] It is not clear whether the repetition is intentional or due to scribal error; note the similar repetition in 69 below.

53. Chenyeis] For the chains of marriage, cf. Chaucer, *Bukton*, 9. *changeis ar sweit]* Proverbial (Whiting, C 144).

58. kynd . . . nature] In the medieval period the two words were almost interchangeable. Dunbar may – as often in this poem – be coupling near-synonyms (see Bennett 1965: 194–212). Love and 'the law of kynde' are associated in Chaucer, *Troilus and Criseyde*, I. 237–8.

60ff.] Alluding to the belief that birds choose their mates on St Valentine's Day (see also 206). Cf. Chaucer, *Parliament of Fowls*, 309–10; also the similar complaint in *The Floure of Curtesy* (Lydgate, *Minor Poems*, II): 'Alas, what may this be, / That euery foule hath his lyberte / Frely to chose after his desyre / Everyche his make thus, fro yere to yere?' (53–6).

65. born] Only the first letter of the word is visible, but this reading (suggested by Burrow 1977) is plausible. For the idiom, cf. *Pearl*, 239; and Hay, *Alexander*, 6813: 'Full wele is me the tyme that I was borne'.

67. curage] This has a wide range of senses, but in this poem one usually present is 'sexual desire' (cf. also 188, 203, 215 and 485).

70ff.] Cf. 474 below. The Wife of Bath delights similarly in going 'To prechyng eek and to thise pilgrimages, / To pleyes of myracles and to mariages' (*CT*, III. 557–8).

77. weild] For the sense 'possess sexually', cf. *Awntyrs off Arthure*, 365: 'the worthiest wight that eny welde wolde'.

79. the yok] The traditional yoke of marriage (cf. Chaucer, *Merchant's Tale*, *CT*, IV. 1285). But the image is revitalized, with the man a yoked animal (either ox or horse) drawing the plough (cf. also 85). Sexual metaphors drawn from ploughing were common; cf. Maitland, MF, no. xxxi.

80. preveit his pith] There is a pun on several senses of the common alliterative phrase, *prove someone's pith*: (1) test his sexual potency, or virility; (2) test his strength, as if in battle; cf. *Rauf Coilyear*, 863: 'Thay preis furth . . . thair pithis to prufe'.

81. kirk . . . markat] A legalism for every public place.

85. forky fure] Both words are obscure. *Fure* may mean 'man, fellow' (so *DOST*), or be an error for *sure*, 'reliable'. *OED* takes *forky* to be a variant of *forcy*, 'powerful, strong', but this is repetitious, and not endorsed by *DOST*.

87] Proverbial. Cf. 47. 58–9; also Whiting, F 306.

89–145] This describes a stock literary type, the *senex amans*, or infatuated old man. Cf. the portrait of January in Chaucer's *Merchant's Tale*; also Lydgate, *Temple of Glas*, 179–95.

90. wolroun] The word is clearly abusive, but its precise sense is not certain. *OED*'s explanation as 'boar' is no longer accepted, and does not seem relevant; *CSD* suggests derivation from *will*, 'wild', and the pejorative suffix -*roun*.

91. flewme] Phlegm, according to medieval theories of physiology, was the humour dominant in old age. See also 272.

92. scabbit] Literally 'having scabs' (linking with *scart* in 93), but also 'worthless'. *scorpioun]* A creature noted for its stinging tail. *scutarde]* Obscure. It might represent an old nickname for the hare (*OED*, *scutarde*[1]); but is usually taken to derive from the verb *scout*, 'shoot, spurt', and to mean 'one who pours out, or defecates'.

96. soft ... silk] An ironic use of a common simile (Whiting, S 313).

97. to the syn assent] A sarcastic use of the terminology of confession. Cf. *Pistel of Susan*, 146: 'ʒif I assent to this sin'.

101ff.] The wife speaks of her husband as if he were a devil, and specifically an incubus.

101. Mahowne] Literally Muhammad, viewed by medieval Christians as a false god; in Dunbar and other Scottish writers often a name for the devil (*DOST*, *Mahoun*).

105–8] Cf. the description of January: 'With thikke brustles of his berd unsofte, / Lyk to the skyn of houndfyssh, sharp as brere' (*Merchant's Tale*, *CT*, IV. 1824–5). A heckle was a tool used in combing flax (see Henryson, *Fables*, 1825–9).

108. as a glemand gleyd] 'As a blazing ember'. A common simile for brightness (Whiting, G 152).

111. bogill] A terrifying spectral creature. Cf. the quotation in note to 54. 161.

112. Belzebub] Beelzebub, 'Lord of Flies', and 'prince of demons' (Matthew 12: 24); hence a popular name for the devil (cf. also 101 and 102).

113. smake smolet] Smake means 'rascal' or 'rascally'; but *smolet* has not been satisfactorily explained. A. J. Aitken (see Burrow 1977) suggested that it might be 'a corruption of *smolt*, mod. Scots dialect *smowt*, "little fellow", here used colloquially of the penis'. Kinsley, following Dobson and Ingham 1967, emends to *smakes molet*, and glosses as 'rogue's muzzle'. But there is no evidence for *molet* in the sense 'mouth'.

114] *Farcy*, or glanders, is a chronic disease of horses, which causes a nasal discharge and other ailments.

120. gib] 'Cat'; in later Scots usage, specifically a castrated male cat.

124. trawe] Probably 'trick', though this sense is not evidenced elsewhere; it may be an error for *traine*, 'trick, stratagem'.

128] 'And is useless at satisfying my sexual needs'. Cf. Maitland, MF, no. cix, 26–8: 'Off Venus play past is the heit / For I may not the mistiris beit / Off Meg nor Mald'. For the use of *bene*, cf. 46. 23.

129] The line is difficult, and has been interpreted very differently. Kinsley places a comma after *yeild*, which is glossed as a verb, 'repay, recompense'; he glosses *yerne* as 'eagerly, gladly' and *gane* as 'impotent'. But this produces a short second half-line that is defective in alliteration; and *DOST* gives no warrant for *gane* in this sense. I follow the explanation of Burrow 1978: 'He thinks that I long for young people because he has become impotent'. The expression 'yeild ... gane' is parallel in construction and sense to 'gane chaist' (293). *Yeild* is very much a Scottish farmyard word (see *OED*, *yeld*, a., and *CSD*, *yeild*); although not otherwise recorded in the sense 'impotent', it has related depreciative senses, such as 'barren, sterile, infertile'.

135–6] For the common sexual innuendo on *pen*, see *DOST*, *pen*, n. 6. In *payis ... pays* there is a play on the senses 'gratifies' and 'gives payment'. Note also the monetary pun on the final syllable of *recom-pense*.

141. raid] See also 194 and 391 below. Dunbar plays on two senses: 'armed incursion', i.e. aggressive act against the woman; and 'act of mounting for sexual intercourse'. The latter was a legalism; *DOST*, *rade*, 5, quotes Skene: '*marcheta mulieris* is the raide of the woman, or the first carnall copulation'.

142. Johne Blunt] A Scottish nickname for a stupid, dull-witted man.

147. leuch apon loft] 'Laughed loudly'. An alliterative phrase commonly used of men carousing: cf. *Rauf Coilyear*, 739: 'lordis leuch upon loft'.

154. to blise or to ban] 'To bless or to curse'. A common antithesis; cf. *Wallace*, II. 292: 'thai blis or ban'.

155] The phrasing is traditional. Cf. Wyntoun, VII. 269: 'Wyth hyr his liff in leil spousse . . . to lede'; and *Rauf Coilyear*, 47: 'I leid my life in this land'.

164] Proverbial. Cf. 'Ane byle lang beilit man breik at the last' (MF, no. xlv, 52).

165–7] Note the similar passage in **56**. 85–8.

183. Venus chalmer] A sexual euphemism (see also 430–31). Cf. Chaucer, *Wife of Bath's Prologue*, *CT*, III. 617–18: 'I koude noght withdrawe / My chambre of Venus from a good felawe'; and Maitland, MF, no. cix, 24. Similar phrases were current in medieval French and Latin. The *chalmer* was a private room, often a bedroom (cf. 194, 370).

186–7] Chaucer likewise compares lecherous 'olde dotardes' to dogs: a hound, 'whan he comth by the roser . . . though he may nat pisse, yet wole he heve up his leg' (*Parson's Tale*, *CT*, X. 856). Chaucer's probable Latin source employs the same image (Wenzel 1974: 372).

194. radis] See 141 above.

195] Cf. *Merchant's Tale*, *CT*, IV. 1851: 'But God woot what that May thoughte in hir herte'.

196] The sense and syntax are difficult. I take *syde*, like *thra*, to modify *spekis*; *how it settis him* is a sarcastic parenthesis; *sege* is not the verb 'say' (there is no evidence for such a form in Scots) but the noun 'man', common in alliterative verse (cf. 469 below). MF's *segis*, 'men', gives better sense and may be correct.

197–8] The sense is very difficult, and the repetition of *bot* suggests corruption. A tentative explanation is: 'unless he himself one evening might make some assault (*say* being taken as aphetic form of *assay*) on one of them; but he is not such a one, not one of those who possess their natural powers (i.e. virility)'. For *nature*, cf. 174 and 392.

206. sanct Valentynis day] St Valentine first figures as patron of lovers and mating birds in late-fourteenth-century courtly poems, such as Chaucer's *Parliament of Fowls* and *Complaint of Mars*, and Oton de Granson's *Le Songe Saint Valentin*. There is no evidence for the common belief that this courtly cult originated as a folk festival, or derived from the Roman Lupercalia (Oruch 1981).

232. geir] For the sexual sense, see **62**. 32.

234] The *straik* is clearly sexual, but the terminology is military; cf. *Golagros*, 992: 'The sterne stakrit with the straik, and stertis on stray'.

238. bird] A poetic term for a young woman, perhaps with a pun on 'young bird'. *bourd]* Literally 'sport, cause for mirth'; in context, perhaps 'share of the sport'.

247. spreit . . . inspir] A pious formula. Cf. *Awntyris off Arthure*, 255: 'enspires iche sprete'.

252. schene . . . schrowd] A common collocation in Scottish alliterative verse. Cf. *Golagros*, 599: 'Schaip the evin to the schalk, in thi schroud (= armour) schene'; also Holland, *Howlat*, 891.

257. lesson] Dunbar plays with various senses: 'lecture, discourse read before an audience'; and also, since the Widow sees herself as a preacher (249), 'portion of Scripture read at divine service'.

261. as tygris be terne] This alliterative variant upon the common 'cruel as a tiger' (Whiting, T 284) is used of women in an anti-feminist Scots poem (B, f. 263^r / 15): 'Als terne as tygir of tung vntollerable'.

262. turtoris] The turtle-dove was believed to remain constant to her mate for ever, and symbolized constancy in marriage. Cf. Chaucer, *Parliament of Fowls*, 355: 'the wedded turtil'; and *Merchant's Tale, CT*, IV. 2079–80. For a sarcastic application of the turtle-dove to women's truth, cf. *Reson and Sensuallyte*, 6855–90. Bitterling 1986 notes in *talk* a possible allusion to Song of Songs 2: 12: 'the voice of the turtle'. *talis]* 'Tails', in the common sense of 'sexual organs'. Cf. Langland, *Piers Plowman*, B. III. 131: 'For she is tikel of hire tail'; and Whiting, T 8. *Brukill*, 'frail, wanton', corresponds to *tikel*. There is also a pun, following *talk*, on 'tales, narratives'.

263–4] This perverts Christ's words to the Apostles: 'Be ye therefore wise as serpents and harmless as doves' (Matthew 10: 16).

263] The *dow*, or dove, was proverbially meek and innocent (Whiting, D 359). Lydgate writes with similar sarcasm of women's meekness: 'as a dowe they ha no galle' (*Reson and Sensuallyte*, 6797).

266. stangand as edderis] Proverbial (Whiting, A 47); cf. **15**. 9.

269. nought worth a hen] A phrase for something of little value (Whiting, H 347).

273. hatit ... like a hund] Proverbial (Whiting, H 585).

274. kissing ... clapping] A common pair. Cf. 483.

275. claw his cruke bak] 'Scratch, tickle his crooked back'. The phrase has the implication 'flatter, cajole'.

277. bler his ... e] A common idiom for 'cheat, hoodwink'; cf. Henryson, *Fables*, 2041: 'I can craft to bleir ӡone carlis ee'; and Whiting, E 217.

284. saif my honour] 'Protect my good name'; cf. 461 below. It was important that a courtly lover should preserve his lady's reputation by being discreet.

289] Proverbial-sounding; cf. *King Hart*, 657–8: 'Quha gustis sweit and feld nevir of the sowre ... How may he seasoun iuge?'

293] The husband treats as his heir another man's child.

295. wichtnes of handis] Physical force. Cf. *Piers Plowman*, B. XIX. 247: 'wynne it ayein thorugh wightnesse of handes'.

305. perfit eild] A common phrase, corresponding to Latin *perfecta aetas*, for the age at which a person attained maturity, or legal competence; this was usually 12 for a girl, 14 for a boy. There is an ironic reference to the sense 'supremely excellent, faultless'. For Scottish uses, see *DOST, perfite*, a., and *elde*, n. 1b; see also Dove 1986. *Pert* combines the sense 'clever, quick-witted' with the derogatory 'bold, impertinent'.

306. knew] This has the common innuendo, 'knew carnally'. (*DOST, knaw*, 12c.)

311. thocht I say it my self] Formulaic, usually a mock-modest preface to a boast. Cf. *Rauf Coilyear*, 236: 'And thocht myself it say'; also Whiting, S 74.

315] For the Widow's notion of mercy, see 501 below.

316] Cf. Chaucer, *Knight's Tale, CT*, I. 1761: 'For pitee renneth soone in gentil herte'; also *Merchant's Tale*, IV. 1986. The Widow claims to possess a refined sensibility, associated with those who are *gentill*, noble by birth or nature. See also **26**. 40–42.

319. sit ... my summondis] 'Disregard my summons'. This legalism (*OED*, *sit*, 34) is also used of marital strife in *Rauf Coilyear*, 99: 'For durst scho never sit summoundis that scho hard him say'.

330. as a best I broddit him] See 79 above, and 354–7 below. For similar imagery see an anti-feminist poem (B, f. 263ᵛ / 27) that describes the man yoked to an evil wife: 'Full oft he feilis the brod and dar not quhryne'.

331. to Rome] A very long way (Whiting, R 182). The tamed horse was a symbol of domination, but it implies a reversal of the usual social norms when women ride men.

344–6] The syntax seems confused. Possibly the anacoluthon is meant to suggest the Widow's angry incoherence.

347. bauchles] The exact sense is debatable, but the word seems a legalism, in apparent contrast to *billis*, 'written documents, contracts concerning the transfer of property'. It is most plausibly explained as 'formal reproaches for breach of faith' (Sellar 1986).

351–2] The sexual role-reversal, latent in the widow's other images for herself (e.g. in 326, 379), is here explicit.

355. cappill ... crelis] A common alliterative collocation. Cf. *Rauf Coilyear*, 43 and Henryson, *Fables*, 2028. The husband is depicted as a packhorse, with baskets slung on his back.

358] Cf. Montgomerie, *Cherrie and the Slae*, 211: 'skorne cummis commonlie with skaith'.

374. me prunya] 'Adorn myself'; the sense 'preen the feathers (of a bird)' is clearly relevant (cf. 379, 382).

379] The peacock was a type of pride (Whiting, P 280).

382] The parrot – like the peacock – was esteemed for its bright plumage, but proverbially proud (Whiting, P 305). Cf. Holland, *Howlat*, 125: 'the proper papejaye, proude in his apparale'. The husband is also a bird: *plukit* signifies both 'stripped of feathers' and 'robbed of money'.

384] This alludes to the proverb: to make a rod with which to beat oneself (Whiting, S 652).

389. thing] A common euphemism for the sexual organs, whether female or male (as in 486 below). Cf. Chaucer, *Wife of Bath's Prologue*, *CT*, III. 121: 'oure bothe thynges smale'.

408. 9] 'Wis men know that evil wives are to be recognized by such behaviour': i.e. cruel treatment of stepchildren, or hostility to kinsmen (403–7).

413ff.] For a widow whose grief is dissembled, cf. the Wife of Bath (*CT*, III. 587–92).

423. As fore in a lambis fleise] Proverbial and ultimately scriptural (Whiting, W 474; Matthew 7: 15).

424. my bright buke] A richly illuminated book of hours. The feminine desire to own such expensive status symbols was satirized by Eustache Deschamps: 'Heures me fault de Nostre Dame ... D'or et d'azur, riches et cointes' (*Oeuvres*, IX, p. 45).

430–31. bancat] For the common equation of sexual appetite with eating, cf. **20**. passim, and **64**. Cf. also *cury* (455). *Venus chalmer]* See 183 above.

432–5] This beautiful but comic simile transforms Chaucer's description of

Criseyde in 'widewes habit blak': 'Nas neuere yet seyn thyng to ben preysed derre, / Nor under cloude blak so bright a sterre' (I. 170–75).

437–9] The sponge may be Dunbar's invention, but it was an ancient charge that women could weep to order. Cf. Ovid, *Remedia Amoris*, 690: *Ut flerent oculos erudiere suos*, and Martial's epigram on Gellia (I. 33).

444] Cf. the proverb, 'Women are in church saints, abroad angels, at home devils' (Tilley, W 702).

449. for the syght] 'To avoid being seen'. Cf. the similar usage in *Pistel of Susan*, 57.

452. bejaip] 'Trick, fool'; here, as often, in a sexual sense. Cf. Chaucer, *Manciple's Tale*, *CT*, IX. 144–5, where a wife bejapes a jealous husband.

454. under Crist no creatur] 'No creature on earth'. *Under Christ* was a common tag in alliterative verse.

462. wise] An epithet favoured by the Widow (cf. 294, 451, 496). For similarly ironic use, cf. Chaucer, *Wife of Bath's Prologue*, *CT*, III. 209, 225 and passim.

465] 'May the woman who reaches the age of a hundred, but remains a foolish girl, be publicly derided'. This perverts a much-glossed text (Isaiah 65: 20): *puer centum annorum morietur, et peccator centum annorum maledictus erit*. On this 'boldly feminized version', see Burrow 1986: 155–6. The Widow pours scorn on the woman who cannot keep her love secret.

469. semelyar sege] Cf. *Rauf Coilyear*, 713: 'servit in that saill seigis semelie'.

476–502] This is the comic climax of the Widow's speech, juxtaposing the courtly and the 'riatus', and illustrating her sovereignty over not one lover but a 'thik thrang'.

477. bachilleris blith] Cf. Holland, *Howlat*, 689.

478. luffaris lele] A common phrase in love verse. *Lover* still retains the sense 'suitor, wooer', as in **20**. 4–5.

479, 484] The skilful pouring of wine and carving of meat were much-esteemed social accomplishments, often performed by young squires.

489. fair calling] 'Warm welcome'. See **47**. 188 and note.

490ff.] This embroiders a popular medieval topos: the lady who flirts with several men simultaneously (Bawcutt 1992a: 343–4).

498. luf unluffit] A common phrase for unrequited love. Cf. Alexander Scott, no. xxviii, 1: 'To luve vnluvit it is ane pane'.

500] For the notion that the unrequited lover will die, cf. **20** and **26**.

501–2] The Widow recalls the Sermon on the Mount: 'Blessed are the merciful, for they shall obtain mercy' (Matthew 5: 7); but she confuses erotic mercy, the woman's favour or 'grace' for which the lover pleads, with the mercy towards those in misfortune that might provoke divine pity.

502. sely saull] See **33**. 25 and note. The best explanation of *sabot* is that it means God, and derives from the biblical *Dominus Sabaoth*, 'Lord God of Hosts' (Dobson and Ingham 1967); cf. Bartholomaeus Anglicus, I. 1, on God's names: 'the thridde name is *Sabaoth*'.

504. legeand] 'Story', with ironic reference to the sense 'saint's life'. Cf. Chaucer, *Shipman's Tale*, *CT*, VII. 145–6: 'Thanne wolde I telle a legende of my lyf / What I have suffred sith I was a wyf'.

511–22] Note the return to the rich descriptive style of the opening.

512. day … daw] A common alliterative phrase; cf. *Golagros*, 609; *Rauf Coilyear*, 924.

515. Silver schouris] Also used of dew in **47**. 14.

516. shoutit . . . schaw . . . schill] Cf. *Tayis Bank*, 115–16: 'The schene birdis full schill cowth schowt / In to that semly schaw'.

526. with my pen did report] 'Put down in writing'. Dunbar uses the phrase in **64**. 69.

530] This ironic question to the audience parallels 41–8.

4
A Ballat of the Abbot of Tungland

1–2] Several of Dunbar's poems open with a reference to Aurora, the dawn goddess, and her crystal eyes (**19**. 2 and **41**. 9) or tears (**47**. 16–18). But *cristall haile* is puzzling: the most likely explanation is that it is a figure for dew-drops. A similar usage occurs in a poem in praise of May: 'Aurora with visage pale / Imbalmes with hir cristall hale' (B., f. 229^v, 23–4). The use of the dawn topos here is comic.

5. a Turk of Tartary] The land of the Turks was variously called Turkiland (see B's title) or Turkey (61). It was vaguely identified with Tartary, the remote Asian country of the Tartars, whose name was mistakenly thought to derive from Latin *Tartarus*, hell. Dunbar thus implies the pagan and diabolic origins of Damian.

8] A *waithman* was a poacher, or outlaw; Scottish writers applied the term to Robin Hood. In 'Still undir thir levis grene' (MF, no. cxxx, 64), a maiden, wearing 'waithman weyd', is dressed in green and carries a bow and arrows.

12. wryte and reid] Damian's literacy enabled him to pose as a friar.

16. Lumbard leid] The language of Lombardy, i.e. Italian. Damian may have come from northern Italy, although in the court records he is usually termed French. The University of Bologna was famous for the teaching of medicine, but also had a reputation for the manufacture of poisons.

17ff.] Satire of greedy and incompetent doctors was common in the Middle Ages; cf. Langland, *Piers Plowman*, B. VI. 269–74.

19. nowthir seik nor sair] 'Neither the sick nor the diseased'. A traditional alliterative phrase.

21. Vane organis] 'Organic', or jugular, veins (*DOST*, organe, n 3, and *MED*, organik, organise). Ironic praise for one who cuts throats under the pretence of phlebotomy.

31. Jow] 'Jew, unbeliever'. Vaguely abusive, but perhaps influenced by the legend of the Wandering Jew, and other tales of evil Jewish alchemists, doctors and sorcerers.

32. generit was of gyans] This phrase, which also occurs in *The Crying of ane Play*, 21, implies evil ancestry. Giants were believed to be the monstrous progeny of the fallen angels and 'the daughters of men' (Genesis 6: 1–5). Cf. **31**. 4 and Henryson, *Bludy Serk*, 35–42.

37] For the simile, cf. Whiting, R 8.

44. hiddy giddy] Dunbar alludes, jokingly, to the churning of the victims' bowels. This unusual reduplicative compound, 'helter-skelter, topsy-turvy', may derive from Holland, *Howlat*, 821.

45. practikis ... put to preif] A common collocation. *Practikis* is used of physicians' professional skills, as in Lindsay, *Meldrum*, 1437–9: 'The greitest leichis of the land ... all practikis on him prouit'. Dunbar ironically combines it with the pejorative sense, 'clever tricks, stratagems'.

49–50] This implies a blasphemous disregard of sacred things: the mass, and its most holy moment, the *sacring*, or consecration, of the eucharist. This was signalled by the ringing of a bell.

53. channoun] Tongland abbey belonged to the Premonstratensians, an order of regular canons. Dunbar may recall Chaucer's satirical portrait of the canon-alchemist, dirty of clothing and fiendish in nature, in *The Canon's Yeoman's Tale*.

54. matynnis channoun] The phrase has been variously interpreted, but seems to refer to the service of matins, 'in accordance with canon law'.

55] The stole was a narrow strip of cloth worn over the shoulders; the fanon, or maniple, was a band attached to the wrist of a priest officiating at mass. They were usually made from rich fabrics, and finely embroidered.

58. quintessance] The chief object of alchemy was to discover the 'fifth essence', a supposed ethereal substance, additional to the traditional four elements. It was confused with the elixir, or philosopher's stone, which was believed to transmute base metals into precious ones, such as gold. Cf. **56**. 55 and note.

65. Dedalus] Daedalus, the legendary skilled craftsman (in some accounts a smith), who made wings from wax and feathers, to help his son escape from the Cretan Labyrinth. Icarus, however, drowned.

66. the Menatair] The Minotaur was half-man and half-bull, and thus, like the feathered abbot, a monstrous hybrid.

67] Vulcan, the god of fire, was blacksmith not solely to Mars but to all the gods; according to some legends he was thrown from the heavens, either by Juno or Jupiter. This allusion has a double point, recalling the abbot's sooty labours at the furnace (51–2), and anticipating his fall from the sky. The mention of Mars may derive from Chaucer's inclusion of the smith among Mars' followers: *Knight's Tale, CT*, I. 2046.

68. Saturnus kuke] The notion is clearly insulting. Saturn was a baleful, 'crabbit' planet (see **47**. 114); and the abbot resembles a cook in his alchemical concoctions.

69. tuschettis] A Scottish word for lapwings. The *tuchet* plays a similarly aggressive role in *Howlat*, 821–4.

73. myttane] An unidentified bird of prey; cf. **57**. 12. *Sanct Martynis fowle]* Probably some kind of fish-catcher. In Caxton's *Reynard the Fox*, p. 20, it is a bad omen when Tybert sees one of 'seynt Martyns byrdes' flying on the left. A bird of this name figures in many languages, and there has been much debate as to its identity. It can be traced, however, to the parable of the diabolic *mergos*, or diving birds, mentioned in the earliest, very influential *vita* of St Martin of Tours (d. 397).

74] Dunbar alludes to a well-known theme, the mobbing of the owl by smaller birds. The epithet 'horned' perhaps indicates the long-eared owl, so called from its prominent ear-tufts; it also implies that the abbot, like a devil, had horns on his head.

80] This fuses two similes, suggesting both ferocity and speed: 'fierce as fire', and 'as fire from flint'. See Whiting, F 167 and F 190.

81. tug for tug] A type of phrase common in battle descriptions; cf. *dynt for dynt* (76).

89] Cf. the similar pairing in Holland, *Howlat*, 191: 'Cryand crawis and cais'.

97–8. skrippit ... skryke ... skornit] Cf. 123 below, and the owl's complaint in *Howlat*, 67: 'Sum skripe me with scorne, sum skrym at myn e'. Chaucer calls the jay 'skornynge' in *Parliament of Fowls*, 346.

100. rawcht him mony a rowt] 'Gave him many a blow'. A common alliterative collocation; cf. 'sic rout he raucht', Barbour, *Bruce*, II. 423.

103. hawkit] A joking use of a descriptive term for cattle that have white spots or streaks.

113. at the plunge] A falconry term; Douglas describes birds diving to escape falcons in *Palice of Honour*, 1707: 'And at the plunge part saw I handillit hait'.

115. The crawis ... cair] Cf. Chaucer, *Parliament of Fowls*, 363: 'the crowe with vois of care'.

122. yawmeris ... yowlis] Cf. Douglas, *Eneados*, VI. xvi. 38: 'ȝowland with ȝammering grisly for to her'. Similar alliterative pairs were common (Cf. *OED*, *yammer*, sb. and v.).

125] A comic variant on the 'wakened by bird-song' topos. Cf. the 'schout' of birds in **41**. 183, and the 'shoutyng' that ends *The Parliament of Fowls*.

5

6. provyd] In addition to 'provide', the specialized ecclesiastical sense, 'grant a benefice', is relevant.

7] The court records list payments to musicians and entertainers of many kinds; some of the story-tellers are named, such as 'Wallass that tellis the geistis to the king', and others called 'Watschod' and 'Widderspune' (*TA*, I, 176, 307, 378).

8. the moryis] There are several references to morris dances being performed at James IV's court. The most detailed evidence concerns one organized by John Damian in January 1504, probably for Twelfth Night: payment is recorded to 'Colin Campbell and his marowis that brocht in the Moris dauns'; also recorded is the purchase of six dancing coats, 'the womanis goun', and other clothing (*TA*, II, 414). The exact nature of the morris at this time is debatable, but it is thought to derive from the *morisque*, 'Moorish dance', that was popular at many European courts in the late fifteenth century. On the theatrical nature of the *morisque*, see Kusie 1989; and on the morris in England, see Heaney 1989.

12] The sense is difficult, but might be explained: 'looks as if he cannot help what he is doing'. I take *with aw* not as 'along with the rest', but as combining with *do* in the idiomatic phrase, 'cannot do the contrary, cannot help it' (see *OED, withal*, 1 and 2; *do*, 54).

19] Cf. **52**. 25, where Dunbar calls the queen an 'advocat', who will speak to the king on his behalf. Line 20 hints at the scandal that might follow such intercession.

21. sempillnes] The word implies both humble social status and innocence, or lack of guile. The poet's apparent self-depreciation conveys a boast.

24. the kyngis grace] Both 'the king's grace, or favour', and an honorific title for James IV. Similar word-play occurs in **66**. 99.

6

1–5] Aberdeen was a flourishing port and royal burgh; see Macfarlane 1985: 266–73, and Lynch *et al.* 1988: 148–60. Poems in commendation of a city belong to an ancient genre. For a later Scottish parallel, cf. Lindsay's praise of Edinburgh and other cities in *Papyngo*, 626–46. Contrast Dunbar's dispraise of Edinburgh in **42**.

3] Most editors accept Laing's conjecture, *ascendit*, as a means of filling the gap in this line. But a preferable verb would be *upheyt*, 'raised, exhalted'; this alliterates, and occurs in a similar sense and construction in **45**. 5: 'On to the sterris upheyt is thyne honour'.

18. a cap of gold and silk] This refers not to headgear but to garments made from cloth of gold; *cap* is a variant of *cape*, and probably here has the specific sense, 'cope'.

21–2] The Salutation of the Virgin, or Annunciation (see Luke 1: 26–33), also figured in Edinburgh's welcome to the queen in 1503.

25–8] Matthew 2: 1–12.

29–31] Genesis 3: 24. The angel was traditionally the Archangel Michael.

33. the Bruce] Robert Bruce, who reigned as Robert I (1306–29). His military success in the War of Independence was celebrated by Barbour (cf. **16**. 61).

37] There is a gap in this line, and we cannot be sure of Dunbar's exact wording. The botanical imagery in 38, however, gives a clue as to the nature of this pageant. It showed a plant or tree representing the kings of Scotland, such as that devised for the 1590 entry into Edinburgh of James VI and his queen: 'the kingis grace genelageie in the forme of a trie from the Bruce till himselff' (Mill 1927: 204). These dynastic trees – secular counterparts to the tree of Jesse – were common in royal entries. A phrase such as 'the stok ryell' (cf. **41**. 151) seems likely.

42] Green clothing was particularly associated with May and its festivities; cf. **47**. 127 and note.

47. halsand] Editors follow Laing in substituting *saluand* for R's *husband*. James is not known to have accompanied the queen on this visit, and it seems unlikely that he would be mentioned so casually. I emend to *halsand*, a formal, slightly archaic word, which is closer to *husband* and is employed by Dunbar in **41**. 11.

58] The provision of wine is mentioned in the Edinburgh entries of 1561 and 1579 (Mill 1927: 190, 194). Maitland mentions the practice nostalgically: 'And at ȝour croce gar wyn rin sindrie wayis / As wes the custome in our eldaris dayis' (MF, no. xvi, 22–3).

61–3] The *propyne* was a lavish gift, of wine, gold or other luxuries, presented to distinguished visitors to a burgh. James II, when he visited Aberdeen in 1448, received two tuns of Gascony wine.

7

1–6] Dunbar's opening is deceptively mild, even devotional in tone. With the phrasing of the first two lines, cf. **44**. 1.

5] Cf. Genesis 1–2.

6. quein of heveyne] A favourite medieval title for the Virgin Mary. Cf. **11**. 6 and note.

8] The king was traditionally the fount of justice; cf. **41**. 106–26.

15–27] This catalogue of rogues contrasts with the *men of vertew and cuning* (11). Syntactically, it breaks off unfinished, but the anacoluthon may be designed to suggest anger at their apparent success. Alliterative and flyting-like, this passage contains many obscure words. Some probably derive from contemporary slang or abuse, but a few may be Dunbar's own coinages.

17] Stuffettis perhaps means 'grooms'; cf. Lindsay, *Beaton*, 373: 'ane stuffat stollin out of ane stabyll'. *Strekouris* may be a figurative use of a word for hounds (*OED*, *streaker*, 1 and 2). *Strummellis* seems the same word as *strumbell* (62 below), and occurs only in Dunbar, as a pejorative epithet for farm animals (**20**. 54).

18. haschbaldis, haggarbaldis] DOST (s.v. *luschbald*) notes the existence of a group of abusive nouns employing the pejorative suffix *-bald*, and suggests their connection with verbs, such as *hasch*, *hag*, that mean 'strike, cut down'. *hummellis]* Perhaps cattle. In later Scottish usage the word was used of polled domestic animals.

21] On mandrakes, see note to **54**. 29; on the ugliness of the mastiff, see **60**. 17.

23. bledder cheikis] This implies fat, swollen cheeks. Cf. the self-indulgent Dominican friar in *Pierce the Ploughman's Crede*, 222: 'With a face as fat as a full bledder'.

26] This line is obscure. *Glaschewe-hedit* is not otherwise recorded, but cf. *glaschane* (59). *Gorge-millaris* appears to be composed of two nouns: *gorge*, 'throat', and *miller*. *OED* (*gorge*, sb.) tentatively suggests '? a glutton'.

28–38] Dunbar lists three different types of unworthy and greedy churchmen; the abbot and bishop, who are interested only in the externals of religion, symbolized by the references to cowl and rochet; and a third, who is not content to be a humble parish priest.

34] The sense is difficult. Kinsley takes *dastart* to be a sarcastic reference to the bishop.

38. My lord] An honorific title for abbots and prelates as well as nobles.

43] The wearer of these cast-offs is a learned, impoverished young noble, who despises the man for whom he runs errands.

49. Saying] Either 'seeing' (of the young noble) or, more probably, 'assaying, trying out' (of the churchman). *his odius ignorance]* This parodies honorific titles such as 'his reverence' or 'his grace'.

51–2] Seating at meals was governed by a strict sense of social hierarchy. Cf. *Pierce the Ploughman's Crede*, 760–61: 'For her kynde were more to y-clense diches / Than ben to sopers y-set first and served with silver'.

52. muk the stabell] 'Remove the dung from the stable'. It was said of James III's low-born counsellors that they were better fitted 'to haue haldin the pleugh or . . . mokit clossittis' (Pitscottie, I, 181).

55. hoppir hippis] The hopper was a wide, funnel-shaped container, through which grain passed into the mill. It was so called because of its shaking, hopping movements. Dunbar's image suggests both shape and motion; perhaps 'protuberant, shaking hips'.

59. glaschane] DOST records no other use, but similar words occur in later Scottish usage as terms for the coalfish (*OED*, *glossan*; *SND*, *glashan*).

60. Mell-hedit] (1) Having a large squarish head, like a mallet; (2) stupid. The comparison to a *mortar stane*, a hollowed-out stone, chiefly used to knock, or beat, barley, reinforces the insult.

62. strumbell] See 17 above. *stand ford]* 'Stand for it, guarantee'. Cf. Henryson's use of this colloquialism in *Practysis of Medecyne*, 8; and see *DOST*, *ford*.

73. wrytting] It is not clear whether this refers to Dunbar's verse, or to work as a professional writer, or clerk, in the royal household. For *writing* in this official sense, see **55**. 69, and **60**. 9.

74. danger ... deris] For this alliterative collocation see Henryson, *Robene and Makyne*, 21: 'So that no denger do the deir'.

75] Whiting treats this as proverbial (D 15) – perhaps because of 'As hes bein herd' – but cites no other instances.

8

1–8] Note the striking alliteration on plosive consonants (b, d, k).

1, 9–10] The dragon and the serpent were traditional figures for the devil. See Revelation 12: 9: 'And the great dragon was cast out, that old serpent, called the devil'; cf. also Revelation 20: 2–3.

3–6] This scene – part of the traditional iconography of the Harrowing of Hell – derives ultimately from two Psalms: 'Lift up your heads, O ye gates ... And the king of glory shall come in' (24: 7); and 'He hath broken the gates of brass and cut the bars of iron in sunder' (107: 16).

4] The cross is the symbol of Christ's triumph, carried like a battle-standard as he liberates hell.

7] The Redemption is visualized as a document, signed on the back with Christ's blood to confirm its legal validity. Cf. Chaucer, *An ABC*, 59: 'And with his precious blood he wrot the bille'; and the ME 'Charters of Christ', in which the charter endowing man with heaven is written on Christ's skin, the ink being his blood (Woolf 1968: 210–14).

8] Cf. Luke 24: 34. These words figure in the mass for Easter Day, and are used in the liturgy in the weeks following Easter. They form the first line of an anonymous Resurrection poem that immediately precedes Dunbar's (see B, f. 34ᵛ).

9. Lucifer] A traditional name for the devil, once the brightest of the angels (*Lucifer* means 'light-bearer'). Cf. also **54**. 6–7.

11–15] The devil is less often represented as a tiger than as serpent or dragon, but the image, which Dunbar develops imaginatively, has a precedent in scholastic commentaries on the Scriptures.

15] *Fang* signified not only the prey of an animal, such as the tiger, but also the plunder of a thief.

17–19] The lamb and the lion were familiar symbols for Christ, occurring frequently in medieval art, hymns and the liturgy. (Cf. Adam of Saint Victor's Easter sequence, *Zyma vetus expurgetur*, or Fulbert of Chartres's hymn, *Chorus Novae Jerusalem*.) The lamb was a type of Christ's sacrifice; and the lion of Judah was taken to foreshadow the Resurrection. Kinsley also notes the influence of the bestiary story of the lion cub brought to life by its father's breath, interpreted as a type of the Resurrection.

20] This image of Christ, the giant, is frequent in medieval Latin hymns, often in proximity to the lamb and lion. Dunbar here, as in **48**, recalls Psalm 19: 5: *Exultavit ut gigas ad currendam viam*, 'He has rejoiced, as a giant, to run his course'. The figure of the giant in this verse was variously interpreted, to signify Christ's great strength, or the mystery of his Incarnation (as in St Ambrose's hymn, *Veni redemptor gentium*), or – as here – the Resurrection. (For fuller discussion, see Bawcutt 1992a: 180–81; and Hill 1978.)

21–3] The metaphors of Aurora, the dawn, Apollo, the sun, and 'the blisfull day' contain a threefold reference to Christ as the light of the world (see also 27–8). In St Ambrose's popular and influential hymn *Splendor paternae gloriae*, Christ is figured similarly: first as *Lux lucis et fons luminis / Dies dierum illuminans*, 'Light of light … O Day illuminating all days'; then as *Verusque sol*, 'the true sun'; and in the final stanza as the dawn: *Aurora cursus provehit / Aurora totus prodeat*, 'Dawn is advancing, May he who is the perfect dawn come forth'. In the Harrowing of Hell there is similar stress on light triumphing over darkness; this derives from Isaiah's prophecy (9: 2) that the people that walked in darkness have seen a great light.

27–8] This alludes to the darkness that accompanied the Crucifixion (Luke 23: 44–5); cf. 1. 84–5.

29] An allusion to the ringing on Easter Day of the church bells, which had been silenced for three days. Langland's vision of the Harrowing of Hell ends with the music of bells, 'That men rongen to the resurexion' (*Piers Plowman*, B. 18. 428).

33. done ceis] On the construction, see Introduction, p. 14.

9

5] 'It seems to me best to be cheerful'. The refrain may be proverbial. Cf. Henryson, *Fables*, 521: 'Be blyith in baill, for that is best remeid'.

6. chynge and varie] Cf. 'The stait of man dois change and vary' (**16**. 9); and Henryson, *The Abbey Walk*, 41–2: 'This changeing and grit variance / Of erdly staitis'.

7] On the personification of Fortune, see **24**.

26–7] 'Who should be despondent (lit. droop or dir) for the loss of something that is nothing but vanity?' *Tynsall* is a different word from modern English *tinsel*; see *OED*, *tinsel*, sb.[1], and cf. **54**. 20.

27–9] Cf. the theme and refrain of **34**.

29. twynkling of ane e] A very brief moment of time; the phrase is proverbial, and ultimately scriptural (Whiting, T 547; I Corinthians 15: 52). Cf. also **47**. 235.

39. farie] Literally 'illusion, dream'; but *MED*, *fairie*, 2, illustrates the application to this world as something illusory.

10

1. Gladethe] 'Rejoice'. An irregular form of the imperative singular, modelled on English imperative plurals in *-eth*. Cf. Chaucer, *Complaint of Mars*, 1: 'Gladeth, ye foules'.

4. perle of price] Cf. also 33. This alludes both to the queen's name and to the scriptural *pretiosa margarita*, or pearl of great price (Matthew 13: 46). Lindsay likewise calls Queen Margaret 'that peirle preclare' (*Papyngo*, 547). Similar word-play was popular in poems addressed to women called Margaret.

5. charbunkle] Carbuncle. A name given to the ruby, and also to a mythical precious stone believed to emit light in darkness. As a symbol of excellence it was popular with Scottish poets; Douglas praises Virgil as 'Chosyn charbukkill' (*Eneados*, I Prol. 7), and cf. also 18. 24.

6. rois riale] Here and in 25 clearly alluding to the red and white badge of the Tudors; cf. 41. 171–2.

10. Lodsteir] Literally 'guiding star', figuratively 'shining example'. The word was common in panegyric, and often coupled with *lamp*; Lindsay called James IV: 'Lode sterne and lampe of libiralytie' (*Papyngo*, 492).

11. Pollexen] Polyxena, daughter of Priam, was beloved by Achilles. Her beauty is mentioned by Chaucer in *Troilus and Criseyde*, I. 454–5.

12. Pallas] A title given to Athena, goddess of wisdom.

17–23] This embroiders an ancient panegyrical topos: that a beautiful woman is Nature's masterpiece. The notion of a work of art is reinforced by such words as 'depictour', 'kervit' and 'depaint'. Cf. Chaucer, *Physician's Tale*, *CT*, VI. 10–31, and *Parliament of Fowls*, 377–8, where Nature (as in 17) rejoices in her handiwork: 'Nature hireself hadde blysse / To loke on hir'.

29–31] A queen's most important duty was to provide an heir. Sir Richard Maitland, writing of Mary Queen of Scots, in 1558, prays similarly: 'To the grit god mak intercessioun / To send our princes gud successioun' (MF, no. xvi, 31–2). *lang desirit]* James IV was slow to marry, and to have a legitimate heir.

33–9] A virtuoso display of lapidary symbolism; the stones' distinctive 'virtues' are here less important than their beauty, brightness, and place within an alliterative pattern. The stanza is governed by the 'outdoing topos': Margaret, the pearl, transcends all other jewels in beauty and preciousness.

38] The ruby was sometimes termed 'king of stones', but this line recalls the scriptural praise of the virtuous woman whose price is 'above rubies' (Proverbs 31: 10).

11

1. Hale] 'Hail', the equivalent of *Ave* or *Salve*, with which Latin poems on the Virgin frequently began. *sterne]* The star was a popular figure for Mary, whose name was sometimes etymologized as *maris stella*, 'star of the sea'. Cf. 'Ros Mary', 9: 'O sterne that blyndis phebus bemes bricht'; and 'Obsecro', 14: 'Sterne of the sey'. Similar images occur later (25–8, 53 and 70).

3] For this image of Mary as a *lucerne*, or lamp, cf. 'Ave gloriosa', 42–3: 'Haill, brichtest sterne, Haill, licht lucern'; and Greene, *Carols*, no. 207: 'O lantern of eternall licht'.

5] The thought resembles Hebrews 13: 8: *heri, et hodie, ipse et in saecula*.

6. Angelicall regyne] Cf. Kennedy, *Passioun*, 123: 'Haill, sueit angelicall regin'. Mary was commonly called queen of heaven (see 52), and of the angels. She received the title of queen in the patristic period, and in the fifteenth century the Coronation of the Virgin became a favourite theme with artists and writers.

8. rosyne] 'Rose'. A nonce-formation. See also note to 40.

11. Yerne] I follow *OED* in taking this as a verb, 'feel, or show compassion'; other editors treat it as an adverb, 'swiftly, soon'. *virgin matern]* The virgin birth was a central paradox of the Incarnation. Cf. line 22 below, and Dante's prayer, 'Vergine madre . . .' (*Paradiso*, 33). See Woolf 1968: 130–33.

12. rute and ryne] Kennedy also applies this formulaic alliterative phrase, which literally means 'root and rind', to the Virgin (*Passioun*, 124).

14. Alphais habitakle] Cf. 'I am Alpha and Omega, the beginning and the end' (Revelation 1: 8).

16. tabernakle] A frequent image for the Virgin, or her womb. Cf. Kennedy, *Passioun*, 128: 'The Haly Gaist schane in hir tabernakill'. The figure derives from the standard exegesis of Psalm 19: 5 (AV 19: 4): *In sole posuit tabernaculum*.

18. his signakle] The sign of the cross.

20. dethis . . . umbrakle] 'The dark shadow of death' (the scriptural *umbra mortis*).

22. but makle] Cf. **41**. 152–4 and note.

26. day sterne] A term more commonly used of Christ, as in **48**. 3.

29–30] There were many medieval stories of the Virgin putting devils to flight (see Woolf 1968: 121–3).

31. plicht] 'Anchor', a symbol of hope. *mekle of mycht]* An alliterative formula, also used in **60**. 17.

34. nychttingale] One of a cluster of bird symbols for the Virgin in Lydgate, *Minor Poems*, I, no. 49, 80.

35] Cf. 'Obsecro', 7: 'Way to thame that wilsum ar'. In Latin verse the Virgin was similarly *via* or *erranti semita*.

38. emprys] 'Empress'. Cf. 61 below, and 'Ros Mary', 7: 'Emprys of hevyne of paradys and hell'.

40. ros of paradys] The rose was one of the most popular images for the Virgin; cf. also 8 and 79, and note to **48**. 4. This refers specifically to the belief that the rose in paradise, before the Fall, was unfading and without thorns.

42. flour delyce] A type of lily, often shown in depictions of the Annunciation, and usually taken to symbolize Mary's royalty and her chastity. Cf. Kennedy, 'Closter of Crist', 1: 'riche recent flour delys'.

43. daseyne] A nonce-form, for the rhyme. Chaucer calls the daisy 'emperice and flour of floures alle' (*Legend of Good Women*, F Prol 185) *hale fro the splene]* On this phrase, see note to **30**. 2.

47–8] The Virgin's role as the supreme intercessor between sinful man and God was much stressed in Marian lyrics: cf. 'Ros Mary', 33–5: 'O madyn meike most mediatrix for man . . . Pray thi son Ihesu'. Kennedy's 'Closter of Crist' ends: 'Beseike thi sone . . . Sen hale suple to Kennedy thow art / O mater dei memento mei thi man'. On the theological background, see Woolf 1968: 119–20.

56. mak our oddis evyne] This seems, contextually, to mean 'pardon our imperfections'. (Cf. *DOST, od* and *oddis.*)

58. ellevyn] Apparently 'eleven', used in an indeterminate sense, 'a large number'. For another possible explanation, see note to 65. 21.

60. Thy name ... nevyne] 'Recite thy name'. A set alliterative phrase; cf. Holland, *Howlat*, 33: 'names to nevyn'.

65. pavys] 'Shield'. This symbolizes the Virgin's protective power against sin and the devil; cf. Lydgate, *Minor Poems*, I, no. 53, 34: 'pavys of my dyffence'.

71. Spyce] The verse 'I gave a sweet smell like cinnamon and aromatic balm' (Ecclesiasticus 24: 15) was often applied to the Virgin.

72. grayne] Literally 'seed'. For the image of Jesus as a seed, or ear of corn, that sprang from a maiden and was reaped on Calvary, see Gray 1972: 77. Here, collocated with spice and paradise, there may be a further sense, 'grain of paradise, the spice cardamom'.

73. wall] The wall symbolizes the Virgin's power to protect sinners; cf. Lydgate, *Minor Poems*, I. no. 54, 68: 'Geyn feendes power our castel and our wal'. The figure derives from exegesis of Song of Songs 8: 9: 'If she be a wall, we will build upon her a palace of silver'; cf. also Luke 10: 38. Swenson (1989) notes how in lines 73–8 'Dunbar's imagery works to bring us through the outer wall into the most intimate chamber of Ecclesia'. *place palestrall]* 'Palatial dwelling'. *DOST* suggests that this erroneous use of *palestral*, 'pertaining to wrestling, athletics', derives from a misunderstanding of 'pleyes palestral' in *Troilus and Criseyde*, V. 304.

75. trone regall] 'Royal throne'. Cf. Holland, *Howlat*, 751: 'Thow seker trone of Salamon'. Solomon sitting upon his throne foreshadowed the Son upon his mother's lap (cf. I Kings 10: 18).

77–8] 'Thy chamber enclosed the lord of all'. This refers to the paradox that God, who encompasses everything, was himself encompassed in the Virgin's womb. Cf. Douglas, *Eneados*, X Prol. 106–8, and Diehl 1985: 204–8. The figure of a *closet*, or small room, derives from exegesis of the *porta clausa* of Ezechiel 44: 1–3, as a reference to Mary's virginity. Cf. Lydgate, *Minor Poems*, I, no. 49, 34: 'Chambyr and closet clennest of chastyte'; and Holland, *Howlat*, 725: 'chalmer of chastite'.

79. ball cristall] Poems praising the Virgin abound in images of jewels and precious stones (cf. 62); crystal commonly symbolized her purity, and specifically the Immaculate Conception. Cf. 'Ave gloriosa', 11: 'Haill cumly cristell cleir'.

80. angell fude] See 1. 54 and note.

83. fall mortall originall] A reference to the doctrine of original sin, and the death-bringing consequences of the Fall.

12

4. wretchitnes] 'Misery', together with the more specialized sense 'miserliness'. In *38.* 29 the word contrasts with *fredome*, 'generosity'.

6. sturt or stryfe] 'Quarrelling or strife'; cf. *36.* 31. Similar alliterative phrases were common, especially in poems attacking women. Cf. Flemyng's 'Be mirry bretherene', on the life of the sailor: 'he knawis nowdir sturt nor stryfe ... Bot he that hes ane evill wyfe / Hes sturt and sorrow all his life' (B, f. 160ʳ / 35–8).

8] Cf. the similar alliterative collocation with *mell* in **3. 56**.

9] For the bond of marriage, cf. **3. 47–8**.

11–14] 'He who has an unblemished wife – a butt (*prop*) for his own arrow-shaft (*genyie*) – and then makes love to a strange woman (lit. shoots at a *schell*, or target), and is wasted by venereal disease'. Cf. Carmichaell, no. 786: 'He that hes a wif of his awin and gois to this town, that is a lown'. Archery was a popular sport, and the king often played 'at the prop' with courtiers (see *TA*, I, 273; II, 401; III, 179 and 366; I, 360). Such sexual applications of the language of archery were common, and in Scottish poets 'shooting at the shell' usually had obscene connotations. Cf. Lindsay's reproof to James V in *Flyting*, 36–7: 'Thocht ȝe rin rudelie, lyke ane restles Ram, / Schutand ȝour bolt at mony sindrie schellis'.

14] This line has been misunderstood. The phrase *fleis of Spenyie* had two contrasted senses. Sometimes it corresponded to Spanish fly, or cantharides, then a popular aphrodisiac, made from crushed beetles. But it was also one of many names given to syphilis, as is illustrated by the Glasgow surgeon Peter Lowe: 'Amongst the Frenchmen it is called the Spanish sicknesse, in England the great pocks, in Scotland the Spanish Fleas, and that for two causes, the one because it began first amongst the Spanyards; the other, because when the infection spreadeth first forth in the body, it is like vnto red spots, called flea-bitings' (*An Easie, certaine and perfect method, to cure and preuent the Spanish Sicknes* (London, 1596), B 1ᵛ–2ʳ). This latter sense is clearly most relevant here.

19. rewth] Cf. **52. 9**.

13

9. confort kyth] This alliterative phrase sometimes carries the implication of giving sexual encouragement (*DOST, kythe*, v. 4b). Dunbar often associates *confort* specifically with erotic pleasure; see **20. 5** and **41**.

14. deyme] 'Pass malicious judgment'. This verb belongs to the vocabulary of the topic; cf. **69. 109**.

17. parramouris] An adverbial use of the noun; in Scots found only in verse, in the phrase 'to luve parramour(is)'.

28. not worth a fle] A common phrase for worthlessness; cf. Henryson, *Fables*, 2045; also Whiting, F 345.

41] With the use of *See* in the final stanza cf. **16** and **38**.

47] Probably proverbial. Cf. Whiting, T 399.

14

1] Editors have long termed *Andro Kennedy* a 'court physician', but the poem provides little support for this, unless *solacia* (57) is taken as 'medical remedies' rather than 'pleasures'. External evidence is also lacking. An 'Andro Kennedy' figures in the court records from August 1502 to September 1503 (*TA*, II, 61, 158 and 393), but seems to have been a humble messenger (cf. 2). The name was fairly common; other Andrew Kennedys at this time include a landowner, mentioned in May 1501; another man, who died in Edinburgh in 1491, *bastardus absque legitimis heredibus* (*Great Seal*, no. 2070), seems a more likely candidate (cf. 5–6). The style *maister* implies that Kennedy was a university graduate, but may be merely jesting.

3–4] An incubus was a devil who had sexual intercourse with a woman. A similar link with friars occurs in Chaucer, who says of the limitour: 'Ther is noon oother incubus but he' (*Wife of Bath's Tale*, CT, III. 880).

9–12] This plays with the testamentary formula *nihil sit certius morte, nec incertius hora mortis*. The thought is a truism; for numerous parallels, see Whiting, D 96.

10] The second half of this line is unsatisfactory in all witnesses. B reads *quhen we haif done*; MF has *dome*, 'fate', instead of *done*, which injures the rhyme.

12. blind Allane] Unidentified, but not necessarily fictitious; cf. Lindsay's 'No more than did blynd Alane of the mone' (*Beaton*, 396), which may echo Dunbar.

15–16] A flippant rewriting of the common formula for a testator's sanity: *eger corpore sanus tamen mente*, 'sick of body but sound of mind'.

24. Cuthbert] Unidentified, but presumably a taverner, or cellar-keeper in a great house.

32. bed of stait] A costly bed, such as the 'gret bed of stait', hung with cloth of gold, prepared for Margaret Tudor in 1503.

35–40] It was not uncommon to stipulate one's burial-place, usually in a church or churchyard. But the *mydding*, or rubbish heap, was a shameful place, where the bodies of criminals or the excommunicated were thrown; cf. Lindsay, *Beaton*, 269.

36. Air] Ayr, a town in which the Kennedys were a prominent family.

41–4] The bequest of one's heart was a feature of lovers' testaments, although they are usually said to be loyal and constant.

44. Jacobe] This represents the dative of *Jacoba*, Andrew's wife or mistress.

46. Verum deum renui] A confession of atheism. The allusion is to Jeremiah 9: 6: *renuerunt scire me, dicit Dominus*, 'they refuse to know me, saith the Lord'.

49–51] The *best aucht* was the most valuable article or animal that a tenant owned; on his death, by feudal custom, the landlord claimed it. The term represents legal Latin *melius averium de conquestu*. It corresponds to, but is not synonymous with, Gaelic *caupe*, used in Carrick and the Highlands for a tribute paid to the head of kin; in 1490 the Scottish parliament abolished the custom of *caupe*, but it persisted into the late sixteenth century, when the lawyer Skene called it 'a notabill oppressioun' (MacQueen 1991 and 1993).

51. hede of kyn] The chief of a family, or clan.

55–6] Proverbial: cf. Carmichaell, no. 199: 'Als sib as seive and riddle that grew baith in a wod'; and Whiting, S 304. Lines 53–6 suggest that Kennedy is the sort of man who boasts, without justification, of being related to great men.

59] This satirically reverses the disclaimer in legal documents that a grantor was acting without fraud or guile.

60–61] St Anthony's, at Leith, was a house of Augustinian canons, who cared for the poor and diseased; the order was founded by St Anthony of Vienne. There may be a covert allusion to the fact that part of the canons' income came from the wine trade; for every tun arriving at Leith they received one quart, either for sale or for their own use. William Gray has not been identified. The most likely candidate, however, is William of Myrtoun, who was elected as 'maister', or preceptor, of St Anthony's in 1489, and whose tenure of office seems to have been surrounded with controversy until he was dispossessed in April 1496.

63–4] Proverbial. Cf. Whiting, H 417.

68. Dispersit, dedit pauperibus] A well-known verse (Psalm 112: 9), associated particularly with St Lawrence, and his generosity to the poor.

73. Jok Fule] Possibly a type-name; yet a real fool of that name was present at court between 1503 and 1505 (*TA*, II, 354; and III, 160).

79. bleris my lordis e] On this common phrase, see note to 3. 277.

81. Johne Clerk] Unidentified. Cf. the poet mentioned in **16**. 58, but the name is common, and they are probably different persons. Kinsley takes him to be an incompetent physician, who 'falsely transcribed *dentes* in some medical context'. But the point of line 88 – literally 'By writing *dentes* (teeth) without the letter d' – remains obscure.

97ff.] Cf. the instructions for a martial funeral befitting a great soldier in Lindsay's *Testament of Squyer Meldrum*.

101. playand cop out] On this phrase, see **51**. 13 and note.

104] 'I mingled my drink with weeping' (Psalms 102: 9).

106. Dies illa, dies ire] 'That day, the day of wrath'; the Last Judgment (cf. 22 above). This may allude to the great thirteenth-century hymn, attributed to Thomas of Celano, which opens *Dies ire, dies illa*. But the word order is closer to the *Libera me* responsory in the Office for the Dead: *Dies illa, dies irae calamitatis et miseriae* (*Sarum Breviary*, II, 270).

107–9] Squire Meldrum similarly rejects *bellis*, or the passing-bell, and requests that 'gret Cannounis' be fired instead (181–2).

110] A wisp of straw was the recognized sign of an alehouse.

116. De terra plasmasti me] The opening of the antiphon *De terra plasmasti me et carne induisti me*, employed in the burial service after the grave was covered with earth (*Sarum Missal*, 448). It derives from Job 10: 8–9: 'Thine hands have made me and fashioned [*plasmaverunt*] me . . . thou hast made me as the clay'.

15

2. sentence conveniable] A wise and appropriate saying that will sum up the nature of the world.

6–15] The repeated coupling of *Yisterday* and *this day* draws attention to the parallelism between these stanzas.

8–9] This striking antithesis resembles a traditional piece of Scottish weather lore: 'When March comes in with an adder's head, it goes out with a peacock's tail' (*OED, peacock's tail*, 1) For *stangis lyke une eddir*, see Whiting, A 47.

10. Concluding] This signifies both 'ending' and 'overcoming in argument'. As if in an imaginary debate, the weather ends by refuting the poet's earlier statement.

15] For the anthropomorphic conceit of birds' bowers, cf. **47**. 11.

16–19] These are four very familiar 'sentences' about mutability; for parallels, cf. Whiting, J 58 and N 108. But the *repetitio* on *nixt* is less common, and may be indebted to a passage in *Troilus and Criseyde*, which ends: 'And next the derke night the glade morwe; / And also joie is next the fyn of sorwe' (I. 951–2).

16. bene] 'Is' (an anglicism); as a different part of speech it forms an acceptable rhyme with the past participle *bene* (20).

16

2–3] I take the poem's occasion to be an actual illness; but Reiss (1979: 29–30) considers the *seiknes* merely symbolic.

4] 'The fear of death troubles me greatly'. These words have a solemn origin in the third Nocturn of the Office of the Dead: *Peccantem me quotidie et non poenitentem timor mortis conturbat me* (*Sarum Breviary*, II, 278). They were often quoted separately, as a moral *sententia* or in epitaphs (Woolf 1968: 333–5; Gray 1972: 6). They also occur in the burdens of several carols (Greene, *Carols*, nos. 369–72).

7. brukle] 'Morally frail'; a traditional epithet for the flesh, here signifying 'sensual nature, or appetite'. According to homiletic tradition, mankind had three principal enemies, the world, the flesh and the devil; cf. Chaucer, *Melibee*, *CT*, VII. 1421ff.

10–11. Now ... Now] A common rhetorical formula, implying mutability; see **34**. 19–22 and note.

13. stait] Dunbar plays on two senses, 'state or condition' (as in 9 also), and 'rank of society', as in *estatis* (17). This introduces the theme of Death the Leveller; cf. Greene, *Carols*, no. 370: 'In what estate so euer I be, / Timor mortis conturbat me'.

15. So waveris] B, MF; P's *wavis* is repetitious and metrically weak. *Waver* is a verb that Dunbar uses elsewhere of mutability: cf. **66**. 1: 'this waverand warldis wretchidnes'.

37. Art-magicianis] 'Practitioners of magic'. This compound also occurs in *Clariodus*, V. 1590ff., which describes the feats performed 'By astrologis and art magicianis, / Grit sortolegis with thair enchantments'.

41–3] The irony is scriptural; cf. 'Physician, heal thyself' (Luke 4: 23).

46. Playis heir ther padyanis] 'Act their parts in life, as if in a drama'. The metaphor was common (see Whiting, P 5), often with reference to life's brevity. Cf. 'I haue pleyd my pagent and now am I past' (*CB XV*, no. 159). Dunbar uses a similar metaphor in **25**. 13.

47. faculte] This refers to the poets as a professional body, or class, and also to their 'professional skill'.

49. done ... devour] 'Devoured'. On this periphrastic construction, also used in 57 and 61, see Introduction, p. 14.

50–51] The list of poets is headed by the traditional trio of great English poets: Geoffrey Chaucer (d. 1400); John Lydgate (d. 1449), who was a monk at the Benedictine abbey of Bury St Edmunds; and John Gower (d. 1408). See the eulogy of these poets in **47**. 253–70.

53. syr Hew of Eglintoun] Usually identified with Sir Hugh Eglinton of that Ilk (d. 1377), who lived in the reign of Robert II. There is no other evidence that he was a poet.

54. Heryot] Unidentified. *Wyntoun]* Andrew Wyntoun (*c.* 1350–1425) was prior of Lochleven, and author of *The Original Chronicle*, the first large-scale vernacular history of Scotland (see Goldstein 1987).

55. this cuntre] That is, Scotland, and distinguishing the Scottish from the English poets.

57] The scorpion was notorious for its poisonous sting, here representing the sting of death (I Corinthians 15: 55).

58. Maister Johne Clerk and James Afflek] An English 'master John Clerk' has been identified as author of the alliterative *Destruction of Troy*. Dunbar was clearly familiar with much alliterative verse, and it has been suggested that he may refer to this poet (Turville-Petre 1988). The name, however, was very common; for another mention of 'master Johne Clerk', see **14**. 81 and note. (Although there are attributions to 'Clerk' of four poems in the Bannatyne manuscript, these are written in a later hand.) *Afflek* (P, B) is a variant spelling of *Auchinlek* (MF); the poet has not been identified, although Lyall (1976b) suggests a candidate in James Auchinleck (d. by 1492), the eldest son of Sir John of that Ilk.

59. trigide] 'Tragedy, tragic narrative'. Henryson applied the term to *The Testament of Cresseid* (4), as did Chaucer to *Troilus and Criseyde* (V. 1786).

61. Holland] Richard Holland was a notary, and a canon and precentor of Moray Cathedral. His fortunes were closely linked with those of his patron, Archibald Douglas, earl of Moray, and he died (c. 1482) in exile in England (Stewart 1972). Dunbar was well acquainted with his *Buke of the Howlat*, an allegorical poem in stanzaic alliterative verse. *Barbour]* John Barbour (c. 1320–95), archdeacon of Aberdeen and author of *The Bruce*, the great historical poem on Robert Bruce and the War of Independence.

63. Schir Mungo Lokert of the Le] No verse survives, but he was probably the 'Sir Mongo Lokart knycht', known to be dead by 27 February 1489. The Lockharts of the Lee were a Lanarkshire family.

65. Clerk of Tranent] Unidentified; Tranent is a small town between Edinburgh and Haddington.

66. the anteris of Gawane] This poem about Sir Gawain, one of King Arthur's most famous knights, has not been identified. A Scottish romance in which he is prominent, however, is the alliterative *Golagros and Gawane*, which was printed by Chepman and Myllar.

67. Schir Gilbert Hay] Author of a substantial Alexander romance, *The Buik of King Alexander the Conquerour* (c. 1460). He also made prose translations of three French treatises (dedicated to William Sinclair, earl of Orkney, in 1456). Hay graduated from St Andrews (1419), and spent many years in France, serving as chamberlain to Charles VII. The date of his death is uncertain, but it probably occurred before 1470.

69. Hary] Poet of *The Wallace* (c. 1475–78); little is known of Hary's life, although he figures in the court records during the 1490s, and his blindness is mentioned by John Major. *Sandy Traill]* Unidentified.

71. Patrik Johnestoun] Patrick Johnston (d. 1495) was a notary, landowner, and official receiver of revenues from Crown lands in West Lothian. He produced entertainments for the court at Yule and Shrovetide between 1476 and 1489. Bannatyne attributes to him *The Thre Deid Pollis*; in the Maitland Folio, however, it is assigned to Henryson.

73. Merseir] This poet receives more prominence than any other in the list; but several of Dunbar's contemporaries bore the surname, and it is not possible to identify him. Lindsay mentions a poet of this name (*Papyngo*, 19), and three 'ballattis of luve' are attributed to him by Bannatyne.

75. quyk] Douglas uses the epithet of Virgil (*Eneados*, I Prol. 12). The line echoes Chaucer's praise of the Clerk (*CT*, I. 306) as 'short and quyk and ful of hy sentence'.

77–8. Roull . . . Roull] Neither poet has been identified, but one was presumably author of *The Cursing*, a blackly comic piece (MF, no. xlvi), dated before 1503.

81–2] Robert Henryson, author of *The Fables* and *The Testament of Cresseid*, flourished in the late fifteenth century; he is believed to have been a schoolmaster and notary at Dunfermline.

83] *Schir Johne the Ros* was a friend of Dunbar's (see **54**. 1 and 39), but has not been identified with certainty. Two candidates have been suggested: Sir John Ross of Montgrenan, king's advocate and a lord of council in the reign of James III, who died in 1494; and Sir John Ross of Halkhead, near Renfrew, 'a convivial companion of James IV' (Kinsley) who had died by 1502 (see Lyall 1976b). No poems are extant.

86. Stobo] John Reid, also known as Stobo, perhaps from his birthplace. He was a long-serving clerk and letter-writer in the royal secretariat, a notary, and rector of Kirkcrist. Described as lying 'seik' in May 1505, he had died by 13 July 1505. No poems survive. *Quintyne Schaw]* A fellow-servitor of Stobo and Dunbar, last mentioned in July 1504. One poem is extant (MF, no. cxlvi), a short satire on court life.

89–91] *Walter Kennedy*, author of *The Passioun of Crist* and other poems, was Dunbar's antagonist in *The Flyting* (see **54** headnote); although these lines suggest that his death was imminent, he seems not to have died until 1518.

93. brether] Brother-poets and fellow human beings. Cf. the reference to 'my bredir all' in **43**. 26.

97] Proverbial; cf. Carmichaell, no. 1523: 'There is remeid for all things bot for sudane deith'; and Whiting, D 78.

98. for dede dispone] 'Make ready for death'. This was achieved by contemplation, by reading treatises like the *Ars Moriendi* (see O'Connor 1942) and by making a will. To die unprepared, in a state of sin, might entail the loss of salvation.

17

5. rink] A poetic word current chiefly in alliterative phrases; cf. Henryson, *Testament of Cresseid*, 432.

14. trew as ony steill] A common simile (Whiting, S 709).

19. the air] Justice ayres, or circuit courts, were held twice-yearly, in spring and autumn, north and south of the Forth. Dunbar alludes to the court held in Edinburgh itself. The treasurer, like the king, often attended the ayres; indeed, an important source of Crown revenues was the dubious traffic in fines, respites, and remissions exacted from malefactors (Nicholson 1974: 567–70; MacQueen 1993: 59–65).

21–2] Pensions were paid twice a year, at Whitsun and Martinmas. The records show that Dunbar usually received his Martinmas 'wage' promptly, on either 11 or 12 November, but in 1512 he did indeed have to wait until Christmas Eve, or Yule.

25ff.] With this *repetitio* on 'Welcum', cf. **45**. 9–25.

18

1. Lodovick] Louis XII of France (1498–1515), whom Bernard Stewart served as ambassador and military commander. *most cristin king]* The style *roi très chrétien* corresponds to *rex christianissimus*, which was first given to the Christian Roman emperors; in the Middle Ages, after a propaganda effort by Charles V, it was reserved solely for the kings of France.

4. most anterous and abill] An echo of **45**. 42.

6. to governe and to gy] A popular alliterative phrase; cf. *King Hart*, 20.

7. weir the sabill] 'Wear black clothes, as a sign of grief'. *Sable* was the heraldic term for black. Cf. **3**. 418 and 447, and Chaucer, *Complaint of Mars*, 284: 'Now have ye cause to clothe yow in sable'.

8. the flour of chevelrie] The slightly varying refrain always ends with this somewhat clichéd phrase for the perfection of knighthood. Dunbar also applies it to Stewart in **45**. 18; cf. *Lancelot*, 2181: 'the flour of knychthed and of chevalry'.

10. douchtie ... in deid] A common collocation (*DOST*, *douchty*, 2).

13. the Turk sey] Presumably the Black Sea. The military power of the Ottoman Turks was then at its zenith, and it was a high tribute to imply that a military commander was feared even by the Turks.

17–18] With the figure of death as a devouring dragon, cf. **25**. 28; also Lindsay, *Magdalene*, 15.

19. The prince of knychtheid] For this phrase, see **45**. 18.

20. The witt of weiris] Cf. *Golagros and Gawane*, 1137: 'Wawane, the wit of our were'.

21. stoir] A variant of *stour*, 'combat' (*OED*, sb.[1]). Common in alliterative phrases commending courage; cf. **45**. 9: 'in stour most strong'.

24. charbuckell] The carbuncle was popular with Scottish poets as a metaphor for excellence; see **10**. 5 and note.

25–32] To end with a prayer for the soul's welfare was a usual feature of medieval laments for the dead.

19

1–16] The idealized spring setting and the elevated style, with its vaguely eulogistic epithets, closely resemble the openings of **41** and **47**. The theme derives ultimately from classical poetry, in which Aurora, the dawn goddess, is described as rising from the sea or her bed, and putting night or the stars to flight.

2. cristall] 'Bright as crystal'. Aurora also has 'cristall ene' in **41**. 9. The phrase was popular with Scottish poets, cf. Henryson, *Orpheus and Eurydice*, 355; and *Testament of Cresseid*, 176. *chasing ... sable]* Cf. **41**. 56.

6. lawry grene] The laurel was a traditional perch for birds singing of love. Cf. *The Floure and the Leafe*, 109, where the nightingale sits 'in a fresh greene laurey tree'.

8. luves service] The phrase belongs to the terminology of courtly love. Cf. *The Kingis Quair*, where birds are busy 'in lufis seruice' (448), and folk renew their 'seruis vnto loue' (831).

9–10] Crystal, symbolizing brightness and purity, was a common image for water. But Dunbar may allude specifically to the river of the water of life, clear as crystal (Revelation 22: 1).

12. persew] This may have the legal sense, 'prosecute a plea, as in a court of law'. Cf. the legal term *pleid* in 115 below.

14] This echoes Chaucer, *Parliament of Fowls*, 356: 'The pekok, with his aungels fetheres bryghte'. Angels, in medieval art and drama, were commonly represented with wings of peacock feathers. The nightingale's appearance is not naturalistic, but symbolizes her spiritual significance.

18ff.] The merle resembles the lark in **41**. 12–14, greeting the dawn and exhorting lovers to awake.

19. rong] 'Re-echoed, resounded'. A popular hyperbole. In Lydgate, *Black Knight*, 45, the birds 'So loude songe that al the wode ronge'. Cf. also **47**. 25, and Clanvowe, *Boke of Cupide*, 99–100.

20. o] Apparently a reduced variant of *on*, 'in, during' (*DOST*, *o*, prep.[2]).

26] The nightingale's song was proverbially merry; cf. Douglas, *Eneados*, XIII Prol. 61; and Whiting, N 110.

31] Proverbial. Cf. Barbour, *Bruce*, VII. 45: 'We haiff tynt this trawaill'.

35] This alludes to the well-known saying, 'Young saint, old devil' (Whiting, S 19). Medieval moralists criticized it as a sinful proverb, and it was usually put in the mouths of devils, or evil counsellors, such as Placebo in Lindsay's *Satyre*, 233–4. On its connotations, see Burrow 1979.

38. makis on] Literally 'makes one', i.e. unites in one person. The merle argues that it is unnatural for a young person to behave like an old one. Cf. 'Youth and age are often at debate', or 'Crabbed age and youth cannot live together'.

44] Genesis 1: 27: 'So God created man in his own image'.

46] 'Was true love shown there, or not'? *Quhithir* functions as an interrogative marker (*DOST*, *quhither*, conj. III. 4). It often introduces rhetorical questions; cf. Henryson, *Fables*, 2564: 'Quhether call ȝe this fair play or nocht?'

47. paramour] 'Lover'. The spiritual application to Christ occurs in other religious verse.

58–60] The thought is orthodox. In Chaucer's *Physician's Tale* (*CT*, VI. 26–7), Nature, praising Virginia's beauty, says: 'I made hire to the worshipe of my lord; / So do I alle myne othere creatures'. Henryson touches on the theme in *Fables*, 2842–6: God is the source of beauty, and causes nature 'To prent and set [it] in euerilk creature'.

61–3] These lines develop a more general reflection on the duty of thanking God for his gifts. Cf. St Augustine, *On Christian Doctrine*, I. 31. 34: 'For every good of ours either is God or comes from God'.

70–71] A perversion of the scriptural commandments: 'Thou shalt love the lord thy God with all thy heart, and with all thy soul, and with all thy mind. This is the first and great commandment. And the second is ... love thy neighbour as thy self' (Matthew 22: 37–9). These were the basis for St Augustine's discussion of love: 'all your thoughts and all your life ... should be turned toward Him from whom you receive these powers ... whatever else appeals to the mind as being lovable should be directed into that channel into which the whole current of love flows. Whoever, therefore, justly loves his neighbour should so act toward him that he also loves God with his whole heart' (*On Christian Doctrine*, I. 22. 21).

70. fro the splene] See **30**. 2 and note.

77. goldin-tressit] This unusual compound epithet perhaps derives from *Troilus and Criseyde*, V. 8: 'gold-tressed Phebus'. (In Latin poetry the sun was termed *auricomus*.)

78] To shine like the sun was a commonplace (Whiting, S 897).

81–7] Love is said to ennoble human beings, and to convert vices into virtues. For similar praise of human love, cf. Clanvowe, *Boke of Cupide*, 151–60; and Gower, *Confessio Amantis*, IV. 2298–2302: 'it doth aweie / The vice ... / It makth curteis of the vilein, / And to the couard hardiesce it yifth'.

89] Cf. Clanvowe, *Boke of Cupide*, 166–7: 'Nyghtyngale, thou spekest wonder faire, / But, for al that, the sothe is the contreyre'.

90] It was a commonplace that Cupid was a blind god who made his servants blind; cf. Gower, *Confessio Amantis*, VIII. 2130–31. The train of thought in lines 90–94 resembles **47**. 203–5.

102. the feindis net] This image of the devil as a fowler who lays snares for man is aptly placed in a bird's mouth. Cf. also Henryson, *Fables*, 2444, and his particularly striking use in *The Preaching of the Swallow* (*Fables*, 1843–5). In the Bible the wiles of the devil are often compared to snares and nets. For the application specifically to love, cf. Douglas, *Eneados*, IV Prol. 246. *tone]* 'Taken, captured'. A hyper-anglicism, or 'form which does not exist in southern English, but might have been supposed to do so' (Aitken 1983: 30). MF has the usual Scots form, *tane*.

103] 'But love the God of love who died for love of mankind'. Cf. 'God is love' (I John 4: 8, 16).

105–12] The birds sing antiphonally. Cf. the similarly patterned description of bird-song in **41**. 164–75.

111. with his deid the bocht] 'Redeemed thee by his death'; the phrase also occurs in **69**. 98.

115. pleid] 'Debate, discussion'. Frequent in legal contexts, with the sense 'disputes at law, litigation'. *in to my thocht is grene]* 'Is fresh within my mind'. For the idiom, cf. 'ay grene in to his mynd', **3**. 317.

117. reconfort] Note the echo – with a difference – of *confortable* (**4**).

118] The listening poet is depicted as an unrequited lover.

20

1. this hynder nycht] For Dunbar's use of this phrase, see note to **63**. 1.

3. my hoip, my heill] 'The source of my hope and well-being'. An alliterative pair popular in Scottish verse. Cf. 'My hop, my heill', Hary, *Wallace*, XI. 569.

6. with danger deill] 'Display coldness to me'. On the significance of *danger* in love poetry, see **47**. 223 and note.

15. sweit as the hunye] A popular simile (Whiting, H 430). Honey is a common endearment; see also lines 3, 30 and 39.

22. Tehe] A derisive laugh (modern *teehee*), particularly associated with women: cf. Chaucer, *Miller's Tale*, *CT*, I. 3740: 'Tehee! quod she'.

23. tuchan] Usually explained as a form of *tulchan*, a calf-skin stuffed with straw and put beside a cow to induce her to give milk; figuratively it was applied to an inferior substitute, and later to a large, fat person (*CSD*, *tulchan*).

30. huny soppis] A dish made of bread steeped in honey and water; the term figures elsewhere as an endearment. *Possodie*, although interpreted by past editors as a form of *powsowdy*, a broth made from a sheep's head, seems more plausibly connected with *possett*, a drink of hot milk curdled with ale or wine, and flavoured with sugar and spices (see *DOST, possodie* and *possett*).

33] To single out the woman's heels has a comic incongruity, particularly since they are unlikely to be white. *Quhalis bane*, or walrus ivory, was a type of extreme whiteness; see Whiting, W 203, and Henryson's *Thre Deid Pollis*, 29.

37. mychane] Unexplained; the context suggests a sense such as 'mouth' or 'belly'.

38. hurle bawsy] Obscure, but possibly related to 'Hurlbasie', the name for a demon.

39. slawsy gawsy] *Slawsy* is not recorded except here and in 41; *gawsy*, 'plump and fresh-complexioned', occurs in later Scots usage (see *CSD, SND*).

43. capirculyoun] *DOST* interprets this as an 'arbitrary variant' of *capercailye*, 'wood grouse' (Gael. *capull coille*, 'horse of the wood').

44. brylyoun] This word has not been explained, but Kinsley takes it to signify the *pudendum muliebre*. It may rather be a scribal error for *rylyoun*, 'shoe of undressed hide', implying that the girl is a simple peasant.

46. tyrlie myrlie] Recorded in later Scots as a term of endearment (*SND, tirl*, n. and v.). Kinsley compares *tirly whirly*, used by Burns and other writers in various senses, some sexual. A similar reduplicative formation is Skelton's *tyrly tyrlowe*, which in *Collyn Clout*, 949, is glossed as 'female genitalia'. *crowdie mowdie]* This may be another playful nonce-formation, although it could be interpreted literally as 'mouldy porridge' (cf. *CSD, crowdie*, 'oatmeal and water, eaten raw').

48. stang] The literal sense is 'pole, stake'; there is an obvious sexual innuendo, similar to that in *yerd* (3. 130 and 220).

51. golk of Marie land] The only other occurrence of this phrase is in *King Berdok*: 'the golk ... of maryland' (14, and 20). This too is a comic wooing-poem, but the phrase is applied not to a man but to the heroine. *Golk* means either 'fool' or 'cuckoo'; the precise sense of *Marie land* (? Mary's land) is unknown.

57. apill rubye] The name for a variety of apple.

60. the dery dan] No other Scots use is known – *dirrye dantoun* (58. 24) is not necessarily the same phrase – but the context implies a jocular euphemism for sexual activity. *DOST* glosses as 'amorous sport'. ME *dery dan* appears to have been the name of a popular song (see Bowers 1955: 219, and *IMEV*, 2700). The prefatory 'Quhilk men dois call' suggests that it was a vulgar or popular catchphrase.

61. myrthis met baythe in ane] 'Their separate pleasures coincided'.

21

2. sabill] A heraldic term for black, also applied to funeral garments (as in **18**. 7). The sky seems to be clad in mourning.

4–5] There is some ambiguity. Dunbar lacks heart both for his own writing and for enjoying that of others. The *playis* were possibly but not necessarily dramatic.

8] *Dule* is dissyllabic.

10. Symmer] For a fuller personification of summer, see Henryson, *Fables*, 1678–84.

17. In tyme provyde] Stock moral advice. Cf. **34**. 5; and an anonymous poem (B, f. 75ʳ) that begins, 'Befoir the tyme is wisdom to provyde'.

20. this court] That of James IV. The poet is here concerned with the practical problems of earning a living.

23–5] 'Let Fortune exhaust her anger (towards you), since no rational argument may mollify (her), until her alloted time (symbolized by Time's hour-glass) is past'. Bad fortune must be endured rather than striven against, since Fortune is not subject to reason.

27] A slight rewording of the proverbial 'Who may hold that will away?' (Whiting, H 413). The things of this world are fleeting.

28] *No space* is adverbial, 'no length of time'.

31–3] This succinctly conveys the poet's reluctance to be closely acquainted with Old Age.

34–5] The necessity for the soul to render accounts after death was a homiletic commonplace (cf. Romans 14: 12). It is a leading theme of *Everyman*; there Death tells Everyman that he must bring his 'boke of counte' when he is summoned to appear before God (103ff.).

36] Cf. Job 38: 17: 'Have the gates of death been opened unto thee?'

38–40] Moralists commonly depicted the grave as a low house that forced those who entered to stoop low. Cf. Lazarus in *The Towneley Plays*, 391: 'Vnder the erthe ye shall thus carefully then cowche; / The royfe of youre hall youre nakyd nose shall towche'. (See Woolf 1968: 83–4.)

48] 'Depressed by the showers of thought'. This recalls the opening stanzas. The showers are both literal and symbolic, fusing the *havy schouris* (7) of winter with the poet's *havy thocht* (12).

49] This resembles the greetings to summer traditionally sung by birds; cf. Chaucer, *Parliament of Fowls*, 690: 'Now welcome, somer'; and *Kingis Quair*, 235.

50. sum disport] *Sum*, as in 47, stresses the limited, partial nature of this delight.

22

1–6] Note the alliteration on sibilants.

7–8] The owl was considered ugly; cf. Lindsay, *Dreme*, 478: 'Foule lyke ane oule'. It usually had an adverse moral significance, and figured as a type of the traitor in a fable from the popular fourteenth-century *Dialogus Creaturarum Moralizatus*; there the owl conspires against his true king, the eagle (cf. **41**), to have lordship over all other birds, but is captured and sentenced to banishment. (For a sixteenth-century translation, see *The Dialoges of Creatures Moralysed*, pp. 179–80.)

12. cowle] Hooded garment worn by monks or friars.

13–14] It was proverbial that treachery turns upon itself (Whiting, T 444).

15–16] Cf. Whiting, G 491: 'The beguiler is beguiled'.

19–24] The sense is difficult and compressed, and I differ from past editors in its interpretation. I gloss *suppleis* as 'supporters' (not 'punishment'): since *gallow treis* is likely to be a plural, I take *he* as the adverb 'high' (not 'he'), and 23–4 as a relative clause of the 'zero' type. It might be paraphrased: 'Donald Owyr has more falsehood than any four of his supporters from around the Western isles and seas, [who] now grimace on high upon gibbets'. Dunbar argues: if the followers have been executed, why should the leader be pardoned?

19. strong] When used of traitors and malefactors, this has the sense 'flagrantly guilty'.

25. Falsett no feit hes] Obscure; Kinsley explains *feit* as 'standing-ground, base'.

29] The phrasing has chivalric connotations; cf. Alexander Scott, *Justing*, 63: 'God schaw the ryght'.

31–2] The fox, by *kynd*, or natural disposition, is crafty and deceitful; cf. Henryson, *Fables*, 402. This analogy dominates the last three stanzas, and voices the received Lowland opinion of Highlanders as thieving, treacherous and, above all, wild. The contrast between 'domesticated' Lowlanders and 'wild and untamed' Highlanders is first recorded in the fourteenth-century chronicler Fordun; cf. Nicholson 1974: 206.

32. reffar, theiff and tratour] A common Scottish inclusive phrase for malefactors.

47–8] A Scottish proverb (Whiting, F 627). It was employed by Henryson, *Fables*, 827, and later applied to another 'crafty fox', Cardinal Beaton, by Knox (*History of the Reformation*, I, 54–5). The sense seems to be that a villain is incorrigible.

23

1. quhytt] The word is deliberately ambiguous. At this time it was less likely to refer to race than to fair-skinned beauty, as in Henryson, *Thre Deid Pollis*, 25: 'ladeis quhyt'.

3. the last schippis] Although topical-sounding, this reference has not been identified. The ships were possibly those of the piratical Barton brothers, who often captured the ships and cargo of the Portuguese, who dominated trade with Africa. (On the Bartons, see Macdougall 1989: 238–41).

5. mekle lippis] According to writers on physiognomy these were not only ugly but a sign of folly. Cf. Hay, *King Alexander*, 10256–8: 'Quha hes thik lippis grete and vngudely . . . Ar oft tyme full of foly'.

6. tute mowitt] 'Having a protruding mouth'. The fifteenth-century writer John Metham described a *tut mouth* as one 'with thyk lyppys, rounde, stondyn owte'; it signified 'a gret devourere off mete and a gret drynker' (*Works*, p. 133). *aep]* The Barbary ape was the one most familiar in medieval Europe. It was regarded as *turpissima bestia*, an evil animal (Janson 1952: 14); cf. also 41. 109 and note.

9. saep] Black soap. Soap, then used chiefly for washing clothes rather than persons, was usually liquid, and made from a mixture of tallow, fish-oil and potash.

12. tar barrell] 'Black as tar' was a common simile (Whiting T 39), but this image also suggests corpulence.

13. the son tholit clippis] The black woman's birth is symbolically associated with the darkness of an eclipse; eclipses were considered portents of evil.

14] 'The night (possibly with a pun on *knight*) fought with gladness on her behalf'. Implicit is a battle between night and day.

19. weld] 'Enjoy, possess'. Here, as in **3**. 77, the verb has a sexual sense.

21. fedle] A scribal form of *feld*, with metathesis.

23. kis hir hippis] With this vulgar gibe, cf. **54**. 131. The 'misdirected kiss' is a common humiliation in folktale and fabliau; cf. also Chaucer, *Miller's Tale, CT*, I. 3730–40.

24

1. Lucina] A name for the moon; in **47**. 2 and 79 she is also linked with Fortune, a similarly inconstant and unreliable goddess. The moon was associated with disturbed mental states; cf. 'ilk mone owt of thy mynd' (**54**. 53).

10. fantasie] This hints at the delusive nature of the dream that follows.

11. dame Fortoun] Fortune was traditionally female, and ruled over 'everie warldlie thing'; the turning wheel was her usual attribute, symbolizing mutability. Cf. Boethius's influential discussion of Fortune's role in human affairs in *The Consolation of Philosophy*, bk 2; for Scottish portraits, see Barbour, *Bruce*, XIII. 635–70, and *Kingis Quair*, 1110–55. Medieval commonplaces about Fortune are listed in Whiting, F 506; see also Patch 1967, and Pickering 1970: 168–222.

26. griphoun] A fabulous beast, which (like the abbot) was a hybrid: half-eagle and half-lion. Griffins were unclean birds (according to the Scriptures), notorious for their love of gold, and therefore symbols of avarice. Their most famous exploit was to draw the chariot of Alexander through the air. See Armour 1989: 15–45.

27] The female dragon perhaps derives from the Dragon mentioned in Revelation 12: 3–17.

29. Antechrist] During the Middle Ages there was enormous interest in the figure of Antichrist, and many bizarre tales circulated concerning his monstrous birth and blasphemous imitation of Christ, including an unsuccessful attempt to emulate the Ascension. The legend originated in Christ's own words about the false Christs and prophets who would appear before his second coming at the end of the world (Matthew 24: 24; I John 2: 18, 22). Medieval writers commonly spelt the prefix *Ante-* rather than the Biblical *Anti-*. The abbot, in his attempt to fly, resembles Antichrist and other evil figures who were believed to prefigure him; he also preaches his coming reign (37).

31. Saturnus fyrie regioun] On Saturn's ominous associations, see **47**. 114–15. The planet was not usually termed 'fyrie'; Henryson speaks of Saturn's 'cald region' (*Orpheus*, 191), and Lindsay of his 'frosty' sphere (*Dreme*, 488). Perhaps there is a confused reference here to the region of fire, thought to surround the earth immediately below the moon's sphere (cf. *Dreme*, 378).

32] *Symon Magus* figures in the Bible (Acts 8: 9–24), and became a type of ecclesiastical greed, or simony. He was even more notorious in the Middle Ages, however, as a sorcerer, who attempted to fly to heaven, and was dashed to the ground through the prayer of St Peter; his fall was a very popular subject in medieval art. He too was viewed as a type of Antichrist, and also of evil preachers (Emmerson 1981: 27–8, 122–4, and passim). *Mahown* was a common name for the devil (see 3. 101), but here is likely to refer specifically to Muhammad, the prophet of Islam. He was believed to have made miraculous flights through the air (Owen 1970: 150–54), and was viewed as a precursor of Antichrist (Emmerson 1981: 67, 197).

33. Merleyn] Merlin, the wizard, who figures in Arthurian legend, and was reputed to be the son of the devil.

34. Jonet] Probably a type-name for a witch.

38. neir the warldis end] Cf. the questions put to Jesus concerning signs 'of the end of the world' (Matthew 24: 3).

49] To see several moons was more commonly a portent of disaster than of 'thrift'; cf. Shakespeare, *King John*, IV. ii. 182; and Lindsay, *Satyre*, 826: 'I see fyfteine Mones in the lift'.

25

1, 8] 'Remember, man, that thou art ash … That thou must return to ash'. These words, ultimately from Genesis 3: 19, were used in Ash Wednesday services; the phrasing *quod cinis* (rather than the Vulgate *quia pulvis*) derives from the Sarum liturgy, then commonly used in Scotland (cf. Wordsworth 1959). The words were often quoted, on their own, as a reminder of human mortality.

5–6] Here (and in 25–6) Dunbar possibly recalls Job 14: 2: 'He cometh forth like a flower, and is cut down; he fleeth also as a shadow'. A shadow was a common image for human mutability (cf. Whiting, S 178 and 182), but *in ane glas* implies a reflection in a mirror, which was less frequent.

7. thocht thy bodye ware of bras] Cf. Job 6: 11–12: 'What is my strength? … Is my flesh of brass?' Brass was proverbial for hardness and durability (Whiting, B 511).

8] See note to line 1.

9–14] Death's power over the greatest of men, scriptural and pagan, is illustrated here. Several – Hector, Alexander and David – were included among the 'Nine Worthies'. Such lists of exemplary figures were also a feature of the well-known *ubi sunt* topos (see Gray 1972: 183–90), to which this passage may be indebted, although it does not use the *ubi sunt* formula. Cf. 'Man, hef in mynd', 12–14: 'For bald hector and achilles / and alexander, the prowd in pres / hes tane thare leif and mony ma'.

9–10] Hector, son of Priam and noblest of the defenders of Troy, was killed in single combat by the Greek warrior Achilles *(Achill)*. *Hercules*, the Greek hero, was noted for his prodigious feats of strength and cunning, the so-called 'Twelve Labours of Hercules'. *Sampsone* (Samson), like Hercules, was famous for his great strength, breaking down the gates of Gaza and destroying the temple of Dagon (Judges 13–16).

11] Alexander the Great alone has a whole line devoted to him. Alexander's prominence perhaps reflects his special popularity in Scotland (the name was given to three kings), but there was a didactic tradition of using him as a prime illustration of Death the Leveller. Cf. *Hamlet*, V. i. 191ff.

12. Meik David … fair Absolone] Both epithets were traditional. Cf. Lydgate:

'Who was ... Meker than Dauid, wiser than Salamon? Or fayrer founde than was Absolon?' (*Minor Poems*, II, no. 72, 57–61.) David was esteemed for his humility; and the beauty of his son, Absolon, was proverbial (Whiting, A 18).

13. playit thair pairtis] 'Played their allotted roles in life, as in a drama'. A similar image occurs in **16**. 45–6.

14. God, that all thing steiris] The phrase recurs in **7**. 3.

15. exceptioun] 'Exemption from the normal rule'; also in the Scottish legal sense, 'plea by a defendant against a decision or judgment'.

20. uglye] MF's *horrible* is perhaps correct: it is better metrically, and the coupling with *ugsum* is traditional.

25–6] Cf. *Everyman*, 17–18: 'Strengthe, Pleasure and Beaute / Wyll fade from the as floure in Maye'.

27–8] On death as a devouring dragon, cf. **18**. 17–18.

29] Cf. **16**. 29–32.

33–6] This common homiletic theme is based on Revelation 14: 13: 'Blessed are the dead ... And their works do follow them' (see Woolf 1968: 317). It is memorably dramatized in *Everyman*, 906–7: 'They all at the last do Everyman forsake, / Saue his Good Dedes there dothe he take'.

41–7] It was a sermon commonplace to compare the perils of human life to a stormy sea voyage (Owst 1961: 68–76). In the Christian tradition the *port* which one seeks to reach is God or heaven (Dunbar uses the figure in **34**. 13). But this sometimes overlapped, not altogether harmoniously, with the classical notion that death is the port to which all are bound. Jesus, the redeemer, offers the only hope of salvation in this *tempest*, and is here symbolized as the ship's main anchor (*plycht anker*) and rudder (*steiris*).

44] 'But violently break apart, disintegrate, like a ship in a storm'. I take *speiris* to be an early use of 'spars' in the nautical sense: 'a general term for all masts, yards, booms, etc.' (*OED*, *spar*, 4; a sense not there recorded till 1640).

45] On the late medieval cult of Jesus's Five Wounds, see **69**. 23 and note.

46] The anchor symbolizes hope; cf. St Paul: 'Which hope we have as an anchor of the soul, both sure and steadfast' (Hebrews 6: 19). The *steiris*, or rudder, symbolizes divine guidance. Chaucer, *Man of Law's Tale, CT*, II. 833, speaks likewise of the Virgin: 'That is to me my seyl and eek my steere'.

26

1. swete ... fo] A traditional oxymoron for a beloved but cruel mistress; cf. Chaucer, *Knight's Tale, CT*, I. 2780, and *Troilus and Criseyde*, I. 874 and V. 228.

2] Cf. Chaucer, *Knight's Tale, CT*, I. 2776: 'Myn hertes lady, endere of my lyf'.

5. man slayar] The same hyperbole occurs in 'Fresche fragrent flour', where the mistress is termed homicide and manslayer.

6. your man am I] The lover is his lady's feudal vassal, a figure common in medieval love poetry. See also lines 13, 21 and 24. Cf. *Kingis Quair*, 435; Chaucer, *Troilus and Criseyde*, I. 427 and V. 939; and *Legend of Good Women*, 1626.

16] Cf. *Troilus and Criseyde*, IV. 302–3: 'O wery gost ... why nylt thow fleen?'

17. dwawmes] 'Swoons, fainting-fits'. Bannatyne says similarly that his heart 'In deidly dwalmys sowpit is for evir' (16).

24] Murder *undir traist*, or homicide *sub praetextu amicitiae*, was regarded as a particularly heinous crime. An instance occurred in the reign of James IV, when the Scottish warden of the Marches was killed by an Englishman during the period of truce (Macdougall 1989: 252).

31. mayne and murning] The same alliterative collocation occurs in Henryson, *Fables*, 1555.

36–7] The *dow*, 'dove', symbolized meekness and humility; it was distinct from the *turtour*, or 'turtle-dove', the traditional type of fidelity in love. Cf. 3. 262–3 and note.

41] Cf. Chaucer's famous line: 'For pitee renneth soone in gentil herte' (*Knight's Tale, CT*, I. 1761; also *CT*, IV. 1986). The saying had semi-proverbial status (Whiting, P 243).

45–8] The *repetitio* on *quhill* is impaired by the change of meaning in line 48.

49] Cf. the end of Troilus's epistle to Criseyde: 'And far now wel, myn owen swete herte' (V. 1421).

27

4. as ony ganyie] This implies a sharp, piercing pain. For similar comparisons, cf. Whiting, A 184–5.

8] The phrasing is close to **15.** 1–4. Ross (1981: 155) comments that 'the poet's search for a 'sentence' . . . tells us something about his method of composition'.

9. Unsleipit] 'Unslept, not having slept'. Apparently parallel to *Dullit. behind]* 'Back of the head'. This was traditionally the seat of memory. Cf. Hay, *Alexander*, 9742–4: [Reason governs the middle part of the brain, and] 'Behind him in the noddill lyis Memor, / As kepare of all thing that cummys before'.

14. danceing nor deray] A common alliterative phrase. Cf. Douglas, *Eneados*, XIII. viii. 75: 'ioy and myrth, with dansyng and deray'.

28

4. corce] This was a highly literary term for a coin, and usually the vehicle for word-play, as in **50.** 21–2. Some Scottish coins bore the St Andrew's cross on one side.

11. lord thesaurair] See headnote to **17.**

29

1] The syntax is difficult, and some editors emend *in* to 'now' or 'may'. *DOST*, however, glosses *in* as 'in spiritual communion with'; *gif* must then be explained as an elliptical form of the more usual *God gif*, 'God grant', employed elsewhere in the poem.

4. hansill] A gift, usually one given at New Year, as a token of good luck. Cf. *Sir Gawain and the Green Knight*, 66, where King Arthur's courtiers at New Year 'forth runnen to reche hondeselle'; and Barbour, *Bruce*, V. 120–21, where the word is ironically applied to plunder: 'Syk hansell to that folk gaiff he / Rycht in ye fyrst begynnyng'.

14–15] Cf. **41**. 106 and note.

18. Fraunce crownes] French *écus*, or gold crowns, were current in Scotland, and finer than the normal Scottish gold coins (Metcalf 1977: 164).

30

2. fro the splene] 'From the heart (lit. spleen)'. The spleen was believed to be the seat of various emotions, including love. This phrase is common in Scottish poets, and indicates heartfelt sincerity; cf. **19**. 70; **41**. 12; and **47**. 106.

3–4] The notion of love as a fire was an ancient commonplace. On its cooling through age, cf. Henryson, *Testament of Cresseid*, 29–30. Venus's *brand*, or flaming torch, is a figure that can be traced to classical mythology, but Dunbar here recalls Chaucer, in *The Parliament of Fowls*, 114; and *The Merchant's Tale*, *CT*, IV. 1727–8, where Venus dances 'with hire fyrbrond in hire hand' at the wedding of May and January.

24. the quarrell to sustene] The sense is difficult. Kinsley takes the reference to be to jousting; *DOST* glosses *quarrell* as 'grievance, cause'; Schipper more plausibly explains it as 'the contention between true and false love'.

28. luvis court] Something of a cliché; the notion of a court of love, presided over by Venus and Cupid, was often embroidered by poets; cf. Gower, *Confessio Amantis*, VIII. 2661–2, where Youth 'Of Loves court was Mareschal'.

33–62] These stanzas illustrate the *truble* that a courtly lover experiences, such as fear of ill-success, jealousy, and the disdain of his mistress.

58. denger] Here and in 64 (though not in 41) this has the special sense common in love poetry, 'disdain, coldness towards a lover' (see note on **47**. 223).

59. sett nocht by a bene] 'Estimate as worthless'. A *bean* was a common measure of low value (Whiting, B 85–92).

65–6. grace, mercy] Divine grace and mercy are contrasted with their erotic equivalent, the lady's pity towards her lover. Cf. Arcite's words in *The Knight's Tale*, *CT*, I. 1120–2: 'And but I have hir mercy and hir grace . . . I nam but deed'.

81–82] Cf. **19**. 103: 'Bot luve the luve that did for his lufe de'. On the theme of Christ, the faithful lover of the soul, cf. *Troilus and Criseyde*, V. 1842–8.

90. in flouris grene] 'In the flower of youth'. Cf. the refrain of Henryson's *Ressoning betuix Aige and Yowth*: 'O 3owth, be glaid in to thi flouris grene'.

31

1] A call for attention in the minstrel manner. Cf. the openings of *Sir Thopas*: 'Listeth, lordes, in good entent', and *A Gest of Robyn Hode* (ed. Dobson and Taylor 1989): 'Lythe and listin, gentilmen'.

2. wys and wycht] The same alliterative doublet is applied to Bernard Stewart (**45**. 11).

4–6] The giant father and *sossery* hint at an evil and diabolic origin. Cf. **4**. 32 and note; and **14**. 1–8. Although a giant and a fairy queen are mentioned in *Sir*

Thopas, their roles are wholly different; several romance heroes had supernatural parents.

7–8] This syntax is characteristic of popular narrative; cf. *Sir Cleges*, 13–14: 'A corteysear kny3t than he was on / In all the land was there non'; and *A Gest of Robyn Hode*, st. 23: 'A soriar man than he was one / Rode never in somer day'.

8. gane] 'Go, walk'. Not an instance of the 'southern' infinitive in *-n*, but a northern verb apparently distinct from *ga*. See *DOST*, *gane*, v.[2], and *SND*, *gaun*.

12. Rois and Murray. Ross and Moray, in the extreme north of Scotland, correspond to the remote lands in which romance heroes demonstrated their courage.

14. Helland gaist] As in **54**. 168, this phrase implies that Highlanders are famished and emaciated.

16. glen Quhettane] Clan Chattan, which consisted of a number of northern clans and families, dominated by the Macintoshes. It is unnecessary to emend *glen* to *clan*, since this style of the name was often employed in the sixteenth century; see also *DOST*, *glen*, n.[2]. Clan Chattan had a fierce and warlike reputation; Dunbar possibly refers to the clan's recent activities, such as a raid on Cromarty and Inverness in 1490, and a revolt in 1502, led by Farquhar Macintosh, that threatened royal estates in Moray (see Nicholson 1974: 542–5; Macdougall 1989: 180).

17. as oxin] Norny turns the tables on the Highlanders, who had a reputation as cattle-thieves.

22–3] Sir Thopas likewise excelled at wrestling (740). This was not solely a plebeian sport, but was practised by nobles. Cf. Bower's encomium of James I: 'he ... would challenge any one of the magnates [of any size] to wrestle with him' (*Scotichronicon*, XVI. 28).

24] In tail-rhyme it was common to place stereotyped assertions of veracity in the 'tail'; but this and 36 are evidently sarcastic.

25. wyld Robein] Robin Hood is mentioned by several Scottish writers, such as Wyntoun, Bower and Douglas (*Palice of Honour*, 1718); see Dobson and Taylor 1989: 4–6. *Under bewch]* 'In the greenwood', suggesting the environment of outlaws and poachers.

26. Roger of Clekniskleuch] Neither person nor place has been identified.

27. bauld a berne] A formulaic phrase. Cf. Henryson, *Fables*, 2110.

28] *Gy of Gysburne* was killed by Robin Hood, after competing with him in feats of archery, casting the stone, and wrestling; see Dobson and Taylor 1989: no. 5. *Allan Bell* is plausibly taken to refer to *Adam* Bell, one of three Inglewood outlaws celebrated in the ballad 'Adam Bell, Clim of the Clough, and William of Cloudesley' (Dobson and Taylor 1989: no. 28).

29. Simonis sonnes of Quhynfell] 'The sons of Simon of Whinfell'. The same phrase occurs in *Colkelbie Sow*, 381, as the title of a dance or song. Two wild and mountainous areas in Cumbria have this name: Whinfell, to the south of Cockermouth, and Whinfell Forest, south-east of Penrith.

31. anterous] 'Adventurous'. A stock epithet for a brave knight. Cf. **45**. 42.

31–3] Traditional chivalric exploits. Cf. Wyntoun, III. 972 (C): 'Thai that mycht the gre thar wyn / Off turnamentis or of justynge'; and the romance *Ipomadon*, 16–18: 'Thereffore in this world wherever he went / In justys or in turnament / Euermore the prys he wan'.

35. Schir Bevis] The hero of *Sir Bevis of Southampton*, a medieval romance, still very popular in Dunbar's time and throughout the sixteenth century. Sir Bevis receives climactic position in this burlesque of the outdoing topos.

37. Quenetyne] Identified by some scholars with an equally mysterious figure, the poet 'Quintine', mentioned by Douglas (*Palice of Honour*, 924); cf. also **54. 34**, where a Quintin is Kennedy's cousin. But the person here mentioned is not necessarily a poet, and may be merely a lowly member of the royal household.

43–8] Curry was a fool, often mentioned in the court records from 1495 until his death, shortly before June 1506 (*TA*, III, 197). He seems to have been a 'natural' fool, and was married to 'daft Anne' (III, 369). Curry's *kneff* was an attendant, employed to take charge of him when the court moved from Edinburgh to other parts of Scotland.

49–50] At Easter and Yule fools, like minstrels and other entertainers, flocked to court to receive rewards; cf. Mill 1927: 38–9. 'Lord of every fool' is an equivocal phrase. If Norny were a knight, he might retain fools in his household and thus be their lord; but Dunbar implies that he is rather the chief of fools, an archetype of folly. There may be an allusion to the Scottish 'Abbot of Unreason', whose festive role was analogous to the English Lord of Misrule.

54] Small bells not only formed part of a fool's costume (cf. *Thre Prestis of Peblis*, 469), but often decorated the clothing of courtiers, and the trappings of their horses. Cf. the bells on Venus's chariot in *The Palice of Honour*, 436–40.

32

7–8] Past editors do not comment on these puzzling lines, which seem to play on the visual and phonological resemblance between *wemen* and *we men*. Puns exploiting the pseudo-etymological analysis of *woman* as 'woe man' were fairly common (see Whiting, W 512, and *OED*, *woman*, 1k). But there is evidence, chiefly from the late sixteenth century onwards, for puns on *women* (often spelt *weemen*) and *we men*. Cf. 'Without women we men cannot be' (Tilley, W 692); also the quatrain (preserved in Fergusson's *Proverbs*, p. 124):

> Women to men ar equall every way.
> And lyk infirmityes in both do stay.
> Wee men are women, women ar wee men
> What differens is tulxt us & women then?

9] 'A curse on (lit. woe befall) the fruit that would destroy the tree (from which it grew)'. Possibly proverbial. The train of thought in 9–12 resembles *The Letter of Cupid*, 173ff.: 'every wicht wot . . . / That of a woman he discendit is / Than is it schame of hir to speik a mis / A wicket tre gude fruct may none furth bring'.

13ff.] A standard topic in defence of women was their suffering in childbirth and loving care of children. Cf. 'For we aucht first to think on quhat maner / Thay bring ws furth and quhat pane thay indure / First in our birth and syne fro yeir to yeir . . . ' ('All tho that list', 8ff.); also Weddirburn, 94–5: 'Ar we nocht maid of wemenis flesch and blud / And in thair bosum we ar bred and borne'.

18. bane] Usually glossed as 'bone'; but to suck from the breastbone (i.e.

sternum) seems an odd and unparalleled phrase. I take *bane* to be the adjective, 'comfortable, hospitable' (*DOST*, *bayne*, *bane*).

21–3] This alludes to the common proverb (Whiting, B 306) condemning the bird that fouls its own nest. This was traditionally employed by those wishing to rebut men's criticism of women; cf. *CB XIV*, no. 110: 'I holde that brid muche to blame / That defouleth his oune nest'; and *Letter of Cupid*, 182ff., on the 'dishonest' bird 'That vsis to defoull his awin nest / Men to say weill of wemen it is best'.

27–30] It was the culminating argument in women's favour that Christ, although his father was God, had a human mother, the Virgin Mary. Weddirburn writes: 'God that knawis wemenis nobilitie / Was of ane woman born as ȝe ma reid / And nocht consaivit be menis polute seid' (12–14). Yet this passage is curiously elliptical; possibly lines referring explicitly to the Virgin have been excised from the original. On Protestant censorship of references to Mary in the later sixteenth century, see MacDonald 1983: 417–19.

29. king of kingis] Cf. **48**. **28**.

33
The Maner of Passyng to Confessioun

1. the fourty dayis] Lent.

2] Confession should be voluntary. Cf. Henryson, *Fables*, 794: 'Do wilfull pennaunce'.

3. haly writ] Jesus fasted for forty days in the wilderness (Matthew 4: 1–2).

10. schrive the clene] A penitential formula. Cf. **69**. **4**.

15–18] It was traditional in penitential literature to speak of sin as a disease or injury, and of the confessor as a spiritual physician, who administered medicine to the soul. Cf. also 22–3, 35 and 54.

17. haill and sounde] 'Completely healthy'. A poetic cliché, used by Henryson (*Fables*, 2943) and common in Chaucer.

25. sely] 'Silly, pitiable', a stock epithet for the soul awaiting God's judgment.

28. circumstance] A good confession had to be complete, and to include all the 'aggravating circumstances', or details that affected the nature of the sin. Lines 40–41 mention a few of these, but the number was not fixed. On the mnemonic verses that listed them, see Tentler 1977: 116–19, and Bitterling 1983.

29. discreit] The stock term for the good confessor, who must 'discerne betuix veniale and dedly syn' (Ireland, 'Penance'; Asloan MS, I, 19). Cf. **69**. **91**.

35] Penitential writers who warned of ignorant priests often employed this proverb: 'When the blind leads the blind, both fall in the ditch' (Whiting, B 350; Luke 6: 39).

48. contrycioun] Contrition, or heartfelt repentance for sin, was the first act of penance; the second was confession to a priest; and the third was satisfaction, or reparation.

54] Proverbial: 'Everie man wats best quhair his awin scho binds him' (Carmichaell, no. 478); Whiting, S 266.

56. all and sum] 'One and all', a common verse tag.

57–70] In the late-medieval period there was growing stress on the importance

of frequent confession. Ireland notes similarly that a man is obliged to make
confession 'anys in the ȝere at Pasche' (cf. 62–3), but that it is better to confess
each month, 'and best of all quhen euer he knawis or doutis to be in dedly syn'
('Penance'; Asloan MS, I, 9 and 19).

57–61] Although the gist is fairly clear, the syntax is difficult. Line 57 is
hypermetrical, and the repetition of *and* suggests corruption. An antecedent,
such as *man*, or *quha*, 'whoever', seems required to explain the later uses of *he*
(59) and *That man* (61).

60] 'And has no thought of his end (i.e. death)'. Cf. **68.** 7.

64–70] Ireland similarly criticizes the young who put off penance to old age,
and risk damnation. Such deferred penance has small merit (cf. 69); see
'Penance'; Asloan MS, I, 3, 6–7.

34

3. freynd . . . fo] God and the devil.

7. vaill of trubbill] A common figure for life's miseries, originating in Psalm
84: 6. Cf. Henryson, *Thre Deid Pollis*, 2: 'the vaill of murnyng and of cair'.

8] 'Vanity of vanities, all is vanity' (Ecclesiastes 1: 2 and 12: 8).

9–11. Walk furth . . . Speid home] Dunbar's phrasing recalls Chaucer's *Truth*,
17–19: 'Her is non hoom, her nis but wildernesse; / Forth, pilgrim, forth!
Forth, beste, out of thy stal! / Know thy contree'. But the notion of human life
as a pilgrimage was a medieval commonplace, well documented in Whiting, P
200–201. It ultimately derived from St Paul: 'here have we no continuing city'
(Hebrews 13: 14), and 'they were strangers and pilgrims on the earth . . . But
now they desire a better country, that is, an heavenly' (Hebrews 11: 13–15).

13. port of grace] Heaven, or salvation. For the background to this common
nautical figure, see note to 25. 41–7. The phrase 'port of grace' may have had a
special piquancy for Scottish readers, since the title was given to Newhaven and
Burntisland, two small harbours on the Firth of Forth; in these cases it represented
a shortened form of *portum Domine nostre gratie*, 'the port of Our Lady of grace'.

19–22] This employs the 'Now this, now that' topos, a rhetorical formula,
common in medieval complaints on mutability or the fickleness of Fortune. See
Whiting, N 179; and for some Scottish uses, cf. Henryson, *Fables*, 2939–47;
Hary, *Wallace*, IV. 336–40; Douglas, *Palice of Honour*, 171 81.

19. blak as sabill] A common intensifier of black (Whiting, S 1–2).

23] This alludes to the power of Death the Leveller; even the wealthy, clad in
cloth of gold, will disintegrate into dust.

35

2. monyast] A superlative of *mony*, common in Scots.

4. the ovirword of the geist] 'The refrain of the song'. Common in later Scottish
usage to indicate a constantly repeated theme, or topic.

5] The King's evil counsellors in Lindsay's *Complaint*, 198, boast: 'Bot we sall
part the pelf amang ws'.

6] The swan symbolizes a rich benefice, the duck one of less value.

11–14] The syntax is difficult. The metaphor of the feast continues, in the form of saints' feast days; line 12 alludes to the liturgical distinction between services commemorating the saints in general (*commune sanctorum*) and those devoted to specific saints (*proprium sanctorum*). The poet sings at such services, requesting charity from the lairds who were patrons of the church livings that he desired.

17] Proverbial-sounding, although there is no close parallel. Lindsay says of evil clerics (*Monarche*, 4752–3): 'Bot thay haif spred thare Net, with huik and lyne, / On rentis ryche'.

19] Proverbial. This is Whiting's only citation (N 176), but cf. Tilley, N 337: 'Where nothing is, nothing can be had'.

20] Dunbar represents himself as a nonentity. The cipher, or zero, metaphorically signifies some person or thing useful to others but of no intrinsic value. Cf. Charles d'Orléans: 'as a syphir now y serve That nombre makith and is him silf noon' (cited by Whiting, C 273).

23] The number of service books, such as missals, breviaries and antiphoners, possessed by a church reflected its wealth. Church bells were constantly being rung, for both liturgical and secular purposes. See McKay 1962: 100–105.

28] For death as a *dragoun* cf. **18**. 17.

29] Cf. Lindsay, *Dreme*, 133: 'quho moste had suld moste repent'.

30] It was a commonplace that after death one must render account to God of all one's actions; cf. **21**. 34–5 and note. For a close parallel, see *Thre Prestis of Peblis*, 1273–4: 'The mair golde and gude that euer we haue, / The mair count thairof this King [God] will craue'.

36

3. trance] A state between waking and sleeping; the term has more solemn connotations than *dream*.

6. Mahoun] A name given to the devil; see notes to **3**. 101, and **24**. 32.

8] *Fasternis evin* was celebrated in medieval Scotland with 'dancing and singing' (Barbour, *Bruce*, X. 443–4); there are also references to football and cockfighting (*Colkelbie Sow*, 943–5). At the court of James IV two entertainments were particularly popular – *gysing*, or masking, and jousting.

11–12] France was seen as the source of the latest fashions. Cf. Lindsay, *Satyre*, 452: 'ane gay gamound of France'.

16] There was no fixed order for the sins, but it was common to start with Pride. Cf. Ecclesiasticus 10. 13: 'For pride is the beginning of sin'.

17–21] Pride is shown in its external manifestations: what Chaucer, following St Gregory, called 'synful costlewe array of clothynge, and namely in to muche superfluite, or elles in to desordinat scantnesse' (*Parson's Tale, CT*, X. 410–15).

17] Pride wears a *bonet*, or cap, fashionably tilted to one side (cf. **3**. 180). *bair wyld bak]* Editors have regularly emended *bair* to *hair*, which weakens the alliterative pattern, and does not markedly improve the sense. If *bair* is retained, the image of Pride is highly grotesque and illustrates 'desordinat scantnesse'; he is part-naked like a savage, or *wyld* man.

18] Pride's extravagance is 'likely to cause impoverished homes'. Preachers, when attacking costly dress, often cited Ecclesiasticus 21: 4: 'the house of proud men shall be made desolate'.

21. kethat] B; *keithe cot* MF. Past glosses – 'cassock', 'voluminous mantle' – are guesswork. Beard suggests that this refers to an upper garment then fashionable, a coat (known also as a *base coat*) with an enormous skirt, made up of organ-pipe pleats radiating from the waist, rather like the spokes of a wheel (cf. the simile in 19).

30] Apparently nicknames for devils. *Blak belly* is not otherwise known; *Bawsy brown* is a name given by Henryson to a dog (*Fables*, 546).

31. sturt and stryfe] An alliterative formula; see **12**. 6.

32] Wrath, in Spenser's *Faerie Queene*, I. iv. 33, makes a similar gesture, symbolizing aggression: 'And on his dagger still his hand he held'.

33. brandeist lyk a beir] The simile suggests the clumsy movements of baited bears, usually restrained by chains (cf. 38).

37] The armour is contemporary: padded leather jerkins, steel helmets, and *stryppis*; these seem to correspond to *splints*, which were plates or strips of overlapping metal, used chiefly to protect the arms at the elbows.

48. wirdis quhyte] A phrase for insincere speech. Cf. Henryson, *Fables*, 601: 'flatteraris with plesand wordis quhyte'.

52–4] Envy was a vice associated particularly with courtiers; in Chaucer, *Legend of Good Women*, Prol. F, 358, Envy is the court 'lavendere', or washerwoman. Acts were repeatedly passed by Scottish parliaments, denouncing 'lesing makaris', or slanderers (Macdougall 1982: 279–80).

55–6] I Timothy 6: 10: 'The love of money [*Cupiditas*] is the root of all evil'. For the saying's currency, cf. Whiting, C 491.

61–6] Force-feeding with molten metal was one of the stock torments of hell (cf. 101), but to swallow gold was peculiarly, and appropriately, a punishment of the covetous. Cf. Henryson, *Orpheus*, 330. For other illustrations, see Owen 1970: 163, 167.

66. of allkin prent] French 'crowns' (**29**. 18) and other foreign coins were current in Scotland.

68. lyk a sow] The sow was proverbially filthy and sleepy (Whiting, S 541). On the traditional aspects of this portrait, see Wenzel 1967: 106ff.

70. belly huddroun] Not otherwise recorded except in **20**. 38. *DOST* explains as 'large-bellied person' and associates the second element with a word meaning 'heifer'.

74. Belliall] Originally an abstract noun, 'iniquity'; but the biblical phrase 'sons of Belial' encouraged the belief that it was the name of the devil.

76. slaw of feit] Wenzel (1967: 109) notes that preachers called sloth a spiritual gout, and that In Dante, *Purgatorio*, 18, the slothful are forced to run incessantly.

78. counyie] Hitherto unexplained. I take the word to represent French *congé*, a term applied to the concluding movement of dances, and sometimes equated with the *branle* (or *braule*), 'the leave-taking at the close of the *basse danse*'.

80. berand] Whinnying was thought to indicate a horse's desire to copulate. *bagit]* There is no evidence for the usual gloss, 'testicled'. The word commonly meant 'swollen, big with young' (see *DOST*, *baggit*; *MED*, *baggen*, v.; *OED*, *bagged*). Past editors assume that Lechery is compared to a stallion; but Sloth resembles a *sow*, and here too the animal may be female. Horses of either sex often symbolized libido: for lustful mares, cf. Virgil, *Georgics*, III. 274; and for stallions, cf. Jeremiah 5: 8: 'they are become as amorous horses . . . each one neighed after his neighbour's wife' (cf. Kolve 1984: 237–48).

87. Lyk turkas birnand reid] 'Glowing red like a smith's pincers'. The simile aptly evokes not merely colour but torment. Devils were represented with pincers, and torturers employed the *turkas* to pull out teeth and finger-nails.

88] Adulterers were sometimes punished by being led publicly with ropes tied to their genitals.

94–5] Gluttony was often associated specifically with drunkenness. Spenser's Gluttony carries 'a bouzing can' (*Faerie Queene*, I. iv. 22). *Collep* has not been explained: the form looks like *collop*, 'fried ham, bacon', but the other items in the line suggest that it too is a drinking-vessel. Possibly the word is a variant of ME *collok*, 'tankard'.

102. lovery] Livery, in the sense 'court allowance of food and wine'. Cf. *Bruce*, XIV. 233–4: 'he maid of wyne levere / Till ilk man'.

103–20] This dance is unaccompanied by music, which is symbolically absent from hell, a place that lacks order and harmony. Dunbar's gibes against murderous minstrels and cacophonous Highlanders are variants upon stock popular jokes concerning the inhabitants of hell.

106–8] A legal joke. The *breif of richt* (Latin *breve de recto*) was a writ which established right to *heretage*, landed property that descended by succession to the heir-at-law. In disputed cases, however, it seems that the plea might be decided, not by an inquest or assize, but by combat. (See MacQueen 1993: 188–214; and Sellar 1984). There is an obvious irony, since manslaughter or murder is not the same as trial by combat, and the heritage in question is hell.

110. Makfadyane] Dunbar perhaps recalled two men of this name: the fictional traitor against whom William Wallace campaigned, and who took refuge in a cave (cf. the *nuke* in 111) before being beheaded (Hary, *Wallace*, VII. 626–868); and an actual Maurice Macfadyane, who in August 1452 attacked the bishop of Argyll, George Lauder, mockingly saluting him in Gaelic and treating him 'dispytfullie' (see McGladdery 1990: 120–21).

111. northwart] Highlanders lived chiefly in the north and west of Scotland. But the north was traditionally associated with devilry and evil. Cf. Chaucer, *Friar's Tale*, *CT*, III. 1413; and Jeremiah 6: 1: 'evil appeareth out of the north'.

115. tarmegantis] 'Devils'. This was the usual ME meaning, but the more recent sense, 'quarrelsome persons', is also relevant (*OED*, *termagant*, 2). Dunbar possibly punningly alludes to the Highland bird later known as a ptarmigan (*OED*, *ptarmigan*).

117. Rowp] A verb often applied to the raven's croaking cry; cf. Holland, *Howlat*, 215.

119. the depest pot] The bottomless pit mentioned in Revelation 20: 1–3.

125. pricklous] A contemptuous term for a tailor.

130–31] These succinct, abusive compounds draw upon the stereotype of tailors as dirty and dishonest. *seme byttaris]* Literally 'biters of seams': in order to make seams smooth, tailors pressed them together with their teeth. *beist knapparis]* 'Those who crack vermin between their teeth or with the shears'. Cf. *DOST*, on *knap*, or *gnap*, an echoic verb, 'break with a snapping sound'. *stomok steillaris]* 'Stealers of stomachers'. The stomacher was an article of dress, worn by both men and women, over a jacket or gown, and laced in front. *clayth takkaris]* 'Stealers of cloth'. Similar charges against tailors are made in Stewart's *Flyting betwix the Soutar and the Tailyour* (cf. Bawcutt 1987: 92–3).

133–6] The banner is a mock-chivalric motif; cf. the comic banners carried by the peasants in *Colkelbie Sow*, 330–32. Craftsmen's banners were not displayed as a prelude to battle, but carried in civic processions; the emblem of the Aberdeen tailors was a pair of shears. Dunbar possibly also refers to a popular jest concerning a dishonest tailor to whom the devil appeared bearing a banner made out of the cloth that the tailor had stolen (Bawcutt 1992a: 188).

137–8] An instance of the impossibility topos; tailors will never be honest, until the tideless Mediterranean flows and ebbs.

147. wicht as mast] 'Strong as a ship's mast'. Proverbial; Whiting, M 397–9.

151] The cowardly tailor awaits his opponent (A, MF); in B, implausibly, he goes to meet him.

155. lyk ony thunner] Mock-chivalric. The simile was common in battle descriptions. Cf. Lindsay, *Meldrum*, 527–8: 'that meiting ... soundit lyke ane crak of thunder'; and Whiting, T 269–71.

157–9] The soutar comes *out of the west*, because he is the *defender*. The challenger would come from the east gate.

164. sanct Girnega] A mock-saint; Crispin and Crispianus were the usual patrons of shoemakers. Elsewhere *Girnega* is a name given to a devil; it is also associated with soutars in Stewart's *Flyting*: 'Sanct Garnega that grym gaist', and '3our girnand god, grit Garnega'.

167–8] A mock-chivalric allusion to a common battle topos. Cf. Barbour, *Bruce*, II. 355: 'The blud owt at thar byrnys brest'. Here a disparaging reference to the cobbler's oil or blacking is substituted for blood.

176. of knychtheid gaif him order] This burlesques the practice of conferring knighthood on the eve of battle. Contrast Hay, *Ordre of Knychthede* (*Prose Works*, III, 31): 'outrageous commoun vicious men ar nocht to be ressauit to the ordre of knychthede'.

193. birnes] 'Coat of mail, breastplate'. This word belongs to the ancient alliterative diction of battle poetry. The anomalous use of the plural form with singular sense is found elsewhere: cf. *Golagros*, 843–4: 'That knight ... braissit in birneis and basnet'. See *DOST*, *birny*; *MED*, *brinie*.

201. strenyt ... in steill] 'Constricted, squeezed in armour'. Apparently modelled on formulaic alliterative phrases, such as 'stuffit in steill' (*Golagros*, 200).

203] Cf. Lindsay, *Satyre*, 2285: 'The devill dryte in thy gambis'. Such coarse sayings were common; cf. Whiting, D 207.

206] Romance combats commonly end in this way, and the line has a formulaic ring.

216. armes] Both 'weapons' and 'armorial bearings'.

221. to my hairt thar socht] With the idiom, cf. *Wallace*, VI. 200: 'paynfull wo socht till his hart'.

227. heir] This may represent either 'heir' or *here*, a poetic word for 'lord'.

37

1. Betwix twell houris and ellevin] 'About midnight'. For similar phrases, cf. Henryson, *Fables*, 1325 and 1780. Here the illogicality suggests something absurd may follow.

2–3] The dreamer is privileged, like St John, to hear an angel's revelations.

4. blist be ye] 'Blessed may you be'. The refrain recalls the Beatitudes (Matthew 5). But Dunbar also plays on the sarcastic use of *blist* to mean 'accursed'.

11. craft] Both the 'skill' characteristic of the good craftsman and also 'craftiness, deceit'.

17. this fair] This apparently alludes to the poem's occasion; most Scottish burghs had fairs, usually on saints' days. MF's colophon implies a different but convivial setting, a craftsmen's feast: 'Quod Dumbar quhone he drank to the Dekynnis for amendis to the bodeis of thair craftis'. Deacons were the officials of the crafts.

30. quhattrak] 'What does it matter?' A colloquial phrase, similar to modern 'so what?'

31. craftis slie] Dunbar purports to praise 'clever skills', but implies 'cunning deceptions'.

39. knavis] Common in the pejorative modern sense, 'rascals, rogues'; but the earlier senses, 'serving men', and 'men of menial rank', were still current.

38

1. Lentren] Lent, the time for penance.

4] 'All earthly joy turns into sorrow'. Cf. Henryson, *Praise of Age*, 26: 'Of erdly ioy ay sorow is the end'. The thought occurs in many medieval writers; see Whiting, J 58 and E 80.

6–7] This paraphrases *Memento homo quod cinis es et quod tu in cinerem reverteris*; see note to 25. 1.

10–11] For death, the devourer, cf. 25. 27–8.

11. grane] This could represent 'branch' (*DOST, graine*²), or 'seed' (*DOST, graine*¹); Douglas couples 'fruyt and grayn' (*Eneados*, XII Prol. 256), to symbolize fecundity.

15. for a trane] Henryson writes similarly of the fowler who covers his nets with chaff to deceive birds: 'he hes it heir layit for ane trane' (*Fables*, 1856). Line 13 specifies the insidious temptations of the world.

17–18] January and May were proverbially opposed; cf. *Kingis Quair*, 765, and Whiting, J 14.

19] Rain after drought is a figure of mutability (Whiting, D 417).

22, 24. nerrest air ... verry air] 'Most immediate heir ... rightful heir'. This type of legal metaphor was popular with Scottish moralists; cf. 'wisdome to virtew is the nerrest air' (*De Regimine Principum*, 130: MF, no. xxxix); *Ratis Raving*, 1310; and *DOST, air*¹, 3.

37–40] The technique resembles that of the last stanza in 16: a slight turn in the thought, introduced by *Sen*, and the fourfold repetition of a key word.

39

1] 'Anyone may see the unpredictability of love'. The syntax of lines 1–4 is loose, but *Quha* is probably an indefinite pronoun rather than interrogative. Small interprets the first line as 'Let him who wills, behold ...'.

2–3] Cf. *Testament of Cresseid*, 225: 'Vnder smyling scho was dissimulait'.

7–8] 'She does not serve Steadfastness'. For Henryson 'continuance' is a feminine virtue; see *Garmont of Gud Ladies*, 15.

9–10] The conduct of lovers is not characterized by discretion and consideration, virtues that Dunbar couples elsewhere; see **47**. 165; and **63**. 56.

11–12] It was a commonplace that love's pleasure does not last long (Whiting, L 524).

13–14] 'She is so ready to make new friends, that old ones are forgotten'. Cf. the proverbial 'new love chases out the old' (Whiting, L 547). New Acquaintance is personified in **47**. 220.

19. tyme mispendit] Moralists commonly reproved the misuse of time. Cf. **66**. 3; and Henryson, *Prayer for the Pest*, 86: 'For we repent all tyme mispent'.

23–4] 'As if one were to order a dead man to dance in the tomb'. This striking image was perhaps suggested by the Dance of Death.

40

1. ane straucht way to deid] 'A direct road to death'. It was a commonplace that life resembled a 'thoroughfare', or a road, on which humans were pilgrims or travellers; cf. **34**. 9, and Whiting, W 663. The depreciative *bot ane*, 'nothing but a', is characteristic of pronouncements about life, which is proverbially 'but a' breath or a dream (Whiting, L 240–41).

2. pas . . . dwell] With this antithesis, cf. **25**. 3–4.

3. A slyding quheill] This image of life as a wheel is closely allied to the better-known figure of Fortune's wheel. For discussion, see Dove 1986: 75, and Burrow 1986: 43–6.

5] For the image of man as death's prey, cf. **16**. 95.

41

1–7] The spring setting and the sustained temporal clause, beginning with *Quhen*, were conventional. Cf. the much-imitated opening of *The Canterbury Tales*: 'Whan that Aprill with his shoures soote . . .'. The dreamer's humorous riposte to May (29–35), however, departs from tradition, and emphasizes the contrast between the actual weather and the idyllic climate of the idealived 'garth' (47) that he enters.

2. Appryll] Probably trisyllabic (see *DOST, aperell*).

4] May is mother 'of monthes glade' in Chaucer, *Troilus and Criseyde*, II. 50, and a 'maternall' month in Douglas, *Palice of Honour*, 65.

5 hegyn thair houris] It was a common conceit to compare bird-song to church services; see also **47**. 10. The closest parallel is in Clanvowe, *Boke of Cupide*, 67–70: 'And sawe the briddes crepe out of her boures . . . / That they began of May to don her houres'.

9. Aurora] Goddess of the dawn. *cristall ene]* 'Bright eyes'. Cf. **19**. 1–2 and note.

11. paill and grene] 'Pale and wan'. The reference is to Aurora, whom Douglas describes similarly in *Palice of Honour*, 1. See also note to **47**. 16. The phrase is often applied to unhappy women: cf. *Troilus and Criseyde*, IV. 1154 and V. 243.

12–14, 24–5] Cf. *The Floure of Curtesy* (attributed to Lydgate), 8–10:

> The same tyme, I herde a larke synge
> Ful lustely agayne the morowe gray:
> 'Awake, ye louers, out of your slombringe'.

Medieval poets commonly depicted the lark as greeting or heralding the dawn; her song was seen as a reproof to indolent lovers. (On the background, see Bawcutt 1972.)

12. fro the splene] On this phrase, see **30**. 2 and note.

19. broun and blew] Cf. *Tayis Bank*, 18: 'blosumes broun and blew'; very dark flowers, such as violets, were called brown.

22] See 36–7 below.

24. done ... proclame] 'Announced, in the manner of a herald'. On this periphrastic tense, also used in 14, 49, 56, and 152, see Introduction, p. 14.

33. Eolus] Aeolus, god of the winds. In Scottish tradition he absorbs the character of Boreas, the north wind; Henryson speaks of his 'blastis boreall' (*Fables*, 1693). On his horn, or bugle (**47**. 230), cf. Chaucer's depiction of Aeolus as the trumpeter of Fame (*House of Fame*, 1571–82).

36–7] Cf. Chaucer, *Knight's Tale*, *CT*, I. 1042–5:

> For May wole have no slogardie anyght.
> The sesoun priketh every gentil herte,
> And maketh it out of his slep to sterte,
> And seith, 'Arys, and do thyn observaunce'.

The Scottish 'observance' of May included the bringing home of flowers and birch branches (Mill 1927: 19–21).

51. bricht as angell] A common simile; cf. Whiting, A 124, 126 and 127.

57–8] On the three hierarchies (or nine orders) of angels, see **48**. 9–10 and note; their music was believed to be supremely beautiful. With this simile, which resembles that used in 51, cf. Douglas, *Palice of Honour*, 443–4: 'it semit nathing ellis / Bot Ierarchyes of Angellis ordours nine'.

64ff.] Nature's role is more than decorative; she is depicted as creator, ruler and educator. Dunbar's ideas, although highly orthodox, were probably influenced by the description of Nature as goddess and queen in Chaucer's *Parliament of Fowls*, and Holland's *Howlat* (see Bawcutt 1992a: 95–8).

64–6] Neptune and Aeolus respectively govern the sea and the winds; their absence or expulsion is a common motif in Scottish depictions of a calm, idyllic scene. Cf. Douglas, *Palice of Honour*, 49–52: 'God Eolus of wind list nocht appeir ... Neptunus nold within that palice hant'; and Lindsay, *Monarche*, 185: 'Neptune that day, and Eoll held thame coye'. Here they also symbolize potential disturbers of the social order; *inhibitioun* and *perturb* are legalisms.

75] Cf. Chaucer, *Parliament of Fowls*, 321: 'As they were woned alwey fro yer to yeere'.

76. mak obediens] A feudal term, 'do homage to one's superior'. Note the parallel with 116–17 below.

78] The swiftness of the roe deer was proverbial; see Whiting, R 170 and 175.

80] The swallow, also a type of swiftness (Whiting, S 923), is a messenger in Holland, *Howlat*, 138–43.

83] Yarrow, or milfoil, was a herb believed to have magical properties, and was used in attempts at divination.

84. swift as ony arrow] Proverbial; see Whiting, A 186.

85. in twynkling of ane e] 'In a moment'. On this proverbial phrase, see note to 9. 29.

91. curage leonyne] The phrase was something of a cliché; cf. Chaucer, *Monk's Tale, CT,* VII. 2646.

92–8] The lion, by long tradition king of beasts, is here described in heraldic terms, with reference to the Royal Arms of Scotland: gold, a lion rampant gules, within a double tressure flory counter-flory (i.e. within a border decorated with fleur-de-lys). Cf. Holland's fuller account of the arms of 'our soverane of Scotland' (*Howlat*, 366–73): 'He bure a lyon as lord of gowlis full gay ... Of pure gold was the ground ... / With dowble tressour about flowrit in fay, / And flourdelycis on loft'.

106. Exerce justice] The king was the traditional fount of justice, and was expected to give special protection to the poor and weak (cf. 107, 124). The theme recurs in Scottish poems belonging to the *speculum principis* tradition; cf. *De Regimine Principum* (MF, no. xxxix), 125–210.

107. skaith na skornis] A common alliterative phrase. Cf. 3. 358.

109] The unicorn, which commonly symbolized virginity, represented the virtuous antitype to the ape, which was associated with lust and sexuality. Their juxtaposition was a frequent motif in late medieval art (Janson 1952: 114–15; 139–40).

110. bowgle] The wild ox, noted for its ferocity and huge horns; cf. *Kingis Quair*, 1093: 'The bugill drawar by his hornis grete'. The domesticated ox, with which it is contrasted, symbolized patient industry.

117. homege and fewte] The formal acknowledgement of allegiance by a vassal to his lord.

119] This line alludes to a Latin distich: *Parcere prostratis scit nobilis ira leonis; / Tu quoque fac simile, quisquis dominaris orbe* ('The noble wrath of the lion knows how to spare those who are prostrate before him; do likewise, each of you who will reign over the world'). This maxim was well known in the Middle Ages, and often placed in the mouths of suppliants. It refers to clemency, the virtue held to distinguish the good king from the tyrant, and one particularly associated with the lion in bestiary lore (see Bawcutt 1986b). There is no evidence that this maxim was the Scottish royal motto; it was, however, associated with the heraldic Scottish lion by Bower (*Scotichronicon*, III. 39) and possibly by Henryson (*Fables*, 930).

120] The eagle was traditionally the king of birds (see Bartholomaeus Anglicus, XII. 2). Chaucer speaks of 'the royal egle' (*Parliament of Fowls*, 330), and in Holland's *Howlat* (313–14) it represents the Emperor. Here the Eagle's symbolic significance does not differ strikingly from that of the Lion; his role is to administer justice impartially. In 57. 26 the eagle also symbolizes James IV, and presides over a court of birds.

122. awppis] DOST glosses *awp* as 'bullfinch' (= ME *alpe*). But no other Scottish use is recorded, and bullfinches, which are small, attractive birds, seem oddly coupled with owls. *Awppis* is possibly an error for *quhawppis*, 'curlews'.

This was in common use (see *DOST, quhap(e; OED, whaup*); and the bird, like the owl, was considered ugly; *DOST* records the insult 'nebbit lyk ane quhaipe'.

123] Peacocks, parrots and cranes are linked as handsome, showy birds. Cranes, which have distinctive red plumage on their heads, appear as cardinals in Holland, *Howlat*, 162–3.

125–6] Birds of prey often symbolized the knightly class. For the notion that every bird has its appropriate prey, cf. **57**. 13–14.

125. fowll of ravyne] A phrase apparently influenced by Chaucer, *Parliament of Fowls*, 323 and 527. This is the only occurrence recorded by *DOST*; the usual Scots term for a bird of prey was 'fowl of reif'.

129] The thistle had been adopted only recently as the Scottish royal emblem. It first appeared on coins in the reign of James III, and figured on James IV's Great Signet. Ornamental thistles abound in the documents associated with the marriage of James and Margaret, and the windows of Holyrood were decorated with 'a Chardon and a Rose interlassed'. (See Macfarlane 1960; Burnett 1983; and Bawcutt 1986b.) Here the Thistle's significance is defensive, symbolizing a king's duty to protect his country from invasion. Cf. the use in **52**. 22–3.

130. busche of speiris] Dunbar alludes to the prickly foliage of thistles, and also to the figurative military sense of *bush*, 'bushy throng'. Cf. Douglas, *Eneados*, VII. xi. 77: 'Amyd a bus of speris in raid thai'.

134–40] The Thistle is urged to discriminate, and – like a gardener – to value plants 'of vertew', such as lilies, more highly than those without 'vertew', such as nettles. The injunction is paradoxical, in view of the thistle's usually adverse symbolism. Implicit is the analogy between a well-governed kingdom and a well-tended garden that figures in the *speculum principis* tradition.

140] Cf. Bartholomaeus Anglicus, XVII. 91: 'the lilye is next to the rose in worthinesse and nobilite'.

141–3] Usually interpreted as advice to James, who had several mistresses, to be faithful to his queen.

143. honesty] 'Honour', and more specifically, 'chastity'.

144–7] Cf. Bartholomaeus Anglicus, XVII. 136: 'Among alle floures of the worlde the flour of the rose is chief and bereth the prys'.

150] 'Illustrious of lineage, higher than the lily'. The reference is to the heraldic Lily of France.

152–4] This echoes words addressed to the Bride in the Song of Songs 4: 7–8 (Vulgate): *Tota pulchra es, amica mea, et macula non est in te. Veni de Libano, sponsa mea, veni; coronaberis*. In the Middle Ages these verses were traditionally applied to the Virgin Mary – cf. **11**. 22 – and associated particularly with her Assumption and Coronation.

171–2. reid and quhyt . . . michty cullouris twane] This is the culmination of earlier references to these colours (6, 142). Flowers or a woman's complexion were traditionally 'red and white', but there is an allusion to Margaret Tudor's lineage: daughter of Henry VII (the red rose) and Elizabeth of York (the white rose).

180. perle] 'Pearl', with a play on the Latin meaning of Margaret, *margarita*. Cf. **10**. 4.

184–5] Dream poems often end abruptly; the shouting of birds similarly wakes the dreamer in *The Parliament of Fowls*, 693.

188–9] It is possible that these lines are literally true, and that the poem was composed in advance of the wedding, in May 1503. It was not uncommon for medieval poets to date poems, especially love epistles: cf. Robbins, *Secular Poems*, no. 189; also Chaucer *The House of Fame*, 63. But Douglas likewise associates his Twelfth Prologue with 'the nynt morowe' of May (268), and *The Quare of Jelusy* (7) has the same date. It seems likely that for Scottish poets 9 May had some special significance: in the church calendar it was the feast of both the Translation of St Nicholas and the Translation of St Andrew, patron saint of Scotland. There also existed a tradition that this date marked the beginning of summer, which would be symbolically appropriate for a poem celebrating a marriage and a peace treaty, a fresh start in human and political terms (see Bawcutt 1992a: 74–5).

42

1. merchantis] Dunbar addresses the wealthy merchants and overseas traders, who formed the powerful oligarchy in control of Edinburgh (cf. Wormald 1981: 46–9). The term *merchant* was also used of smaller retailers and shopkeepers, as in 38.

4. commone proffeitt] See note to 71–2.

11. feusum] 'Foul, offensive'. This is a variant spelling of a word more usually spelt *fowsum*. Although this form is not otherwise attested, alternations between *ou/ow* and *eu* spellings are not uncommon. Cf. *piteuslie* (46), and *feulis*, instead of *foulis*, in **3**. 10.

15. Stinkand Stull] Despite the scribal alteration of *t* to *c*, *stull* seems correct and corresponds to *Styll* (38). In the midfifteenth century a tenement of several storeys was built along the north side of St Giles; it was pierced by passages, one of which, the *Stinkand Styll*, or Stinking Style, led directly to the north door of the church. Here and in 38 the term seems to indicate not just the passage but the surrounding buildings, which made the church dark and were overcrowded with small businesses. The pejorative epithet 'stinking' was commonly applied to the closes and wynds of early Edinburgh.

16. parroche kirk] St Giles, in the High Street, which became a collegiate church in 1466.

17. foirstairis] External staircases to the second floor of a building, usually made of wood.

23. ?] The Market Cross stood to the north-east of St Giles; it was the symbolic centre of the burgh, where proclamations were made and punishments carried out.

24–5] In Scottish burghs the *Trone*, or public weigh-house, often stood beside the market cross; in Edinburgh its site was at the corner of West Bow and Castle Hill.

25. Pudingis] These resembled haggis in being made from the entrails of sheep or other animals, stuffed with oatmeal and inferior meat or offal. Like *pansches* they were food of low status; cf. Henryson, *Fables*, 727–9. *Jok]* A generic name for a low-born man, and invariably derisive in Dunbar (see **14**. 73 and **57**. 66). Coupled with another name, it signifies 'men of the common class'.

29–30] Most important Scottish burghs maintained public musicians, or minstrels; Dunbar criticizes their limited repertory. *Now the day dawis]* The name of a song long popular in Scotland. Cf. Douglas, *Eneados* XIII Prol. 182: 'As menstralis playng "The ioly day now dawys"'; for a pious version, see *The Gude and Godlie Ballatis,* p. 192. *Into Joun]* No song with this opening is now known. But cf. Alexander Scott's 'In June' (no. xxvii), which perhaps derives from an earlier song.

31–2] These lines are difficult to explain, largely because no saint called *Cloun* is known to have existed; he is mentioned elsewhere only in jocular oaths (see Lindsay, *Satyre,* 1371 and 4388). Possibly *Cloun* (like *Girnega* in 36. 164) belongs to the comic tradition of mock-saints. It is tempting to connect the word with *clown,* 'peasant, fool'; unfortunately this word is not recorded until the latter sixteenth century in English, although *DOST* records the adjective *clunish,* 'boorish, stupid'. The overall sense is difficult. It might be paraphrased: 'More skilled men (such as myself?) must act as clowns (or wait upon clowns), and never have the right to other occupations'.

34] 'To retain in your service such gallows-birds'. *Mowaris on the moyne* means 'those who make grimaces at the moon'; it derives from a ME slang phrase, applied to criminals hanging on the gallows (see Bawcutt 1987: 93–4; also Whiting, M 767).

36] For Dunbar's low opinion of the *craftis* of tailors and soutars, see also 36.

39. ane hony came] This suggests the crowded quarters of the merchants, and also their busy activity.

57. the Sessioun] See note to 2. 7.

67–8] The syntax is difficult. It might be paraphrased: 'So that there may be no extortions (i.e. illegal exactions of money), denounce all fraudulent and shameful conduct'.

71–2] Singular *proffeit* signified private and selfish interests; *common proffeit* signified the welfare of the whole community. These somewhat clichéd phrases were regularly opposed to each other; cf. 'than gais singlere prouffit before the commoun prouffit' (Hay, *The Gouernaunce of Princis: Prose Works,* III, 61).

74. Jerusalem] Historically, the place where Jesus was crucified; morally and spiritually, the City of God, and thus a model for earthly cities.

77] Editors have filled the blank variously: *reconqueis, win back to,* and *restore to.* Yet none seems idiomatic or sufficiently climactic.

43

5] Proverbial; see Whiting, E 120.

6. unto Ynd] 'As far as India', part of a stock tag (Whiting, I 35), which here implies 'in the whole world'. India was regarded as fabulously wealthy; cf. 66. 66.

11. My brother] 'My fellow human being'. With this usage, common in didactic verse, cf. 26 below, and Henryson, *Fables,* 2910: 'My brother, gif thow will tak aduertence'.

13] A version of the proverbial 'Thank God for whatever he sends' (Whiting, G 262). Cf. Henryson's refrain to *The Abbey Walk:* 'Obey and thank thi God of all'.

17] 'With rancour in heart, concealed by sweet words'. Gall, a secretion of the liver, was a type of intense bitterness, and a figure for malice. It was often contrasted with the sweetness of honey (Whiting, G 12 and H 433).

18] 'Whoever serves the world most will have most to repent (after death, at the Last Judgment)'. Cf. **35**. 29.

19. subchettis] Obscure. The word may represent *subcharges*, 'second courses, extra dishes at a dinner'; such luxuries (cf. 12) were criticized by moralists. For a similar thought, cf. Henryson, *Fables*, 345–6: 'thy gansell [garlic sauce] sour as gall; / The subcharge off thy seruice is bot sair'.

28. langour . . . lent] An alliterative formula; cf. Douglas, *Eneados*, VIII Prol. 14: 'Langour lent is in land'.

29] Proverbial; Whiting, C 295.

31–3] Proverbial. Cf. Whiting, C 494: 'He that is covetous is poor'.

44

1–2] Dunbar implies that he lacks not just a friend in whom to confide but someone who might assist him. The first line is formulaic; cf. the opening of **7**, and Lindsay, *Bagsche*, 1: 'Allace, quhome to suld I complayne'.

2] *Ane or mo*, literally 'one or more', is an inclusive tag, meaning 'in their full extent'.

5] The falseness and unreliability of 'this warld' was a medieval commonplace. For many parallels, see Whiting, W 671.

6. Lord] On the ambiguity of this word, see 81 and note.

7] It was a common complaint that long service went unrewarded; cf. **63**. 53, and Whiting, S 165.

11] Falsehood, riding on horseback and followed by a retinue of attendants, is clearly prosperous.

19] Wit (understanding) and reason are often coupled by Dunbar; see **49**. 4 and note.

21] The word order is ambiguous. I take it to be the court that has shown contempt for virtue, by advancing unworthy people (the *rebald*, *carlis* and *bumbardis*) to high office. On *done dispys*, see Introduction, p. 14.

28] A legal metaphor: *fredome*, or liberality, is not esteemed, because he has been sentenced to forfeiture, or confiscation of his lands.

29] For the association of pity with princes, cf. **3**. 442.

36–9] This revivifies ancient commonplaces on the banishment of virtue from society. Cf. Isaiah 59. 14: 'justice standeth afar off; for truth is fallen in the street, and equity cannot enter' (see Wenzel 1986: 174–5).

36. ane furrit goun] A gown lined or trimmed with fur was a sign of wealth, and implies the rewards of flattery.

41–2] The contrast is traditional; cf. Psalms 5: 9; 12: 2–3; and Whiting, M 755: 'Mouth and heart do not agree'.

44. gud deidis] Cf. **25**. 35.

46–9] This witty cluster of images for those who lack charity embroiders proverbial notions of the heart hard as stone or flint; cf. **20**. 40, and Whiting, F 284, H 277. Whalebone, or ivory made from walrus tusks, was a popular image of whiteness, but not normally applied to the tongue. *Asure*, or *lapis lazuli*, calls attention to the hardness as well as the blueness of eyes. *Adamant* was a type of extreme hardness (Whiting, A 40); here, as often, it is also associated with the lodestone, through confusion with Latin *adamare*, 'have attraction for'. Dunbar alludes to people who are reluctant to *dispone*, or bestow their goods, in charitable giving.

51–3] On the necessity of obeying Death's summons, cf. *Everyman*, 85–6; on the resurrection of the body at the Last Judgment, see II Corinthians 5: 10.

56] The construction is difficult, and the referent of *this* unclear. Perhaps *this* refers to the untrustworthy world, ruled by Fortune (57–9), which 'in short, demands nothing (no other end?) but death'.

57–9] Fortune was traditionally depicted as a whore; for her alternation between smiles and frowns, cf. Barbour, *Bruce*, XIII 636–8; *Kingis Quair*, 1124–5.

59] 'Whose false promises pass hence like the wind'. For similes of this type, cf. Whiting, W 330 and W 341.

63] This image of the angel blowing a trumpet at the Last Judgment derives from St Paul: I Corinthians 15: 52; and I Thessalonians 4: 16.

64] 'Which (i.e. the wrongfully acquired goods) being unrestored to their owner, no confession will avail'. The doctrine that absolution could not be granted to a sinner, if stolen goods had not been restored to their rightful owner, held an important place in medieval confessional theory. It is a recurrent theme in *Piers Plowman*.

71–4] These lines evoke the horror of hell: 'where burning souls, forever saying, Woe! Woe!, shall cry, alas that women bore them. O, how great is that darkness'. The words have a liturgical origin, in a passage associated with the *Libera me* responsory in the Office of the Dead (see *Sarum Breviary*, II, 280). Line 73 also recalls Job 3: 3: 'Let the day perish wherein I was born'.

76–9] This draws upon popular beliefs concerning the signs that would precede the Day of Judgment. The effective alliteration on plosives resembles that in **47**. 235–43 and the final stanza of **63**.

76. warldis wrak] A contemptuous phrase for worldly wealth, literally meaning 'world's dross, rubbish'.

81] The *Lord* addressed in line 6 might have been a secular prince, but there is no doubt that this *Lord* is God. With the use of *sen*, 'since', cf. the final stanzas of **13**, **16** and **38**.

83] It is now clear that the speaker is a churchman. He answers his earlier question (6), and rejects worldly ambitions for advancement, in the shape of a benefice.

45
The Ballade of Barnard Stewart

Title. Beaumont Roger] The *comté* of Beaumont-le-Roger, near Bernay in Normandy. *Bonaffre]* Long unidentified, this represents Benaffre, the French form of Venafro, near Capua, of which Bernard Stewart was made earl in 1501. *his ordoure]* Stewart received from Charles VIII the Order of the Cockle, or of St Michael, which was instituted by Louis XI.

8] The refrain echoes the Palm Sunday processional hymn, *Gloria laus et honor tibi sit*, composed by Theodulf of Orléans.

9ff.] Anaphora on 'Welcum' was common in poems of greeting; cf. **17**.

12. the soun of Mars] A popular phrase for courageous soldiers; cf. **73** below.

17. the secund Julius] 'An equal to Julius Caesar'. Cf. the description of Troilus as 'Ector the secounde' in *Troilus and Criseyde*, II. 158.

50. Fleys on weyng] Alluding to the classical notion of *Fama*, or Rumour, as a winged goddess; cf. *Aeneid*, IV. 173, and Chaucer, *Troilus and Criseyde*, IV. 659–61: 'the swifte Fame . . . with preste wynges'.

57–62] Stewart is compared to six of the world's great military commanders, three of whom (Hector, Arthur and Julius Caesar) figure in the Nine Worthies topos.

57. Achill] The Greek hero Achilles. 'Fierce' is a fixed epithet, possibly deriving from Ovid, *Metamorphoses*, XII. 592–3; cf. Douglas, *Palice of Honour*, 1208 and 1627.

58. Hector] The great Trojan hero; *invincible* is an odd epithet, since he was ignominiously killed by Achilles.

59. Arthur] Scottish poets and historians showed great interest – mingled with disapproval – in the legendary history of King Arthur.

60. Agamenon] Agamemnon, leader of the Greeks in the Trojan War.

61. Henniball] Hannibal (247–182 BC), the great Carthaginian general, who fought against Rome in the Second Punic War.

67. lawry] 'Laurel'. The symbol of military glory; cf. **4** above, and Chaucer, *Knight's Tale, CT*, I. 1027: 'With laurer crowned as a conquerour'.

68. olyve greyn] The traditional emblem of peace; see Whiting, O 32. It was also the attribute of envoys; cf. Douglas, *Eneados*, VII. iii. 15–16.

73–9] An imaginary horoscope. Hay, in *The Gouernaunce of Princis (Prose Works*, III, 115), notes the influence upon a man 'of the sternis and planetis that concurris in his natiuitee'. Dunbar attributes Stewart's courage to Mars and Saturn, his personal attractiveness to Venus, his eloquence to Mercury, and his overall good fortune to Jupiter. Chaucer provided similarly impressionistic horoscopes for the Wife of Bath (*CT*, III. 609–16) and Hypermnestra (*Legend of Good Women*, 2576–93). Lindsay's Squire Meldrum says likewise that Mars, Venus and Mercury 'rang the day of my natiuitie' (*Testament*, 64–91).

73–4] Mars 'reigned' as the dominant planet; Mars, although usually astrologically malevolent, as god of war was the appropriate patron of soldiers. (Mars gave the Wife of Bath her 'sturdy hardinesse'.) *Armipotent*, 'mighty in battle', was his stock epithet; cf. **47**. 112 and note.

75–6] Saturn seems partly assimilated to Mars, often depicted with red or fiery eyes. Traditionally, Saturn is cold and aged (as in **47**. 114–15); in Henryson's *Testament of Cresseid*, 157, he has rheumy, sunken eyes.

76] This line is metrically clumsy, but others (e.g. 9, 63) are also hypermetrical. The correct reading may be *men manasing to de*, 'threatening men with death'. For this archaic idiom, see *DOST*, *manace*, v. 2a.

77. keist hir amourouse e] Cf. Venus's 'blenkis amorous' in *Testament of Cresseid*, 226.

78] Mercury was traditionally the god of eloquence; cf. **47**. 116–17.

79. Fortuna major] 'The greater fortune', an astrological term for the beneficent planet, Jupiter. Douglas, discussing the 'gud influens' of Jupiter, says: 'Ioue is clepit "Fortuna major" and Venus "Fortuna minor"' (*Eneados*, I.

v. 2 note). Jupiter is likewise termed *fortuna major* in an astrological treatise cited in Curry 1923.

82] This echoes *Troilus and Criseyde*, V. 1591: 'O swerd of knyghthod, sours of gentilesse'. Cf. also 69 above.

85. Bertan] Britain. The allusion is to the battle of Bosworth, 1485.

89–93] The acrostic was a very popular device in late-medieval panegyric: it was used in love poems; in religious verse, especially poems on the Virgin; and also, as here, in praise of kings and noblemen.

94–5] Cf. Lydgate, *Fall of Princes*, IV. 371, who says of the Roman hero Marcus Manlius that his name ought 'With goldene lettres to been enlumynyd'.

46

1. Ask Wedinsday] The first day of Lent; for more solemn poems with an Ash Wednesday setting, see 25 and 38. The eating of meat was prohibited in Lent; there was more latitude as to the drinking of wine, but abstinence was practised by the austere.

2] *Cummar* originally meant 'godmother', but acquired the more general sense 'close female friend, gossip'.

5. lang Lentrin] Highly sarcastic, since Lent has only just begun.

12] *Megirnes* alludes to the first woman's complaint of leanness, and is clearly ironic.

14] Malmsey, a sweet fortified wine, originally came from a part of Greece known as *Malvasia* (in Italian) and *Malvesie* (in French). The boozy gossips of Noah's wife in the third play of *The Chester Miracle Cycle* likewise prefer malmsey. See also note to 70. 13.

23] The bean was a conventional image of worthlessness (Whiting, B 92); cf. the similar use in 3. 128.

30] A slight change in the refrain – as often in Dunbar – signals the poem's end, and represents the women's unvoiced 'hoip'. In Ab the line is hypermetrical; MF, which omits *lang*, is better rhythmically.

47
The Goldyn Targe

1–9] Note the threefold naming of the sun as 'day star', 'candill' and Phoebus. There is a similar triple patterning of the syntax; the poet's rising parallels that of the sun and the lark.

1. stern of day] 'Day star'. This phrase was commonly applied to the sun, although sometimes also used of the planet Venus.

2. Vesper] A name given to the evening star. Cf. Douglas, *Eneados*, I. vi. 119: 'Vesper, the evyn starn brycht'. *Lucyne]* Lucina, one of many names for the moon. Cf. Douglas, *Eneados*, XIII Prol. 68: 'hornyt Lucyn castand bot dym lycht'.

4. the goldyn candill matutyne] Cf. Chaucer, *Complaint of Mars*, 7: 'the sunne, the candel of jelosye'. Dunbar's phrase is imitated, rather clumsily, in *Clariodus*,

II. 1395–6: 'Richt as the lustie candill matutine / Begouth with cristall visage for to schyne'.

7] Cf. Ovid's description of the sun in *Metamorphoses*, II. 23–4: *Purpurea velatus veste sedebat / In solio Phoebus*. The diction also has ecclesiastical connotations: *cape* could signify 'cope'; and a common sense of *revest* was 'dressed in ecclesiastical vestments'. The sun is depicted partly as an emperor, partly as a dignitary of the church.

8] On the lark's association with the dawn, see note to **41**. 12–14.

10. sang thair houris] For this conceit, see note to **41**. 5.

14. perly droppis] A common phrase for dew. Cf. Henryson, *Ressoning betuix Aige and Yowth*, 3: 'perly droppis of the balmy schouris'.

15] This recalls *Troilus and Criseyde*, II. 53: 'And ful of bawme is fletyng every mede'.

16–18] Dunbar introduces the theme of pain in love. Dew-drops are imagined to be the tears of Aurora, the dawn goddess. Cf. Lydgate, *The Floure of Curtesy*, 38–40: 'Whan Aurora, for drery complaynyng, / Can distyl her chrystal teeres wete / Vpon the soyle'. Aurora, according to classical poets, was grieving for the death of her son, Memnon; here, however, she weeps on being separated from Phoebus. This notion derives from the common medieval confusion of Tithonus, the name of Aurora's lover, with Titan, a name for the sun god in Ovid and Virgil. Chaucer alludes to this separation of 'Titan' and the dawn goddess in *Troilus and Criseyde*, III. 1464–70.

18] Cf. Chaucer, *Knight's Tale*, *CT*, I. 1493–6: 'And firy Phebus ... with his stremes dryeth in the greves / The silver dropes hangynge on the leves'. Dunbar's verb, *drank*, is more audaciously anthropomorphic.

20. tender croppis] A Chaucerian phrase; cf. *CT*, Prol. I. 7.

21. Venus chapell clerkis] 'Choristers of Venus'. Cf. **10** above.

23. beriall droppis] Echoed by Douglas, *Eneados*, XIII Prol. 26. Beryl was a term for crystal (see **10**. 34).

26. ourscailit in silvir sloppis] A difficult phrase, which may mean 'oversprinkled with silver patches of cloud'. *DOST* tentatively glosses *ourscailit* as 'scattered over, sprinkled', deriving the word from *scale*, v., 'scatter, disperse'; but a link with *scaled*, 'furnished with scales', seems possible. The precise sense of *sloppis* is uncertain: it may be a figurative use of a word for various types of loose clothing (*OED*, *slop*, sb.[1]); cf. the clothing metaphors in 7, 12, 42 and 48. But it might, alternatively, refer to breaks in the clouds (*OED*, *slap*, sb.[2]).

27. lef] A singular in a collective sense, 'foliage'; of the similar use of *branch* in 15.

28–33] This passage influenced Douglas's description of reflected light in *The Palice of Honour*, 40–42, and *Eneados*, XII Prol. 59–62.

30. as lamp] A very common simile (Whiting, L 54–5).

36. clere as stern in frosty nycht] A vivid but proverbial simile; cf. Chaucer, *CT*, Prol. I. 267–8; and Whiting, S 673, S 685.

39. emerant bewis] Cf. Chaucer, *Parliament of Fowls*, 175.

48. Florais mantill] Cf. the opening lines of Lydgate's *Complaint of the Black Knight*, and Hary, *Wallace*, IX. 147: 'fresch Flora hir floury mantill spreid'. It was traditional to describe the earth in spring as clad in a garment made by Flora, goddess of flowers, or by Nature (see 42, and 87–90).

51. quhite as blossum] A common simile (Whiting, B 383).

52. merse] A ship's top-castle, a sort of circular platform surrounding the masthead.

54] Dunbar gives an ominous twist to an ancient image (see Job 9: 26 and Whiting, F 30–31).

56. rispis and the redis] 'Sedge and reeds'. An alliterative phrase common in Douglas: see *Eneados*, II. ii. 142; and XII Prol. 152.

64–72] Dunbar heightens his subject's value by asserting the impossibility of describing it adequately. On this rhetorical 'inexpressibility' topos, see Curtius 1953: 159–62.

67, 69. Omer ... Tullius] Homer and Marcus Tullius Cicero. These great writers are chosen as models of literary excellence, the one in Greek poetry, the other in Latin prose. Cicero was much admired in the Middle Ages for his treatises on rhetoric.

73. Thare saw I] A stock descriptive formula, much used by Chaucer; cf. *Knight's Tale, CT*, I. 1995ff., and *House of Fame*, 1214–81.

75. Juno] Jupiter's wife, and goddess of the sky in **41**. 69. *Appollo]* The presence of Apollo in this list of female deities (cf. **58** above) has puzzled scholars. Dunbar clearly knew that Apollo was a name for the sun (see **8**. 22 and **19**. 78); and one would expect him to know also that Apollo was a god rather than a goddess. But mistakes as to the sex of classical figures were not uncommon in medieval authors: Hymeneus is a goddess in *The Quare of Jelusy*, 59; and Marcia (= Marsyas) is female in *The House of Fame*, 1229. The author of *Clariodus*, what is more, distinguishes between the god Apollo and a goddess, called 'Apolleine', to whom the beautiful princess Meliades is twice compared (IV. 960 and V. 1901). This could be a misunderstanding, but it might represent a mythographical tradition, known also to Dunbar, and, if so, the correct reading in this line would be *Apolleine*. *Proserpyna]* Ravished while gathering flowers by Pluto (125), Proserpina is both a spring goddess and queen of hell.

76] A close echo of Chaucer, *Knight's Tale, CT*, I. 2297: 'O chaste goddesse of the wodes grene'.

77] Clio is strictly the Muse of history rather than poetry, but Dunbar recalls Chaucer's invocation, in *Troilus and Criseyde*, II. 8: 'O lady myn, that called art Cleo'. Cf. also *Kingis Quair*, 128.

78. Thetes] Thetis, goddess of the sea. *Pallas ... Minerva]* The Greek Pallas Athene, tutelary goddess of Athens, was identified with the Roman goddess Minerva. But Dunbar and his contemporaries were aware that the two goddesses were originally distinct. They are distinguished by Stephen Hawes in *The Pastime of Pleasure*, 3320ff. and 4965.

81. Lucifera] A feminine form of Lucifer, 'light-bearing', a name sometimes given to the planet Venus. 'Bright as Lucifer' was proverbial.

87–90] This ultimately derives from Alan of Lille's influential description of Nature and her marvellous robe in *De Planctu Naturae*, prose 1 (Sheridan 1980: 85). Cf. Chaucer, *Parliament of Fowls*, 316–18; and *Reson and Sensuallyte*, 347ff. For the personification of Nature, see **41**. 64ff.

94–9] Cf. the similar passage in **41**. 71–7.

110] Cupid is called a king by Henryson (*Testament of Cresseid*, 144) and other Scottish poets. Cf. the portrait of Cupid, with 'bow in hand that bent full redy was' and 'grundyn' arrows, in *Kingis Quair*, 653–65. On medieval conceptions of Cupid, see Panofsky 1962: 95–128.

112. armypotent] The stock epithet for Mars. Cf. **152**, and **45**. 73; also *Knight's Tale, CT.* I. 1982 and 2441.

114–15] This represents the traditional conception of Saturn as an old man – *ald* is a fixed epithet – whose astrological influence was malign. Cf. the fuller portrait in Henryson, *Testament of Cresseid*, 151–68.

115] In *The Knight's Tale, CT*, I. 2469, Saturn says likewise: 'My lookyng is the fader of pestilence'. Cf. Douglas, *Eneados*, VII Prol. 30, where he causes 'darth and infectioun'.

116–17] Mercury is commonly patron of rhetoric and eloquence; cf. **45**. 78; Henryson, *Orpheus*, 213; and Lindsay, *Dreme*, 393–4. For a complex portrait of this many-sided god, see Henryson, *Testament of Cresseid*, 239–52.

117] Douglas praises Virgil for being 'inuentive of rethorik flowris sweit' (*Eneados*, I Prol. 70). Cf. 253 and 275 below.

118–19] Priapus, god of enclosed gardens (as in Chaucer's *Merchant's Tale, CT*, IV. 2035), is coupled with Faunus, god of open countryside (the link with 'wildernesse' occurs in *Troilus and Criseyde*, IV. 1544). Both were fertility deities: the phallic Priapus was viewed as an emblem of aroused lust, and the lustful Fauni (as a class) were associated with Satyrs, and sometimes identified with *incubi* (see 125–6).

120] Janus was the god of gateways and the beginning of new enterprises. Chaucer apostrophizes him similarly at the start of Troilus's love affair: 'Now Janus, god of entree, thow hym gyde' (*Troilus and Criseyde*, II. 77).

122. Eolus] See 229–30 and note.

125–6] Pluto, god of the Underworld, was often equated with the devil. Here, because of his rape of Proserpina, he is called an *incubus*, a demon who had intercourse with a woman. In medieval legend Pluto and Prosperpina were also regarded as the king and queen of faery.

127. in grene arayit] The green clothing of both courts is stressed: see 60, 126 and 139. Dressing in green, although not unknown in everyday life, was particularly associated with hunting, and also with May rites and festivities: Malory's Guinevere and her knights wore green, when they went a-maying; young men in Aberdeen had green coats for the Robin Hood games; and Wallace and his followers dressed in green 'for the sesson' (Hary, *Wallace*, VI. 125–6). Cf. also **6**. 42, where maidens 'claid in greine' greet the queen on her May visit to Aberdeen. Symbolically, green is highly ambivalent. It is, logically enough, associated with the natural world and with youth; cf. the references to green foliage (11, 35, 39, 56, 76), and the figurative freshness of the participants (86, 105, 155). The colour also sometimes symbolizes inconstancy or lust (cf. *King Hart*, 330; *Testament of Cresseid*, 221). Pluto's green cloak thus does not necessarily imply his faery nature; as a devil he might rather have been expected to wear *sable*, or black.

131–2] On the 'observance' of May, see **41**. 37 and note.

135] Love traditionally began at 'first sight'. *boucht full dere]* With the phrasing, cf. Chaucer, *Anelida*, 255: 'Alas! youre love I bye hit al to dere'.

139–41] The ladies until this point concealed their bows in the cloaks that they wore – as was customary – over their kirtles.

145ff.] The attackers personify various feminine qualities: some of these, such as Beauty and 'Danger', often figure in medieval love allegory; others, such as 'Comparison' and 'Presence', are not common personifications. For an excellent analysis of their significance, see Fox 1959: 327–30.

151] Reason's shield, or targe, figures at important points in the allegory (157, 169, 183, 200), and gives the poem its title. In homiletic writing an allegorical shield usually derives ultimately from the Scriptures: cf. 'the shield of faith' (Ephesians 6: 16) or 'He shall take holiness for an invincible shield' (Wisdom 5: 19). But in this passage another shield, that of Pallas Athene, seems a more likely source, especially since it figures in Gower's version of the Perseus story (*Confessio Amantis*, I. 390–435). Perseus uses the shield of Pallas, or 'wisdom', to protect his sight from the sin of 'mislokynge'; this receives an explicitly erotic interpretation, when Amans confesses that he has misused his senses, reason has failed him, and he is 'topulled in [his] thoght' (565).

174. Comparison] Perhaps 'evaluation of the merits of different suitors'; but Kinsley suggests 'the lady's assessment of how far the lover falls short of the ideal'.

187. plicht anker] The plight anchor was a ship's principal anchor; here it is a figure for the strongest, most reliable member of the company.

188. Fair Callyng] 'Friendly Greeting or Reception'. In Scottish verse this phrase corresponds to French *Bialacoil*, one of the personifications that aid the lover in *Le Roman de la Rose*. 'Fair Calling' is Venus's 'uschere' in *Kingis Quair*, 673; cf. also **3**. 489.

195. rappit on as rayn] Similar collocations are common in battle descriptions: cf. Douglas, *Eneados*, V. viii. 76: 'Als fast as rayn schour rappys on the thak'.

203. kest a pulder in his ene] Like the modern 'threw the dust in someone's eyes', this means 'duped, deluded'.

205] Cf. the Chaucerian *Romaunt of the Rose*, 3336, where the lover becomes 'forwandred as a fool' when Reason departs.

215] The syntax is ambiguous: when Reason is blinded, love – which is a hell-like experience – briefly seems a paradise. Love was commonly described in such paradoxes: 'a swete hell . . . And a soroufull paradys' (*Romaunt of the Rose*, 4743–4).

216. mercy . . . grace] Stock terms for the lady's favour; cf. **3**. 315 and 501. The dreamer's love is unrequited.

221. quhill men mycht go a myle] That is, a very short time.

223. Dangere] It is difficult to find a single modern equivalent for this word; it signifies the lady's coldness towards her suitor, and reluctance to yield her love, with connotations of scorn and contempt. *Dangier* is the Rose's guardian in *Le Roman de la Rose*, and the lover's chief enemy; it is a personification that figures repeatedly in medieval love poetry (on the word's significance, see Barron 1965 and Lewis 1936: 123–4, 364–6). For Dunbar's other uses, cf. **20**. 6 and **30**. 58.

226. Departing] Many editors treat this as a participle, presumably describing *Dangere*. I take it to signify 'Parting' or 'Departure', and to imply the lover's estrangement from his mistress; cf. *depart* in 16 above, and contrast the earlier role of *Presence*.

229–30] Aeolus, god of the winds, commonly symbolizes bad or stormy weather in Scottish poetry (see note to **41**. 33). The change in the weather parallels the lover's emotional state, now in the care of *Hevynesse*.

235] See note to **9**. 29.

238–43] The violent awakening resembles the end of **63**.

245–52] The diction of this idealized spring scene is highly conventional;

'halesum' and 'attemperit' were favourite epithets with Chaucer and Lydgate.

252] This echoes line 82 above.

253–70] This is the first Scottish tribute to the traditional trio of great medieval English poets, although preceded by James I's praise of Gower and Chaucer (*Kingis Quair*, 1373–9). Cf. **16**. 50–51.

253–5] The general sense of this apostrophe is clear: for those who read correctly, or perceptively, Chaucer is the finest of all the poets that have ever flourished in Britain. But the syntax is difficult, and editors punctuate the lines differently. I take 254 as a parenthesis, and *evir* (255) as modifying what precedes. The line-filler, *quho redis rycht*, was common in alliterative verse; cf. *Golagros*, 561: 'quha sa right redis'.

253. rose] Figuratively 'supreme exemplar'. Douglas later calls Chaucer 'roys ryall' (*Eneados*, I Prol. 342); and Lindsay praises Douglas similarly (*Papyngo*, 24).

258. illumynit] A key word; cf. *enlumynit* (45) and *illumynate* (266). It derives from the art of the illuminator, who painted manuscripts with gold and bright colours (cf. **3**. 425). Transferred to the natural world, it has the sense 'bright, glowing with light' (see 45, and **41**. 21). Here and in 266 it signifies the great poet's power to embellish a subject, a style, or a whole language. Dunbar may recall Chaucer's praise of Petrarch, 'whos rethorike sweete / Enlumyned al Ytaille of poetrie' (*Clerk's Prologue*, *CT*, IV. 32–3). But the word was common in the critical vocabulary of Lydgate, who praised Chaucer in similar terms (Ebin 1988: 20–24).

262. morall] A fixed epithet for Gower, first used by Chaucer in *Troilus and Criseyde*, V. 1856. *laureate]* 'Worthy of the laurel crown bestowed on poets'. Cf. Henryson, *Fables*, 1377.

263. sugurit] 'Sweet, melodious', Cf. also lines 69, 106 and 265. The figure is much used by Lydgate (Ebin 1988: 28).

271–9] The farewell to one's book was popular with late-medieval poets; cf. *Kingis Quair*, 1352–65. But in this highly Chaucerian context Dunbar clearly recalls Chaucer's envoi to *Troilus and Criseyde*, V. 1786: 'Go, litel bok'. On this 'modesty' topos, see Curtius 1953: 411, and Bawcutt 1976: 170.

272] Cf. *Troilus and Criseyde*, V. 1790: 'But subgit be to alle poesye'.

278–9] *Rude* implies 'coarse' (of a garment) and 'crude, unpolished' (of diction). Dunbar fears to have the inadequacy of his style exposed, Douglas, in an envoi to *The Palice of Honour*, 2161–9, similarly disparages the 'russet weid' of his poem.

48

1] 'Send down dew from above, you heavens' (Isaiah 45: 8). This was a recurring versicle in Advent services, and used in the mass for the fourth Sunday in Advent.

3. the brycht day ster] Cf. Revelation 22: 16, where Jesus is called 'the bright and morning star' (*stella matutina*). The same image is used of the Virgin Mary in **11**. 26.

4. the ros Mary] Cf. 44 below, and 11 passim; also the poem that begins 'Ros Mary most of wertew virginale' (Asloan MS, II, 271). The rose, which was considered the most beautiful of flowers, was a particularly popular image for Mary. It figures in the burdens of several carols: 'Ther is no rose of swych vertu / As is the rose that bare Jhesu' (Greene, *Carols*, no. 173). *flour of flouris]* An image of perfection, corresponding to Latin *florum flos*; cf. Chaucer, *ABC*, 4. The construction, which parallels *of kingis king* (28), is modelled on Hebrew.

5–7] Christ, the son of God, is the light of the world, far superior to *Phebus*, the earthly sun. The sun symbolism, much used in the liturgy, derives from the exegesis of Malachi 4: 2. Line 7 alludes to Psalm 19: 6: 'His going forth is from the end of the heaven [Vulgate *A summo coelo egressio ejus*], and his circuit unto the ends of it'. Psalm 19, which opens 'The heavens declare the glory of God', resembles this poem in its jubilant tone, and was used in Advent services.

8] 'And unto us a child is born' (Isaiah (9: 6). These words were employed in the introit for the mass of Christmas Day; they are also employed in the burdens of several Nativity carols (see Greene, *Carols*, nos. 19, 20 and 36). In later stanzas Dunbar slightly modifies the refrain, to fit in with their syntax.

9–10] Angels were traditionally divided into nine different orders, arranged in three hierarchies: angels, archangels and virtues; powers, princes and dominations; thrones, cherubim and seraphim. Cf. the list in Lindsay, *Dreme*, 519–32, where they make similar 'Louyng with sound melodious'.

12. firmament] The eighth sphere, which contained the fixed stars.

13] The four elements, of which the universe was traditionally composed. Cf. Lindsay, *Dreme*, 379–80.

14. most and lest] 'Of highest and lowest rank'; an inclusive phrase, meaning 'all, without exception'.

28. of kingis king] Cf. Revelation 19: 16.

38. Aurora] The Dawn. On some implications of this image for Christ, see *8*. 21 and note.

43. blissit frute] This recalls the angelic salutation *Ave Maria . . . benedictus fructus ventris tui* (Luke 1: 28, 42).

47. prince] Cf. Isaiah 9: 6: 'the prince of peace' (*princeps pacis*).

49. hevin imperiall] The *coelum empyreum*, or highest heaven, was believed to be the dwelling of God and to shine with a pure, brilliant light. Cf. Douglas, *Palice of Honour*, 1878.

53. gloria in excelsis] 'Glory be on high'. These are the opening words of the *Gloria* in the mass, which derives from the angels' greeting to the shepherds (Luke 2: 14).

49

1. sensualite] Indulgence in the pleasures of the senses. Cf. Henryson, *Fables*, 1118–24, who says that sensuality turns men to 'brutall beistis' unless they are governed by reason.

4] Wit, 'understanding, intelligence', and Reason, the power that makes moral decisions, are frequently coupled by medieval writers (cf. *53*. 20 and *44*. 19), since they are closely allied mental faculties. 'First Witt consavis, syne Ressoun gevis the domes' (Hay, *King Alexander*, 9745). Cf. also *King Hart*, where Reason and Wit arrive together (578) and Reason advises the heart similarly: 'Schir king, I reid ȝe ryse' (761).

5. *clips and cryis]* An alliterative collocation that also occurs in Douglas, *Eneados*, VII. vi. 134.

6. *amend my mys]* 'Make amends for my sin'. A common phrase in penitential verse. The line resembles Henryson, *Prayer for the Pest*, 49: 'Thow grant ws grace for till amend our mis'.

50

1] An imprecation: 'Holy saviour, may silver be accursed!' Saint Salvator was a devotional title given to Christ.

3. *cheritie]* Charity, both in the general sense 'benevolence, kindness' and also specifically, 'almsgiving'.

5. *panefull]* A purse in a healthy state (cf. 16) would be full of money, but this one is filled only with pain. Cf. Whiting, P 449: 'To be purse sick and lack a physician'. Some critics (Reiss 1979: 42; Scott 1966: 94) perceive a further, sexual innuendo in *purs*, presumably as 'scrotum' (*DOST*, *purs*, 3), but do not explain the point of such an allusion.

22. *cors]* (1) The Cross on which Christ died; (2) a coin having a cross stamped on one side. Such puns were common, in both English and French, and were associated with the proverbial saying that the devil dances in an empty purse or pocket (Whiting, D 191). Dunbar here inverts the orthodox belief that an image of the Cross, or making the sign of the Cross (as in 3. 103), could expell the devil.

24] 'In whatever circumstances'. For this common jingle on *tyne/win*, cf. Barbour, *Bruce*, XII. 374: 'Quhile for to wyn and quhill to tyne'; also Whiting, W 284 and W 39.

33–5] Dunbar delays his appeal to the king, as in 5. The king, who alone can heal the poet's malaise, is envisaged as a physician. For other uses of this metaphor, cf. 57. 56; and 63. 49–50.

51

1. *Schir]* This mode of address is respectful and deferential, but not obsequi-ous; it is common in letters to Scottish kings, together with honorific titles, such as 'your grace' and 'your highnes'. The word opens several of Dunbar's petitionary poems. 51, 52, 53, 55, 56 and 57; it features also, slightly displaced, in 27, 35, and 66. 90.

3–4] Cf. the similar treatment of this theme in 63. 61–5.

6. *quhiddir]* An interrogative marker, used to introduce rhetorical questions or dilemmas. It is a variant of *quhithir* (19. 46 and note).

9. *a-thrist]* 'Suffering from thirst'. This probably represents the participial adjective (*OED*, *athirst*).

11–12] Cf. the proverb: 'It is na play where ane greits [weeps], and another laughs' (Fergusson, p. 62).

11. *collatioun]* Dunbar puns on two senses: (1) light evening meal (cf. 62. 14 and note); and (2) the act of a bishop by which he confers a benefice upon a churchman, in Scotland specifically the nominee of a patron (such as the king).

See *DOST, collatioun,* and Donaldson 1960: 19.

13. playis cop out] 'Competes in drinking the cup empty'. The phrase implies convivial carousing. Cf. **14.** 101; and Douglas, *Eneados,* I. xi. 91–2: 'al the nobillis tharof drank abowt – / I wil nocht say that ilkman playt cop owt'.

15] Banesoun, or benison, implies 'approval, goodwill' as well as the more specific sense, 'benediction, grace', appropriate to a meal.

52

1. Schir] See **51.** 1 on this mode of address. *your grace]* Primarily an honorific title, but there is a play on other senses; the poet prays that the king should have divine grace, and that he himself should obtain favour.

4] 'God grant that you might be John Thomson's man'. *Johne Thomsounis man* was a semi-proverbial phrase, signifying a man dominated by his wife. This is the first recorded use of what became among later Scottish writers a common and highly contemptuous taunt for a hen-pecked husband. The phrase's origin is not known. There is no evidence to support the usual explanation as *'Joan* Thomson's husband'; the phrase might possibly be interpreted as 'a man of the type of John Thomson'. It may derive from a lost Scottish tale or anecdote, related to the English 'mery jest of John Tomson and Jakaman his wife' (*Roxburghe Ballads,* II, 136–42), in which John's wife is a jealous shrew.

19. vowit to the Swan] The chivalric practice of making binding vows to a noble bird, such as a swan or peacock, became extremely fashionable, both in romances and in actual courts, in the late Middle Ages. Dunbar alludes to a specific incident, the great feast held at Pentecost 1306 by Edward I, at which vows were taken upon two swans to avenge the murder of John Comyn and Robert Bruce's oath-breaking to the English king. This is the first recorded instance of the custom, and the only known case of vowing to a swan (see Bullock-Davies 1978: xviii–xxxviii).

21–2] Dunbar employs heraldic symbolism to allude to Margaret Tudor, the *Rose,* and James IV, the *Thirsill* (Thistle), as in **41.** Line 23 (like 29) implies that he is out of favour with the king.

31. sweit sanct An] St Anne, mother of the Virgin Mary, was the object of great veneration in the fifteenth century. But her name was often used in asseverations, as here, chiefly to supply a rhyme. Cf. Chaucer, *Friar's Tale, CT,* III. 1613: 'by the sweete seinte Anne'.

53

1. Schir] See **51.** 1 and note.

2] Mure has not been identified, but Dunbar implies that he takes after his father in being a vagabond and a thief.

3. magellit] The figurative use is rare, but Douglas requests scribes not to 'maggill nor mysmetyr my ryme' (*Eneados,* vol. IV, p. 194). *making]* Cf. Chaucer, *Troilus and Criseyde,* V. 1789: 'But litel book, no makyng thow n'envie'.

6. hyne to Calis] 'From here to Calais'. A stock phrase for a long distance (Whiting, C 6).

9. salpeter] The chief use of saltpetre, or potassium nitrate, was as a constituent of gunpowder. Regarded as a poison and possessing an unpleasant taste and smell, it symbolizes slander and defamation. There is an implicit contrast with sugar and honey, the traditional figures for fine writing (cf. **47**. 263–5).

10–17] Slanderous rumours were taken very seriously by Scottish parliaments, and were the subject of frequent legislation in the fifteenth and sixteenth centuries. Cf. **36**. **52**.

11. collouris] A common term for rhetorical figures of speech. Cf. Chaucer, *Clerk's Prologue, CT*, IV. 16–18: 'Youre termes, youre colours, and youre figures, / Keepe hem in stoor til so be that ye endite / Heigh style'.

18. far owt of seasoun] Cf. Skelton, *Garnesche*, 130: 'ye rayle all out of seson'. It was the custom for fools and entertainers to gather in court at the feasts of Easter and Yule (cf. 25).

19] Fools are often depicted with close-cut hair.

20] On the coupling of wit and reason, see note to **49**. **4**.

24. Cuddy Rug] A fool first mentioned in September 1504, when the king visited Dumfries, for which *Drumfres* was then the usual spelling (*TA*, II, 457–8). He is listed on several occasions, the last being 1512. He should be distinguished from another *Cuddy* then at the court, an English luter.

26. yallow and reid] There were no fixed colours for the dress of lower servants in the reign of James IV. But court fools seem to have worn yellow and red garments: Curry (cf. **31**. 44) had coats and hose of 'rede and yallow' wool (*TA*, I, 342; III, 93), and John Bute (cf. **58**. 19) had a coat in the same colours (*TA*, IV, 50).

27] The sport of baiting bulls is mentioned in *Christis Kirk on the Green* (MF, no. xliii), 211.

54
The Flyting of Dumbar and Kennedie

1. Schir Johine the Ros] Dunbar's friend and confidant, whose death is mourned in **16**. 83; unfortunately nothing is known for certain of his life. Lines 39–40 imply that he had collaborated with Dunbar in some work; 'your making' contrasts with '*thy* ryming' in 32.

2. Quinting] Quintin here figures as a collaborator with Kennedy in some lost invective, vaguely called *ane thing* (1). He is Kennedy's kinsman and his *commissar* (34, 131), the term for a deputy in judicial or legal matters. It may indicate the professional relationship between the two men. Nothing else is known of Quintin, except that he may be the poet praised by Douglas in *Palice of Honour*, 924, and Lindsay, *Papyngo*, 19. He is unlikely to be the same person as 'Quintyne Schaw' (**16**. 86).

6–7] Cf. Isaiah 14: 12–13: 'How art thou fallen from heaven, O Lucifer . . . For thou hast said in thine heart, I will ascend into heaven, I will exalt my throne above the stars of God'. Lucifer's pride was proverbial; cf. Whiting, L 587.

8. harmis hynting] An alliterative formula; cf. 'thai hynt grete harmys' (*Golagros*, 703).

9–15] Mock-apocalyptic. Cf. 'For the stars of heaven ... shall not give their light ... I will shake the heavens, and the earth shall remove out of her place' (Isaiah 13: 10–13).

16. the commoun bell] Most burghs had a public alarm bell, tolled in cases of fire, riot or invasion.

25. blawis ... boist] 'Utters boasts arrogantly'. A common phrase; cf. *Rauf Coilyear*, 369: Thow ... greit boist blew'.

27. roist] Literally, 'roast meat', here apparently in a transferred sense, 'occasion of riotous feasting'.

28. laureat lettres] Probably alludes to the classical Latin phrase *litterae laureatae*, a dispatch, bound with laurel leaves, that announced a victory (*DOST, laureat*, 4).

29. Mandrag] Mandrake, a plant whose forked, fleshy root was believed to resemble a man.

30. Thrys scheild] The phrase is agricultural in origin: thrice-shilled (or -sheeled) barley has been put three times through the mill (cf. *schilling* in 147) to remove the outer husk.

36] Apes and owls were considered ugly, evil creatures; see **22**. 7 and **23**. 6.

37] The *skaitbird* has not been identified, but is also mentioned in *King Berdok*, 26–7: 'ane howlat nest / Full of skait birdis'. Kinsley compares *skatie goo*, a later term for the skua, a bird thought to steal other birds' eggs and to live on their excrement.

43. walidrag] Vaguely opprobrious, but the later sense, 'undersized person or animal', seems relevant (see *CSD, wallydrag*). *verlot of the cairtis]* A menial servant, who loads carts (cf. the contemptuous *cart fillaris* in **7**. 25).

50. Cuntbittin] Kinsley explains as 'poxed', but *MED* records a similar compound, glossed as 'impotent' (Bawcutt 1987: 85).

51. Densmen on the rattis] Dunbar may allude to the capture and execution of thirty-six Danish pirates in Edinburgh in 1489 (Macdougall 1989: 228). The *ratt*, or wheel, was a barbarous mode of execution, in which the criminal was placed upon a large wheel, and, as it turned, the limbs were fractured.

65, 97] Possibly these are responses to claims made in Kennedy's earlier invective, mentioned in 1–2.

66. Dagone] The Philistine god, or idol, that fell to the ground before the ark of the Lord (I Samuel 5). *dowbart]* Obscure; *DOST* and *CSD* suggest a connection with the later *dulbert*, 'stupid person, fool'.

73. crop and rute] 'Supreme example (lit. topmost shoots and root)'. An unorthodox use of a poetic cliché; cf. Chaucer *Troilus and Criseyde*, II. 348: 'of beaute crop and roote'.

74. fathir and moder] Each of these words had the figurative sense 'source, origin'; their coupling (which anticipates modern usage) provides a comic parallel to 'crop and rute'.

77–8] 'You planned to destroy our principal lords (B's *our lordis cheif*) in Paisley with a deadly poison'. MF's variant, *the lord thy cheif*, however, may be correct: to poison the chief of one's clan would be a heinous act of treachery. (Kennedy's chief was his elder brother, John, Lord Kennedy.) Such allegations of poisoning were common, whenever great persons mysteriously fell ill or died. In fifteenth-century Scotland there were various rumours of attempts to poison James III, or his brother, Albany, or his queen (see Macdougall 1982: 118, 185 and 194). The accusation is later denied by Kennedy, and seems groundless, although the reference to Paisley suggests some lost topical allusion.

80. on the I sall it preif my sell] 'I myself shall prove, or substantiate, the charge against you.' Cf. 86 below.

81–2] Cf. Henryson, *Fables*, 2830–32: 'Ane thrawart will, ane thrawin phisnomy. / The auld prouerb is witnes of this *lorum: / Distortum vultum sequitur distortio morum'*. On Scottish interest in the quasi-science of physiognomy, see Mapstone 1994.

83. Ganyelon] MF. Ganelon, who betrayed his kinsman Roland at the battle of Roncesvalles, was a medieval archetype of treachery, on a par with Judas Iscariot. Cf. Hary, *Wallace*, XII. 843–4: 'the traytour Ganʒelon / The flour off France he put till confusion'; also Chaucer, *Book of the Duchess*, 1121–3. Earlier editors retain B's *glengoir loun*, 'poxed'. But this latter phrase, although offensive, is less relevant, since the main charge here is treachery (see 73, 77–8 and 86).

84. fowlar than ane fen] 'Filthier than a dungheap'; cf. Whiting, F 120.

90–96] This voyage may be factual, but has not been dated.

91–2] This recalls, imperfectly, a scene in Virgil (*Aeneid* I. 81–141), where Aeolus, god of the winds, shatters the ships of Aeneas and black clouds obliterate the sun. On the coupling of Aeolus and Neptunus as a symbol of storms and bad weather, see **41**. 65 and note.

94. Holland, Seland, Yetland and Northway coist] Holland, Zeeland (at the mouth of the Scheldt), Shetland and the coast of Norway. The counties of Holland and Zeeland were important trading partners of Scotland; *Yetland*, or *Zetland*, was the usual Scottish form of the name Shetland. We are not told where Dunbar intended to sail, only that his ship was blown off course by hundreds of miles, first in a southern direction, then far north, to the empty sea around Shetland and west of Norway, the climactic *sey desert* (95).

97. goldin lippis] Cf. **47**. 263.

99. gluntoch] The sense is difficult. Murison (1974: 79–80) linked the word with 'gluntow' in Holland, *Howlat*, 796, and explained as 'black-kneed', from Gaelic *glundubh*, an epithet for Niall, the high king of Ireland. But this latter word, according to Prof. W. Gillies (in a private communication), was 'a fixed epithet, coined to sneer at the kneeling (i.e. devout) proclivities of a well known figure'; what is more, if written in Scots it would be more likely to be spelt *glundow*. He suggests that *gluntoch* represents Gaelic *gluinteach*, from *glun*, 'knee', and means 'having big or protuberant knees'.

105. of all the warld reffuse] 'Rejected by all'. Cf. *Troilus and Criseyde*, I. 570.

112. Carrik] See also 134, 158 and 211. Carrick is the southernmost part of Ayrshire.

123–6] Kennedy is compared to the persecutors of saints, who were depicted as ugly, with hooked noses and wrinkled brows.

123] St Lawrence was martyred by being burnt on a gridiron.

124.] St John the Baptist was beheaded; a blindfold was commonly placed over the eyes of a criminal who was about to be executed.

125. Augustyne] St Augustine of Canterbury (d. 604); the metre suggests the shortened form 'Austin'. Dunbar alludes to the legend, originating in the twelfth century, that when St Augustine preached to the English he was insulted, and pelted with fish tails. The story was famous (cf. Whiting E 109), but Dunbar may have known the version told by Bower, *Scotichronicon*, III. 33.

126. Bartilmo] St Bartholomew was flayed alive and then crucified.

127. The gallowis gaipis] A low catchphrase; cf. 222, and Pistol's 'Let gallows gape for dog' (*Henry V*, III. vi. 41).

128] In the Middle Ages haggis was not associated solely with Scotland; for a medieval English recipe, using chopped entrails, spices, eggs and milk, cooked in a sheep's stomach, see *Two Fifteenth-Century Cookery Books*, p. 39.

129. Commirwarld] 'Useless person, one who encumbers the world'. Cf. Chaucer, *Troilus and Criseyde*, IV. 279: 'I combre-world, that may of nothyng serve'. *comptis the ane kers]* A common idiom; Whiting, C 546.

141. gallow breid] 'One bred for the gallows'; with a pun on *Galloway*.

143. wathemanis weid] 'Outlaw's dress'. See note to 4. 8.

145] The line sums up the Lowlander's view of the Highlander's character and appearance. *Ersch katherene]* 'Gaelic-speaking robber'. *polk breik]* The bag in which Highlanders carried their supplies (*DOST*, *poke braik*). *rilling]* A rough shoe of undressed hide; in the Middle Ages it was regarded as an attribute of the Scots, particularly the Highlanders, and often ridiculed. See *Wallace*, I. 215–19; Lawrence Minot's verses attacking the Scots (*c.* 1333), which couple both insults: 'Rughfute riveling, now kindels thi care! Berebag with thy bost' (*Poems*, no. 2); and Bawcutt 1988b.

153. owt of repair] 'Unfrequented, lonely'. Hospitals were often sited in remote places, or at the entrances to glens.

155. of blis als bair] 'Devoid of bliss'. A common phrase; cf. Henryson, *Fables*, 1701; and Chaucer, *Anelida*, 213.

158. dowsy] This has been explained as the substantival use of a rare adjective, meaning 'stupid' (*OED*, *dowsy*; *DOST* has no entry). I take the reference to be to Kennedy's wife or mistress – drowning was more commonly a punishment for women than men (cf. 61. 15) – and interpret the word as 'harlot' (cf. *MED*, *douce*, a. and n.).

160. swetar than secrrind bell] A bell rung at the *sacring*, or consecration, of the eucharist marked the most sacred part of the mass. Cf. 4. 50.

161. Lazarus] In the Middle Ages Lazarus, whom Christ raised from the dead (John 11: 1–44), was confused with the beggar who lay at the rich man's gate, full of sores, and was believed to be a leper (Luke 16: 20). Both aspects of this composite figure are relevant: Kennedy is depicted in 161–72 as a resurrected corpse; but there are many references to him as a beggar, and 154 associates him with lepers. (On the background, see Woolf 1968: 318–20; Bawcutt 1992a: 194). *tramort]* 'Corpse, skeleton'. This passage is echoed by William Stewart, describing a wedding feast interupted by 'ane laithlie lene tramort / . . . Like ane bogill, all of ratland banis' (*Croniclis*, 46, 885–8).

162–72] This burlesques the solemn genre of warnings from the dead, represented by a poem such as Henryson's *Thre Deid Pollis*. With 162 and 167 cf. *Thre Deid Pollis*, 14–16: 'haif mynd of deth, that thow mon dy: / This sair exampill . . . Sowld caus all men fra wicket vycis fle'.

164. holkit is thyne ee] Cf. *Thre Deid Pollis*, 4, and *Awntyrs off Arthure*, 116.

165. blaiknit is thy ble] A formulaic phrase. Cf. *Golagros*, 1133: 'othir bernys . . . blakynnit thair ble'.

171. lyk ane saffrone bag] This implies dry, yellow skin. Small bags containing saffron were worn, suspended from the neck, for various medicinal purposes – to prevent miscarriages, or to expel poison.

172. spreit of Gy] Guido, or Guy, of Corvo was a ghost who in 1323 returned to haunt his wife, and to describe the horrors of Purgatory. There were versions of this story in Latin, English and other languages, and it was well known in Scotland; see references in *Crying of ane Play*, 14; Lindsay, *Dreme*, 16. Dunbar may have read the vivid account in Bower, *Scotichronicon*, XIII. v–ix.

179] Possibly an echo of Henryson, *Fables*, 903: 'The hardbakkit hurcheoun and the hirpland hair'.

182. lene as ony treis] A common simile (Whiting, T 456).

191–2] The grotesque image is culinary. Kennedy lies, as if in a saffron sauce, sprinkled with powder made from primroses, and scenting the air with cloves. For saffron in sauces, cf. *Testament of Cresseid*, 421; and *Two Fifteenth-Century Cookery Books*, 15. On powdered primroses, see ibid., 25 and 29.

196] A comic use of stereotyped phrases for a large number: with *gers on grund* cf. Whiting, G 426. *Leif on lind* was a common phrase (Whiting, L 139), in verse used vaguely for 'leaves on trees'.

198–9] The sense is difficult, and the text seems corrupt. A possible paraphrase is: 'You will [do it] again with more witnesses than myself. You cannot rid yourself of it, because of your past jaundice'.

202. caprowsy] An unidentified article of clothing; previous suggestions include 'upper garment, or short cloak' (Laing); 'rough cap' (Small); 'cape with a hood' (Mackenzie); and 'undergarment' (Kinsley).

205. rubbit quheit] Wheat rubbed between the hands to extract the grain. Cf. 116–17.

209. Strait Gibbonis air] 'Heir to (i.e. resembling) Strait Gibbon'. Payments were made to a man of this name in 1503 (*TA*, II, 378, 395); he may be identical with 'Quhissil Gibbone' (*TA*, I. 371), and, if so, an entertainer.

211. Edinburgh cors] Cf. note to **42**. 22.

212. hard as horne] A common simile (Whiting, H 481).

213] This refers to the practice of putting straw inside boots, as an insole in cold weather.

217. as beis out thrawis] Cf. Chaucer, *Summoner's Prol.*, *CT*, III. 1693: 'as bees out swarmen from an hyve'; Whiting, B 177.

219] Kennedy resembles an owl 'mobbed' by crows; cf. **4**. 74.

220] The *brachis* are excited by the scent of Kennedy's boots, made in the Highland manner from raw deer hide.

221. laidis and lownis] A common term for servants, or menials; cf. *Colkelbie Sow*, 416.

233–48] The climactic use of internal rhyme was popular with Scottish poets. Cf. Henryson, *Prayer for the Pest*, and Douglas, *Palice of Honour*, 2116–42. The need for rhymes often, as here, led to inventive word-coinages but strained syntax. This passage draws together many of the leading themes and images of *The Flyting*.

240. ledder] The ladder to the gallows.

241. byt buttoun] An obscure term of abuse; literally 'bite-button'. *air to Hilhous]* Hillhouse is a common Scottish place name, but this is usually taken to refer to Sir John Sandilands, laird of Hillhouse in Linlithgowshire. The point

is unclear, unless the proximity of *gluttoun* implies that he was a big eater.
242. Rank beggar] Cf. *Testament of Cresseid*, 483: 'ane rank beggair'. *flay-fleggar]* 'Flea scarer, chaser'; connotes infestation with vermin (cf. 102, 121, 148 and 195).
243. Chittirlilling] An obscure term of abuse, Kinsley takes it to be a 'playful variant' of *chitterling*, 'pig's guts'. *rilling]* See note to 145 above. *likschilling]* 'One who licks up discarded husks of grain' (cf. 147).
245. rak-sauch] 'One who stretches a withy, when hanged', i.e. 'gallows-bird'.
247] For a similar sequence, cf. *Colkelbie Sow*, 153–4: 'A lunatik, a sismatyk, / An heretyk, a purspyk'. *carlingis pet]* This insult recurs in later Scottish verse; cf. 'nocht bot ane carlingis pet' (*Satirical Poems*, viii. 14). The phrase is usually explained as 'old woman's favourite', *pet* being glossed as 'domestic animal; petted child' (*DOST*, *pett*, n.¹). Yet this insult seems curiously mild, and the sense is likely to be scatological. *Pet* is probably an instance of *pett*, n.³, 'fart'; cf. French *pet*.

55

2. ane Yowllis yald] 'A Yule horse'. No early occurrence of this phrase is known, apart from Dunbar's; but *Yule's yaud* and *Yule's yawll* are recorded in Scotland in the eighteenth and nineteenth centuries, and signify someone who leaves work unfinished before Christmas or the New Year, or who has no new clothing to celebrate the season. The full implications of the phrase are now obscure, but it was clearly derisive.
3] Most references to the *aver*, or draught-horse, are contemptuous. Cf. James VI (cited in *DOST*): 'A kindely auer will neuer become a good horse'.
4] The sense is difficult. Literally, the line appears to mean 'Shot forth over the cliff to squash the clover', which suggests the fate of a dead or dying horse. A tentative explanation is: 'Thrown out unceremoniously to lie on the clover'.
5] Perhaps 'And had as pasture all the rocky fastnesses of Strathnaver (*Strenever*)'. Strathnaver, the valley of the river Naver, is in Sutherland. The point may consist in its extreme remoteness, and its distance from court.
6. housit] Provided with a *hous* (cf. 65), or horse-cover. These were made from a variety of fabrics, ranging from canvas and wool to silk, velvet and white damask. *stald]* Provided with a stall, or stable; there is also (as in 11) a pun on the ecclesiastical sense of *stall*. A canon's stall in a cathedral would be highly desirable.
10. drug and draw] 'Drag and pull'; an alliterative phrase commonly used of draught-horses. Cf. Henryson, *Fables*, 2750: 'To drug and draw in cairt and cariage'.
11–12] The horse is pushed from the stall (where he would be fed on hay) and has to eat *fog*, rank grass left in the fields during winter, which was chiefly used to thatch houses (cf. Henryson, *Fables*, 198). *firthe and fald]* 'Wood and enclosed field'; cf. Douglas, *Eneados*, VII Prol. 162: 'baith firth and fald'.
16. pastouris] 'Pasterns', the part of a horse's foot between the fetlock and the hoof (*DOST*, *pasture*, n.³). The sense 'pastures, grazing-land' is possible, but repetitive after *feild*.
18] The sense is obscure. Editors usually interpret *bekis* as 'corner teeth'; this

is plausible in the context, but receives no support from dictionaries (see *DOST*, *beke, bek*; *MED, bek*, n.[3]; *OED, beak*). *Spruning* is also difficult; it may represent an erroneous form of *sprungin*, or a variant (by metathesis) of *spurning*, 'projecting, sticking out'. *he and bald]* Literally, 'high and bold'.

33. suppois my thrift be thyne] 'Although my resources may be scanty'. Cf. the proverbial 'His thrift waxes thin that spends more than he wins' (Whiting, T 250).

34] Cf. the Scottish proverb: 'In some mannis aucht mon the auld horse die' (Carmichaell, no. 847; Tilley, H 680). It implies that a dead horse is a liability.

36] Cobblers chewed hide to make it supple. *Pierce the Ploughman's Crede*, 752–3, describes a soutar filthy with grease, who has teeth 'with toylinge of lether tatered as a sawe'.

41. trapperis] Cf. Douglas's description of richly embroidered horse 'trappuris', in *Eneados*, VII. iv. 191–4.

42] *Spurrit* reinforces *forridin*: the overworked horse is prepared to suffer more cruelty, if only he is well treated at Yule.

45] 'Now that liveries are bestowed, accompanied with loud cries of "largess!" (from the heralds)'. Dunbar plays on two senses of *livery*: the Christmas allowance of clothing given to courtiers, and an allowance of provender for horses. (*DOST, luveray, luferay*, documents the sense-range, and the large number of spelling-variants; see also *OED, livery*).

46] Palfreys were conventionally *prowd*; cf. *King Hart*, 898. *Prowd* has a vague sense, referring to magnificence of dress or appearance.

47. gillettis] In a double sense: 'mares' and 'wanton women'. Cf. the ME proverb: 'The smaller pesun, the more to pott, The fayrer woman, the more gylott' (Whiting, P. 102).

48. riddin] In addition to the literal sense, there is an innuendo, 'mounted for copulation'; cf. **64**. 6, and Skelton, *Bowge of Court*, 402 and 409.

52. gammaldis] A variant of *gamountis* (**36**. 11). The term was applied both to the high leaps of human dancers, and to the bounds or curvets of a horse.

53–4] A protestation of loyal service. Dunbar implies that the kings of neighbouring countries wished to employ him.

57–60] The old horse would prefer to associate with *gentill* horses – ones of good breed – but is forced to join those that are of inferior status and diseased.

60. scabbit] Suffering from scab, a contagious disease of horses, a type of mange.

69–76] Some critics query James IV's authorship of these lines, and attribute them to Dunbar. There is no external evidence to prove, or disprove, the attribution.

69] On the *thesaurer*, see headnote to **17**. His responsibilities included providing liveries for the royal household, as well as the stabling and equipment for horses.

72. lyart] 'Silvery-grey', an epithet primarily for horses, but also applied to men's hair and beards.

74] Bishops and abbots commonly rode on mules, whose expensive trappings were criticized by moralists. Cf. Lindsay, *Papyngo*, 1050–52: 'More ryche arraye is now, with fren3eis fyne, / Upon the bardyng of ane Byscheopis Mule / Nor euer had Paule or Peter agane 3ule'.

56

1. Schir] On this form of address, see **51**.1 and note.

6. Astrologis] Most courts at this time had official astrologers.

9] The numerous payments made to minstrels, trumpeters, luters, fiddlers and harpers show that there was much music-making at the court of James IV. *Menstralis* were instrumental musicians. Cf. 'menstralis *blawing*' (6. 22).

10] *Cawandaris* is obscure. *Flingaris* is usually explained as 'dancers', but I take it, like *chevalouris*, to have a military sense, 'missile-throwers'.

12. barkis and ballingaris] An inclusive phrase for seagoing ships; cf. Douglas, *Eneados*, IV. vii. 72: 'mony gret schyp, ballyngar and bark'. James IV implemented a huge and costly naval building programme; see Macdougall 1989: 223–46.

16. Pryntouris] In September 1507 James issued a licence to the first Scottish printers, Chepman and Myllar, and it has been suggested that the poem was therefore composed after this date. But *printers* is ambiguous, and Dunbar may be using it in the still current sense, 'workers in the mint, those who stamp impressions on coins'. Kinsley notes that Dunbar had already referred to coiners (11); but there are similar repetitions elsewhere ('knychtis', 'chevalouris').

30] The terminology is drawn from scholastic philosophy: *forme* is 'the essential, determining principle of a thing'; it contrasts with the *mater*, or *substance*, of which it is made.

41. groukaris] Obscure. *gledaris]* Also obscure, although Kinsley suggests a link with *gled*, 'kite', implying someone ravenously greedy. *gunnaris]* James IV's interest in firearms is well documented. Many of the gunners at his court were foreign, coming from France and Germany.

42. Monsouris] An often sarcastic title for French noblemen. *Clarat cunnaris]* Expert judges of claret, a term not for red wine from Bordeaux but for any wine of yellowish or light-red colour; the phrase is modelled on *ale cunner*, someone appointed by the burgh to assess the quality of ale.

46. hall huntaris] Those who hunt wildfowl in the hall (rather than in more orthodox locations).

55] On James IV's interest in alchemy, see headnote to **4**.

56. multiplie] There is a pun on (1) 'increase' and (2) the alchemical sense, 'transmute base metals into gold'. For similar irony, cf. Chaucer, *Canon's Yeoman's Tale*, *CT*, VIII. 731, and 834–5: 'Whoso that listeth outen his folie / Lat hym come forth and lerne multiplie'.

59. last additioun] The reference is to the alchemists, introduced by *eik* (55).

60] The Tolbooth of a Scottish burgh had a triple function: it was the usual meeting-place of the council, the seat of the burgh court, and also the prison. See Lynch *et al.* 1988: 63–4.

65–6. Cokelbeis gryce] Dunbar refers to the poem *Colkelbie Sow*, which describes a long list of fools who were invited to feast on a *gryce*, or little pig; his pell-mell list of rogues and fools is close in technique to *Colkelbie Sow*, 119–72.

73. panence] This is a usual Scots spelling of *penance*, yet it does not make good sense here, unless the poet says that if he were rewarded he would close his eyes to others' faults, and this would entail punishment (in purgatory). The sense would be improved by emending to *pacience*.

83–5] The poet suffers from melancholy, which was thought to be caused by
an excess of black bile, due to an imbalance of the 'humours'. One remedy then
advocated was purging (cf. 85); figuratively, this corresponds to flyting, or
venting one's spleen. Dunbar suggests, however, that he might be healed by a
sweet medicine, or *tryackill* (87), i.e. more generous treatment by the king. For
this favourite figure of the king as physician, see **50**. 33–5 and note. The tone
is half-comic, half-threatening. Cf. a similar passage in 3. 162–7.

57

2. is done forloir] On this periphrastic construction, see Introduction, p. 14.
5. thocht] 'Anxious thought, distress'. Cf. **21**. 12. *dois me mischeif]* 'Harms,
injures me'. *Mischeif* is best interpreted as a verb; cf. its unambiguous function
in 60.
6, 31. servit] 'Served with food (i.e. rewarded)'.
7–9] Dunbar compares himself to a hungry hawk who, although his feathers are
starting to moult, is not given leave to come to the lure. Hawks were fed from
the *lure*, a feathered apparatus, resembling a bird, that was used to train them
to return; during the moulting season they were kept in mews.
7. rid halk] Literally 'red hawk'. Apparently a yearling hawk, so called from its
red plumage; see *OED*, *sore*, a.²; *red*, a. 17 (b); *DOST*, *red(e*, 3b.
11] 'Noble birds, of the same breed as the falcon, are forgotten'. The falcon was
a small but highly esteemed bird of prey; the term was sometimes restricted to
the peregrine falcon. Cf. Holland, *Howlat*, 321: 'the falcone farest on flicht'.
12. myttell] Unidentified except as the name of an inferior bird of prey. An act
of parliament (1457) coupled kites with 'myttallis' as 'foulys of reif', which
destroyed crops and wild fowl (*DOST*, *mittal*, n.). *hard in mynd]* 'Re-
membered'. *Hard* may be the participle, 'heard', or the adverb, 'hard, fast'.
13–14] The *gled*, or kite, was not esteemed. It was regarded as greedy and
cowardly (see Bartholomaeus Anglicus, XII. 27), and its natural prey was
carrion, or frogs and mice (cf. Henryson, *Fables*, 2896–902). Partridges were
considered food more fitting for a goshawk than a kite; goshawks were large,
short-winged hawks that preyed on low-flying birds. They play a martial role
as 'chiftanis chevalrous' in Holland's *Howlat*, 326–9.
16–19] The harsh voice of the magpie is contrasted with the heuny of the
nightingale's song. The magpie symbolised the bad poet, because of its ugly
song and thieving ways.
16. pairtie cote] This refers to the magpie's striking black and white plumage,
and also to the particoloured clothing worn by humans, such as the Fool in *The
Thre Prestis of Peblis*, 469: 'With club and bel and partie cote with eiris'.
18. the corchet cloiff] Literally 'split the crotchet'. Dunbar possibly alludes to the
rapid singing of many short notes in polyphonic vocal music.
21–3] Dunbar refers implicitly to foreign favourites and also to the fashion,
common in the fifteenth century, for kings to have menageries, and to keep
exotic birds like peacocks and parrots.
21] The first record of a proverb later in common use; see Whiting, F 573, and
Tilley, F 625.
23. but greif] 'Without physical discomfort'. This stresses the birds' privileged

position, and contrasts with the poet's own 'grief' (3 and 63).

24] Dunbar complains that the offspring of Scottish families are scorned. *Kynd* and *native* are here virtually synonymous; cf. Douglas, *Eneados*, VI. xiv. 39: 'His kynd natyve land'. The owl was regarded as 'odious' (**22**. 7). Its appearance and its cry were considered hideous: Douglas describes its 'laithly' form and 'ugsum' shriek (*Eneados*, VII Prol. 105–8).

26. gentill egill] The eagle symbolizes James IV, as in **41**. 120–6. *Gentill* (as in 14 and 32) has several senses: high in rank (of humans); of a good breed (of birds, animals); and pleasant, kindly (of disposition).

26–9] The eagle was celebrated for its high flight and generosity in sharing its own prey with other birds; see Bartholomaeus Anglicus, XII. 2. The king's exercise of patronage is here symbolized as a feast, as in **35** and **51**.

32. Gentill and sempill] Formulaic for 'those of every rank'.

33] 'Of the same type as Rauf Coilyear and John the Reeve'. Note the similar use of *kynd* in 11. Ralph, a charcoal burner knighted by Charlemagne, was the low-born hero of a late-fifteenth-century Scottish alliterative romance. John the Reeve, or village overseer, was also a 'carle', knighted by Edward I; he figures in a medieval English tale with a similar structural pattern to *Rauf Coilyear*. Dunbar couples them as instances of social upstarts rewarded by kings.

36. refuse] Usually glossed as 'refusal'; but there may be a further sense, 'something cast aside as worthless'. Dunbar says both that his requests are denied, and that he is rejected by the court.

38] This was a proverb usually employed to support arguments for social equality; cf. Whiting, A 37.

46–8] Dunbar's self-depreciation is ironic.

47. flattir and feynye] A common alliterative doublet.

48. ballattis breif] A Scottish phrase for writing poems; cf. **50**. 6.

49] The poet is guided by *barnheid*, 'childishness'; i.e. he lacks worldly wisdom.

52. mercye . . . rycht] 'Out of mercy, not as a right'; the antithesis was common (cf. Whiting, M 508–9).

54] 'That you would give some medicine'. This figure of the king as physician to the ailing poet continues in 56–60; cf. also **50**. 34 and **63**. 49–50.

62] The context and rhythm suggest a reference to some song or lullaby; cf. the refrain to a mid-sixteenth-century English song: 'Singe danderlie Distaffe, and danderlie' (Rollins 1924: 48).

64. vicar] The service of a parish was committed to a vicar when, as often happened, the rector was non-resident, or the church was 'appropriated', or gifted to a monastery or cathedral. On the poverty of vicars, see Donaldson 1960: 12–16.

66. Jok] A generic name for a rustic or low-class man. *Michell* (71), 'Michael', is used similarly.

67–8] The figurative language derives from card-playing. One sense of *cleik* is 'haul or sweep of cards' (*DOST*, *cleke*, 2); and line 68 refers to cheating. Cf. Skelton, *Speke Parott*, 429: 'He caryeth a kyng in hys sleve'; also Whiting, S 381, and modern 'to have an ace up one's sleeve'.

69. ballattis under the byrkis] Cf. the similar phrase in **41**. 28. Both present the poet as a semi-pastoral figure.

72. dispensationis] Papal licences to a churchman, most commonly to hold several benefices simultaneously.

74. totum . . . nychell] 'All . . . nothing'. There is a punning reference to a game of chance – as *playis* suggests – with a teetotum, 'a four-sided disk made for a spinning toy, with a letter inscribed on each side: T (*totum*) . . . N (*nihil*), the player's fortune being set by the letter uppermost when the toy fell' (Kinsley).

81–4] Dunbar compares his misery to the pains of purgatory, and thus implicitly compares the king to God.

58

1. Sir Jhon Sinclair] Sir John Sinclair of Dryden, present at court throughout James IV's reign. He is not known to have travelled to France (2), although he was in England in September 1501 (*TA*, II, 121). He is recorded as playing bowls and cards with the king (II, 112, 459).

2. France] Dunbar mocks the common view of France as the home of high fashion; cf. 34, and 36. 12. In *Christis Kirk* (MF, no. xliii, 56) the minstrel 'counterfutit France'.

8. maistir Robert Schau] Probably the Master Robert Shaw who spent several years at the University of Paris in the 1490s, and was a court physician. On one occasion he prescribed a 'ressait' (remedy) for the queen, when her nose bled (*TA*, II, 477), and there are references to him in the records between 1502 and 1508.

13. fra Sterling to Stranaver] 'From Stirling to Strathnaver (in Sutherland)', i.e. throughout the whole of Scotland. The phrase is a variant on a common formula for geographical inclusiveness.

15. maister almaser] This term was usually applied to the king's chief almoner, or dispenser of charitable gifts to the poor. Throughout James IV's reign the office was held by Sir Andrew McBrek (see *TA*, I, pp. ccxxxiv–v, on his duties).

16] A rhythmically effective line. *Hommiltye jommeltye*, possibly Dunbar's invention, is a reduplicating form like modern 'higgledy-piggledy'. A *juffler* was someone who moved awkwardly, dragging his feet along the ground.

19. John Bute] There are many references to this court fool, the first dated 3 November 1506 (*TA*, III, 301). He is sometimes called 'John of Bute' (III, 319), which may indicate his place of origin. He had an attendant called Synch, and his clothing seems to have been rich and elaborate.

22–7] Dunbar puts himself at the centre of the poem. He sees his court role as 'the mackar', but the self-portrayal is strikingly comic.

24. dirrye dantoun] Presumably the name of a dance, but no other reference is known. Cf. 20. 60.

25. pillie wanton] Editors have assumed that this must be an animal (as with the similes in 11 and 17), and made various guesses: 'turkey-cock', 'filly' or 'colt'. *DOST*, however, glosses as 'person who is amorous, lecherous or "randy"', and connects with *pillie*, n.[1], 'penis'.

26, 29–34] There are many references to Mistress Musgrave, chiefly between 1511 and 1513, when she is listed among the queen's attendants (*TA*, IV, 230), and – along with the wife of Sir John Sinclair – receives rich clothing and New Year gifts (*TA*, IV, 324, 401). It seems likely that she is the woman called 'Agnes

Musgrave' (IV, 430) and the wife of Sir John Musgrave (IV, 125).

36. Dounteboir] Not apparently a surname, but a nickname for a court lady. John Knox refers contemptuously to 'old downtybowris . . . that long had served in the court' (cit. by *DOST, duntibour*).

44. The quenis Dog] A punning reference to James Dog, who was in the queen's service after 1511. See **60** and **61**.

47. mastevlyk] Dunbar applies the same pejorative image to Dog in **60.** 17.

48] Proverbial. Cf. Whiting, H 592.

59

1–2] Roses and lilies are images commonly linked in poems describing beautiful women; cf. **3.** 28–9. Here they symbolize not only beauty but feminine virtue. For the rose as a symbol of the Virgin, see **11.** 40 and **48.** 4.

2. of everie lustynes] Cf. the same phrase in **10.** 10.

3. bontie . . . bewtie] Twin attributes of the ideal woman. Cf. **19.** 61, and *The Floure of Curtesy* (Lydgate, *Minor Poems*, II), 215–16: 'my lady is so auysee / That bountie and beautie bothe in her demeyne'. The pairing was traditional; see Whiting, B 152.

4] Most editors alter MS *is deir* to *is held most deir.* But the line is grammatically correct as it stands, and is not necessarily defective metrically.

6–10] The garden may be literal as well as metaphorical. Note the parallelism with stanza 1. The flowers (like roses and lilies) are red and white; they too combine beauty and virtue, being 'lusty' and 'halsum'; and the solitary defect is reserved for the last line.

10. rew] This puns on *rue,* a herb with strong-scented leaves, and *rue,* the virtue of pity, compassion. Similar word-play occurs in other Scottish verse: in *The Lay of Sorrow,* 51–2, a lady, complaining of her lover's unkindness, says: 'In my garding quhare I sewe / All peiciens [= patience; also the herb, dock] now fynd I nocht bot rewe'; and in Rolland's *Court of Venus,* I. 172, Despair carries a clearly emblematic bush of rue. One 'halsum' property of the herb, according to Bartholomaeus Anglicus (XVII. 141), was to repel venomous animals from gardens; he also noted that although it was said to diminish amorous desire in men, it produced the opposite effect in women.

60

1. wardraipper] Dog was not the Master but a lesser official of the Wardrobe (18). This was an important royal department, concerned with the clothes of the queen and her household, and also with tapestries, bed linen and other moveable items. Between 1511 and 1513 he received payment for the purchase of velvet, taffeta and other rich fabrics for the queen's gowns, kirtles, hats and 'tepatis'. *Venus boure]* A compliment to the queen, and her apartments (cf. 23 below).

2–3] Doublets for the queen's servitors usually required two and a half ells of cloth (a Scottish ell was about a metre); their price varied according to the cloth, black velvet being much more expensive than 'fustiane'. A *frog* (Scottish form of *frock*) was a voluminous cloak or mantle, often worn over armour; it would clearly be more expensive than a doublet.

4. dangerous] Dunbar plays on various senses: 'causing danger to others'; 'stingy, reluctant to give'; and 'surly, unobliging'.

5. markis] The signs on a document, such as a seal, that proved its authenticity.

7] Cf. *Christis Kirk* (MF, no. xliii), 198: 'As thay had worreit lambis'.

17. mastive] The mastiff was large, ugly and powerful, and used chiefly as a guard dog. It was regularly confined by leashes and iron collars (see Gilbert 1979: 65–6, and 106). Dog is compared to a mastiff in **58**. 44–8, which may have been written about this time.

19. Gog Magog] Probably the legendary British giant Goemagot, first mentioned in Geoffrey of Monmouth's *History of the Kings of Britain*, I. xvi. Dunbar may recall the account in Wyntoun, I (E), 335–6: 'Amang thaim ane wes mekle of mycht / Goge Magoge to name he hecht'. But *sowdan*, or sultan, usually referred specifically to an eastern ruler, and *Gog Magog* may here represent a blending of Goemagot with the sinister biblical figures Gog and Magog, or with the mysterious oriental giant descended from 'God Magoz' who is included in a list of 'sowdanis' in Hay's *King Alexander*, 6049–67.

61

4. he is a lam] Ostensibly high praise, since the lamb was a type of innocence and humility (Whiting, L 26–32). But in fables (cf. **64**) the lamb was regularly the victim of stronger beasts, and therefore connoted less admirable qualities in a man, such as weakness and inability to defend himself against a shrewish wife.

9–11] These lines sneeringly imply that Dog is performing tasks more fitted for a woman.

18. bayth syd and back] 'All over her body'. For this inclusive formula, cf. 1. 57.

19. barrou tram] One of the poles or shafts by which a hand-barrow was carried. For their use as weapons by peasants, cf. *Christis Kirk* (MF, no. xliii), 193–4: 'Thai forsy freikis . . . Bet on with barow trammis'.

21. doin me obey] On the construction, see Introduction, p. 14.

62

2. courte] Both the royal court and a court of justice. *Kend* has a double sense: 'well known' and 'known carnally'.

5. gudmen] 'Husbands', and also, ironically, 'good men'.

8. meynis . . . mak] 'Make their complaints'; but the sense 'make intercession, act as intermediaries' seems present (see *DOST*, mene, n.[1] 6).

11. myld and moy] A common alliterative phrase. Douglas describes Venus as 'myld and moy' (*Eneados*, XIII. xi. 2).

14. collatioun] A refreshment taken in the evening, often including wine and sweetmeats; cf. Henryson, *Testament of Cresseid*, 418: 'Spycis and wyne to thy collatioun'. The term connoted luxury and amorous intimacy. Cf. Lindsay, *Satyre*, 437–8: 'he maks ȝow supplicatioun / This nicht to mak with him collatioun'.

19. Traist as the steill] A version of a common simile (Whiting, S 707 and S 709). For similar irony in its application to women, cf. the refrain to Greene, *Carols*, no. 400: 'Wemen be as trew as stele'.

28. grathit up gay] A common alliterative collocation. Cf. **3**. 365; and *Golagros*, 131 and 903.

31. spend] 'Expend money (in bribes)', but a sexual innuendo seems likely.

32. geir] 'Property', with the further sense, 'sexual apparatus' (*DOST*, *gere*). Lindsay likewise refers to a woman's 'gallant geir' (*Satyre*, 465), although it was more commonly applied to men (cf. **3**. 232).

35–40] *Compositouris* were legal officers who regularly attended the circuit courts, or *ayres* (on these see 17); they bargained with those found guilty of theft, manslaughter or oppression, who were allowed to pay atonement for their crimes. The treasurer was usually one of the *compositouris*, and a high proportion of his receipts came from 'this remunerative treatment of disorder' (Nicholson 1974: 567–70).

41. All haill almoist] Perhaps 'almost unimpaired', although the sense 'whole' is also present (cf. 'litle loist'). In 44 *all haill* has an adverbial function, 'entirely'.

42. sobir] All witnesses have this spelling, but it may be a misreading of *sovir*, 'sure, certain', required by the context.

47. supprys] The primary sense seems to be 'harm, damage' (the women's reputation); but Dunbar alludes also to the further sense, 'ravish, rape'.

48. honeste] Dunbar plays ironically on the word's various implications: honour, moral worth; woman's chastity; and the outward show of such virtues.

63

1. This hinder nycht] Corresponding to ME 'this endres day', this is a ritualized phrase, like 'Once upon a time'. For Dunbar it seems primarily a device for distancing himself slightly from what follows, and often introduces a dream. Cf. **20, 64** and **65**.

2. ane new aray] This implies that the poet's room was not normally so luxurious; marvellously transformed, it is decorated with paintings or wall-hangings. Cf. Chaucer, *Book of the Duchess*, 321–30; Lindsay, *Meldrum*, 883–4.

5. oure first father] Alluding to the creation of Adam (Genesis 2: 7).

11. phary] 'Supernatural experience, perhaps of fairy origin'. The word is repeated in 111 below.

20. Sad as the leid] 'Heavy as lead'; cf. Whiting, L 123.

25. wallowed as the weid] 'Faded, discoloured, as weeds' (*weid* is a collective singular). Henryson describes Eurydice's 'hew' similarly: 'wan and walowit as the wede' (*Orpheus*, 350). For other Scottish uses, see Whiting, W 172.

27. Nobilnes] The quality particularly desirable in the king, which can give the poet 'lecheing' (50); see 42, 72 and 108.

48–9] On the poet's metaphorical illness, cf. **50**. 34–5.

56] Dunbar regularly couples *Discretioun* (48) and *Considerance*; see **39**. 9 and **47**. 165.

58. Effectioun] 'Partiality, undue affection for kin or friends'. This was a vice commonly criticized by moralists. In *De Regimine Principum* (MF, no. xxxix),

120, the king is advised to exclude 'all effectioun singulare'.

62. sessioun] 'Season', rhyming with *Ressoun*.

63ff.] On this theme of the equitable and rational *distributioun* of benefices, cf. **51**. 1–5.

73] This line is hypermetrical. *Ressoun* may be an error (perhaps originating in a marginal gloss); *my brother* resembles the usage elsewhere (cf. 30, 56 and 106).

74–5] The sense seems to be that it would be highly advantageous to have Reason participating in the judicial system. The sentence might be paraphrased: 'You would be worth a great deal to this kingdom, if you sat on the platform with officers of the law'. With the idiom in 75, cf. Skelton, *Bowge of Court*, 157: 'Ye be to her, yea, worth a thousande pounde'.

74. lordis at the cessioun] The Lords of Session were members of the king's council appointed to hold 'sessions', or sittings, for the hearing of civil causes or complaints.

81–2] Proverbial-sounding, but Whiting (A 215) cites only this use.

83] 'And he who asks, loses nothing but his words'. Cf. Chaucer, *Troilus and Criseyde*, V. 798: 'I shal namore lesen but my speche'; and Whiting, S 614.

86. Schir Johne Kirkpakar] Sir *John* was a mocking term for a priest; cf. 'drounkin schir Iohne Latynelesse' (Lindsay, *Kitteis Confession*, 76). *Kirkpakar* seems a nonce-formation for a greedy pluralist churchman, who amasses churches, as if he were a *pakar*, or trader. There may be a side allusion to Scottish surnames beginning with *Kirk-*, such as Kirkpatrick.

90. yone ballet maker] A contemptuous phrase: 'that ballat-maker, or versifier'. It is not Dunbar's view of poetry, but imputed to the philistine cleric.

91] 'And then, sir, destroy the church, so long as I may prosper'. Previous editors punctuated the line differently, treating *schir Bet the Kirk* as a second personification, although no satisfactory explanation was provided for this difficult phrase. I take *schir* to be parenthetic and vocative – cf. 'And now, schir, laitlie' (27. 6). *Bet* may be a form of *bete*, v., 'beat, or beat down'. For a similar construction, cf. the proverbial '(tyr (strip) the kirk and theik (thatch) the queir', which roughly corresponds to 'rob Peter to pay Paul'.

91–5] This stanza is a continuation of Kirkpakar's shameless speech. It was common for ambitious clerics to have agents at Rome and elsewhere, who kept them informed of vacancies caused by the deaths of bishops and other churchmen. In the next stanza Reason's 'thow' shows that he is addressing one man, not two, and 'kirkis sevin' picks up the earlier use of the phrase by Kirkpakar (88).

96. The ballance gois unevin] A pair of scales was the usual attribute of Justice, and it was a common notion that those in authority should hold the balance even; cf. 'Thus sowld ane lord the ballance evinly hald', Henryson, *Hasty Credence*, 15.

102–4] Kinsley takes the referent of *him* and *he* to be Dunbar, who 'Intemperately' asks for more than one benefice. But Temperance is replying to Reason, and employs the same figure of the *ballance*; both refer to the greedy Kirkpakar, who is not satisfied with one cure, and causes the balance to sway in his direction.

105] The point of this is obscure. Perhaps 'Whoever can best rule should have most authority'.

109–10] Patience says that the king would not, even for his own profit, delay the nomination of someone to a vacant bishopric, if this in turn delayed the poet's own preferment. As long as a bishopric was vacant the crown enjoyed its revenues.

111–15] There is alliteration on voiceless plosives, especially /k/, to denote loud noise or explosions.

114] Leith, in James IV's reign, was the port where foreign guns first entered the country, and a place where they were also manufactured and stored. In July 1506 a bombard, or cannon, was taken to Leith sands, and shot in the presence of the king (*TA*, III, 203–4).

64

1–2] Cf. the opening of *The Thre Prestis of Peblis*: 'In Peblis towne sumtym as I herd tell'.

1. This hindir nycht] On this opening, see **63**. 1 and note. Dunfermline was an important burgh, where the king had a residence. It was famous for its great abbey, which contained the tombs of several Scottish kings and the shrine of St Margaret.

7. ferly cace] Similar in sense to *windir thing* (2). The refrain comments ironically on the oddities of the story.

11. todlit] 'Played amorously', a sense not otherwise recorded for this verb (*OED, toddle*). Dunbar puns also on *tod*, 'behaved in a tod-like manner', and there may be some connection with the later phrase *tail-toddle*, recorded by *SND* in the sense 'sexual intercourse'.

12. grace] In the amorous sense, of a woman's favour.

13. Lady] Apparently a call to the Virgin for help.

16. reid-haird] The fox's fur is commonly called red. There was an ancient distrust, inherited from the physiognomy treatises, of people who had red hair. Hay, *King Alexander*, 10134–9, associates them with falsehood: 'to begyle thai ar richt wounder sle'. *lowry]* 'Knavish, crafty person', with an allusion also to the Scottish nickname for the fox, first recorded in Henryson (*Fables*, 952). There may be some play on the verb *lour*, 'crouch low', often used of the fox (cf. 12).

18. silly] A stock epithet for lambs and sheep, implying innocence and foolish simplicity. It is frequent in Henryson; cf. *Fables*, 2620, 2625 and passim.

19. tribbill ... bace] A punning use of musical terms. In part-song the treble was sung by high voices, the *bace*, or bass, by low voices. One would expect the female lamb to sing the treble, but there is a *double entendre* on *tribill*, upper position in sexual intercourse, and *bace*, lower position. For a similar innuendo, cf. Maitland (*MF*, no. xxxi): 'fresche Maii and cauld Ianuarye / Aggreis nocht vpone ane sang in Iwne / The tribbill wantis that sould be swng abwne'.

23. ane morsall] This combines the literal sense, 'small mouthful of food', with the metaphorical sense, 'pretty young woman'. The ominous equation between devouring women and making love to them continues in 24–5.

26] *Race* is used of a charge in a tournament; cf. Lindsay, *Justing*, 57: 'ather ran at vther with new raicis'.

34. girnand] 'Snarling'. Cf. the wolf's 'girnand teith' in Henryson, *Fables*, 2630.

36. be the hals] The fox holds the lamb by her neck; the phrase could imply a lover's embrace, but often connoted murderous intent. The wolf treats the lamb similarly in Henryson, *Fables*, 2699: 'he hint him be the hals'.

39. prenecod] Literally 'pincushion', with a clear sexual innuendo.

44. jangleris] 'Those who spread malicious gossip'; cf. Henryson, *Robene and Makyne*, 101–2.

45] The sense is difficult. Perhaps it might be paraphrased, 'But in some way or other they were marred (i.e. morally compromised)'.

47. gaif hir grace] Probably 'showed her mercy'.

50–51] The thought is a commonplace (Whiting, J 58), but the wording recalls the union of the lovers in *Troilus and Criseyde*, III. 1221: 'For out of wo in blisse now they flete'.

58–62] The fox concealed in a lambskin is a figure for duplicity in Dunbar (2. 37 and 3. 423) and other Scottish writers; it corresponds to the scriptural wolf in sheep's clothing (see Whiting, W 474). The image here is peculiarly sinister, and seems to imply – on one level of the fable – that the fox has killed the lamb. The sheep do not raise the alarm because they fail to perceive the deception.

66. tod] Mackenzie and Kinsley adopt MF's variant, *bell*, although the point is not clear, unless it refers to the curfew. But the fox is presented as a mass-slaughterer and multiple seducer. *Strikkin*, like other words in this poem, has a double meaning: 'struck, killed', and 'copulated with' (for this sense, cf. *OED*, *striker*, 2d).

69. report . . . pen] Cf. the similar usage in 3. 526.

65

2. Sanct Francis] St Francis of Assisi (*c.* 1181–1226), founder of an order of friars, dedicated to poverty and simplicity of life.

13] 'You who have long given instruction in the laws of Venus'. This refers jocularly to Dunbar's love poems. For Venus as a lawgiver, cf. *Kingis Quair*, 708, 734.

20. confessour] The term for saints, such as Francis, who made a strong affirmation of their faith but were not martyrs. Here it has a further point, since the friars' right to hear confessions was much resented.

21. allevin] The sense is uncertain. 'Eleven' seems curiously precise, but occurs elsewhere in Dunbar as an indeterminate large number (11. 58; 63. 89). It might possibly be better analysed as *all evin*, an adverbial phrase similar in function to the common line-filler *full even*, with the vague sense 'of a truth, indeed'.

22] 'Seven times as many saints among bishops as among friars'. This has a specious truth, since the orders of friars were instituted late in the history of Christianity.

26] Dunbar usually introduces new speakers in a dialogue with 'Quod', but this is not invariable (see **19.** 65). Similarly unassigned speeches occur in Henryson's *Robene and Makyne*, and *Fables*, 447 and 472.

33–5] Although Franciscan friars took a vow of poverty, they were much criticized for their good living and enjoying the hospitality of the wealthy. Cf. Chaucer, *Summoner's Tale*, *CT*, III. 1765–77.

33. place] 'Mansion, wealthy dwelling'. The rhyme with *Kalice* suggests that the original reading may have been *palice*.

34. frome Berwick to Kalice] This symbolizes the extremities of England: Berwick on Tweed was finally won from the Scots in 1482, and Calais was in English possession until 1558. For this formula, indicating wide extent, see Whiting, B 260.

38. Derntoun kirk] The collegiate church at Darlington, County Durham. In the fourteenth and fifteenth centuries many Scots, using the east-coast route that this place-name implies, made pilgrimages to St Thomas's shrine at *Canterberry*.

44. haly watter] The mention of holy water, ritually used to exorcize evil spirits, might well alarm the devil. Cf. Whiting, D 208.

48–9] Discomfited devils traditionally left ruin in their wake.

66

7. sweit abayd] Literally 'sweet waiting, or delay'; a cryptic phrase, perhaps referring to the eagerly expected but long-deferred benefice. Cf. 61–84.

10. faceis twa] A traditional image of duplicity; cf. Whiting, F 12: 'Trust not him that has two faces'.

21] A commonplace; cf. Whiting, W 132 and 133.

22] 'The honorable mode of life, [that] is all gone'. The structure of the stanza requires this relative construction; *ago*, 'gone', is a Chaucerism, found chiefly in rhyme position.

23] 'Everywhere': *hall and bour* is a common inclusive phrase, usually referring to a great household; *burgh and plane* means 'town and country'.

27. change as wynd or rane] People are as unreliable as the weather.

29. the Bordour] Specifically the border between Scotland and England, an area notoriously lacking in law and order.

31. swane] Apparently a nonce-plural, for the rhyme.

37–9] In order to grab earthly wealth and power the son is willing to dispossess his father of his property, and reduce him to bankruptcy.

42–3] The closest parallel occurs in Carmichaell, no. 425: 'Cairts and waines may gang on that conscience'. The apparent implication is that a corrupt conscience is capacious, and tolerates a multitude of sins.

43] The eight-ox team was the usual unit on Scottish farms from the fifteenth to the nineteenth century.

49–50] 'And one man, unworthy of possessing a stall (in a cathedral), wishes to be promoted to cardinal'. This may be a general attack on ambitious churchmen. But Dunbar perhaps refers specifically to bishops like Robert Blacader and Andrew Forman, who had unfulfilled hopes of becoming cardinals.

55. Sum with ane thraif playis passage plane] This line has long been misunderstood. *Thraif*, an agricultural term, signified two stooks of corn, usually containing twelve sheaves; the word figuratively meant 'a large number, a lot' (*OED*, *thrave*). *Passage* was the name given to a game of dice, corresponding to French *passe-dix* and Italian *passa-dieci* (*OED*, *passage*, 15). Dunbar imagines a churchman openly (*plane*) playing dice with a large number (of *kirks*); the sense is either that he wins them by gambling (for a similar image, cf. **57**. 66–9), or squanders their revenues on trivial pursuits.

57. It] The referent here – and comically throughout 57–83 – is the long awaited *kirk*, or benefice.

62. Calyecot] Calicut (now Kozhikode), the important port on the south-west coast of India; jewels, spices, and cloth (later known as calico) were brought there, and thence transported to Europe. *the new fund yle]* It is difficult to identify such a vague phrase with certainty. Although long explained as Newfoundland, discovered by Cabot in 1497, it may quite as plausibly refer to Columbus's far more famous discoveries in the Caribbean; these were reported in *The Letter of Columbus*, or *Epistola de insulis nuper inventis* (1493), of which at least eighteen editions or translations appeared within four years. The structure of Dunbar's phrase resembles the titles of these works.

63. The partis of transmeridiane] No other use of this technical-sounding phrase is known. *Transmeridiane* literally means 'beyond the meridian', and *OED* explains as 'the region beyond the meridian in the Atlantic which separates the New from the Old World; the Western Hemisphere'. For Scottish writers at this time, however, *meridiane* and *meridionall* signified the south or the equator (see *DOST*'s citations for these words), and it is possible that Dunbar may refer to the southern hemisphere.

66. Ynde] India symbolized both wealth and extreme remoteness (cf. **43**. 6).

67. grit se occeane] This phrase corresponds to Latin *magnum mare oceanum*, the great sea surrounding the central land-mass, as contrasted with the Mediterranean.

69–71] Some scholars have been reluctant to accept *Paris* at its face value, suggesting it is an error for Persia or Paradise. But these lines may symbolize the old threefold division of the world into Europe, Asia and Africa.

71. ylis of Aphrycane] Probably the Atlantic islands of Madeira, the Canaries and Cape Verdes, all of which were known by 1460.

74. gane will] 'Gone astray'; this phrase is used by Douglas of ships lost at sea (*Eneados*, I. i. 56).

78. unicornis] Gold coins, stamped with a unicorn on the obverse, first issued in 1486 by James III. *crownis of wecht]* Crowns, or gold coins, of the standard weight, as opposed to 'lycht crownis'.

81. provydit] 'Arranged in advance', with allusion also to the ecclesiastical sense of *provide*, 'to grant a benefice'.

86] Heather was used to thatch the roofs of small, rural churches, but would not have been used for wealthy Scottish abbeys, such as Dunfermline or Melrose. *Scant* is probably the adverb, 'barely, scarcely', but as the adjective, 'poor, meagre', might describe the church itself.

87] This implies the poet's poverty. Cf. Fergusson, p 14: 'a poore man is fain of little'.

89–93] Ironic. If the poet does not possess many *curis*, or benefices, he is not guilty of pluralism, and his soul will not undergo spiritual death or suffer punishment for this sin in purgatory.

91. sillie saule] See note to **33**. 25.

95. flytis lyk ane phane] 'Is changeable as a weather-vane'. Cf. Whiting, V 5 and 6.

99. your grace] Here, as in 90, an honorific title for the king, with a play also on the sense 'mercy, favour'. *crop and grayne]* 'Totally, wholly', possibly a rhyme-determined variant on the more common *crop and rute* (**54**. 73).

67

2] Fortune's gifts, such as wealth and prosperity, were distinguished from those of Nature and Grace.
4] Proverbial; cf. Whiting, S 608: 'In much speech sin lacks not'.
5] 'And strive never to tell lies, out of malice'. The double negative, here and in 6, is used for emphasis.
8] A commonplace. Cf. Whiting, M 414, R 231, and G 407, which puts it in the negative: 'He may not govern many people that cannot govern himself'.
9–12] Cf. Whiting, F 635: 'Tel no man what thou wilt do; That now is frend may be fo'.
15. cum sancto sanctus eiris] 'With the holy you will be holy' (Psalm 18: 25).
19] Cf. the proverbial refrain of 43.
21] Cf. 'sotell deth knokyd at my gate, / And on-avysed he seyd to me, chekmate!' (*CB XV*, no. 149). Metaphors from chess were popular with medieval writers; see Whiting, C 169.
25–8] Very common advice. Cf. 13–15 above, and Whiting C 395: 'Draw to such company as you would be like'.
33–4] Cf. Ecclesiasticus 21: 28: 'A whisperer defileth his own soul, and is hated wheresoever he dwelleth'.
35–6] Proverbial. Cf. Whiting, S 92: 'He that scorns other men shall not go unscorned'.
43–4] The theme is common in the Psalms; cf. Psalm 18: 1–6.

68

7. considdering not the fyne] There is a play on two senses of *fyne*: (1), end, final purpose, and (2) final event of life, death. Cf. the well-known maxim, *respice finem*, 'remember the end' (Ecclesiasticus 7: 36), and Whiting, E 84.
8] The refrain sounds proverbial, but no exact parallel has been noted. Moralists commonly warned that prosperity was delusive. Cf. Henryson, *Fables*, 291, and Whiting, P 420–23. The change of wording in 16 may be an error, *lyfe* being repeated from 14.
9–13] Dunbar alludes to specific university subjects, such as logic, rhetoric, natural philosophy, astronomy and theology.
12. dirk apperance] 'Obscure appearance'. This suggests suspicion of that branch of astronomy that we call astrology. Cf. Lindsay, *Monarche*, 674: 'dirk Iugementis of Astronomye'.
13. fablis] 'Fictions, fictitious stories'. Cf. Henryson, *Fables*, 1: 'feinȝeit fabils of ald poetre'.
15. dry] 'Wither'. The fading flower is a common emblem of mutability.
19. myrrouris] 'Models, exemplary figures'. With the imagery in 19–20, cf. Lydgate, *Testament*, 117–18 (*Minor Poems*, I): 'To eyen blynde light, lanterne and spectacle, / And bryghtest merour of alle felicite'.

20. lamps] 'Sources of light, intellectually and spiritually'. The figure is biblical; cf. II Samuel 22: 29.

22] Proverbial; cf. Whiting, W 642.

23] This recalls the role of conscience at Judgment Day; cf. 1. 123.

69
The Tabill of Confessioun

3] The speaker is praying before an image of the Crucifixion, as in the first stanza of 1.

4. meik] The rhyme with *sweit*, etc., is not imperfect. Rhymes between *k* and *t* are found elsewhere in Scottish verse; cf. Henryson, *Bludy Serk*, 81–3 (*serk* and *harte*).

8] The refrain voices the common medieval fear of dying in sin, without time to repent. Cf. **34**. 5 and **49**. 6.

18–20] Cf. the depiction of the Seven Deadly Sins in **36**.

23. Rew on me, Jesu, for thy woundis five] Cf. **167**. Devotion to the five wounds of Jesus (in his hands, feet and side) was at its height in the late fifteenth century. The wounds were regarded as a sign of his compassion for sinners; they were honoured in prayers, and depicted in paintings and other images. The cult of the wounds was commonly associated, as here, with veneration and repetition of the name of Jesus.

26–30] The corporal works of mercy were traditionally seven: feeding the hungry, giving drink to the thirsty, visiting the sick, ministering to prisoners, lodging strangers, clothing the naked and burying the dead (Matthew 25: 35–6).

33–9] The seven spiritual works of mercy were: instructing the ignorant, converting sinners, counselling the doubtful, comforting the sorrowful, praying for the living and the dead, bearing wrongs patiently and forgiving injuries.

35. distitud] Literally 'destitute', perhaps here in a strained sense, 'spiritually impoverished'.

38] This apparently refers to the patient endurance of others' wrongdoing. The phrasing, which is clumsy, seems to anticipate the next line.

42–5] In Catholic theology the sacraments were traditionally seven: eucharist, baptism, penance, confirmation, matrimony, ordination and extreme unction. Cf. Ireland's list in 'Penance' (Asloan MS, I, 77), and his detailed exposition of their significance in *The Meroure of Wyssdome* (III, 1–104). The Reformers, however, reduced the number of sacraments to two: baptism and the holy supper. MF omits most of this stanza; in Bd and B it is altered, and only two sacraments are mentioned.

49] The ten commandments had scriptural authority: Exodus 20: 1–17; Deuteronomy 5: 6–21.

57–69] The twelve articles of the Creed, traditionally composed by the twelve apostles.

73–80] Hope, faith and charity (I Corinthians 13: 13; Galatians 5: 5–6) were the theological virtues; the cardinal, or chief moral, virtues were fortitude, prudence, temperance and justice.

73. strang as wall] A common simile; cf. Whiting, W 17.

76] This image of spiritual armour against sin derives from St Paul: Ephesians 6: 13–17.

81–8] The commandments of the church were tabulated in the Middle Ages, but their number seems to have fluctuated. The seven that Dunbar lists were traditional: to pay tithes, to avoid excommunication, to observe religious feasts and days of fasting, to hear mass on Sunday, to attend the parish church, to go to confession, and to receive the eucharist once a year at Easter. The stanza is omitted by Bd, B and MF.

89] The sin against the Holy Ghost was commonly regarded as despair; cf. Chaucer, *Parson's Tale*, 692–5; and Mark 3: 29.

91. undiscreit] A good confessor should be discreet, able to distinguish between venial and mortal sins.

92] The reference is to receiving the eucharist when in a state of sin.

94] Ireland lists the gifts of the Holy Ghost as: 'the gift of wisdom of science of counsall of vnderstanding of strenth of prudence of pete and of dreid to tyne the luf and the favour of god' (Asloan MS, I, 77). The scriptural basis was Isaiah 11: 2–3.

95] The Lord's Prayer begins *pater noster*, 'Our Father'; see Matthew 6: 9–13. It was traditionally divided into seven clauses.

111. rent on rude] A traditional phrase in religious verse; cf. Henryson, *Prayer for the Pest*, 39.

133. fals seling] Attempts to pervert justice by the use of counterfeit seals.

134. sessioun] See **2**. 7 and note.

145–50] Mary Magdalene was the object of great devotion in the Middle Ages. She ranked with the apostles as a 'co-apostle', since she was the first to see the risen Christ; she was also identified with the unnamed woman who washed his feet with her tears (Luke 7 and 8). Because of her great contrition for her sin (symbolized by copious tears), she was regarded as a model for the penitent.

151–2] This refers to the doctrine that one should not receive the sacrament while in a state of sin (cf. 92).

153–9] The tone and phrasing are similar to **1**. 97–112.

161–2] Ireland similarly stresses the need to detest not only the sins one remembers but also those one has forgotten (Asloan MS, I, 12).

163–4] Ireland, discussing penance in *The Meroure of Wyssdome* (III, 61), expatiates on this theme of God's two courts: at the moment of death the soul 'enteris in the court of extreme iustice / And euir for a litle payn that wauld deliuer it heir in the court of mercy / thou sal susteyne thar excedand intollerable and inymaginable payn'.

165–6] On this traditional notion of the soul as a voyager, see **25**. 41–7 and note.

70

3. Commendis us] 'Send greetings (lit. recommend ourselves)'. It was usual to begin letters in this formulaic way.

13] Several deliveries of beer were made to the Stirling friary 'be the kingis command' (*TA*, II, 256, 269); but the friars' reception from him, in Lent 1502, of a gallon of malmsey (*TA*, II, 140) does not suggest the ascetic life.

18. stok and stone] 'Lifeless objects'. A common alliterative phrase, originally applied contemptuously to idols.

23. dirige] Matins of the Dead was known as *dirige*, from the first word of the opening antiphon, *Dirige, Deus meus, in conspectu tuo viam meam* ('Direct, O God, my life in your sight'). The word was at first trisyllabic in the vernacular, as in Latin, and this pronunciation is rhythmically excellent here and in line 28.

24. doing beseik] On the construction, see Introduction, p. 14.

31] On the nine orders of angels, see note to 48. 9–10. *ordour nyne]* The plural would be more usual, but the singular occurs elsewhere, and may be a special Scots idiom.

36. welthe and weilfair] A common phrase (repeated in 74), signifying material prosperity, or the good things of life.

38. Say ... chirritie] A pious formula, often used at the end of poems: cf. Lindsay, *Squyer Meldrum*, 1593: 'Say ʒe Amen, for cheritie'.

39. Tu autem, domine] A liturgical formula, representing *Tu autem domine miserere nobis*, 'Do thou, O Lord, have mercy on us'.

44. Iube, domine] A shortened form of *Iube domine benedicere*, 'Give blessing, O Lord', usually followed by a benediction.

47. Patriarchis] The founding fathers of Israel, especially the twelve sons of Jacob.

48. Confessouris] A term applied to saints, such as St Francis (**65.** 20), who confessed, or avowed, their faith but were not martyrs.

55–8] The importation into Scotland of Rhine wines and claret (see note to **56.** 42) is well documented. Wines from Orléans and Anjou (in the Loire region) were also popular with the Scottish court (*TA*, I, ccix–ccxi).

62. sanct Geill] St Giles, appropriately invoked, since the parish kirk of Edinburgh was dedicated to him. His feast day (1 September) was celebrated with a procession through the streets of Edinburgh. St Giles was believed to have special power in obtaining forgiveness for sinners.

70. sternis sevin] Not a constellation of stars, such as the Pleiades, but the seven planets (*OED, seven stars*). God and the saints dwelt in the highest heaven, the *coelum empyreum*, above the planets and the *primum mobile*; cf. **48.** 49 and note.

78. Gabriell] The archangel Gabriel, God's messenger, who announced the birth of John the Baptist and Jesus.

85–90] This recalls Chaucer, *Troilus and Criseyde*, I. 638–9: 'For how myghte evere swetnesse han ben knowe / To him that nevere tasted bittirnesse.'

103–118] This passage parodies the conclusion of Lauds, which was sung directly after Matins of the Dead. See *Sarum Breviary*, II, 281; also Bawcutt 1992a: 201–2.

103–4] This parodies petitions from the Paternoster.

112–13] This is the opening verse of Psalm 102, one of the Penitential Psalms, which occurs in some versions of the Office of the Dead. *Domine*, like its vernacular equivalent, 'Lord', might be addressed to a king as well as to God. Dunbar hints that James alone can authorize the court's departure from Stirling.

Index of Titles and Refrains

Some readers may be more familiar with Dunbar's poems under the titles devised for them by Kinsley and other editors since the eighteenth century. This index lists the more common titles given to these poems, together with the refrains that provide the basis for many of them. Italics indicate titles that occur in an early witness; R indicates a refrain.

Abbreviations and Bibliography

Abbreviations

A	Asloan Manuscript.
Ab	Aberdeen Sasine Register.
Ar	Arundel Manuscript.
B	Bannatyne Manuscript.
Bd	Bannatyne Draft Manuscript.
Beard	C. R. Beard, *Dictionary of Costume and Armour*, unpublished MS, copy in *DOST* office.
CB XIV	Carleton Brown (ed.), *Religious Lyrics of the Fourteenth Century*, Oxford, 1957.
CB XV	Carleton Brown (ed.), *Religious Lyrics of the Fifteenth Century*, Oxford, 1939.
CM	Chepman and Myllar prints.
CSD	*The Concise Scots Dictionary*.
CT	*The Canterbury Tales*.
DOST	*A Dictionary of the Older Scottish Tongue*.
EETS: ES, OS	Early English Text Society: extra series, original series.
IMEV	*Index of Middle English Verse*.
Kinsley	James Kinsley (ed.), *The Poems of William Dunbar*, Oxford, 1979.
Laing	David Laing (ed.), *The Poems of William Dunbar*, Edinburgh, 1834; supplement, 1865.
Mackenzie	W. Mackay Mackenzie (ed.), *The Poems of William Dunbar*, London, 1932; rev. edn 1960.
ME	Middle English.

MED	*Middle English Dictionary*.
MF	Maitland Folio.
MS	Manuscript.
OED	*The Oxford English Dictionary*.
P	Early Scottish print (? 1507).
R	Reidpeth Manuscript.
Schipper	J. S. Schipper (ed.), *The Poems of William Dunbar*, Vienna, 1892–94.
Small	J. Small, with W. Gregor and AE. J. G. Mackay (eds), *The Poems of William Dunbar*, STS, 1884–93.
SND	*The Scottish National Dictionary*.
STS	Scottish Text Society.
TA, Treasurer's Accounts	*Accounts of the Lord High Treasurer of Scotland*, ed. T. Dickson and J. Balfour Paul, 4 vols, Edinburgh, 1877–1902.

Bibliography I: primary texts

Ailsa Muniments, SRO GD. 25 (Register House, Edinburgh).

Alan of Lille, *De Planctu Naturae*, trans. J. L. Sheridan, Toronto, 1980.

Alliterative Poetry of the Later Middle Ages, ed. Thorlac Turville-Petre, London, 1989.

Asloan Manuscript, The, ed. W. A. Craigie, 2 vols, STS, 1923–5.

Augustine, Saint, *On Christian Doctrine*, trans. D. W. Robertson, New York, 1958.

Awntyrs off Arthure, The, ed. Ralph Hanna III, Manchester, 1974.

Bannatyne Facsimile, The Bannatyne Manuscript, introd. D. Fox and W. A. Ringler, Scolar Press, London, 1980.

Bannatyne Manuscript, The, ed. W. Tod Ritchie, 4 vols, STS, 1928–34. (Cited by folio.)

Barbour, John, *Barbour's Bruce*, ed. M. P. McDiarmid and J. A. C. Stevenson, 3 vols, STS, 1980–85.

Bartholomaeus Anglicus, *On the Properties of Things*, trans. John Trevisa, ed. M. C. Seymour *et al.*, Oxford, 1975. (Cited by book and chapter.)

Blamires, Alcuin (ed.), *Woman Defamed and Woman Defended: an Anthology of Medieval Texts*, Oxford, 1992.

Bower, Walter, *Scotichronicon in Latin and English*, ed. D. E. R. Watt *et al.*, Aberdeen and Edinburgh, 1987–. (Cited by book and chapter. Seven of a projected nine volumes have been published.)

Burrow, John (ed.), *English Verse 1300–1500*, London, 1977.

Carmichaell, James, *The James Carmichaell Collection of Proverbs in Scots*, ed. M. L. Anderson, Edinburgh, 1957.

Caxton, William, *The History of Reynard the Fox*, ed. N. F. Blake, EETS: OS 263, 1970.

Chaucer, Geoffrey, *The Riverside Chaucer*, ed. L. D. Benson, Oxford, 1988.

Chepman and Myllar Prints: A Facsimile, The, introd. William Beattie, Edinburgh, 1950.

Clanvowe, John, *The Works of Sir John Clanvowe*, ed. V. J. Scattergood, Cambridge, 1965.

Clariodus: A Metrical Romance, 3 vols, Maitland Club, Edinburgh, 1830.

Colkelbie Sow and the Talis of the Fyve Bestes, ed. Gregory Kratzmann, New York, 1983.

Complaynt of Scotland, The, introd. A. M. Stewart, STS, 1979.

Crying of ane Play, The. In *Bannatyne Manuscript*, ff. 118^v–119^r.

Deschamps, Eustache, *Oeuvres complètes*, ed. Q. de Saint-Hilaire and G. Raynaud, Paris, 1878–1903.

Devotional Pieces in Verse and Prose, ed. J. A. W. Bennett, STS, 1955.

Dialoges of Creatures Moralysed, The, ed. Gregory Kratzmann and Elizabeth Gee, Leiden, 1988.

Douglas, *Eneados. Virgil's Aeneid Translated by Gavin Douglas*, ed. D. F. C. Coldwell, 4 vols, STS, 1957–64.

Douglas, *Palice of Honour*. In *Shorter Poems*.

Douglas, Gavin, *The Shorter Poems of Gavin Douglas*, ed. Priscilla J. Bawcutt, STS, 1967.

Everyman, ed. A. C. Cawley, Manchester, 1961.

Fergusson's Scottish Proverbs from the Original Print of 1641, ed. Erskine Beveridge, STS, 1924.

Floure and the Leafe, The, ed. Derek Pearsall, London, 1962.

Geoffrey of Monmouth, *History of the Kings of Britain*, trans. Lewis Thorpe, London, 1969. (Cited by book and chapter.)

Golagros and Gawane. In *Scottish Alliterative Poems*, ed. F. J. Amours, STS, 1897.

Gower, John, *The Works*, ed. G. C. Macaulay, Oxford, 1899–1902.

Greene, R. L. (ed.), *The Early English Carols*, Oxford, 1935; 2nd edn 1977.

Gude and Godlie Ballatis, The, ed. A. F. Mitchell, STS, 1897.

Hary's Wallace, ed. M. P. McDiarmid, 2 vols, STS, 1968–69.

Hay, Gilbert, *The Buik of King Alexander the Conquerour*, ed. John Cartwright, 2 vols, STS, 1986–90. (Vol. I, containing Introduction and Glossary, forthcoming.)

Hay, Gilbert, *The Prose Works of Sir Gilbert Hay*, ed. J. A. Glenn, STS, 1993–. (Vol. III contains *The Buke of the Ordre of Knychthede* and *The Buke of the Gouernaunce of Princis*.)

Henryson, Robert, *The Poems*, ed. D. Fox, Oxford, 1981.

Higden, Ranulf, *Polychronicon*, ed. C. Babington and J. R. Lumby, 9 vols, Rolls Series, London, 1865–86. (Cited by volume and page.)

Hoccleve, Thomas, *The Minor Poems*, ed. F. J. Furnivall and I. Gollancz, EETS: ES, 61, 73, 1970.

Holland, Richard, *The Buke of the Howlat*. In *Longer Scottish Poems I*.

Ipomadon, ed. E. Kölbing, Breslau, 1889.

Ireland, John, *The Meroure of Wyssdome*: vol. I (books 1–2), ed. C. Macpherson, STS, 1926; vol. II (books 3–5), ed. F. Quinn, 1965; vol. III (books 6–7), ed. Craig McDonald, 1990.

Kennedy, Walter, *The Passioun of Crist*. In *Devotional Pieces in Verse and Prose*.

King Berdok. In *Bannatyne Manuscript*, ff. 142^v–143^r.

King Hart. In Douglas, *Shorter Poems*.

Kingis Quair, The, ed. J. Norton-Smith, Oxford, 1971; Leiden, 1981.

Knox, John, *John Knox's History of the Reformation in Scotland*, ed. W. Croft Dickinson, 2 vols, London, 1949.

Lancelot of the Laik, ed. Margaret M. Gray, STS, 1912.

Langland, William, *The Vision of Piers Plowman: The B-Text*, ed. A. V. C. Schmidt, London, 1978.

Lay of Sorrow, The, ed. K. G. Wilson, *Speculum*, vol. xxix (1954), pp. 708–26.

Leland, John (with additions by Thomas Hearne), *De Rebus Britannicis Collectanea*, London, 1774.

Leslie, John, *The History of Scotland*, Bannatyne Club, 1830.

Lindsay, Sir David, *The Works*, ed. D. Hamer, STS, 1931–36.

Longer Scottish Poems I: 1375–1650, ed. P. Bawcutt and F. Riddy, Edinburgh, 1987.

Lydgate, John, *Lydgate's Fall of Princes*, ed. H. Bergen, EETS: ES, 121–4, 1924–7.

Lydgate, John, *The Minor Poems*, ed. H. N. MacCracken, Parts I and II, EETS: ES, 107, 1911, and OS, 192, 1934.

Maitland Folio, The, ed. W. A. Craigie, 2 vols, STS, 1919–27.

Maitland, Sir Richard. Poems cited by number from *Maitland Folio*.

Metham, John, *Works*, ed. H. Craig, EETS: OS, 132, 1916.

Minot, Lawrence, *Poems*, ed. J. Hall, Oxford, 1914.

Montgomerie, Alexander, *The Poems of Alexander Montgomerie*, ed. J. Cranstoun, STS, 1887.

Parlement of the Thre Ages, The. In *Alliterative Poetry of the Later Middle Ages*.

Pearl, ed. E. V. Gordon, Oxford, 1953.

Penguin Book of Latin Verse, The, ed. F. Brittain, Harmondsworth, 1962.

Pierce the Ploughman's Crede. In *The Piers Plowman Tradition*, ed. H. Barr, London, 1993.

Piers Plowman. See Langland.

Pistel of Susan, A. In *Alliterative Poetry of the Later Middle Ages*.

Pitscottie, Robert Lindesay of, *The Historie and Cronicles of Scotland*, ed. AE. J. G. Mackay, 3 vols, STS, 1899–1911.

Ratis Raving and Other Early Scots Poems on Morals, ed. Ritchie Girvan, STS, 1939.

Rauf Coilyear. In *Longer Scottish Poems I*.

Reson and Sensuallyte, ed. Ernst Sieper, EETS: ES, 84, 89, 1901–1903.

Rolland, John, *The Court of Venus*, ed. Rev. W. Gregor, STS, 1884.

Roxburghe Ballads, ed. W. Chappell, 9 vols, London, 1871–99.

Sarum Breviary, ed. F. Proctor and C. Wordsworth, 3 vols, Cambridge, 1879–86.

Sarum Missal, The, ed. J. Wickham Legg, Oxford, 1916; 1969.

Satirical Poems of the Time of the Reformation, ed. J. Cranstoun, 2 vols, STS, 1891–93.

Scott, Alexander, *The Poems*, ed. J. Cranstoun, STS, 1896.

Secular Lyrics of the XIV and XV Centuries, ed. R. H. Robbins, Oxford, 1952.

Sir Gawain and the Green Knight, ed. Norman Davis, 2nd edn, Oxford, 1979.

John Skelton: The Complete English Poems, ed. J. Scattergood, London, 1983.

Stewart, William, *The Buik of the Croniclis of Scotland*, ed. W. B. Turnbull, Rolls Series, London, 1858.

Tayis Bank. In *Bannatyne Manuscript*, f. 229^r.

Tilley, M. P., *A Dictionary of the Proverbs in England in the Sixteenth and Seventeenth Centuries*, London, 1950.

Thre Prestis of Peblis, The, ed. T. D. Robb, STS, 1920.

Towneley Plays, The, ed. G. England and A. W. Pollard, EETS: ES, 71, 1897.

Two Fifteenth Century Cookery Books, ed. T. Austin, EETS: OS, 91, 1888.

Whiting, B. J., with H. W. Whiting, *Proverbs, Sentences, and Proverbial Phrases from English Writings Mainly before 1500*, London, 1968.

Winchester Anthology, The, introd. Edward Wilson and I. Fenlon, Cambridge, 1981.

Wynnere and Wastoure. In *Alliterative Poetry of the Later Middle Ages*.

Wyntoun, Andrew, *The Original Chronicle*, ed. F. J. Amours, 6 vols, STS, 1903–14.

Bibliography II: secondary works

Aitken, A. J. (1971), 'Variation and Variety in Written Middle Scots', in A. J. Aitken, A. McIntosh and H. Palsson (eds), *Edinburgh Studies in English and Scots*, London, pp. 177–209.

——— (1977), 'How to Pronounce Older Scots', in A. J. Aitken, M. P.

McDiarmid and D. S. Thomson (eds), *Bards and Makars*, Glasgow, pp. 1–21.

—— (1983), 'The Language of Older Scots Poetry', in J. D. McClure (ed.), *Scotland and the Lowland Tongue*, Aberdeen, pp. 18–49.

Anglo, S. (1992), *Images of Tudor Kingship*, London.

Archibald, Elizabeth (1981), 'William Dunbar and the Medieval Tradition of Parody', in Lyall and Riddy (1981), pp. 328–44.

—— (1992), 'Tradition and Innovation in the Macaronic Poetry of Dunbar and Skelton', *Modern Language Quarterly*, vol. liii, pp. 126–49.

Armour, Peter (1989), *Dante's Griffin and the History of the World*, Oxford.

Auden, W. H. (1933), Review of Mackenzie, *The Criterion*, vol. xii, pp. 676–8.

Aulén, Gustaf (1970), *Christus Victor*, London.

Barron, W. R. J. (1965), 'Luf-Daungere', in F. Whitehead (ed.), *Medieval Miscellany Presented to Eugene Vinaver*, Manchester, pp. 1–18.

Barrow, G. W. S. (ed.) (1974), *The Scottish Tradition: Essays in Honour of R. G. Cant*, Edinburgh.

Bawcutt, Priscilla (1972), 'The Lark in Chaucer and Some Later Poets', *Yearbook of English Studies*, vol, ii, pp. 5–12.

—— (1974), 'Aspects of Dunbar's Imagery', in Beryl Rowland (ed.), *Chaucer and Middle English Studies*, London, pp. 190–200.

—— (1976), *Gavin Douglas: A Critical Study*, Edinburgh.

—— (1981), 'The Text and Interpretation of Dunbar', *Medium Aevum*, vol. l, pp. 88–100.

—— (1983), 'The Art of Flyting', *Scottish Literary Journal*, vol. x, no. 2, pp. 5–24.

—— (1986a), 'Dunbar's Christmas Carol', in D. Strauss and H. W. Drescher (eds), *Scottish Language and Literature, Medieval and Renaissance* (Scottish Studies, 4), Frankfurt, pp. 381–92.

—— (1986b), 'Dunbar's Use of the Symbolic Lion and Thistle', *Cosmos*, vol. ii, pp. 83–97.

—— (1987), 'Dunbar: New Light on Old Words', in C. Macafee and I. Macleod (eds), *The Nuttis Schell: Essays on the Scots Language*, Aberdeen, pp. 83–95.

—— (1988a), 'A Medieval Scottish Elegy and its French Original', *Scottish Literary Journal*, vol. xv, no. 1, pp. 5–13.

—— (1988b), 'A Miniature Anglo-Scottish Flyting', *Notes and Queries*, vol. ccxxxiii, pp. 441–4.

—— (1991), 'The Earliest Texts of Dunbar', in F. Riddy (ed.), *Regionalism in Late Medieval Manuscripts and Texts*, Woodbridge, pp. 183–98.

—— (1992a), *Dunbar the Makar*, Oxford.

———— (1992b), 'Images of Women in the Poems of Dunbar', *Etudes Ecossaises*, vol. i, pp. 49–58.

Baxter, J. W. (1952), *William Dunbar: A Biographical Study*, Edinburgh, 1952.

Bennett, J. A. W. (1965), *The Parlement of Foules*, Oxford.

———— (1982), *Poetry of the Passion*, Oxford.

Bitterling, Klaus (1983), 'William Dunbar's *The Maner of Passyng to Confession* and the "Circumstances" of the Medieval Confessional', *Notes and Queries*, vol. ccxxviii, pp. 389–91.

———— (1986), '*The Tretis of the Tua Mariit Wemen and the Wedo*: Some Comments on Words, Imagery, and Genre', in D. Strauss and H. W. Drescher (eds), *Scottish Language and Literature, Medieval and Renaissance* (Scottish Studies, 4), Frankfurt, pp. 337–58.

Bloomfield, M. W. (1952), *The Seven Deadly Sins*, Michigan.

Bowers, R. H. (1955), 'Three Middle English Poems on the Apostles' Creed', *PMLA*, vol. lxx, pp. 210–22.

Boyle, Leonard E., OP (1985), 'The Fourth Lateran Council and Manuals of Popular Theology', in T. J. Heffernan (ed.), *The Popular Literature of Medieval England*, Knoxville, Tenn., pp. 30–43.

Buchanan, P. (1985), *Margaret Tudor: Queen of Scots*, Edinburgh.

Bullock-Davies, Constance (1978), *Menestrellorum Multitudo: Minstrels at a Royal Feast*, Cardiff.

Burness, Edwina (1986), 'Female Language in … *The Tua Mariit Wemen and the Wedo*', in D. Strauss and H. Drescher (eds), *Scottish Language and Literature, Medieval and Renaissance* (Scottish Studies, 4), Frankfurt, pp. 359–68.

Burnett, Charles (1977–78), 'The Development of the Royal Arms to 1603', *Journal of the Heraldry Society of Scotland*, vol. i, pp. 9–19.

———— (1983), 'The Thistle as a Symbol', in *The Thistles of Scotland*, Glasgow Museums and Art Galleries, pp. 8–13.

Burrow, J. A. (1978), 'A Further Note on Dunbar', *Forum for Modern Language Studies*, vol. xiv, pp. 85–6.

———— (1979), '"Young Saint, Old Devil": Reflections on a Medieval Proverb', *Review of English Studies*, n.s. vol. xxx, pp. 385–96.

———— (1981), 'The Poet as Petitioner', *Studies in the Age of Chaucer*, vol. iii, pp. 61–75.

———— (1983), '*Sir Thopas* in the Sixteenth Century', in D. Gray and E. G. Stanley (eds), *Middle English Studies Presented to Norman Davis*, Oxford, pp. 69–91.

———— (1986), *The Ages of Man: A Study in Medieval Writing and Thinking*, Oxford.

Conlee, John W. (ed.) (1991), *Middle English Debate Poetry: A Critical Anthology*, East Lansing and Woodbridge.

Cruttwell, P. (1954), 'Two Scots Poets', in Boris Ford (ed.), *The Age of Chaucer*, London, pp. 175–87.

Cummins, John (1988), *The Hound and the Hawk: The Art of Medieval Hunting*, London.

Cunningham, I. C. (1994), 'The Asloan Manuscript', in *The Renaissance in Scotland: Studies in Literature, Religion, History and Culture*, ed. A. A. MacDonald, M. Lynch and I. B. Cowan, Leiden, pp. 107–35.

Curry, Walter (1923), 'Fortuna Maior', *Modern Language Notes*, vol. xxxviii, 94–6.

Curtius, E. R. (1953), *European Literature and the Latin Middle Ages*, trans. W. R. Trask, London.

Davenport, W. A. (1991), 'Bird Poems from *The Parliament of Fowls* to *Philip Sparrow*', in J. Boffey and J. Cowen (eds), *Chaucer and Fifteenth-Century Poetry*, London, pp. 66–83.

De Comminges, Elie (ed.) (1976), *Traité sur l'Art de la Guerre de Bérault Stuart*, The Hague.

Dickinson, W. C. (1977), *Scotland from the Earliest Times to 1603*, 3rd edn, rev. A. Duncan, Oxford.

Diehl, P. S. (1985), *The Medieval European Religious Lyric*, London.

Dobson, E. J., and Ingham, P. (1967), 'Three Notes on Dunbar's *The Tua Mariit Wemen and the Wedo*', *Medium Aevum*, vol. xxxvi, pp. 58–9.

Dobson, R. B., and Taylor, J. (1989), *Rymes of Robyn Hood: An Introduction to the English Outlaw*, Gloucester.

Donaldson, Gordon (1960), *The Scottish Reformation*, Cambridge.

Dove, Mary (1986), *The Perfect Age of Man's Life*, Cambridge.

Drexler, R. D. (1978), 'Dunbar's "Lament for the Makaris" and the Dance of Death Tradition', *Studies in Scottish Literature*, vol. xiii, pp. 144–58.

Ebin, Lois (1972), 'The Theme of Poetry in Dunbar's "Goldyn Targe"', *Chaucer Review*, vol. vii, pp. 147–59.

—— (1979–80), 'Dunbar's Bawdy', *Chaucer Review*, vol. xiv, pp. 278–86.

—— (1988), *Illuminator Makar Vates: Visions of Poetry in the Fifteenth Century*, Lincoln, Nebr.

Eddy, E. R. (1971), 'Sir Thopas and Sir Thomas Norny: Romance Parody in Chaucer and Dunbar', *Review of English Studies*, n.s. vol. xxii, pp. 401–9.

Edwards, Paul (1992), 'The Early African Presence in the British Isles', in J. S. Gundara and I. Duffield (eds), *Essays on the History of Blacks in Britain*, Aldershot, pp. 9–29.

Eliot, T. S. (1957), *On Poetry and Poets*, London.

Emmerson, Richard K. (1981), *Antichrist in the Middle Ages*, Manchester.

Fowler, Alastair (1970), *Triumphal Forms: Structural Patterns in Elizabethan Poetry*, Cambridge.

Fox, Denton (1959), 'Dunbar's *The Golden Targe*', *ELH*, vol. xxvi, pp. 311–34.

—— (1960), 'The Chronology of William Dunbar', *Philological Quarterly*, vol. xxxix, pp. 413–25.

—— (1966), 'The Scottish Chaucerians', in D. S. Brewer (ed.), *Chaucer and Chaucerians*, London, pp. 164–200.

Fradenburg, Louise (1991), *City, Marriage, Tournament: Arts of Rule in Late Medieval Scotland*, Madison, Wis.

Geddie, William (1912), *A Bibliography of Middle Scots Poets*, STS.

Gilbert, J. M. (1979), *Hunting and Hunting Reserves in Medieval Scotland*, Edinburgh.

Gillies, W. (1988), 'Gaelic: The Classical Tradition', in *The History of Scottish Literature I: Origins to 1660*, ed. R. D. S. Jack, Aberdeen, pp. 245–62.

Goldstein, R. James (1987), '"For he wald Usurpe na Fame": Andrew of Wyntoun's Use of the Modesty Topos and Literary Culture in Early Fifteenth Century Scotland', *Scottish Literary Journal*, vol. xiv, no. 1, pp. 5–18.

Gray, Douglas (1972), *Themes and Images in the Medieval English Religious Lyric*, London.

—— (1974), 'A Scottish "Flower of Chivalry" and his Book', *Words*, vol. iv, pp. 22–34.

—— (1984), 'Rough Music: Some Early Invectives and Flytings', *Yearbook of English Studies*, vol. xiv, pp. 21–43.

Green, Richard F. (1980), *Poets and Princepleasers*, Toronto.

Hay, Bryan S. (1973–74), 'William Dunbar's Flying Abbot: Apocalypse Made to Order', *Studies in Scottish Literature*, vol. xi, pp. 217–25.

Heaney, M. (1989), 'Kingston to Kenilworth: Early Plebeian Morris', *Folklore*, vol. c, pp. 88–104.

Hill, Thomas D. (1978), 'Dunbar's Giant: "On the Resurrection of Christ", Lines 17–24', *Anglia*, vol. xcix, pp. 451–6.

Holmyard, E. J. (1957), *Alchemy*, London.

Hughes, J., and Ramson, W. S. (1982), *Poetry of the Stewart Court*, Canberra.

Hyde, I (1956), 'Primary Sources and Associations of Dunbar's Aureate Imagery', *Modern Language Review*, vol. li, pp. 481–92.

Jack, R. D. S. (ed.) (1988), *The History of Scottish Literature I: Origins to 1660*, Aberdeen.

Janson, H. W. (1952), *Apes and Ape Lore*, London.

Jones, G. F. (1953), '"Christis Kirk", "Peblis to the Play" and the German Peasant-Brawl', *PMLA*, vol. lxviii, pp. 1101–25.

Jung, A. (1989), 'William Dunbar and the Morris Dancers', in D. McClure and M. Spiller (eds), *Bryght Lanternis: Essays on the Language and Literature of Medieval and Renaissance Scotland*, Aberdeen, pp. 221–243.

Kolve, V. A. (1984), *Chaucer and the Imagery of Narrative*, London.

Kratzmann, Gregory (1980), *Anglo-Scottish Literary Relations 1430–1550*, Cambridge.

Lampe, D. (1979), '"Flyting no Reason hath": The Inverted Rhetoric of Abuse', in A. S. Bernardo (ed.), *The Early Renaissance*, New York, pp. 101–20.

Lehmann, P. (1963), *Die Parodie im Mittelalter*, 2nd edn, Stuttgart.

Lewis, C. S. (1936), *The Allegory of Love*, Oxford.

Lyall, R. J. (1974a), 'Moral Allegory in Dunbar's "Goldyn Targe"', *Studies in Scottish Literature*, vol. xi, pp. 47–65.

—— (1974b), 'Some Observations on the *Dregy of Dunbar*', *Parergon*, vol. ix, pp. 40–43.

—— (1974c), 'William Dunbar's Beast Fable', *Scottish Literary Journal*, vol. i, pp. 17–28.

—— (1976a), 'Politics and Poetry in Fifteenth and Sixteenth Century Scotland', *Scottish Literary Journal*, vol. iii, no. 2, pp. 5–29.

—— (1976b), 'Two of Dunbar's Makars: James Afflek and Sir John the Ross', *Innes Review*, vol. xxvii, pp. 99–109.

—— (1977), 'Dunbar and the Franciscans', *Medium Aevum*, vol. xlvi, pp. 253–8.

—— (1983), 'Complaint, Satire and Invective in Middle Scots Literature', in N. Macdougall (ed.), *Church, Politics and Society: Scotland 1408–1929*, Edinburgh, pp. 44–63.

—— (1991), 'The Court as a Cultural Centre', in Wormald (1991), pp. 36–48.

—— and Riddy, F. (eds) (1981), *Proceedings of the Third International Conference on Scottish Language and Literature (Medieval and Renaissance)*, Stirling and Glasgow.

Lynch, Michael (1981), *Edinburgh and the Reformation*, London.

—— (1992), *Scotland: A New History*, London.

——, Spearman, M., and Stell, G. (eds) (1988), *The Scottish Medieval Town*, Edinburgh.

Macafee, Caroline (1981), 'A Stylistic Analysis of Dunbar's "In Winter"', in R. J. Lyall and F. Riddy (eds), *Proceedings of the Third International Conference on Scottish Language and Literature*, Stirling and Glasgow, pp. 359–69.

—— (1992–93), 'A Short Grammar of Older Scots', *Scottish Language*, nos. 11–12, pp. 10–36.

McArthur, T. (ed.) (1992), *The Oxford Companion to the English Language*, Oxford.

MacDiarmid, Hugh (1927), *Albyn, or Scotland and the Future*, London.

McDiarmid, M. P. (1980), 'The Early William Dunbar and his Poems', *Scottish Historical Review*, vol. lix, pp. 126–39.

MacDonald, A. A. (1983), 'Poetry, Politics and Reformation Censorship in Sixteenth-Century Scotland', *English Studies*, vol. lxiv, pp. 410–21.

—— (1987), 'William Dunbar, Mediaeval Cosmography, and the Alleged First Reference to the New World in English Literature', *English Studies*, vol. lxviii, pp. 377–91.

Macdougall, Norman (1982), *James III: A Political Study*, Edinburgh.

—— (1989), *James IV*, Edinburgh.

—— (1991), 'The Kingship of James IV of Scotland', in Wormald (1991), pp. 25–35.

Macfarlane, Leslie (1960), 'The Book of Hours of James IV and Margaret Tudor', *Innes Review*, vol. xi, pp. 3–21.

—— (1985), *William Elphinstone and the Kingdom of Scotland 1431–1514*, Aberdeen.

McGladdery, Christine (1990), *James II*, Edinburgh.

McKay, Denis (1962), 'Parish Life in Scotland 1500–1560', in *Essays on the Scottish Reformation 1513–1625*, ed. D. McRoberts, Glasgow, pp. 85–115.

McKenna, S. R. (1989), 'Drama and Invective: Traditions in Dunbar's "Fasternis Evin in Hell"', *Studies in Scottish Literature*, vol. xxiv, pp. 129–41.

Mackie, R. L. (1958), *King James IV of Scotland*, Edinburgh.

Maclaine, A. H. (1964), 'The *Christis Kirk* Tradition: Its Evolution in Scots Poetry to Burns', *Studies in Scottish Literature*, vol. ii, pp. 3–18.

MacQueen, John (1970), *Ballattis of Lufe*, Edinburgh.

MacQueen, Hector L. (1982), 'The Brieve of Right in Scots Law', *Journal of Legal History*, vol. iii, pp. 52–70.

—— (1991), 'The Laws of Galloway: A Preliminary Study', in *Galloway: Land and Lordship*, ed. R. D. Oram and G. P. Stell, Edinburgh, pp. 131–43.

—— (1993), *Common Law and Feudal Society in Medieval Scotland*, Edinburgh.

Mapstone, Sally (1986), 'The Advice to Princes Tradition in Scottish Literature 1450–1500', D.Phil. diss., Oxford.

—— (1991), 'Was there a Court Literature in Fifteenth-Century Scotland?', *Studies in Scottish Literature*, vol. xxvi, pp. 410–22.

—— (1994), 'The Scots *Buke of Phisnomy* and Sir Gilbert Hay', in *The Renaissance in Scotland: Studies in Literature, Religion, History and Culture*, ed. A. A. MacDonald, M. Lynch and I. B. Cowan, Leiden, pp. 1–44.

Martineau-Génieys, C. (1978), *Le Thème de la mort dans la poésie française de 1450 à 1550*, Paris.

Metcalf, D. M. (1977), *Coinage in Medieval Scotland*, British Archaeological Report, 45, Oxford.

Mill, Anna J. (1927), *Mediaeval Plays in Scotland*, Edinburgh.

Munro, Jean (1981), 'The Lordship of the Isles', in L. Maclean (ed.), *The Middle Ages in the Highlands*, Inverness, pp. 23–37.

—— and Munro, R. W. (eds) (1986), *Acts of the Lords of the Isles 1336–1493*, Scottish History Society, Edinburgh.

Murison, D. D. (1974), 'Linguistic Relationships in Medieval Scotland', in G. W. S. Barrow (ed.), *The Scottish Tradition: Essays in Honour of R. G. Cant*, Edinburgh, pp. 70–83.

Nicholson, Ranald (1974), *Scotland: The Later Middle Ages*, Edinburgh.

Norman, Joanne S. (1981), 'Thematic Implications of Parody in William Dunbar's "Dregy"', in R. J. Lyall and F. Riddy (eds), *Proceedings of the Third International Conference on Scottish Language and Literature*, Stirling and Glasgow, pp. 345–58.

—— (1989a), 'Sources for the Grotesque in William Dunbar's "Dance of the Sevin Deidly Synnis"', *Scottish Studies*, vol. xxix, pp. 55–75.

—— (1989b), 'William Dunbar: Grand Rhétoriqueur', in *Bryght Lanternis: Essays on the Language and Literature of Medieval and Renaissance Scotland*, ed. J. D. McClure and M. R. G. Spiller, Aberdeen, pp. 179–193.

O'Connor, Sister M. (1942), *The Art of Dying Well: The Development of the Ars Moriendi*, New York.

Orme, Nicholas (1984), *From Childhood to Chivalry*, London.

Oruch, Jack B. (1981), 'St Valentine and Spring in February', *Speculum*, vol. lvi, pp. 534–65.

Owen, D. D. R. (1970), *The Vision of Hell: Infernal Journeys in Medieval French Literature*, London.

Owst, G. R. (1933; rev. edn 1961), *Literature and Pulpit in Medieval England*, Oxford.

Panofsky, Erwin (1962), *Studies in Iconology: Humanistic Themes in the Art of the Renaissance*, New York.

Parkinson (1986), 'Mobbing Scenes in Middle Scots Verse: Holland, Douglas, Dunbar', *Journal of English and Germanic Philology*, vol. lxxxv, pp. 494–509.

Patch, Howard R. (1967), *The Goddess Fortuna in Mediaeval Literature*, London.

Pearcy, R. (1980), 'The Genre of Dunbar's *Tretis of the Tua Mariit Wemen and the Wedo*', *Speculum*, vol. lv, pp. 58–74.

Pfeffer, Wendy (1985), *The Change of Philomel: The Nightingale in Medieval Literature*, New York.

Pickering, F. P. (1970), *Literature and Art in the Middle Ages*, London.

Read, John (1938–46), 'Alchemy under James IV of Scotland', *Ambix*, vol. ii, pp. 60–67.

Reiss, Edmund (1979), *William Dunbar*, Boston, Mass.

Rice, W. H. (1941), *The European Ancestry of Villon's Satirical Testaments*, New York.

Riddy, F. (1988), 'The Alliterative Revival', in R. D. S. Jack (ed.), *The History of Scottish Literature: Origins to 1660*, pp. 39–54.

Ridley, Florence H. (1973), 'Middle Scots Writers', *A Manual of the Writings in Middle English 1050–1500*, ed. A. E. Hartung, vol. iv, New Haven, Conn.

Rigg, A. G. (1963), 'William Dunbar: The "Fenyeit Freir"', *Review of English Studies*, n.s. vol. xiv, pp. 269–73.

Robbins, R. H. (1969), 'John Crophil's Ale-Pots', *Review of English Studies*, n.s. vol. xx, pp. 182–8.

Rollins, Hyder E. (1924), 'An Analytic Index to the Ballad-Entries in the Register of the Company of Stationers of London', *Studies in Philology*, vol. xxi, pp. 1–324.

Rosie, Alison (1989), '"Morisques" and "Momeryes": Aspects of Court Entertainment at the Court of Savoy in the Fifteenth Century', in C. Allmand (ed.), *Power, Culture and Religion in France c. 1350–1550*, Woodbridge, pp. 57–74.

Ross, Ian S. (1981), *William Dunbar*, Leiden.

Roth, Elizabeth (1981), 'Criticism and Taste: Readings of Dunbar's *Tretis*', *Scottish Literary Journal*, Supplement 15, pp. 57–90.

Sanderson, Margaret H. B. (1987), *Mary Stewart's People*, Edinburgh.

Sandison, Helen E. (1913), *The Chanson d'Aventure in Middle English*, Bryn Mawr, Penn.

Scammell, G. V., and Rogers, H. L. (1957), 'An Elegy on Henry VII', *Review of English Studies*, n.s. vol. viii, pp. 167–70.

Scheps, Walter, and Looney, J. A. (1986), *Middle Scots Poets: A Reference Guide to James I, Robert Henryson, William Dunbar and Gavin Douglas*, Boston, Mass.

Scott, Tom (1966), *Dunbar: A Critical Exposition of the Poems*, Edinburgh.

Sellar, D. (1984), 'Courtesy, Battle and the Brieve of Right, 1368: A Story Continued', *Stair Society Miscellany II*, pp. 1–12.

—— (1986), 'Bauchlis', *Scottish Literary Journal*, vol. xiii, no. 2, pp. 90–91.

Shuffelton, F. (1975), 'An Imperial Flower: Dunbar's *The Goldyn Targe* and the Court Life of James IV of Scotland', *Studies in Philology*, vol. lxxii, pp. 193–207.

Singh, C. (1974), 'The Alliterative Ancestry of Dunbar's "The Tretis of the Tua Mariit Wemen and the Wedo"', *Leeds Studies in English*, n.s. vol. vii, pp. 22–54.

Smith, Janet M. (1934), *The French Background of Middle Scots Literature*, Edinburgh.

Snyder, F. B. (1910), '*Sir Thomas Norray* and *Sir Thopas*', *Modern Language Notes*, vol. xxv, pp. 78–80.

Spearing, A. C. (1976), *Medieval Dream-Poetry*, Cambridge.

—— (1985), *Medieval to Renaissance in English Poetry*, Cambridge.

Stevens, John (1961; 1979), *Music and Poetry in the Early Tudor Court*, Cambridge.

Stewart M. (1972), 'Holland of the Howlat', *Innes Review*, vol. xxiii, pp. 3–15.

Swenson, K. (1989), 'Mary as Wall in Dunbar's "Ane Ballat of Our Lady"', *English Language Notes*, vol. xxvii, pp. 1–6.

Szittya, Penn R. (1986), *The Antifraternal Tradition in Medieval Literature*, Princeton, NJ.

Tentler, Thomas N. (1977), *Sin and Confession on the Eve of the Reformation*, Princeton, NJ.

Ting, J. (1987), 'A Reappraisal of William Dunbar's *Dregy*', *Scottish Literary Journal*, vol. xiv, no. 1, pp. 19–36.

Turville-Petre, Thorlac (1977), *The Alliterative Revival*, Cambridge.

—— (1988), 'The Author of *The Destruction of Troy*', *Medium Aevum*, vol. lvii, pp. 264–9.

Utley, Francis L. (1944; 1970), *The Crooked Rib: An Analytic Index to the Argument about Women*, New York.

—— (1972), 'Dialogues, Debates and Catechisms', *A Manual of the Writings in Middle English*, vol. iii, ed. A. E. Hartung, New Haven, Conn.

Walther, Hans (1920; 1984), *Das Streitgedicht in der Lateinischen Literatur der Mittelalters*, Munich.

Wenzel, S. (1967), *The Sin of Sloth: Acedia in Medieval Thought and Literature*, Chapel Hill, NC.

—— (1974), 'The Source of Chaucer's Seven Deadly Sins', *Traditio*, vol. xxx, pp. 351–78.

—— (1986), *Preachers, Poets and the Early English Lyric*, Princeton, NJ.

Williams, A. (1953), 'Chaucer and the Friars', *Speculum*, vol. xxviii, pp. 499–513.

Wilson, Edward (1994), '*The Testament of the Buck* and the Sociology of the Text', *Review of English Studies*, n.s. vol. xlv, pp. 157–84.

Woolf, Rosemary (1968), *The English Religious Lyric in the Middle Ages*, Oxford.

Wordsworth, J. (1959), 'Dunbar's *Quod cinis es*', *Modern Language Review*, vol. liv, p. 223.

Wormald, Jennifer (1981), *Court, Kirk and Community: Scotland 1470–1625*, London.

—— (ed.) (1991), *Scotland Revisited*, London.